Intersecting
Child Welfare, Substance Abuse, and Family Violence

Intersecting
Child Welfare, Substance Abuse, and Family Violence

Culturally Competent Approaches

ROWENA FONG   **RUTH MCROY**

CARMEN ORTIZ HENDRICKS

COUNCIL ON SOCIAL WORK EDUCATION
ALEXANDRIA, VIRGINIA

CSWE PRESS

Library of Congress Cataloging-in-Publication Data

IISBN 0-87293-119-6 (alk. paper)

1. Child welfare—Cross-cultural studies. 2. Substance abuse—Cross-cultural studies.
3. Family violence—Cross-cultural studies.   I Fong, Rowena   II McRoy, Ruth G.
III Hendricks, Carmen Ortiz.

HV713.I58 2005
362.7—dc22

2005013288

Printed in the United States of America on acid-free paper that meets the American National Standards Institute Z39-48 Standard.

Council on Social Work Education, Inc.
1725 Duke Street, Suite 500
Alexandria, VA 22314-3457
www.cswe.org

Contents

Foreword

The production of this book is a noteworthy milestone for social work education. It represents the result of an initiative that began in 1996 when the board of directors of the Council on Social Work Education approved a proposal from its Cultural Diversity Subcommittee to sponsor an invitational conference. The purpose of the conference would be to assess past and present contributions to multicultural curriculum projects in social work practice, human behavior, social welfare policy, research, field education, and international social work. This successful event, led by Dr. Doman Lum, Dr. Maria Zuniga, and Dr. Lorraine Gutierrez, was held at the University of Michigan in December 1998. The leaders of the event and the 80 invited participants at this conference were unanimous in their expressions that this effort required continuation in order to address more thoroughly the important work being undertaken to enhance cultural competence within our practice and in our programs in social work education.

In 2001 the Council on Social Work Education and Casey Family Programs, in collaboration with the University of Texas at Austin School of Social Work, produced the conference that is encapsulated in this book. It was apparent that the conference went beyond the traditional didactic approaches used in events of this nature. The opportunity that was made available for exchange and learning was equaled by the goal of giving appreciation and acknowledgment to those whose knowledge, scholarship, and service can be used for the enhancement of all peoples.

The Council on Social Work Education's mission—to define and uphold standards in social work education that will ensure the preparation of competent, committed social work practitioners—is illustrated in these two important events, and members of the boards of directors deserve our gratitude for their approval and support. Cultural competence, in my opinion, is the future blueprint for all 21st-century practice.

As a former president of the council, I am honored to have been a participant in the conference, and I applaud the organizers whose insight led them to this alliance between practice and education that must occur in many forums and formats if we are to accomplish our mutual objectives.

The scholars whose works are presented in this publication demonstrate that there is within our profession a breadth of vision, a depth of scholarship, and a general eloquence that can define the dimensions of cultural competence that are most critical for effective social work practice. I commend the authors, and especially Drs. Rowena Fong, Ruth McRoy, and Carmen Ortiz Hendricks, who provided such superb editorship of this volume. I know that readers will gain tremendous insight into the intersection of different fields of practice in our goal to advance cultural competence.

Barbara W. White, PhD
Dean, School of Social Work
University of Texas at Austin

Preface

With the Census 2000 statistics indicating that 1 out of every 10 people in the United States is foreign born, most likely a person of color, culturally competent social work practice is mandatory in the education of current and future social workers.

The Council on Social Work Education (CSWE) in its 2001 Educational Policy and Accreditation Standards required that all schools of social work prepare social workers for practice in diverse and cultural contexts. The National Association of Social Work also adopted in 2001 Standards for Cultural Competence in Social Work Practice. This awareness and concern of the Council on Social Work Education has resulted in two task force meetings and two publications, one of which is this book, *Intersecting Child Welfare, Substance Abuse, and Family Violence: Culturally Competent Approaches*.

In 1998 the Council on Social Work Education and the University of Michigan sponsored the first task force meeting where culturally competent practice was examined throughout the various curriculums and interest areas of practice, community organization, policy, research, fieldwork, human behavior in the social environment, and international social work. The cochairs of the meeting were Lorraine Gutierrez, professor at the University of Michigan; Maria Zuniga, professor at San Diego State University; and Doman Lum, professor at California State University at Sacramento.

The outcome of the task force meeting was a publication, titled *Education for Multicultural Social Work Practice*, edited by Lorraine Gutierrez, Maria Zuniga, and Doman Lum, to be published by the Council on Social Work Education in 2004.

Realizing the importance of continuing the examination of culturally competent practice in the various fields of social work, the Council on Social Work Education in collaboration with the University of Texas at Austin and Casey Family Programs, a private, nonprofit foundation committed to improving the well-being of children in child welfare through permanency, transition, and prevention, sponsored a second task force meeting at the University of Texas at Austin in 2001. The conference was cochaired by Rowena Fong, professor at the University of Texas at Austin; Ruth McRoy, professor at the University of Texas at Austin; and Carmen Ortiz Hendricks, emeritus professor at

Yeshiva University of New York. The purpose of the conference was to examine the intersection of child welfare, substance abuse, and family violence. Invited keynote speakers at the task force meeting were Christine Lowery and Oliver Williams. At the follow-up CSWE presentation Robert Hampton offered the keynote address.

Eighty percent of child welfare cases also have problems with substance abuse and domestic violence. Disproportionately high numbers of child welfare cases also involve minority families, especially African American. Missing among social work practitioners, educators, and researchers is the dialogue among African Americans, Latinos, First Nations Peoples, and Asians and Pacific Islanders on how child welfare in their respective groups is affected by substance abuse and domestic violence. This task force meeting allowed that interactive discussion to happen. The outcome is this book, *Intersecting Child Welfare, Substance Abuse, and Family Violence: Culturally Competent Approaches.*

The linkage of chapters among all four ethnic groups occurred in the outline requirements of addressing the sociodemographics; the history of the issues in child welfare, substance abuse, and family violence; the problems encountered; and the recommendations for future directions in practice, policy, and research for each of the ethnic groups. The majority of the chapters focus discussion on direct practice, but some address policy and organizational issues (chapters 11 and 17). Keynote speeches are included but were revised as chapters. Terry Cross and Kathleen Earle Fox were invited to contribute a chapter to the book.

The recommendations for future directions from all four ethnic groups challenge educators, policy makers, and researchers to examine the impact of institutional racism and poverty in their role of perpetuating the oppression of people of color. The disproportionate number of children in the child welfare system and the kinds of stressors families of color face that promote substance abuse and lead to family violence need continued advocacy. This book is intended to guide national efforts in education and research, organizational change, and policy making to arrest this growing phenomenon.

Many people and organizations assisted in the production of this book. The authors want to thank Dean Barbara White, former president of the Council on Social Work Education and dean of the School of Social Work at the University of Texas at Austin, and Ruth Massinga, former chief executive officer for Casey Family Programs, for financially and administratively supporting the task force meeting in Austin. Dorothy Van Soest, professor at the School of Social Work at the University of Washington, Carolyn Rodriguez, director, Texas State Strategy with Casey Family Programs; and Hollee Ganner, administrative assistant at the University of Texas at Austin School of Social Work were all instrumental in organizing the conference presentations, which made this book possible. The Casey Family Programs' funding of the collaboration with the Substance Abuse and Mental Health Services Administration (SAMHSA) allowed the research in chapter 7, and the various Starting Early Starting Smart (SESS) sites and steering committee need to be acknowledged in the contribution of that chapter.

This book was produced by the input of many. However, it is one of many more efforts needed to promote culturally competent social work practice to ensure that families of color are understood, respected, and treated with the integrity and dignity they deserve despite troubling societal-induced problems such as child welfare, substance abuse, and domestic violence.

The increasing use and illegal manufacturing of methamphetamine, an extremely addictive and very potent artificial stimulant, commonly referred to as "ice," "crystal," "glass," "meth," and "speed" is putting children at great risk and is a factor in the removal of growing numbers of children from their birth families and placement in foster homes. This drug, initially was consumed primarily by Whites in rural areas and small urban communities in the West and Midwest, but is now spreading across the country and is beginning to be used also by Hispanic and Asian populations (Rawson, Gonzalex, & Brethen, 2002, p. 145). Besides the risk of fires or explosions, children living in homes with meth labs, inhale toxic fumes, absorb dangerous chemicals into their skin and their clothing, and consequently, are at high risk for respiratory and neurological problems. In many states, child abuse and endangerment statutes now include manufacturing the drug in the presence of a child (Riggs, 2004).

References

Rawson, R., Gonzales, R., & Brethen, P. (2002). Treatment of methamphetamine use disorders: An update. *Journal of Substance Abuse Treatment, 23*, 145–150.

Riggs, D. (2004) *Meth Gives Rise to a New Tide of Child Endangerment*. Adoptalk. North American Council on Adoptable Children: St. Paul, Minnesota.

About the Editors

ROWENA FONG is a professor at the University of Texas at Austin School of Social Work. She also served as the Director of the Center for Asian American Studies at The University of Texas at Austin from 2003 to 2005. A graduate of Harvard University (EdD), University of California at Berkeley (MSW), and Wellesley College (BA), she has taught at the University of Hawaii at Manoa (1990–2002), Ohio State University (1989–1990), Bethel College (1981–1988), and Nankai University in Tianjin, China (1988–1989), where she did her dissertation research on China's Only-Child Policy. She is the coeditor and coauthor of four books, *Culturally Competent Practice with Immigrant and Refugee Children and Families* (published by Guilford Press, 2004); *Children of Neglect: When No One Cares* (written with Dr. Margaret Smith, published with Brunner-Routledge Press, 2004); *Culturally Competent Social Work Practice: Skills, Interventions, and Evaluations* (written with Dr. Sharlene Furuto at Brigham Young University, published by Allyn & Bacon, 2001); and *Multisystem Skills and Interventions in School Social Work Practice* (coauthored with Edith Freeman, Cynthia Franklin, Gary Shaffer, and Elizabeth Timberlake, published by National Association of Social Workers Press in 1998). She has another book in progress, *Culturally Diverse Human Behaviors and Social Environments*, to be published by Brooks/Cole.

Dr. Fong's areas of teaching, writing, and research are concentrated on children and families, specifically in adoptions and child welfare; immigrant and refugee children and families; Chinese children and families; and culturally competent practice. She has taught classes on social work practice with children and families, child welfare, family preservation, children of divorce, human behavior, and the social environment. She has published widely and has done teaching, consultation, and training in the United States and in the People's Republic of China on foster care, adoptions, parenting skills, child development, social work curriculum development, sociology of the family, and sociology of education.

In 2001 she received the University of Hawaii Regent's Teaching Award and the Hawaii Chapter of the National Association of Social Work's Award for Social Worker of the Year in Education and Training. She served on the Commission on Practice of the Council on Social Work Education and is serving as consulting editor on several journals, such as *Social Work, Journal of Ethnic and Cultural Diversity in Social Work, Public Child Welfare,* and *Research and Social Work Practice.* She has been involved with Casey Family Programs serving in the capacity of Chair of the National Diversity Advisory Committee and member of the Hawaii and Texas Divisions' Community Resource Councils. Previous to her academic career, she was a preschool teacher, a clinical social worker at a residential treatment for adolescent boys, and the founder and director of a Chinese bilingual, bicultural preschool in San Francisco. She has been actively involved in the Chinese immigrant communities in Boston, San Francisco, and Hawaii.

Her current research projects focus on immigrant and refugee families' marriage and parenting conflicts, problems in the social service delivery system for refugee resettlement providers, and employability and microenterprise developments for refugees. Child welfare services for immigrants and refugees is a new area of research being developed.

RUTH MCROY is an emeritus professor at The University of Texas at Austin. She held the Ruby Lee Piester Centennial Professorship in Services to Children and Families and was the Associate Dean for Research and Director of the Center for Social Work Research at the School of Social Work at the University of Texas (UT) at Austin. She also held a joint appointment in the UT Center for African and African American Studies and was a member of the University of Texas Academy of Distinguished Professors.

Dr. McRoy received her BA in psychology and sociology and her master's degree in social work from the University of Kansas in Lawrence. She received her PhD in social work from the University of Texas at Austin (1981). Prior to joining the UT faculty in 1981, Dr. McRoy taught at the University of Kansas, School of Social Welfare, and at Prairie View A&M University in Prairie View, Texas.

Dr. McRoy has been involved in adoptions practice for many years. In the 1970s she worked as an adoptions and birth-parent counselor at Kansas Children's Service League in Wichita and as project coordinator of Black Adoption Program and Services in Kansas City. She later was a technical assistance specialist for the Region VI Adoption Resource Center at the University of Texas at Austin. Currently, she provides consultation on a variety of adoption practice issues and serves on the boards of several adoption and foster care programs in the Austin area and other parts of the United States.

Dr. McRoy's research interests include the following: family preservation, open adoptions, emotionally disturbed adopted children and adolescents, transracial adoptions, cross-cultural relationships, sexual abuse, adolescent pregnancy, cultural diversity, domestic violence, African American families, racial identity development, African American adoptions, special needs adoptions, and adoptive family dynamics.

She has authored or coauthored seven books and numerous articles and book chapters on adoptions and has presented many invited papers at national and international conferences. Her books include *Transracial and Inracial Adoptees: The Adolescent Years* (with L. Zurcher, 1983); *Emotional Disturbance in Adopted Adolescents: Origins and Development* (with H. Grotevant and L. Zurcher, 1988); *Openness in Adoption: New Practices, New Issues* (with H. Grotevant and K. White, 1988); *Social Work Practice with Black Families* (with Sadye Logan and Edith Freeman, 1990); *Openness in Adoption: Exploring Family Connections* (with H. Grotevant, 1998); *Special Needs Adoptions: Practice Issues (1999)*; and *Does Family Preservation Serve a Child's Best Interests?* (with H. Altstein, 2000). She is currently writing a new book on transracial adoptions.

At the University of Texas at Austin, Dr. McRoy taught undergraduate and graduate students and has recently taught such courses as the African American Family, Cultural Diversity, Group Dynamics and Methods, Qualitative Methods, Strategies of Intervention, Contemporary Issues in Adoption and Foster Care, and Social Work Practice with Children and Families. In 1984, she won the Lora Lee Pederson Teaching Excellence Award, and in 1990 she was selected as the recipient of the Texas Excellence Teaching Award.

As part of the U.S. Children's Bureau's Collaboration to US Adopt Kids Project, Dr. McRoy was selected to lead a five-year, nationwide research project examining barriers to adoption of special needs and factors associated with adoptive placements. The findings of this research project will help public and private agencies change practices, which may lead to an increase in the pool of prospective adoptive parents.

CARMEN ORTIZ HENDRICKS is professor and associate dean at Yeshiva University Wurzweiler School of Social Work. She was an Associate Professor at Hunter College School of Social Work and a faculty member since 1980. She has taught Social Casework Practice, Advanced Multicultural Social Work Practice, Advanced Social Work Practice with Immigrants and Refugees, Human Behavior in the Social Environment, and the Seminar in Field Instruction. She served as chair of the school's Curriculum Committee (2001–2003) and the Promotion and Budget Committee (2000–2003).

Dr. Hendricks is coauthor of *Learning to Teach, Teaching to Learn: A Guide to Social Work Field Education* (Council on Social Work Education, 2005) and coeditor of *Social Work and Women's Health* (Council on Social Work Education, 2006). Her research and consultation focus on culturally competent social work education and practice. Her most recent publications include "Learning and Teaching Culturally Competent Social Work Practice," published in the *Journal of Teaching in Social Work* (2003, *23*[1/2], 73–86) and "A Community Building Perspective in Social Work Practice," written with Glynn Rudich and published in the *Journal of Community Practice* (2000, *8*[3], 21–36). Dr. Hendricks has written extensively and made numerous presentations on diversity and cultural competence and is a consultant for agencies evaluating their cultural competence standards of performance.

Dr. Hendricks is very active in the National Association of Social Workers (NASW) and the Council on Social Work Education. She has served as the regional representative to NASW's National Committee on Nominations and Leadership Identification (2001–2004). As a member of NASW's National Committee on Racial and Ethnic Diversity, she contributed to the development of NASW's Standards for Cultural Competence in Social Work Practice, which were adopted by the board of directors in 2001. She also served as President of the New York City chapter of NASW from 1996 to 1998 and is active with the chapter's Committee on Latino Affairs. Dr. Hendricks was honored to receive the New York City Chapter of NASW's Chapter Service Award in 2001. Dr. Hendricks has served on the Board of the Council on Social Work Education (1997–2000) and on the Council on Social Work Education's Commission on Educational Policy (2001–2004). She also served as President of the Association of Latino Social Work Educators (2001–2003). Dr. Hendricks received her doctoral degree from Yeshiva University's Wurzweiler School of Social Work and her master's in social work from Adelphi University.

About the Contributors

PORTIA ADAMS, MSW, PhD is an assistant professor at the Graduate School of Social Service, Fordham University, New York, New York. She received her doctorate in social work from Washington University in St. Louis, Missouri. Her research interests center on Black communities and social work practice, currently focusing on the strengths of urban African American adolescent females and HIV prevention. Publications on her research have appeared in *Social Work* and *African American Research Perspectives*, and in *Working with Multicultural Families* (Congress & Gonzalez, 2005).

LARRY BENNETT, PhD, is associate professor at the Jane Addams College of Social Work, University of Illinois at Chicago. His research interests include the implementation of evidence-based practice in social service agencies, the relationship between substance abuse and domestic violence, the structure and effectiveness of community-based batterers' intervention systems, and the developmental/structural links among various forms of men's violence such as bullying, sexual harassment, dating violence, and adult partner abuse. Dr. Bennett is coauthor of *Evaluation of Domestic Violence and Sexual Assault Services* to be published by Sage.

KIMBERLY BROOKS, PhD, is a clinical psychologist at the Children's National Medical Center in Washington, DC. As director of prevention services for a federally funded national research project, titled Starting Early Starting Smart (SESS), her goal was to identify best practices for the delivery of integrated services for at-risk preschool children and their families. She has been an associate in the private practice of Psychological and Educational Associates, Inc., for seven years. Dr. Brooks is an adjunct faculty member at the George Washington University School of Professional Psychology.

TERRY L. CROSS, MSW, ACSW, an enrolled member of the Seneca Nation of Indians, is the Executive Director and developer of the National Indian Child Welfare Association. He is the author of several Indian child welfare curricula and publications on cultural competence in social services. His 29 years of social work practice in both Indian and non-Indian settings give him unique skills and expertise in the field of Indian child welfare, cultural competence, and training.

YOLANDA DAVIS, MSW, is a social worker in the Children and Families Services Unit of a county department of social services in eastern North Carolina. Ms. Davis has provided both clinical and indirect services to children and families and has experience in several service sections of child welfare, namely, intake/crisis, foster care, adoptions, and investigations, and is committed to improving the service delivery system for children. Ms. Davis received her BA and MSW degrees from East Carolina University in Greenville, North Carolina. While pursuing her graduate degree, she was a North Carolina Child Welfare Scholar.

DAVID DEERE, MTh, MSW, holds a master of theology from Southern Methodist University, Dallas, Texas, and a master of social work from University of Arkansas at Little Rock. He is a Licensed Certified Social Worker and is employed by Partners for Inclusive Communities, a University Center of Excellence on Developmental Disabilities at University of Arkansas for Medical Sciences. He serves as the Associate Director and Social Work Coordinator for Partners. Mr. Deere is also an adjunct faculty member of the School of Social Work at the University of Arkansas at Little Rock.

KATHLEEN EARLE FOX, PhD, LMSW, has worked and published widely in the area of American Indian research for the past decade. A native of New York state, she moved to Maine in 1996, where she has taught social work and completed two national studies on the abuse and neglect of American Indian children.

TERESA EVANS-CAMPBELL, PhD, MSW, is an enrolled citizen of the Snohomish Tribe of Indians. She is an assistant professor at the University of Washington School of Social Work, where she directs the Institute for Indigenous Health and Child Welfare Research. Her research interests include: indigenous family wellness, resilience in indigenous families, historical trauma, and Indian child welfare.

EDITH FREEMAN, PhD, is an emeritus professor at the University of Kansas, School of Social Welfare, where she was chair of the clinical practices sequence. She is widely published in the areas of the Black family, children, and families in general; alcohol abuse; and teenage pregnancy. She is best known for *Social Work Practice with Black Families*, which she cowrote with Sadye M. L. Logan and Ruth G. McRoy.

MERIPA GODINET, PhD, is an assistant professor at the University of Hawaii School of Social Work. Prior to that, she was a joint faculty associate specialist with the University of Hawaii School of Social Work and the Hawaii State Hospital. Her research interests include juvenile delinquency and Pacific Islanders, and cross-cultural competency practice in mental health.

LINNER W. GRIFFIN, PhD, is a professor in the School of Social Work and Criminal Justice Studies at East Carolina University (ECU). Dr. Griffin is the project director of the East Carolina University Office of the North Carolina Child Welfare Education Collaborative, which is part of the statewide child welfare practitioner training initiative. She has published widely in the areas of elder abuse/elder maltreatment, adult protective services, and organ transplantation. Dr. Griffin is a member of the Steering Committee of the Institute on Domestic Violence in the African American Community. Dr. Griffin received her BA from the University of North Carolina at Greensboro, her MSW from the University of North Carolina at Chapel Hill, and her doctorate from the University of Houston.

ROBERT L. HAMPTON, PhD, is professor, Department of Social Services York College, and a special assistant to the executive vice chancellor, City University of New York. He previously served York College as its president. Prior to joining York College he served as associate provost for Academic Affairs and dean for Undergraduate Studies, professor of family studies, and professor of sociology at the University of Maryland. A Hartman Mentoring Scholar, he has published extensively in the field of family violence, including five edited books: *Violence in the Black Family: Correlates and Consequences*; *Black Family Violence: Current Research and Theory*; *Family Violence: Prevention and Treatment* (2nd ed.); *Preventing Violence in America*; and *Substance Abuse, Family Violence, and Child Welfare: Bridging Perspectives*. He is the one of the founders of the Institute on Domestic Violence in the African American Community. His research interests include intimate partner violence, family abuse, community violence, student success in higher education, and social change.

LORI HANSON, PhD, is the director of research, evaluation and training of The Children's Trust in Miami, Florida. A Licensed Clinical Psychologist and voluntary assistant professor of clinical pediatrics at the University of Miami School of Medicine, she holds a doctoral degree in clinical psychology from Saint Louis University and specialized in pediatric/clinical child psychology during her internship at the University of Miami Mailman Center for Child Development. Dr. Hanson served as the project coordinator of Miami's Families: Starting Early Starting Smart Initiative and supervised the prevention and early intervention behavioral health services provided to families with young children (0–5) who have caregivers affected by substance abuse and/or mental health difficulties.

IRENE JILLSON, PhD, is an adjunct assistant professor at Georgetown University, School of Nursing and Health Studies. She was the principal investigator for Starting Early Starting Smart in Maryland.

CAROL AMUNDSON LEE, MA, LPC, ACADA, is the director of behavioral health grants for Child Development, Inc. She received her MA from Northwestern State University, Natchitoches, Louisiana. She was the project director for Child Development, Inc., Starting Early Starting Smart in Arkansas. She is a Licensed Professional Counselor with National Certified Counselor status and is an Advanced Certificate Alcohol and Drug Counselor with International Certification.

GWAT-YONG LIE, PhD, is an associate professor of social work at the School of Social Welfare, University of Wisconsin-Milwaukee. She teaches courses in social work methods and domestic violence. She has done research and published in the areas of intimate partner violence, multicultural social work practice, and women's issues, including those concerning Asian and Southeast Asian women and their families.

GORDON LIMB, PhD, is an assistant professor in the Department of Social Work, Arizona State University–West, Phoenix. He received his doctorate in social welfare from the University of California at Berkeley. His research interests center on child welfare issues and policies. His work addresses service utilization, adequacy of services received, outcome predictors, and cultural identification with a primary focus on American Indians and the Indian Child Welfare Act. Publications on his research have appeared in *Children and Youth Services Review, Journal of Social Service Research, Child Welfare,* and *Social Work Perspectives.* He was the assistant director of the Kathryn M. Buder Center for American Indian Studies at the George Warren Brown School of Social Work at Washington University in St. Louis, Missouri.

CHRISTINE LOWERY, PhD, is an associate professor at the University of Wisconsin and an enrolled member of the Laguna Nation of Indians.

LUCIA MAGARIAN, MFA, MS, is a licensed marriage and family therapist in Maryland. Her areas of interest and expertise are in domestic violence, immigration, trauma and recovery work, religion and cultural competence, and emergency preparedness protocols. She has a master of fine arts in creative writing from American University and has written over a dozen plays.

FLAVIO MARSIGLIA, PhD, is associate professor at the Arizona State University School of Social Work. He is the principal investigator of the *Drug Resistance Strategies: The Next Generation* project. Funded by the National Institutes of Health/National Institute on Drug Abuse, the project conducts contextual analysis on the outcomes of the Keepin' It Real program. Dr. Marsiglia has received numerous recognitions and awards such as The Silberman Award for innovative social work research and *La Vida* Award for pioneering efforts on HIV/AIDS prevention and education among Latinas/Latinos. He received his doctorate in 1991 from the Mandel School of Applied Social Sciences at Case Western Reserve University.

CLAUDIA L. MORENO, PhD, MSW, is an assistant professor at Rutgers University. She was a faculty member at Columbia University School of Social Work (CUSSW) and was chair of the Human Behavior in the Social Environment sequence. She is a research fellow at the Social Intervention Group at CUSSW and has published in the area of partner abuse, substance abuse, and developmental disabilities among Latinos. She has conducted national and international research on HIV/AIDS among Latina women and their male sexual partners. She has received numerous awards for her work in the Latino community, including recognition by the U.S. House of Representatives for Outstanding Service to the Latino Community in New Jersey.

JOHN NAKASHIMA, PhD, MSW, is a researcher at the Greater Los Angeles Veterans Affairs Healthcare System in California, specializing in national and local studies on services for homeless veterans. Previously, he worked at National Asian Pacific American Families Against Substance Abuse (NAPAFASA), a nonprofit organizing, research, and advocacy group based in Los Angeles.

ROBERT ORTEGA, PhD, MSW, MA, is an associate professor at The University of Michigan, School of Social Work. He received his BA, MSW, and interdisciplinary PhD in social work and psychology degrees from the University of Michigan. His research interests are in the areas of mental health and child welfare, relationship development, group work practice, treatment interventions, and service utilization. Dr. Ortega is codirector of the Program for Research on Latino Families and Communities and is the principal investigator of the first national study of Latinos and child welfare. He is currently involved in several national research projects and organizations focusing on child welfare, adoption, and child well-being issues.

CAROLYN SEVAL, RN, MPH, LMHC, is a consultant, teaches at Quincy College and North Shore Community College, and is working as a high school nurse at Dover Sherborn High School in Dover, Massachusetts. She did work at Boston Medical Center (formerly Boston City Hospital) serving high-risk families from neighboring urban communities. She was the principal investigator and clinical director of a Substance Abuse and Mental Health Services Administration (SAMSHA) and Casey Family-funded program, Starting Early Starting Smart. Ms. Seval has developed and implemented model treatment interventions for high-risk families, including pregnant and parenting addicted women. She lectures on a wide range of topics, including parenting, addiction, and trauma; program development; and maternal/child health. She is the coauthor of *Families In Recovery: Coming Full Circle*, which presents a family-focused model of approaching substance abuse treatment and recovery.

JOCELYN TURNER-MUSA, PhD, is an assistant professor in the Department of Psychology at Morgan State University. She completed a doctoral degree in social psychology from Howard University and a postdoctoral fellowship in mental health services research at The John Hopkins University Bloomberg School of Public Health. She is currently the principal investigator of an NIMH-funded undergraduate training program in prevention research. She recently served as a research associate and program director on the Starting Early Starting Smart program conducted at Johns Hopkins University. She is a social psychologist with primary interests in psychosocial factors implicated in disease prevention and health promotion among African Americans.

HALAEVALU VAKALAHI, PhD, is the accreditation specialist at the Council on Social Work Education. Previously, she was an educator at San Francisco State, New Mexico State, and Brigham Young University-Hawaii. Her research interests include adolescent substance abuse, juvenile delinquency, and violence, particularly in the context of ethnic minority families as sources of risk and protection. She is currently working on coediting a book, *Women of Color in Social Work Education*.

JENNIFER VICK, LMSW, PhD, completed her doctoral studies at Columbia University. She was working as the research and evaluation coordinator for the Texas Fragile Families Initiative and was a consultant for the Peer Assistance Network of Texas mentor program. She graduated from University of Texas at Austin School of Social Work with a specialty in child and family practice.

KARINA L. WALTERS, PhD, is associate professor at the University of Washington School of Social Work and is an enrolled citizen of the Choctaw Nation of Oklahoma.

At the University of Washington School of Social Work, she is the director of the Wellness Center, where she conducts research on cultural strenghs in indigenous populations that buffer the effect of historical trauma and discrimination on health. She has published and presented nationally in the areas of urban American Indian health and mental health, specifically on the identification of cultural factors that act as buffers between trauma and wellness outcomes (i.e., HIV risk, substance use, physical/mental health). Her research interests include traumatic stress, substance use, HIV risk, and physical/mental health among American Indian and Alaska Native populations; identity development among oppressed populations; and development of culturally relevant measures and sampling methodologies.

JAMES HERBERT WILLIAMS, PhD, is an associate professor and holder of the E. Desmond Lee Chair for Racial and Ethnic Diversity, associate dean for the master's program, and the assistant to the chancellor for Urban Community Initiatives at the George Warren Brown School of Social Work of Washington University in St. Louis, Missouri. He received his doctorate in social welfare from the University of Washington-Seattle. His research interests explore racial differences in risk and protective factors for childhood and adolescent antisocial behavior, race disparities in the juvenile justice system, mental health services in urban public schools, and the relationship of family management and structure to antisocial behavior for African American youths. Publications on his research have appeared in *Social Work Research, Social Work, Violence and Victims, Journal of Quantitative Criminology, Health Promotion Practice, Annals of Behavioral Medicine,* and *Families in Society.*

OLIVER J. WILLIAMS, PhD, is executive director of the Institute on Domestic Violence in the African American Community and associate professor in the Graduate School of Social Work at the University of Minnesota in St. Paul. He has been involved in the field of domestic violence for more than 25 years as a child welfare and delinquency worker, working in battered women's shelters, and developing and conducting counseling with partner abuse treatment programs. His research and publications have centered on creating effective service delivery strategies that will reduce violent behaviors among African Americans. Dr. Williams serves on several national advisory boards focused on the issue of domestic violence.

MICHAEL YELLOW BIRD, PhD, is a citizen of the Sahnish and Hidatsa First Nations. He is the director for the Center for Indigenous Nations Studies and associate professor of American studies. He has held faculty appointments in the schools of social work at the University of British Columbia, Arizona State University, and University of

Kansas. He is currently coediting a textbook with Dr. Waziyatawin Angela Wilson, entitled *For Indigenous Eyes Only: The Decolonization Handbook* and *Decolonizing Social Work With First Nations Peoples: Strategies for Justice and Libratory Praxis* with Drs. Hilary Weaver and Charlotte Goodluck. His research focuses on indigenous peoples, critical thinking and indigenous foreign policy, oral histories of Native Vietnam combat veterans, colonialism and methods of decolonization, indigenous men, and Native prisoners.

MIEKO YOSHIHAMA, PhD, is associate professor of social work at the University of Michigan, School of Social Work. She teaches and conducts research on violence against women, immigrants and refugees, mental health, and community organizing. Dr. Yoshihama's work at local, state, national, and international levels combines research and action to promote the safety and well-being of marginalized communities. In Michigan, through participatory action research projects, she has helped establish two community-based organizations, the Hmong Women United of Michigan, Inc., and New Visions: Alliance to End Violence in Asian/Asian American Communities. In Japan, she co-founded the Domestic Violence Action & Research Group, whose efforts prompted newly emerging battered women's movements in that country. Dr. Yoshihama serves on the boards of various national, state, and local organizations committed to ending violence against women. She has conducted numerous community-based studies of domestic violence in both the United States and Japan. She serves on the Steering Committee of the Asian and Pacific Islander Institute on Domestic Violence.

Part 1

Introduction and Background

Intersecting Child Welfare

Substance Abuse and Domestic Violence

RUTH MCROY and JENNIFER VICK

Introduction

Often in the research and practice literature, substance abuse, child welfare, and domestic violence are examined independently with only vague references to their interdependence. In practice, child welfare workers may be trained to identify child abuse, but often are not trained to detect substance abuse, as just as often those involved in batterer's programs may not be trained to look for child abuse and the interaction effect of substance abuse. The outcomes for many families and children are linked to the criminal justice system's handling of these substance abuse and domestic violence cases.

Moreover, since disproportionately high numbers of families being served by each of these systems are families of color, staff must also be prepared to provide culturally competent services for these diverse populations. For example, in 2000, African American children numbered 14.7% of the population of children under 18 in the United States, but 38% of the children in foster care. Hispanic children represented 17.1% of the child population and 15% of children in foster care, Native American or Alaskan Native represented .9% of the U.S. child population and 2% of those in foster care, and Asian or Pacific Islander children represented 3.5% of the U.S. child population and 1% of the foster care population (O'Hare, 2001).

This chapter introduces many of these issues by reviewing the literature on substance abuse and family violence, as well as the impact on the criminal justice system. Emphasis is placed on the need to provide culturally competent services to these populations.

During the past decade an unprecedented number of children from single-parent families entered the child welfare system because a parent had an identified substance abuse problem (Azzi-Lessing & Olsen, 1996). Adults between the ages of 18 and 25, a common childbearing age range for women, have a higher rate of cocaine and other illicit substance use than any other age group, and the rate appears to be increasing in recent years (National Institute on Drug Abuse [NIDA], 2000; Substance Abuse and Mental Health Services Administration [SAMHSA], 2000). McNichol (1999) found that cocaine was the predominant drug affecting infants placed in family foster care. Crack, the cheapest and most addictive form of cocaine, in particular has gained in popularity with women more than the drugs of the past (Kelley, 1992; Morrison Dore, Doris, & Wright, 1995). Alcohol was followed by cocaine as the two most prevalently abused substances in another study of families adjudicated for child maltreatment (Murphy et al., 1991). In the same study, the use of hard drugs (heroin or cocaine) was present in 22% of the families, and 43% of the families evidenced at least one type of substance abuse (Murphy et al., 1991). Further complicating the picture, and the ability of child welfare workers to intervene with families, is the association of crack cocaine's use with a number of risk factors outside child maltreatment, including interpersonal violence, crime, sexual exploitation of children and adults, and transmission of the AIDs virus (Morrison Dore et al., 1995).

The apparent connection between parental substance abuse and severe family dysfunction, and in turn a higher risk of child maltreatment, seems increasingly obvious (Besinger, Garland, Litrowinik, & Lansverk, 1999; Famularo, Kinscherff, & Fenton, 1992; National Association of Public Welfare Administrators, 1991; National Center on Child Abuse Prevention Research, 1991; *Spectrum*, 1999). However, the nature and extent of this relationship between chemical dependency and parenting behaviors has yet to be clearly delineated (Besinger et al., 1999). Studies connecting substance abuse and child maltreatment have not demonstrated any causal relationship and may be the result of a third variable such as poverty (Murphy et al., 1991). One study demonstrated a significantly greater rate of substance abuse among children whose families received Aid to Families with Dependent Children (AFDC); however, when the effects of poverty were controlled, the results suggested that substance abuse was associated with greater risk of maltreatment regardless of economic status (Murphy et al., 1991). Current estimates of caregiver substance abuse among families of maltreated children vary widely, and methodologies for classifying substance abuse are not often standardized and frequently

lack operational definitions (Besinger et al., 1999). In addition to methodological concerns, terms such as substance abuse, substance involvement, and substance use have
been used interchangeably (Besinger et al., 1999), and many studies vary in terms of
which caregivers are included in the substance abuse classification (e.g., perpetrators,
mothers, fathers, stepparents, and/or guardians) (Besinger et al., 1999).

Despite methodological and definitional debates substance abuse appears to be one
of the most common family problems associated with the abuse or neglect of a child and
entry into the child welfare system (Haack, 1997). One relatively large study of child protective service cases by Besinger et al. (1999) found that approximately 8 out of 10 children who entered the child welfare system because of maltreatment had caregivers who
abused substances. Famularo, Kinshcerff, Bunshaft, Spivak, & Fenton, (1989) found that
the most common court referrals for parents involved in the child welfare system were
aimed at drug or alcohol treatment. In addition, state child protective service agencies
have noted the apparent relationship between increases in substance abuse and increases
in reports of child abuse (National Center on Child Abuse Prevention Research, 1991).
Cases with documented substance abuse are more likely to have repeat involvement with
the child protective services system (Murphy et al., 1991). Additionally, the relationship
between specific substance use and maltreatment may be substance specific. Interestingly,
one study found that families with parents who abused cocaine or heroin had numbers of
prior reports of abuse and mean years of prior protective history that were virtually
identical to families with no documented cocaine or heroin use (Murphy et al., 1991).
However, those parents who abused only alcohol had significantly more reports of maltreatment and longer protective service histories.

More than substance abuse alone, the combination of factors and sequelae associated
with substance use and abuse affects the well-being of children and their families. There
is not sufficient evidence available to untangle the environmental effects such as poor
nutrition, poverty, and a lack of prenatal care resulting from substance abuse on children
(Center for Substance Abuse Treatment [CSAT], 1994). For those children who were
exposed to drugs before birth, it is as yet not possible to determine with certainty which
illicit substances produce which effects at what levels (CSAT, 1994). Also, characteristics
of drug-dependent parents and drug-exposed infants place the relationship between the
mother and child at further risk of abuse and neglect (Kelley, 1992). Many infants
exposed to substances possess such characteristics as behavioral problems and health
needs, which make them more difficult to care for (Delaney-Black et al., 1998; Kelley,
1992; McNichol, 1999; Morrison Dore et al., 1995). No studies purport proof of causation between prenatal cocaine exposure and subsequent behavioral effects because it is
highly likely that other maternal and environmental factors play a significant role in
determining child behavior (Delaney-Black et al., 1998). Beyond the effects that

substance abuse has on the family, the increased difficulty associated with caring for pre-natal substance-exposed children has an impact on other caregivers such as foster families and relatives who may be caring for these children in the event the biological parent cannot (McNichol, 1999), and on the child welfare system as a whole.

The striking rise in the number of parents with substance abuse issues has taxed the already overburdened child protective service system (Kelley, 1992). High numbers of child abuse reports and high caseloads have led the system to concentrate almost exclusively on investigative activities and the provision of foster care, with little time for prevention or in-home services (Haack, 1997). Uncoordinated federal and state efforts to provide substance abuse treatment to women, as well as a lack of development of new program models to serve women with children, have left the substance abuse treatment system unprepared to serve the influx of substance-abusing women who are pregnant or who have young children (Finkelstein, 1994). Moreover, even when treatment is available, compliance with court-ordered substance abuse treatment is lower than any other form of court referral (Famularo, et al., 1989). In addition, one study found that when substance abuse was documented among parents involved in child protective services, the parents were half as likely to accept services as compared to parents without substance abuse issues (Murphy et al., 1991)

Many forms of child abuse, including neglect, physical abuse, prenatal drug exposure, and sexual abuse, appear to be connected with child maltreatment. Children exposed to parental and other adult substance abuse can be at increased risk for lapses in care, protection, and more direct forms of abuse (Famularo et al., 1992). Substance use may cause the parent to be less attentive to children's needs, reduce the parent's ability to control abusive impulses, and divert household finances from basic necessities (Azzi-Lessing & Olsen, 1996).

In disadvantaged areas, many women receive inadequate prenatal care and counseling despite the well-known risks of substance abuse (Berger, Sorensen, Gendler, & Fitzsimmons, 1990; Brownsberger, 1997), thus putting their children at higher risk for in utero drug exposure, often considered prima facie evidence of child maltreatment. This initial exposure of a child to substances before birth may be followed by other forms of abuse. In Kelley's (1992) study of drug-exposed children and their mothers, 40% of the drug-exposed infants were in foster care because of maternal neglect or abuse. In this same study, substance-using mothers were significantly more likely to be found by child protective services to have neglected or abused their children as compared to controls, not including the drug-positive toxicology screen report following birth. Kelley also found that substance-using mothers were more likely than controls to inadequately immunize their children because of failure to keep routine appointments and were more likely to be homeless at the time of the study. Besinger et al. (1999) found that children removed from families with caregiver substance abuse issues were more likely to be removed because of neglect than because of other forms of abuse, as compared to those children without substance-abusing caregivers. Parental neglectful action, or rather inaction, seems to be a risk even after a child is placed into alternative care. McNichol (1999) found that the frequency of biological parent visits for infants in the foster care system with verified prenatal drug exposure was significantly less than that of controls. Famularo et al. (1992) found that alcohol abuse was significantly associated with physical maltreatment, and cocaine abuse was significantly associated with sexual abuse in their sample of child abuse and neglect cases in which the state took legal custody of children.

Gender also seem to play a role in familial substance abuse issues. One study found that maternal, rather than paternal, substance abuse played a more important role in findings connecting parental substance abuse and child maltreatment (Murphy et al., 1991). Women face unique circumstances in light of their reproductive capacity. According to the 1999 National Household Survey on Drug Abuse among pregnant women aged 15 to 44 years, 3.4% reported using illicit substances in the month prior to the interview (SAMHSA, 2000). Since 1985 at least 200 women have been criminally prosecuted for using illicit drugs or alcohol during pregnancy (Haack, 1997). Policies encouraging the prosecution of women based on harm to their child in utero enjoy considerable public and political support (Berger et al., 1990; Haack, 1997), but may result in some unintended effects. Such policies may discourage pregnant substance-abusing women from seeking appropriate medical care for fear of prosecution or child welfare sanctions (Berger et al., 1990; Haack, 1997; Roth, 1991), and the number of mothers of young children in the criminal justice system may increase. Moreover, the removal of a child based on the mother's substance use during pregnancy may not be in the best interest of the child given the shortage of foster care homes (Roth, 1991). Many children entering the foster care system as infants with substance-abusing mothers are placed in alternative care directly from the hospital and have special needs and require consistent caregiving, which the child welfare system may not be able to provide (Haack, 1997). Removing a child from his or her family can result in a series of placements for extended periods of time (Murphy et al., 1991). In spite of the negative impact that substance abuse can have on families, child welfare involvement is neither feasible nor desirable for every family with a substance-abusing parent (Haack, 1997; Morrison Dore et al., 1995). Despite women's unique position as bearers, and often caretakers, of children it is important to recognize that successful substance abuse treatment programs should include both mothers and fathers (Tracy & Farkas, 1994).

What is more important is a comprehensive, coordinated response between child welfare and public health systems to address the difficulties faced by substance-abusing parents and their children (Haack, 1997). The need for decisive action to remedy the negative effects of parental substance abuse is apparent. Children of substance abusers remain in the foster care system longer than other populations, are moved from one placement to another more frequently, and are less likely to return home to their parents (Haack, 1997). Parents who use substances are the least compliant with court-ordered referrals (Famularo et al., 1989). Making matters more difficult is the pervasiveness of substance abuse issues. Whole families may be immersed in the drug culture, and few stable adults may be available for child care and kinship placements (Morrison Dore et al., 1995).

Although men continue to have a higher rate of current illicit drug use than women (SAMHSA, 2000), unique barriers prevent women from seeking substance abuse treatment, including stigma, particularly for pregnant women and mothers who use substances; denial, often stemming from the shame and guilt of using; and a lack of gender-specific treatment services (Finkelstein, 1994; Roth, 1991). Female substance abusers are treated with rejection, disgust, prejudice, and apathy (Pape, 1993). Even practitioners may have stigmatized attitudes toward substance-abusing mothers (Tracy & Farkas, 1994). Mothers and, it could be argued, custodial fathers as well may fear that if they seek treatment they will lose custody of their children (Pape, 1993). In addition, most substance abuse treatment programs were designed initially by and for men (Azzi-Lessing & Olsen, 1996; Finkelstein, 1994, NIDA, 2000; Root, 1989; Roth, 1991), resulting in a relative lack of consideration for the different emotional, social, and economic realities of women's lives (Azzi-Lessing & Olsen, 1996, Finkelstein, 1994, Sun, 2000). Treatment approaches such as the traditional confrontation model may be inappropriate for women who may already be struggling with self-esteem and feelings of powerlessness (Pape, 1993). Furthermore, women are neither being identified nor entering treatment at the same rate as men (Pape, 1993). Issues such as female sexuality and victimization may be ignored (CSAT, 1994; Root, 1989). This lack of consideration for female, and family, issues becomes a particular stumbling block for women who have child rearing responsibilities because of a lack of programs that offer women the opportunity to have their children with them while in treatment (Finkelstein, 1994). In addition to the low availability of treatment programs (CSAT, 1994; Haack, 1997), the lack of affordable and consistent child care and the fear of interference by the department of social services in the family may be important barriers to treatment for substance-abusing women with children (CSAT, 1994; Pape, 1993; Roth, 1991). Finkelstein (1994) has noted that the recovery process for mothers works best when the treatment program is designed for women and their children. The low-income status of many substance-abusing women with children results in more barriers in the form of inadequate transportation and a lack of basic resources that results in a seemingly endless string of small crises that demand immediate attention and interrupt treatment (Azzi-Lessing & Olsen, 1996).

Women and families with substance abuse issues are often facing multiple problems, including inadequate financial resources (Azzi-Lessing & Olsen, 1996; CSAT, 1994; Finkelstein, 1994; Murphy et al., 1991), particularly after the recent feminization of poverty and increase in single-female-headed families (CSAT, 1994; Roth, 1991); substandard housing and violent environments (Finkelstein, 1994); few job skills (Azzi-Lessing & Olsen, 1996; Finkelstein, 1994); low levels of education (Murphy et al., 1991); inadequate transportation (Azzi-Lessing & Olsen, 1996); limited child care options (Azzi-Lessing & Olsen, 1996); and limited support systems (Azzi-Lessing & Olsen, 1996; Finkelstein, 1994; Murphy et al., 1991). The possible role of emotional or psychiatric issues, dual diagnoses, and medical issues should also be considered when treating substance-abusing women (CSAT, 1994). Ongoing stress experienced by single mothers puts them at high risk for many physical and emotional illnesses and, in turn, at high risk for substance use as a coping mechanism (Roth, 1991).

Finkelstein (1994) recommends that women's substance abuse treatment programs should be viewed within the context of their relationships with others, unlike the individual-focused programs of the past developed for men. A family-centered approach would assist women in carrying out their roles as parents; focus on the needs of their children; and consider the social isolation, lack of education, and relatively low level of job skills of many women with substance abuse issues (Azzi-Lessing & Olsen, 1996). Many women with substance use histories often do not live in traditional family settings and do not have extensive social networks to seek support from (Barth, Pietrzak, & Ramler, 1993). Access to resources, such as housing, and the opportunity to develop life skills, including literacy, may also be integral pieces of treatment programs for pregnant and parenting women (Barth et al., 1993). Treatment programs should encourage mothers' positive motivation, such as their children, nurturing instincts, and access to the social support systems that promote and sustain their roles as mothers (CSAT, 1994). A mother may do for her child what she would not do for herself (Roth, 1991). Frequent visitation is critical if women are separated from their children to maintain bonds and enhance motivation toward recovery (Azzi-Lessing & Olsen, 1996). The support provided by caregivers can make a large difference in women's ability to face their emotional issues surrounding their children and to deal with parenting in light of substance abuse (CSAT, 1994; Finkelstein, 1994). Moreover, other significant persons (spouse, boyfriend, partner, etc.) in the woman's life should be involved in the treasment as well (Finkelstein, 1994).

Link Among Criminal Justice, Substance Abuse, and Child Welfare

In 1999 an estimated 721,500 state and federal prisoners were parents to 1,498,800 children under age 18 (Bureau of Justice Statistics, 2000). The process of incarceration is especially difficult for custodial parents. Those who enter jail as pretrial detainees often do not know how long they are likely to be away from their children, thus making it difficult for parents to arrange for appropriate care for their children, and jails may not ask incoming inmates if they have made adequate arrangements for their children's care or even if they have children (Covington Katz, 1998). Children may be shuffled from placement to placement without much information about their mothers' situation (Covington Katz, 1998). When children are placed in alternative care, caseworkers are expected to make concentrated efforts toward the preservation of family ties and family reunification (Beckerman, 1994). However, custodial parents in jail present a particularly difficult population for child welfare service workers. Characteristics common among inmates, such as substance abuse, long histories of victimization, and recurring criminal justice involvement, put children at an increased risk of child abuse or neglect (Covington Katz, 1998) and out-of-home placements.

A father's imprisonment is less likely to threaten the continuity of children's living arrangements, because the mother is likely to assume responsibility for his children (Beckerman, 1994). The reverse however, is seldom the case (Beckerman, 1994), and children of incarcerated mothers are more likely to be placed with a relative, oftentimes a grandparent (Singer, 1995). Despite the apparent lesser role of fathers' incarceration and subsequent absence from their children's lives, future research is needed to further understand the interrelationship among criminal justice, substance abuse, and child welfare of all parents. The current body of research regarding parents and child welfare primarily focuses on mothers.

The number of female prisoners has risen dramatically in recent years (Beckerman, 1994; Singer, 1995). In the United States, the rate of growth of the number of female inmates has exceeded that for male inmates each year since 1981 (Singer, 1995). In 1998 an estimated 3.2 million arrests of women accounted for 22% of all arrests that year, and more than 950,000 women were under correctional supervision (about 1% of the female population) (Bureau of Justice Statistics, 2000). As a result child protective services caseworkers are more and more often encountering situations in which the mother is incarcerated (Beckerman, 1994). Many of these women are facing multiple barriers, including impoverished backgrounds, alcohol and drug addiction, and emotional and mental health problems (Singer, 1995). Major contributors to the increasing incarceration of women have been drug and alcohol and the advent of mandatory minimum sentences for most drug offenses (CSAT, 1994). Society, however, seems to have paid little attention to the female inmate population as evidenced by the few clinical and research investigations and limited services (Singer, 1995) despite increasing attention on understanding why more women are entering the criminal justice system (CSAT, 1994). Singer (1995) hypothesized that the dearth of research literature dedicated to female criminality is attributable to three reasons: (1) women tend to commit nonviolent crimes and therefore are not considered a significant threat, (2) women constitute only a small proportion of inmates, and (3) women have unequal economic and political status.

A mother's incarceration limits her ability to participate in the permanency planning of her child (Beckerman, 1994). Many mothers rarely correspond with or telephone caseworkers, and in one study 30% of the mothers surveyed reported that they did not receive a copy of their child's case plan (Beckerman, 1994). Many jail facilities severely limit inmate access to telephones, local calls typically cost more than regular pay phones, and long-distance calls have to be made collect at a cost that may be difficult for families to afford (Covington Katz, 1998). Moreover, illiteracy limits many mothers' ability to correspond, and the policies of the correctional facilities limit telephone calls (Beckerman, 1994). It is also difficult for mothers to attend court hearings. They must be given sufficient notice of hearing dates to make special arrangements for permission and transportation in order to attend (Beckerman, 1994). Less than half (47%) of the mothers in Beckerman's (1994) study were familiar with the procedures necessary for them to attend court hearings.

In Beckerman's (1994) study of incarcerated women, half of the mothers had children between the ages of two and seven years, and 45% of the children were living in foster care at the time of the mother's arrest. In Singer's (1995) study of female inmates, most of the women (73%) had children and nearly 14% were pregnant. A little more than a third (39%) reported having legal custody of all of their children, about half (51%) had legal custody of none of their children, and just under 10% had legal custody of some of their children.

Studies addressing alcohol and other drugs and crime have demonstrated the interrelatedness of the two issues (Held, 1998), and it seems that the majority of women in jail are addicted to alcohol or other drugs (Covington Katz, 1998). Jails frequently hold women who have been convicted of minor crimes, oftentimes misdemeanors with short-term sentences (Covington Katz, 1998). In Beckerman's (1994) study the greatest percentage of the mothers (43%) surveyed were jailed because of a drug-related offense and were serving a sentence of less than 25 months (58%). In Singer's (1995) study the most common offense of the incarcerated women surveyed was prostitution (50%), followed by drug-related offenses (13%). In this same study, 61% of the women reported having used cocaine at least once a week prior to arrest. Cocaine or cocaine combined with another drug was the most commonly used substance for most of the women who reported drug use in this study (62%), followed by alcohol (26.2%). Nearly half the incarcerated women in Singer's study reported receiving treatment for a drug or alcohol problem at some time in their lives, and 33% (66) of the respondents stated that drug treatment or rehabilitation was the service needed most after release from prison. However, jails do not generally have the rehabilitative programs such as drug treatment, education, and parenting classes found in prisons (Covington Katz, 1998).

Fifty-six percent of the incarcerated women in Singer's (1995) study had comorbid substance abuse and mental health problems. Seventy-five percent reported being threatened with physical violence over the past year, and 69% reported actual violence. In addition, 68% reported forced sexual activity as adults, and almost half (48%) reported sexual victimization in childhood. In total, including adult and childhood sexual abuse, 81% of the women reported sexual victimization.

Although fathers' incarceration may have a relatively smaller impact on their children's entry into the child welfare system, many incarcerated men suffer from the combined effects of substance abuse, incarceration, and mental illness (Abram & Teplin, 1991). The influence of these issues upon the well-being of their children is also important to consider.

Ethnicity

When examining the relationship among child welfare, substance abuse, and criminal justice issues, ethnicity becomes an important factor to consider. Studies indicate that children of color are more likely to be overrepresented in child maltreatment reports in relation to the general population and may be more likely than their Caucasian counterparts to have substantiated cases of abuse once a child maltreatment report has been made (Courtney & Barth, 1996). The incarcerated mothers in Beckerman's (1994) study were primarily either African American (47%) or Hispanic (28%). In Singer's (1995) study of incarcerated females, most of the women (72%) included were African American. Variations in patterns of substance use and dependence have also been noted between ethnic groups by age, gender, and initiation (SAMHSA, 2000). In addition to differences in patterns of use, ethnic minority groups face lingual and cultural barriers that may prevent them from receiving adequate services once they are identified as being affected by substance abuse (Azzi-Lessing & Olsen, 1996). It is impossible to develop effective prevention interventions without understanding culturally tied beliefs and behaviors of the community (Roth, 1991). However, the relationship among ethnicity, child abuse, criminal justice, and substance abuse is complicated and calls for more focus in future research efforts.

There have been methodological issues highlighted in the literature examining the relationships between ethnicity and social issues. Few studies attempt to account for differences in the economic and social well-being of families when examining the effects of ethnicity, and those that do show a reduced or nonexistent effect of ethnicity when social class was factored into the model (Courtney & Barth, 1996). In addition, Azzi-Lessing and Olsen (1996) warn about the racism and media stereotyping that can have an effect on child welfare workers', judges', and other professionals' judgment about drug involvement and minority populations. Also, differences between children in the child welfare system based on ethnicity are most often greatest between Caucasian and African American children; therefore, it may blur the picture to focus on differences between Caucasian children and all other children (Courtney & Barth, 1996). Moreover, as families of color are overrepresented among the poor, it is important for researchers to recognize the relationship in their interpretations of findings.

Despite these methodological concerns, researchers have noted relationships among ethnicity, substance abuse, and child maltreatment. Besinger et al. (1999) found that children with caregivers who abused substances were significantly less often Latino or "other minority" and more often African American. Once in the child welfare system it appears that families and children of color may not receive the same level of service as Caucasian families and children (Courtney & Barth, 1996). Evidence suggests African American children are less likely to exit the child welfare system once they are placed in alternative care (Courtney & Barth, 1996).

Rates of substance dependence and treatment utilization also vary according to ethnicity. Data from the 1999 National Household Survey on Drug Abuse (SAMHSA, 2000) indicate that Native Americans are the ethnic group reporting the highest rate of illicit substance use (10.6%) and dependence (4.7%), followed by African Americans (7.7% and 2.3%), Hispanics (6.8% and 1.9%), and Caucasians (6.6% and 2.3%). Interestingly, those respondents who reported multiethnic backgrounds also reported the highest level of illicit substance use (11.2%) but not dependence (2.6%). As compared to each group's rate of reported substance dependence, the group with the lowest treatment participation was Asians. All other ethnic groups were fairly similar in their rates of treatment as compared to dependence.

For ethnic minority women the barriers become more complicated as they fight both ethnic and gender stereotypes and discrimination. Racism and sexism are persistent conditions in American society (Roth, 1991). The issues that place African American women at risk for problems substances are the same issues that affect their ability to seek help (Roth, 1991). The same might be said for other ethnic minority groups, including Hispanic American women (Barth et al., 1993), who are overrepresented among lower socioeconomic-level families living in urban areas where access to appropriate services and treatment may be limited.

Gender roles and role expectations exist within each culture, but oftentimes are not recognized in research (Roth, 1991). Little is known about the substance use and abuse patterns of Asian Americans, and less is known about Asian American women (Roth, 1991). Similarly, little is known about the substance use patterns of female Mexican Americans (Roth, 1991). Studies may fail to disaggregate data by gender when examining issues related to substance abuse and, furthermore, rarely acknowledge diversity within large ethnic groups such as Asian Americans or Latinos (Roth, 1991). There are likely distinct differences between patterns and characteristics of Korean American versus Chinese American substance use or Mexican American versus Puerto Rican substance use.

Implications for Policy, Practice, and Research

Many of the same issues that should be addressed in order to combat substance abuse are the issues that must be addressed to fight child abuse and neglect. In order to successfully address parental substance abuse issues, dramatic social change and a broad health response is needed in many areas, including financial support, housing, health care, employment, child care, children's services, family supports, and legal rights (CSAT, 1994; Finkelstein, 1994). An array of comprehensive services beyond the narrow focus of substance abuse, including medical, psychological, and social services, is needed (CSAT, 1994). Other related issues such as sexuality and family violence must also be addressed in the treatment of substance abuse (CSAT, 1994). Poverty, violence, and substance abuse are among the factors fueling the growth of child maltreatment and, as result, protecting children requires more than merely enhancing child protective services. Children need to live in adequate housing in safe environments and have access to proper nutrition and health care (National Center on Child Abuse Prevention Research, 1991). Although advances toward the facilitation of state social services to collect detailed and uniform statistics on the children and families they serve has been slowly progressing, there is still a lack of data on problems related to substance abuse (Curtis & McCullough, 1993). However, anecdotal evidence suggests that increases in the actual number of children involved in substantiated reports of abuse and neglect in which parental use of substances was a factor has resulted in an increased number of placements in out-of-home care (Curtis & McCullough, 1993). In addition, Famularo et al. (1992) found that two-thirds of the cases in its study of families whose children had been placed in alternative care by the state involved parental substance abuse.

Oftentimes child welfare workers are not trained to identify substance abuse problems and are ill prepared to intervene in this problem (Curtis & McCullough, 1993;

Gregoire, 1994; Morrison Dore et al., 1995; Pape, 1993) as well as other community gatekeepers such as law enforcement officials and health care providers (Pape, 1993). However, caseworkers may be the only constant and stable resource in the lives of substance-abusing and maltreating parents, and may be in the unique position to help parents move toward treatment because of the legal sanctions adhering to child protective investigations (Morrison Dore et al., 1995). Even though child welfare workers do not generally treat clients' substance abuse issues directly, the well-being of children is inevitably interwoven with the well-being of their parents (Sun, 2000). More training is needed for child welfare staff to improve knowledge and skills in addressing issues related to substance abuse (Curtis & McCullough, 1993, Gregoire, 1994; Haack, 1997; Sun, 2000; Tracy & Farkas, 1994). Also, more efforts are needed toward the recruitment, training, and support of foster care parents, kinship caregivers, and adoptive parents who care for children affected by problems related to substance use and abuse (Kelley, 1992). Likewise, jail staff, oftentimes working with women who are in jail because of substance abuse issues, may not receive any training to address the family-related issues that women face in jail (Covington Katz, 1998). Moreover, rarely do staff members in substance abuse programs have any training in parenting skills, addressing child maltreatment issues, or child welfare (Tracy & Farkas, 1994). Clinicians, practitioners, foster parents, and other stakeholders have to become generalists, rather than specialists, if they want to be more successful with their clients. The sheer number of serious issues facing families in the child welfare and criminal justice systems demands a level of training and knowledge about several issues, including substance abuse, and the other agencies and systems that interact with these same clients. Substance abuse programs and child welfare services have ignored their overlapping populations and remained very separate from one another (Tracy & Farkas, 1994).

Parental substance abuse can lead to longer stays in the child welfare system and create obstacles to family preservation and reunification. Unfortunately, not enough is known about successful interventions with substance-abusing parents to facilitate recovery from chemical dependency while ensuring child safety and family stability (Haack, 1997), as research has failed to demonstrate which interventions are most successful with which clients, particularly women (Pape, 1993). Working toward sobriety is a long and difficult process for substance-abusing and maltreating parents, requiring constant encouragement and support (Morrison Dore et al., 1995). Many researchers have expressed the need for more efficient evaluation mechanisms and prevention programs to address substance abuse (Held, 1998).

Disentangling the effects of different factors such as ethnicity, poverty, and substance abuse upon the child welfare system is difficult and complicated. Estimating the extent of the consequences of maternal substance abuse alone, given the pervasiveness of polysubstance abuse, poor maternal nutrition, and sexually transmitted diseases among women of childbearing age is complex (NIDA, 2000). It seems unreasonable to expect the child welfare system alone to counter the effects of poverty, discrimination, and the subsequent sequelae of these difficult issues (Courtney & Barth, 1996). The interconnectedness and the self-perpetuating and cyclical nature of these issues is apparent. The use of stimulants and other illicit substances may be a form of self-medication in an attempt to escape from feelings of depression (Kelley, 1992). It is not hard to imagine the possibility of depression among young, often unmarried, parents who are struggling financially, have little social support, have a history of personal experience with violence, face discrimination, and/or have little education and few job skills. Mothers of children with prenatal exposure to substances have reported more stress, depression, health problems, and social isolation than mothers of children who were not drug exposed (Kelley, 1992). The ripple effects of substance abuse and child abuse and neglect reach even farther costing the general public in the form of taxes that support programs to treat children suffering prenatal exposure to drugs and to care for children exposed to other forms of abuse (NIDA, 2000). Drug-exposed infants stand a better chance of escaping the detrimental effects of their prenatal substance exposure in strong, supportive, loving homes. However, even when children are removed from abusive or neglectful homes, they may have difficulty finding foster or adoptive homes because of the fear that drug-exposed infants are too risky (NIDA, 2000). It becomes particularly important, when substance abuse issues are involved, for child welfare workers to determine the degree to which parental substance abuse poses a risk to the child and necessitates removal (Tracy & Farkas, 1994) and balance this with the instability of the out-of-home care system. A number of children with substance-abusing families are reunified only to return to placement, possibly evidencing the lack of strong reunification or aftercare services and the difficulty involved in determining if a family is genuinely prepared for reunification (Tracy & Farkas, 1994).

Despite this quagmire of interconnected issues, causes, effects, and outcomes, some movement has to be made beyond after-the-fact interventions. We must focus on improving services at the front end to remedy problems that lead to child removal (Courtney & Barth, 1996).

Suggestions have been made by several researchers with regard to the best practices and improvements. However, the roots of child abuse and neglect, poverty, discrimination, and substance abuse are much more difficult to get at. Few research studies currently published address substance abuse prevention outside of education and public schools, despite the clear connection emerging between tobacco, alcohol, and other drug use, and other human service systems including health and criminal justice (Held, 1998).

Families are often dealing with multiple issues and agencies, including the child welfare system, unemployment, juvenile justice, and substance abuse treatment, and agencies are often interacting with the same families (Azzi-Lessing & Olsen, 1996; "Beyond the boundaries," 1999). However, there is a separation or disconnect in the governance of these agencies and programs that are striving toward different goals and work within different timelines resulting in a categorical, rather than a holistic, approach (Azzi-Lessing & Olsen, 1996; Covington Katz, 1998; Haack, 1997; "Beyond the boundaries," 1999). When chemical dependency is also a part of the picture, time mandates become even more difficult to balance because the cycle of recovery, which is painstakingly slow and erratic, does not easily mesh with the child's needs or the timelines for child welfare decision making (Azzi-Lessing & Olsen, 1996; Haack, 1997). Court mandates and case plans require evidence of abstinence from drug use within a certain amount of time, perhaps unfairly holding women dealing with issues of poverty to an unattainable standard (Azzi-Lessing & Olsen, 1996). Low-income substance-abusing parents involved in the child welfare system must successfully combat the daily crises of living with inadequate transportation, housing, and other basic needs while attempting to keep treatment appointments and maintain abstinence at the risk of losing their children (Azzi-Lessing & Olsen, 1996). However, the needs of the child must be balanced with those of the parent and family unit. As the substance-abusing parent is working toward a recovery, which may or may not be successful, the child is in the care of the child welfare system, growing older and less likely to be adopted.

Federal and state human services and health care bureaucracy often do not support multidisciplinary, jointly administered and funded, and family-focused treatment systems; rather, funding is problem-centered, focusing on only one area of service at a time, and families are inundated by a tangled maze of local, state, and federal agencies and programs that require separate contact and many forms (Barth et al., 1993; Finkelstein, 1994). The lack of flexibility in child welfare systems' responding to the particular needs of children and families, policies establishing time limits for children in care, and sentencing guidelines all affect outcomes for children and families. For example, mandatory sentencing for drug offenses has kept mothers in jail longer yet often returns women to their communities without adequate efforts toward addressing the drug addiction that led to their incarceration (Covington Katz, 1998). Practitioners have learned that single problem-oriented, client-focused approaches are not especially effective with families with many service needs (Barth et al., 1993).

Research efforts have also followed a similar pattern of compartmentalization of issues. Researchers often focus on a problem or event and not its connection to other problems or events (Roth, 1991). For example, studies may note the use of alcohol or other drugs, but they rarely include information about the amount, frequency, or types of use and less about their relationship to, or interrelationship with, other problems (Roth, 1991). Those studies that do include multiple variables suggest complicated patterns of relationship among them and that interventions need to take multiple factors into account (Roth, 1991).

To address the issues involved in substance abuse, criminal justice, and the child welfare system, agencies and professionals need to collaborate more closely as a comprehensive, culturally, and ethnically appropriate, child- and family-centered service system at the policy, program, and practice levels (Azzi-Lessing & Olsen, 1996; Barth et al., 1993; Besharov, 1990; Besinger et al., 1999; Finkelstein, 1994; Haack, 1997; National Association of Public Child Welfare Administrators, 1991; "Beyond the boundaries," 1999). Although the recent trend has been toward collaboration, many agencies have not embraced this principle (Barth et al., 1993). The child welfare system is a loose conglomeration of hundreds of family service agencies and thousands of independent, private agencies, not necessarily in harmony. Tracy and Farkas (1994) recommended jointly sponsored continuing education efforts to reinforce didactic information and foster professional relationships, case consultations, and collaborative projects. Child welfare decision making entails complex weighing of medical, social work, child development, and legal considerations, and is easier and more accurate when it is made in consultation with a diversity of professionals who have the skills and experience to help assess the situation (Besharov, 1990). If the child welfare and criminal justice systems collaborate toward treating mothers with substance addiction and healing fractured families, the criminal justice system can reduce recidivism rates, and the child welfare systems can preserve and reunify more families (Covington Katz, 1998). Parents also need to be a part of this collaborative team effort. Allowing parents to actively participate in their children's placements and case plans will decrease their anxiety and ease the transition for their children (Covington Katz, 1998). Also, a parent's arrest offers a unique opportunity for intervention in that incarcerated parents may find themselves consistently sober for the first time in a long time and may be better able to see the consequences of their actions (Covington Katz, 1998). Based on research there is increasing evidence that substance abuse prevention efforts are not successful when implemented in isolation (Held, 1998).The service delivery system's underfunding and the considerable family needs that often extend far beyond the scope of what service providers can individually offer highlight the critical need for interagency collaboration (Azzi-Lessing & Olsen, 1996).

Unfortunately the overlap in issues has caused some unintended side effects that must also be addressed in order to improve services to children and families. The mission of child welfare is to protect children and ensure healthy development, not function as a law enforcement system (National Association of Public Child Welfare Administrators, 1991). However, the focus on the drug crisis has been on enforcement, not treatment, placing child protective services workers in a punitive rather than supportive position when addressing substance abuse issues (National Association of Public Child Welfare Administrators, 1991). The move toward collaboration should be monitored so as not to abuse or distort the mission or the role of each agency.

New, more collaborative, family- and community-oriented, female-sensitive programs have been recommended by researchers. Although substance abuse treatment and child welfare are overlapping areas of practice, they have not traditionally been viewed as such (Tracy & Farkas, 1994) and thus require concurrent treatment. Researchers have recommended that substance abuse treatment centers take a more holistic approach toward treating women and mothers, including thorough physical examinations (Pape, 1993), psychological assessment and treatment addressing mental illness issues (Pape, 1993), family involvement (Pape, 1993; Tracy & Farkas, 1994) and work around issues of sexuality (Pape, 1993), past victimization (Pape, 1993; Tracy & Farkas, 1994), family violence (Pape, 1993), and parenting (Tracy & Farkas, 1994). Finkelstein (1994) advocated the development of family support centers strongly connected to the community that could work to empower parents, provide them with a range of formal and informal support services from staff and each other, and connect families with long-term support and other specialized services such as substance abuse counseling. Some researchers have further advocated for substance abuse treatment programs to shift from male-centered models to family-centered models (National Center on Child Abuse Prevention Research, 1991). Treating the family unit when there is a substance-abusing parent would allow the parent to enter a treatment program without forcing that parent to choose between recovery and caring for the children (Roth, 1991). Covington Katz (1998) recommended community-based alternatives to incarceration for substance-abusing women so that they may have contact with their children while seeking treatment. Expanded educational support services to pregnant women and new parents are needed (National Center on Child Abuse Prevention Research, 1991), and more treatment options for pregnant women (Berger et al., 1990) and parents with children are needed.

Other researchers have made specific recommendations to existing social service systems. Famularo et al. (1989) recommend that child welfare workers and courts establish a clear hierarchy of mental health and social service needs in each case of child abuse, particularly when working with substance-abusing parents who have low rates of compliance, and communicate to parents the specific concrete expectations of the court. Prison-based therapeutic communities aimed at treating substance abuse have been successful in reducing recidivism rates for males and females (Wexler, Falkin, & Lipton, 1990), and readily available drug- and alcohol-screening and treatment services (Covington Katz, 1998; Singer, 1995) have been recommended for incarcerated women. Other recommendations have included mental health services sensitive to issues such as victimization being available during incarceration (Singer, 1995), education about parental rights (Covington Katz, 1998), medical services appropriate for pregnant women (Singer, 1995), parenting education (Singer, 1995), supervised mother-child visitation (Covington Katz, 1998; Singer, 1995), and treatment and service referrals, including follow-ups and support upon and following release (Covington Katz, 1998; Singer, 1995). Most of these recommendations could be extended for incarcerated fathers as well. Covington Katz (1998) recommends making new jail facilities more child- and family-friendly.

More research is yet to be done to address several areas to better serve families. The lack of gender-specific treatment outcome data hinders the valid design or adaptation of treatment methods specifically for women (CSAT, 1994). Also, future studies should use standardized measures to assess substance abuse among caregivers and a higher level of specificity (including type, frequency, and duration) to clarify how substance abuse relates to child maltreatment (Besinger et al., 1999).

A parent's involvement in child protective services or with the criminal justice system may offer a unique opportunity to address many issues that affect the family, such as substance abuse (Roth, 1991). It is important to take advantage of this opportunity and serve children and their families in a collaborative, gender-sensitive, community-oriented, and culturally appropriate manner.

References

Abram, K. M., & Teplin, L. A. (1991). Co-occurring disorders among mentally ill jail detainees: Implications for public policy. *American Psychologist, 46*(10), 1036–1045.

Azzi-Lessing, L., & Olsen, L. J. (1996). Substance abuse-affected families in the child welfare system: New challenges, new alliances. *Social Work, 41*(1), 15–23.

Barth, R. P., Pietrzak, J., & Ramler, M. (Eds.). (1993). *Families living with drugs and HIV: Intervention and treatment strategies.* New York: Guilford Press.

Beckerman, A. (1994). Mothers in prison: Meeting the prerequisite conditions for permanency planning. *Social Work, 39*(1), 9–14.

Berger, C. S., Sorenson, L., Gendler, B., & Fitzsimmons, J. (1990). Cocaine and pregnancy: A challenge for healthcare providers. *Health and Social Work, 15*(4), 310–316.

Besharov, D. J. (1990). *Combating child abuse: Guidelines for cooperation between law enforcement and child protective services*. Washington, DC: American Enterprise Institute Press.

Besinger, A., Garland, A. F., Litrownik, A. J., & Lansverk, J. A. (1999). Caregiver substance abuse among maltreated children placed in out-of-home care. *Child Welfare*, *78*(2), 221–239.

Beyond the boundaries of child welfare: Connecting with welfare, juvenile justice, family violence, and mental health systems (1999). *Spectrum: the Journal of State Government*, *72*(1). JK 2403 S7, 14–18.

Brownsberger, W. N. (1997). Prevalence of frequent cocaine use in urban poverty areas. *Contemporary Drug Problems*, *24*(2), 349–371.

Bureau of Justice Statistics. (2000). Retrieved on September 28, 2005, from www.ojp.usdoj.gov/bjs/abstract/incarceratedparentsandtheirchildren

Center for Substance Abuse Treatment. (1994). *Practical approaches in the treatment of women who abuse alcohol and other drugs*. Rockville, MD: Department of Health and Human Services, Public Health Service.

Courtney, M. E., & Barth, R. P. (1996). Race and child welfare services: Past research and future directions. *Child Welfare*, *75*(2), 99–136.

Covington Katz, P. (1998). Supporting families and children of mothers in jail: An integrated child welfare and criminal justice strategy. *Child Welfare*, *77*(5), 495–511.

Curtis, P. A., & McCullough, C. (1993). The impact of alcohol and other drugs on the child welfare system. *Child Welfare*, *72*(6), 533–542.

Delaney-Black, V., Covington, C., Templin, T., Ager, J., Martier, S., & Sokol, R. (1998). Prenatal cocaine exposure and child behavior. *Pediatrics*, *102*(4), 945–950.

Famularo, R., Kinscherff, R., Bunshaft, D., Spivak, G., & Fenton, T. (1989). Parental compliance to court ordered treatment interventions in cases of child maltreatment. *Child Abuse and Neglect*, *13*(4), 507–514.

Famularo, R., Kinscherff, R., & Fenton, T. (1992). Parental substance abuse and the nature of child maltreatment. *Child Abuse and Neglect*, *16*(4), 475–483.

Finkelstein, N. (1994). Treatment issues for alcohol and drug-dependent pregnant and parenting women. *Health & Social Work*, *19*(1), 7–15.

Gregoire, T. K. (1994) Assessing the benefits and increasing the utility of addiction training for public child welfare workers: A pilot study. *Child Welfare*, *73*(1), 69–81.

Haack, M. R. (1997). (Ed.). *Drug dependent mothers and their children: Issues in public policy and public health*. New York: Springer Publishing.

Held, G. A. (1998). Linkages between substance abuse prevention and other human services. Retrieved July 18, 2005, from http://www.nida.nih.gov/about/organization/DESPR/HSR/da-pre/HeldLinkagesPartA.htm

Kelley, S. J. (1992). Parenting stress and child maltreatment in drug exposed children. *Child Abuse and Neglect, 16*(3), 317–328.

McNichol, T. (1999). The impact of drug-exposed children on family foster care. *Child Welfare, 78*(1), 184–196.

Morrison Dore, M., Doris, J. M., & Wright, P. (1995). Identifying substance abuse in maltreating families: A child welfare challenge. *Child Abuse and Neglect, 19*(5), 531–543.

Murphy, J. M., Jellinek, M., Quinn, D., Smith, G., Poitrast, F. G., & Goshko, M. (1991). Substance abuse and the serious child mistreatment: Prevalence, risk, and outcome in a court sample. *Child Abuse and Neglect, 15*(3), 197–211.

National Association of Public Child Welfare Administrators. (1991). Working with substance abusing families and drug-exposed children: The child welfare response. *Public Welfare, 49*(4), 37–38.

National Center on Child Abuse Prevention Research. (1991). *Current trends in child abuse reporting and fatalities: The results of the 1990 annual fifty state survey*. Chicago: National Committee for Prevention of Child Abuse.

National Institute on Drug Abuse. (2000). Research Report Series. Cocaine Abuse and Addiction. Retrieved July 18, 2005, from http://www.drugabuse.gov/researchreports/cocaine/cocaine.html Reports/Cocaine/cocaine2.html

O'Hare, W. (2001, June). *Child Population: First Data from the 2000 Census*. Baltimore, MD: Annie E. Casey Foundation and Population Reference Bureau.

Pape, P. A. (1993). Issues in assessment and intervention with alcohol and drug abusing women. In S. L. A. Straussner (Ed.), *Clinical work with substance abusing clients* (pp. 251–269). New York: Guilford Press.

Root, M. P. (1989). Treatment failures: The role of sexual victimization in women's addictive behavior. *American Journal of Orthopsychiatry, 59*(4), 542.

Roth, P. (Ed.) (1991). *Alcohol and drugs are women's issues, volume 1, A review of the issues*. New Jersey: Women's Action Alliance and Scarecrow Press.

Singer, M. Bussey, J., Song, L., & Lunghofer, L. (1995). The psychosocial issues of women serving time in jail. *Social Work, 40*(1), 103–112.

Singer, M. I. (1995). The psychosocial issues of women serving time in jail. *Social Work, 40*(1), 103–113.

Substance Abuse and Mental Health Services Administration. (2000). 1999 National Household Survey on Drug Abuse. Retrieved July 18, 2005, from http://www.health.org/govstudy/6kd376/default.aspx#topofpage

Sun, An-Pyng (2000). Helping substance-abusing mothers in the child-welfare system: Turning crisis into opportunity. *Families in Society: The Journal of Contemporary Human Services, 81*(2), 142–131.

Tracy, E. M., & Farkas, K. J. (1994). Preparing practitioners for child welfare practice with substance abusing families. *Child Welfare, 73*(1), 57–68.

Wexler, H., Falkin, G., & Lipton, D. (1990). Outcome evaluation of a prison therapeutic community of substance abuse treatment. *Criminal Justice and Behavior, 17*(1), 71–92.

2

The Mark of the Urchins

ROBERT L. HAMPTON and LUCIA MAGARIAN

Introduction

Across America, two issues that cut across economic, social, and racial lines are substance abuse and domestic violence. Like characters out of Dickens's *A Christmas Carol*, these are the twin urchins that hide under the coat of a contemporary America, running wild, stealing, not loaves of bread or copper pennies, but family life and stability.

Much like 19th-century England, America is a society that would prefer not to see or deal with these issues, that is, of course, unless it is in a comfortable seat at the local movie house, watching Hollywood's latest morality play. Underneath the exclamations of today's politicians and managed care teams, one can almost hear the murmurings, "Are there no prisons? Are there no workhouses?" "Are there no shelters? Are there no treatment programs?" The effect of much of this lamentation is in both the quantitative data and the qualitative impact on family life. For instance, according to the Bureau of Justice (Rennison & Welchans, 2000):

- In 1998, about one million acts of intimate partner violence (IPV) were committed—85% of which were against women.
- About 4 out of 10 of these female victims had children in their household. Conservatively, that would mean at least half a million children were exposed to

domestic violence. Some experts believe that the range is even higher, closer to three million, and that these kids are 15 times more likely to be at risk for child abuse or death.

- Sixty percent of domestic violence occurs between dinnertime (6 p.m.) and early morning (6 a.m.), when children are most likely to be around.
- And, of the 1,830 deaths as a result of IPV, 1,300 of those murdered were women.

Moreover, the statistics from the National Violence Against Women (NVAW) Survey (Tjaden & Thoennes, 2000) paint an even bleaker picture, for included in the definition of abuse are the categories of sexual assaults and stalking. They learned that:

- Over a half million women are stalked annually.
- Each year, husbands and/or boyfriends rape approximately 322,000 women.

Unfortunately, these statistics do not present the entire story, for, of the more than 300,000 women who were raped by intimate partners (spouse, boyfriends, lovers), the NVAW survey discovered (Tjaden & Thoennes, 2000, p. 53):

- Only 55,000 will report it to police.
- About 53,000 will get a temporary restraining order (TRO).
- Close to 36,000 will painfully discover that the TRO was violated.
- Twenty-six thousand women will succeed in having their perpetrator arrested.
- Twenty-four thousand will seek criminal prosecution.
- Less than *half* of the rapists/abusers (only 10,000) will be convicted.
- And a mere 7,000 abusers will go to jail or serve any sentence.

All in all, abusers face roughly a *13% conviction rate*, frightening odds for a sexually abused individual seeking justice versus the risk that reporting the abuser will trigger a retributive rage. The scenario for physical assault is even worse; less than 5% of women who seek help from the police will be able to have their perpetrator put in prison. If we repeat the above Scrooge-like slogan to these women as a way of *serving* them (i.e., telling them to seek a shelter or legal recourse) without acknowledging their reality (that is to say, that justice is often denied them), then we, as service providers, are collectively asking these women not only to risk being abused again but to risk greater and more severe abuse than before. In some ways, this perpetuates an emotional roller-coaster for our most vulnerable women. It lulls them into a short-lived, false sense of safety and empowerment, only to have true reality plummet them back into fear of their abusers who, in all likelihood, will "teach them a lesson" about asking for help, or "get even" because these women attempt to seek justice.

The Link Between Violence and Substance Abuse

Against this societal backdrop, the link between violence and substance abuse remains an enigma for the reason that substance abuse differs between men and women, as well as between victims and perpetrators. For instance, we know that men do not batter *because* they are drunk or high. According to Larry Bennett (2001), there is "a link between substance abuse and woman abuse, but not a direct link." He has suggested that substance abuse and intimate partner violence have multiple paths of risks and reinforcement (Bennett & Williams, 2003). Unfortunately, the common misconception is that there is a causal relationship between the two. The result, as Bennett points out, is that this incorrect belief only increases the danger for women by (among other things):

•providing the abuser with an excuse, thereby relieving him of responsibility for his own actions
•intensifying his motivation for personal power
•increasing his risk (of abuse) in particular situations
•altering his brain chemistry
•magnifying particular perpetrator characteristics
•or creating dysfunction in his family across generations

Bennett sees a problem with superficial treatments for battering. He asks, "What do you get when a batterer makes 90 AA meetings in 90 days?" And he responds, "A sober batterer." One can see similar results from the quick solutions that medication yields. The question, "What do you get when a doctor puts a batterer on Prozac?" is appropriate. The response, "A happy batterer," is telling (personal communication, February 22, 2001). Unfortunately, only victims emerge from this kind of relationship. The treatment of choice does not address the fundamental issues.

The enigma for most service providers, shelters, and treatment programs is a misunderstanding of the gender differences regarding the interplay between substance abuse and domestic violence for women. Unlike men, battered women often use alcohol or drugs as a way to cope with their abuser, a way to dissociate themselves from painful emotions or memories, a way to numb the very real pain they are enduring. This is not to say that women may not have problems with substance abuse independent of their abusive relationship. Rather, it is to note that the role drugs and alcohol play in the lives of these women is complicated and cannot be limited to the simple notion of addiction.

It may, in fact, be part of their overall survival plan, a point that the U.S. Department of Health and Human Services (Fazzone, Holdon, & Reed, 1997) underscored in the *Treatment Improvement Protocol* (TIP). It goes on to conclude that in the absence of alcohol or drugs, survivors can develop other severe psychological conditions, including eating disorders, obsessive-compulsive behaviors, or somatic conditions, such as migraines or backaches (p. 23). Simplistic perspectives do not provide us with a solid foundation for either practice approaches or social policies (Bennett and Williams, 2003). For perpetrators and victims of intimate partner violence there are usually multiple risk and protective factors that mediate the relationships with substance abuse.

Children at Risk

Children are frequently present in households where there is substance abuse and intimate partner violence. This adds another layer of complexity for those who wish to address the problems created by the twin urchins. Chasnoff (1998) cites that there are more than 500,000 children now in foster care and that substance abuse is the dominant characteristic in child protective services' (CPS) caseloads. When we factor in the long-term effects on the children who are the silent and invisible victims of domestic violence and substance abuse (i.e., the social modeling, the learned behavior that they are being exposed to at home), it is understandable how these twin urchins will terrorize our children and our children's children well into the future.

In his literature review, "Children's Witnessing of Adult Domestic Violence," Edleson (1999) culls quotes from different studies to offer the reader a chance to hear the voices of children who are the secondary victims of domestic violence and substance abuse. The following excerpts provide a vivid window into their world:

> I wouldn't say anything. I would just sit there. Watch it . . . I was just, felt like I was just sitting there, listening to a TV show or something . . . It's like you just sit there to watch, like a tapestry, you sit there. (p. 841)

> I really thought somebody got hurt. It sounded like it. And I almost started to cry. It felt really, I was thinking of calling, calling the cops or something because it was really getting, really big banging and stuff like that. (p. 841)

The revelation of this study on family assault is that violence, of any kind, becomes more normalized and seductive.

Responsibility/Consciousness of This Generation

If we are going to fight the twin urchins of drugs and violence, we must first face the frightening reality of modern American society and how pervasive these two things are in it. Violence is on television, in video games, cartoons, and songs. Substance abuse is glamorized as a way of life, especially when it is associated with beauty, action, wealth, or some other idealized lifestyle. The production of illegal substances is often a major cash crop in some third world countries. The trafficking in drugs provides fast money to a population that has little prospect of climbing the economic ladder, and it has become a lifestyle choice for children who are bored, lonely, and/or curious. The truth is, whether the culprit is substance abuse and/or domestic violence, we have a problem. The traffic in and use of drugs transcend socioeconomic, racial, national, and other boundaries: Black or White, American or Asian, illegal immigrant or citizen, old or young, rich or poor, male or female, educated or illiterate, employed or unemployed, married or single, God-fearing or atheistic. None of these boundaries matters much because the two urchins of domestic violence and substance abuse do not discriminate when they plant their "bombs" in the family home. They are creating victims and abusers at earlier and earlier ages.

Consider another finding from the NVAW survey (Tjaden & Thoennes, 2000): more than half (54%) of female rape victims identified by the survey were under 18 years of age when they first experienced rape. Thirty-two percent were between the ages of 12 and 17, and 22% were children under the age of 12—that is 22% *under* the age of *12* when they *first* experienced rape. That's first, as in *first in what will become, from a statistical viewpoint, a lifetime of more assaults and abuse,* for the correlation between adult survivors of sexual trauma and abuse and women who experience intimate partner violence has long since been established. In fact, the U.S. Department of Justice, Bureau of Justice Statistics (Rennison & Welchans, 2000) reports that over a five-year period (1993–1998), the highest rate for victimization of women by physical, intimate violence occurs between the ages of 16 and 24, which, interestingly, corresponds to when our young people are usually exploring drugs and alcohol. According to the National Institute on Drug Abuse (NIDA), in 2000, the annual illicit drug use for 10th and 12th graders was 26% and 41%, respectively. The annual use of alcohol for these groups was 65% and 73%, respectively. More disturbing is that *8th* graders, 12- or 13-year-olds, were annually using alcohol at a rate of 41%.

The cadres of teachers, youth group leaders, social workers, and drug counselors are soldiers in the war, trying to heal the wounded, comfort the grieving, and encourage the survivors to overcome their daily battle. In fact, these cadres are the experts. Their voices ought to be heard by the legislators, researchers, and policy analysts who are looking for solutions. They know something that other kinds of experts, those in the halls of academia or in the political chambers of Washington, don't know. They see and deal with the reality behind the statistics:

- the tremendous struggle to accomplish the simplest change in behavior
- the overwhelming energy it takes to be upbeat, empathic, and encouraging when you know that the client sitting in front of you will, despite all of the hours in therapy, all of the threats of jail time, or all of the pleadings of family and friends, relapse into the world of drugs, alcohol, or an abusive relationship

And then the questions begin to arise: What separates one abuser from the other? What distinguishes who will succeed in treatment from who will fail? What mark of Cain protects one victim of violence from all the rest? These are, if one can use the word in this context, the "mystical" questions that haunt the souls of those of us who live and deal with this reality. It is as if we are operating on blind faith, the hope of redemption, and the belief that with enough love and perseverance everyone can be reclaimed. After all, isn't that part of the American identity?

Too often, those of us who serve on the front lines of this battle operate just under the radar. We struggle to make a difference in the lives of those whom we serve, and our successes and failures frequently go unnoticed. Part of this discussion is philosophical, maybe even provocative. The questions or ideas posed within this writing are meant to stimulate thinking about our personal relationship to the problems of substance abuse and domestic violence. It won't necessarily give us the one "right" method, treatment protocol, or intervention for dealing with these issues, for that is delusional folly. Rather, we should acknowledge that there is no magic elixir. The reality is in identifying a problem that is both multifaceted and widespread.

Whose Reality? Whose Point of View?

Maybe we would benefit from considering the meaning of some of our greatest philosophical assumptions. For instance, in our quest for theoretical and moral social justice, should we continue to bow down and genuflect at the statue of *Blind Justice* holding her scale, impartial to all? We, quite rightly, equate fairness and equality with goodness, but then we are at a loss on how to operationalize this in our social policies and treatment approaches. We somehow think that it means we must treat everyone the same.

Underneath our advanced degrees, professional licenses, or other designations is a notion that "if we could reach a point when everyone was treated the same, then we could fix the problem."

We therefore quantify issues like intimate partner violence and substance abuse to determine all of the variables so that we can direct money and resources toward the right solutions. After all, this is America, where our hearts have been planted in a soil that is watered by capitalism and the belief that "*Yes!* Money solves it all!"

More beds

More treatment centers

More education programs

More jails

More teachers

More day care centers

More counselors

More housing vouchers

More medications

More, more, more

In fact, some service providers are just as driven as any Wall Street corporate executive. The difference is that we measure wealth in lives instead of stock options, but the bottom line is that we are still measuring. We measure lives as if each were a product that had somehow been broken and come into the shop for repair—our shop. This viewpoint triggers our own dalliance with fantasy and notions of success, for all of us want to be the one who can repair the damaged person! We secretly yearn to be the one who develops the magic approach, who can produce good numbers for bigger and better grants. We nod our heads during intake or rounds, as if we have answers and strategies: this one has a learning disability; that one comes from a broken home; this one needs Narcotics Anonymous meetings for an X period of time; and that one needs job training. When we meet the repeat offender who should be responding to interventions or treatment but isn't, or the woman who can't seem to get her act together despite extra sessions, extra resources, and extraordinary effort on our part, then *we* get frustrated. We console ourselves that there will always be a few who will fall through the cracks. Shortcomings are sometimes rationalized just as easily as the alcoholic justifies one more drink. To us, *our* myth is acceptable, as long as it keeps the story line moving. After all, we need to be able to sort the characters quickly when their profiles land on our desks and then get them onto the conveyer belt before the end of the fiscal year:

•Sexual addicts and partner abuse down this track
•Domestic violence with alcohol down that track
•Drug abuse and repeat battering down the track over there

Sort, send, serve and we create a second chance! A second chance that may allow the individual to be a model citizen, stamped with the mark of "the same as everyone else."

In his book, *God Is a Verb*, Rabbi David Cooper (1997) recounts a wonderful Hasidic tale that exemplifies this approach perfectly. It is the story of a king who discovers that his entire supply of grain has been contaminated by a strange fungus. The grain looked and tasted the same as normal grain. There was no way to know that anything was different, except for one little problem. Anyone who ate this grain lost all contact with reality and became deranged.

The king and his advisor were the only ones who knew about this problem. They discussed their options. They were rapidly running out of uncontaminated grain, and there were no alternatives for feeding the nation. In two more days they would have to open the contaminated storehouse, or all the people in the kingdom would starve. A new grain supply would not be ready for almost a year, and there was no assurance that even that would be safe.

At first they thought that they would give the grain to the people but would not eat it themselves, so that at least two people in the kingdom would maintain their sanity. Then the king realized that he would not be able to govern the masses if he did not understand what the people were thinking. So he suggested that he should eat the grain but that his advisor should stay sane. Then the advisor realized that it would be impossible to give advice to the king if he was seeing true reality and the king was not. They understood that in order to rule a kingdom of people with a different reality, they both had to eat the contaminated grain so that they could see things like everyone else.

The only hope for the future of the people was the possibility that someone would be able to realize that the world they were experiencing was not true reality. So the king and his advisor put out an edict to the people that everyone was required by law to put a mark on their forehead, and every morning when they saw that mark in the mirror, they were to ask themselves, What does that mark mean? Their hope was that people would wonder why they were all obligated to ask themselves this question, and eventually, at some point in the future, this mark would lead the nation to the realization that its reality was illusory.

That is where the story ends. The wisdom of this story is not to focus on the stamp of sameness on each forehead, trying to make sure that we all have the same mark, which would imply that there is one answer for everyone. Rather, the pearl of this parable lies in redirecting our focus to the actions of the king and his servant. He knew that in order to still serve, to still guide, to still *be*, he had to ingest the grain, too. He had to *see the people's reality from their point of view.* This doesn't mean that one should rationalize an abuser's behavior, nor does it justify overindulging in alcohol or legitimizing the use of illegal substances. But it does mean that we have to realize the reality of our clients, our population samples, and our communities. Like it or not, they are full of individuals who view the world completely differently from us. The grain they eat may not be contaminated. Instead, to borrow a phrase from the research and development crowd, it might be "genetically engineered," meaning that victims, abusers, and addicts could be seeing the world through a cultural lens that has traditions, values, behavior patterns, and belief systems that have been cultivated over generations to produce odd malformations relative to our own.

It is their choice, their reasoning, their behaviors, and their attitudes nevertheless, and we have to respect that. If we are to help them, we cannot judge them. This is hard! Their actions may look completely insane, inappropriate, or stupid to some of us. Yet just as we tell clients to watch how they make attributions toward each other, we need to curb our own tendency to engage in the same behavior even as we mask it under the label of making an assessment or diagnosis. The point is that we have to be sensitive to the bread that our families are eating: how it is made, what is in it, and who the baker is. We may even have to eat some of the bread ourselves, studying the cultural differences between not only Black, White, Hispanic, and Asian, but between Nigerians and Ethiopians, Hungarians and Italians, Mexicans and Puerto Ricans, or Japanese and Koreans.

For example, the NVAW survey revealed a significant difference in reporting behavior among various cultures and ethnic groups. It found, for instance, that Native American and Alaskan women were far more likely to report rapes than women from other groups, and that Asian/Pacific Islander women were least likely to report physical abuse. Our task is to explore all the variables that play a role in individuals' experience with abuse and why they do so. For instance, we need more research on just how race, culture, religion, and ethnicity affect intimate partner violence.

Race, Ethnicity, Religion, Culture, and Intimate Partner Violence

Bograd (1999) describes taking these multiple dimensions into account in the process of research and therapy as "intersectionality." He cites several real-life situations where these factors have a profound impact on the victim's decision either to seek help or stay in an abusive situation. For instance, imagine the dilemma for a Jewish woman who keeps kosher. He writes, "As she grapples with domestic violence itself, she must also decide whether to honor herself as a woman deserving of safety or as a Jew—as if she is not both." (p. 281)

In a diverse society such as our own, when our roles as service providers often put us in contact with individuals from different cultures, we have to learn how to navigate that intersection with sensitivity. If we are to be true to our original desire to be fair, then as researchers and clinicians, we need to develop a culturally competent approach that will help us to see the reality of our clients without betraying our professional standards. The efforts to identify culturally competent interventions or evidence-based practices inevitably will raise questions about what constitutes culture generally and the importance of acculturation (Bell & Mattis, 2000; Hampton & Avery 2001).

To discuss cultural competence in this context is to be willing to be vulnerable. We must be unafraid and unashamed to say to our client, to our fellow colleagues, and to our research subjects, "We may not understand, but you can help us to try." To do this, we should:

- acknowledge culture as a predominant force in shaping behaviors, values and institutions;
- acknowledge and accept that cultural differences exist and have an impact on service delivery;
- believe that diversity within cultures is as important as diversity between cultures;
- respect the unique, culturally defined needs of various client populations;
- recognize that concepts such as "family" and "community" are different for various cultures and even for subgroups within cultures; and
- understand that people from different racial and ethnic groups and other cultural subgroups are usually best served by persons who are part of, or in tune with, their culture. (Bureau of Primary Health, 1999)

In order to accomplish these goals, the first thing that we have to create is an atmosphere in our work settings, schools, and programs where cultural competence is intrinsically valued. According to Cross, Bazron, Dennis, and Isaacs (1989), there are five essential elements of a culturally competent system. These elements, including how they are related to both practice and research, are as follows:

First, value diversity. It is imperative that both researchers and practitioners recognize and respect the value of diversity and acknowledge that people from different backgrounds and cultures will make different choices for different reasons. There is no "one-size-fits-all" approach. For instance, one of the areas where this is most apparent is in religion. Being open to the multiple ways people can choose to participate in a religious faith cannot only broaden our own understanding of people, but it is also, for must of us, the original source of values.

If a client's spirituality and belief system are overlooked, be it because of a clinician's own ambivalence toward his or her faith or because of institutional policy, then this not only limits the work that can be accomplished, but could skew one's interpretation of the client's choices. A woman may stay with her abuser because her religion does not approve of divorce. Perhaps it is because she will be shunned by a subculture that denies women any autonomy or because she truly believes that faith is redemptive. The point is not to become a substitute for the client's pastor, priest, or rabbi. The point is to demonstrate a respect for the client's choices, so that she has the freedom to explore various options and which choices work best with who and where she is.

The second factor is to know your own culture. A system, whether it is a system of care providers or of researchers, must be able to assess itself and have a sense of its own culture before it can truly serve a diverse population. So part of becoming culturally competent is to ask yourself:

- Who are you?
- What are the values that reside in your cultural blind spot?
- What assumptions are being made on the institutional level that presume certain behaviors are normative and others are not?

Unless one understands the historical impact of institutional racism, it may be difficult to understand why Black women are more reluctant to report physical abuse to police or social service agencies than their White counterparts. Manetta (1999) writes, "African-American women may under-report the amount of abuse they experience in close relationships. As they are too keenly aware of the racial problems experienced by African-American men in the wider society, they may not want to admit there is anything wrong in the home for fear of compounding this problem" (p. 518). Are they any less traumatized? Do they feel any less desire for help? One must examine any assumptions about Black women that might get in the way of serving them. For instance, do you take their reticence in filing a temporary restraining order as a sign that they are still enmeshed with their abusers? Like the Jewish woman who struggles with her kosherness, the African American woman might be struggling with a sense of betraying her race.

The third factor is to understand the dynamics of difference. It is important for care providers to be conscious of the dynamics that are inherent when different cultures interact and to be constantly vigilant about the dynamics of misinterpretation and misjudgment. In terms of practice, such vigilance will reduce the possible frustration felt by the client and the service provider. In terms of research, it can help prevent the misinterpretation of results. As anyone who works with the Spanish-speaking population knows, the terms "Latina" and "Hispanic" are labels more for the convenience of *institutional record keeping* than an accurate descriptors of the multiple groups of people who are categorized by such terms. Think about the message sent to children and families when, for the sake of budgets, programs, and political campaigns, diverse individuals are blurred into a single fuzzy group, dehumanized and distorted.

The lone El Salvadoran who is working amid a group of Mexicans is not only scraping by to earn a living, to adjust to American culture, and learn a new language. He also has to struggle with the intense emotions that are stimulated by working in a group that is culturally and historically hostile to his.

- What does he do with that repressed anger?
- How does he cope with the hundreds of slights that are perceived as being deliberate and representative of historical tension?
- Who becomes the lightning rod for his emotions: *his wife, children?*
- What does the wife do to cope: *drink, shoot up?*

Of course, there is a pragmatic need to quantify priorities, but as researchers and clinicians, we need to remind ourselves that there is more to interpersonal interactions than we are immediately aware of. Often, the commonality of language can be a chimera, distracting us from understanding individuals on a deeper level, and may weaken the efficacy of our interventions or lead us to inaccurate conclusions in our research.

The fourth element urges us to institutionalize cultural knowledge. Practitioners and researchers must sanction and, if necessary, mandate the incorporation of cultural knowledge in the frameworks of both service delivery and research. This needs to happen at every level so that the appropriate questions will be asked and the research findings will be interpreted in a way that makes sense for the community being served. In most clinical or research settings, it is de rigueur to hold clinical reviews and/or staff meetings on a periodic basis. Why not use these meetings as opportunities to learn more about different cultures?

- Invite members to talk about their own families of origin.
- Present monthly cultural updates about events or histories of different people, especially those groups most represented in one's area.
- Plan activities that will heighten staff awareness of different cultures and traditions.

The fifth and final concept is to promote an adaptation to diversity. Adaptations should aim to reflect an understanding of cultural diversity. This doesn't just mean translating the forms into Spanish, Tagalog, or Arabic. It also means recognizing the power of tradition, symbols, and heritage, then incorporating that awareness into one's therapy or research. This can be accomplished by simply using examples or metaphors that culturally resonate with a client or population that is being studied. In the popular *Chicken Soup for the Soul* series (Hansel, 1999), a story sums up the concept quite nicely. It is an account of an actual incident submitted by Tim Hansel, and it seems an appropriate metaphor for how we can accomplish great things by working together, as clinicians and researchers, addiction counselors, and domestic violence workers, the medical and mental health community, and the court systems. It's called "The Sound of One Hand Clapping" and is about the famous entertainer, Jimmy Durante.

As the story is told, Jimmy Durante was asked to be part of a show for World War II veterans. He told them his schedule was very busy and he could afford only a few minutes, but if they wouldn't mind his doing one short monologue and immediately leaving for his next appointment, he would come. Of course, the show's director happily agreed.

> But when Jimmy got on stage, something interesting happened. He went through the short monologue and then stayed. The applause grew louder and louder and he kept staying. Pretty soon, he had been on fifteen, twenty, then thirty minutes. Finally, he took a last bow and left the stage. Backstage, someone stopped him and said, "What happened?"
>
> Jimmy answered, "I did have to go, but I can show you the reason I stayed. You can see for yourself if you'll look at the front row."
>
> In the front row were two men, each of whom had lost an arm in the war. One had lost his right arm and the other had lost his left. Together, they were able to clap, and that's exactly what they were doing, loudly and cheerfully. (p. 133)

To many of us who work in the field of domestic violence and substance abuse, the image is aptly provocative, for often we leave feeling as if we, too, have had one arm amputated. The key is to work together, to help the families and individuals who land in our offices bleeding from the war, to heal. The way to do this is in unison and in unity. When we do work together, ultimately it will be good for all.

References

Bell, C. C., & Mattis, J. (2000). The importance of cultural competence in ministering to African American victims of domestic violence. *Violence against Victims, 6,* 515–532.

Bennett, L. (2001). Deck the halls: Substance abuse and male partner violence (personal communication, February 22, 2001).

Bennett, L., & Williams, O. J. (2003). Substance abuse and men who batter. *Violence Against Women, 9,* 558–573.

Bograd, M. (1999). Strengthening domestic violence theories: Intersections of race, class, sexual orientation, and gender. *Journal of Marital and Family Therapy, 25,* 275–289.

Bureau of Primary Health. (1999). Guidelines to help assess cultural competence in program design application and management. Retrieved March 5, 2003, from http://www.bphc.hrsa.gov/omwh/omwh_7.htm

Chasnoff, I. (1998). Silent violence: Is prevention a moral obligation? *Pediatrics, 102,* 145–149.

Cooper, D. A. (1997). *God is a verb: Kabbalah and the practice of mystical Judaism*. New York: Riverhead Books.

Cross, T., Bazron, B., Dennis, L., & Isaacs, M. (1989). *Towards a Culturally Competent System of Care, 1*. Washington, DC: CASSP Technical Assistance Center.

Edleson, J. L. (1999). Children's witnessing of domestic violence. *Journal of Interpersonal Violence, 14*, 839–870.

Fazzone, P. A., Holdon, J. K., & Reed, B. G. (1997). Substance abuse treatment and domestic violence: Treatment improvement protocol (TIP) series 25. Rockville, MD: U.S. Department of Health and Human Services, Public Health Service. Retrieved January 14, 2003, from www.nmcadv.org/dv/tip25.html

Hampton, R., & Avery, M. (2001). Working toward a culturally competent model of research for domestic violence in the African American community. In *Domestic violence: Culturally specific treatment interventions for African Americans. Valuing differences and commonalities* (pp. 49–64). Washington, DC: U.S. Department of Health and Human Services.

Hansel, T. (1999). The sound of one hand clapping. In J. Canfield, M. V. Hansen, and H. McNamara (Eds.), *Chicken Soup for the Soul*. Deerfield Beach, FL: Health Communication, Inc.

Manetta, A. A. (1999). Interpersonal violence and suicidal behavior in midlife African American women. *Journal of Black Studies, 29*, 510–522.

National Institute on Drug Abuse. (2000). High school and youth trends. U.S. Department of Justice. Retrieved March 3, 2003, from www.nida.nig.gov/infofax/HSYouthtrends.html

Rennison, C. M., & Welchans, S. (2000) Intimate partner violence. Bureau of Justice Statistics, Special Report. Washington, DC: U.S. Department of Justice. Retrieved May 5, 2003, from www.ojp.usdoj.gov

Tjaden, P., & Thoennes, N. (2000). Extent, nature, and consequences of intimate partner violence: Findings from the National Violence Against Women Survey. Washington, DC: National Institute of Justice, Centers for Disease Control and Prevention. Retrieved May 5, 2003, from http:/www.ojp.usdoj.gov/bjs/ pubalp2.htm111:10,1–3. Available Online Database: Academic Search Elite.

3

Everything Is Connected and Understanding the Center

CHRISTINE LOWERY

Introduction

I appreciate this opportunity to speak from my own cultural perspective as a Laguna (New Mexico) woman and a social worker. My goal is not to present anything new, but to remind you that, essentially, our work is spiritual work. This work is about who we are and who we may become as much as it is about who we serve. In this spirit, I want to dedicate this chapter to my dear friend and social work colleague, Roselyn Mike, a member of the Moapa Paiute tribe of Nevada. She and I attended the University of Utah master's in social work program from 1976 to 1978. Unlike many of us Indian people, she fulfilled the promise of returning and working for her people, which is not an easy job by any means. She served as tribal chair for four years and was the Moapa housing director most recently. Roselyn Mike died of late-diagnosed colon cancer in a hospice in Las Vegas on January 19, 2001. She was 52 years old. She was a good mother, a good social worker, and a good person.

Paguate, New Mexico

When I was small, my Laguna grandmother made these robust turnovers called moon pies. These were crescent-shaped pies filled with the dark, intense flavors of dried peaches or apples. These pies revived memories of fruit lying open, drying in the sun from midsummer into early fall. In the chill of winter, the fruit was revitalized in boiling water and baked into moon pies. In this way, the fruit realized the life of the dormant orchard through the snows of winter.

Does anyone still make moon pies?" I asked Jackie Gonzalez, the Laguna social worker at the Acoma-Laguna Indian Health Service hospital. Hungry for my past, I had searched the Laguna feast in September and saw only fake moon pies, glistening with the sugared sheen of canned blueberry or cherry pie filling. "It depends on who has dried fruit," Jackie responded thoughtfully. When I first heard the answer, it jarred me. Moon pies were made of dried fruit from the orchards.

"Which villages still have orchards?"

Sociocultural change is both life-giving and life-taking. The community orchards in Paguate have fallen into neglect for 20 years or more. A long time ago, you could see grandparents and their grandchildren picking fruit in the spring through summer and into the fall. In season, fields of beans, squash, pumpkins, and corn bordered the orchard where trees produced pears, peaches, apricots, and several varieties of apples. Now young people drive the dirt roads on either side of the old orchards on their way to the dam. The dam is now a source of community frustration because it attracts drinking parties and requires patrol power the tribal police do not have. The water from the dam is primarily for household use, although there is hope of a small fishery in the planning stages. Every once in a while, you can hear the water gurgling through the irrigation ditches that border the village fields, and there are still "ditch officers" who are responsible for maintaining the small irrigation canals. Still, many fields lie fallow or overgrown.

Social gatherings and collective interaction were by-products of planting and harvesting. A trip to the tribally owned grocery store at Casa Blanca, or the Wal-Mart in Grants, New Mexico, does not build relationships in the same way we enjoyed when we worked together in family groups to prepare our fields, plant and harvest our food, or hunt deer in the fall.

Feast days in the pueblos, a combination of honoring Catholic-inspired patron saints and holding social traditional dances, still require family sharing and cooking, and the gatherings include many non-Indian visitors as villagers open their homes. And one can buy moon pies at the Laguna-owned and operated bakery at Casa Blanca, one of seven Laguna villages. These pies are large, made with canned pie filling in thick, sugared crusts. Our eating habits have changed drastically, from community deer stew dinners, rich chili stews, roasted lamb, and boiled tripe to hamburgers, chicken strips, french fries, ice cream, and soft drinks. The rate of diabetes on our reservation, as with other reservations, is high. Small groups of elders are transported to Grants, New Mexico, 20 minutes away, to spend hours in dialysis clinics 3 times a week. In 2001, a two-chair dialysis clinic was opened at the Indian hospital near the Acoma Casino. The elders see dialysis as a good thing, because it helps them feel better and there is cohesion among the elders who ride in the vans weekly. Type II diabetes now affects elementary school children whose families consume carbonated drinks by the case and drive everywhere. Junk food abounds at home, on the ball fields, and at school, and MTV, videos, and video games are as much a part of the culture of the young as in most parts of the United States. The older elders, 78 and over, whose lifelong eating and working habits are different, are slender by comparison, but their children at 58, grandchildren at 38, and great-grandchildren under 18, deal with obesity, not unlike 40% of the U.S. population. The number of young children with asthma is increasing.

In its effort to swallow small towns whole, Wal-Mart had a grand opening in 1999. Wal-Mart sits on the eastern edge of Grants (20 to 30 minutes away depending on which village one comes from), positioned to draw the buying power of Laguna and Acoma families, many with two-parent earners. In December 2000, the Pueblo Market, an old trading post with gas tanks out in front, closed. By summer 2001—up the road from Pueblo Mart and just off the freeway—a new minimart with gas pumps took its place. During the opening months, a wall of soft drinks, six-packs stacked five deep, disappeared at bargain prices.

Dominant cultural elements find their way into our ceremonial dances. The Laguna village of Encinal in New Mexico sponsored its usual masked dances or Katsina dances one weekend this past summer. Twelve dancers in all came and danced prayers for the people of the village under a blue, blue sky. The only gifts that were given during this solemn series of dances, drumming, and singing were two pairs of handmade Pueblo moccasins. Two young males, junior-high age, were called forward into the plaza and received these gifts to reinforce their ceremonial life. Earlier that summer, in the village of Mesita, the Katsinas brought baskets and baskets of homemade bread and baked goods, fruit, vegetables, and even a rabbit marked for a young boy.

In contrast, at Moencopi—my Hopi village near Tuba City, Arizona—in July, there were 50 male dancers, all dressed in white, trimmed in pine boughs, with red, black, and green sashes singing in low, trance-weaving tones. In the afternoon, the ceremony was broken when the dancers brought boxes and boxes of store-bought food and handed gifts to the children. Young Hopi children compared the contents of three or four large, ziplock bags filled with candy products and junk food. The Katsinas used to bring life-giving food from the fields, in season, and the gifts were handmade or home-baked goods and were modest in quantity.

In early 2000, the Dancing Eagle Casino opened in Casa Blanca, New Mexico. By summer, the Laguna tribal council voted to sell liquor at the casino to make it more competitive with the well-established Acoma Sky City Casino and truck stop, six miles west toward Grants. The Acomas do not sell liquor in their casino, yet. This past summer, as the new Acoma cultural center and hotel were constructed, the tribal laundry, across the road from the casino, suffered random closings because of water shortages, a sign of future trauma. About a mile from the Acoma casino, right next to the Indian Health Service hospital, the Lagunas and Acomas share one of the government's regional adolescent substance abuse treatment facilities. Here, we treat our children for the trauma related to the disempowerment and disconnection that masks the trauma of some of our own choices made within the context of dominant cultural values and practices and pressures.

Everything is connected. And there is always hope. This past summer, *mayordomos* (*medromos*) or leaders at New Laguna villages, encouraged young men in their 30s to clean out the irrigation ditches, haul manure, and clear and plant a large field. For some, it was the first time they worked a field since they were young children. In the evening, driving west on the old Route 66, you could see them working in the field long after they had returned from work, darkening figures against a setting summer sun. Some of their younger brothers in the treatment center would do well to work beside them, not for the product expected, but for the relationships that must be nurtured throughout their lifetimes.

Dominant Society: A Cultural Analysis

Punishment and coercion, societal violence, domestic violence, child abuse, substance abuse, mental illness, the exploitation of women and the environment—these are all connected. It is good to talk about these things from a social work perspective and the perspective of liberation pedagogy. According to Paulo Freire (2000) in *Pedagogy of the Oppressed*, the ultimate goal is to become human. As social workers, among our goals is to contribute to conditions that strengthen the people, to join them in recognizing that their oppression is our oppression, and to struggle together in authentic dialogue to make our lives more human and saner. Archbishop Desmond Tutu captured the essence of this work in his culturally balanced way in the word *ubuntu*, which means your humanity is my humanity; your inhumanity is my inhumanity. I hope that when we say cultural diversity, we automatically link diversity with social injustice and an awareness of the histories of oppression perpetrated against people of color, including all forms of violence.

In 2000, the Color of Violence conference marked the first national event in which a multiracial, multiethnic progressive group of activists, students, academics, and service providers met to discuss and plan alternative ways to address violence in the lives of women of color. Andrea Smith, a Native American graduate student at the University of California at Santa Cruz, was the conference coordinator. Like other radical feminists of color, she was fed up with what she called the "professionalization of the anti-violence movement and its marginalization of women of color" (Smith, 2000, personal communication). A longtime rape crisis activist, Smith was critical of the movement's increasing social service orientation, an adapted, co-opted, politically correct position that had ceased to advocate for the structural changes that a culture of nonviolence requires. This conference was a sign of health. Social workers and social work educators need to participate in authentic dialogue in this matter.

When we say cultural competence, I think it is important to ask: Whose culture? Under what acculturation pressures or adaptations or oppressions? And perhaps more important, whose standard of competence? We have to honestly examine how we operate in our cultural frameworks, how these frameworks operate in which realities, on whose behalf, and for what purposes. In spite of where we come from, we have all integrated dominant cultural values at one level or another. Let us be aware of that and start there.

Anne Wilson Schaef wrote an honest and accurate cultural analysis of our society in two books: *Women's Reality* published in 1985, and *When Society Becomes an Addict*, published in 1987. A year later, Anne Wilson Schaef and Diane Fassel (1988) wrote *The Addictive Organization*. Schaef delineates the White male system in the first book. In the second book, she recognizes that the White male system is synonymous with the addictive system. In the third book, she and Fassel focus on organizations where they are not surprised to find the same elements of the addictive system. There is denial, established to maintain a closed system and to minimize the threat of new information to organizational identity. There is the scarcity model—not enough to go around, which breeds competition. There is dishonesty or at least indirect communication and an emphasis on corporate survival leading to ethical deterioration and spiritual bankruptcy (Schaef & Fassel, 1988, pp. 67, 207). Characteristics of an addictive system or White male system are dualistic thinking, perfectionism, self-centeredness, the illusion of control, crisis orientation, depression, and stress. I will weave macro, mezzo, and micro examples to demonstrate the addictive system.

DUALISTIC THINKING

Basic to the addictive system is dualistic thinking: either/or, on or off, black or white, good or evil, right or wrong, male or female. If one part is affirmed to be true, the other is automatically thought to be false. Haitian leader Jean-Bertrand Aristide (2000), in his small book, *Eyes of the Heart*, gives a wonderful example of a child who when given two options always created a third. " 'What do you prefer,' he teased a young child, 'rum or cola?' 'I prefer juice,' she answered. 'Is the pool big or small?' he asked. 'It is beautiful,' she answered" (pp. 19–24). Creating a third way is refreshing, creative, and alive. It moves us away from the limited "either/or" of addictive dualistic thinking. Imagine being open to learning, with the creativity of a child.

One of the characteristics of the addictive system is to invalidate. One invalidation is not enough to destroy, but consider systemic invalidation through bureaucratic social control and cultural invasion. Social workers in community work will recognize invalidation of the people's reality in the rabid pursuit of a positivist evaluation exercise, for example. "When we think we can break something that has many complex facets into two clear dimensions [or duality], it feeds our illusion of control," writes Schaef (1987, p. 112).

ILLUSION OF CONTROL

Key to an addictive system, at the individual and national levels, is self-centeredness and arrogance combined with the illusion of control. This stance permits the godlike status of doctors in the Western medical model, in spite of managed care and the illusion of control manifested there. This stance permits the idea that "man is to have dominion over everything," including women and the environment. This stance permits the United States to violate human rights in our prison systems and to exploit labor markets in the Mexican *maquiladora* system. And this stance allows us to think that we can control crime and violence without examining how the structural elements in our society create and maintain these patterns and for what purposes. Friere (2000) names this the oppressor consciousness or the tendency to transform everything into possessions to be dominated, to be owned, to be bought and sold, with money the measure of all things and profit the primary goal.

LIVING IN CRISIS

Schaef (1985) asserts that living in crisis gives families in addiction the illusion of being alive. If we have created the crisis, a crisis gives us the illusion of control. Depression is concomitant with the illusion of control. If we have been taught that we can control the behavior of other people, our colleagues or our clients or our children, we are set up for failure. If we believe we can control others, we set ourselves up for a great deal of stress. An addictive system is dishonest, and this can be subtle and destructive in families suffering addiction. At the individual level, keeping one's distance from one's feelings prevents honesty with self and with others. Dishonesty affects the family and community by lying to the world, by presenting only the best public image when the chaos of addiction is eating at the family like a cancer. By masking reality, one loses the ability to distinguish between truth and lying. With practice the addict doesn't need a reason to lie, and sometimes an addict may not even know he is lying. Culturally, we con ourselves, we practice "impression management" (Schaef, 1985, p. 52)—fake it until you make it, living beyond our means, pretending to be someone we think others will like or pretending to have knowledge that we don't have.

Dishonesty is so destructive that an addict cannot afford dishonesty in any form. It is not just lying about the drugs or the alcohol, it is not being honest about anything, even small things, in a culture that sanctions cheating, stealing, and lying—just do not get caught. On a very simple level, think about how many times we say, "It's OK," in an effort to be polite or not to hurt someone else's feelings. And we do not think this is dishonest, because we cannot see our own piecemeal destruction. Honesty may not always be pleasant, but it is not destructive. Healthy people will still like us, even when we speak out on our needs or set our limits clearly. Dishonesty is the norm in an addictive society. Consider the hidden agenda, the need for spin doctors and a whole press corps in our government in the name of political righteousness. Consider the duplicity in our places of work, duplicity that we characterize as "politics as usual." This leads us to distorted thinking or what people in Alcoholics Anonymous call "stinkin' thinking": innuendos, assumptions, vague statements, planned misinformation, statements that honestly make no sense at all, and denial. "When reality does not support our confused thinking, we distort reality" Schaef says (1987, p. 63), and sometimes we create confusion, or worse, paranoia. On the contrary, "significant communication is any information that could make employees more effective, decisions more strategic, and change more likely in an organization. Significant content simply does not get through in an addictive organization" (Schaef & Fassel, 1988, p. 143). Schaef and Fassel analyzed the helping services organizations in one example. A group of nurses felt anger and confusion because what they thought they should be doing and what they were doing were in conflict. The mission of the hospital was to promote health, to be responsive to the needs of the people, to provide high-quality care, and develop new forms of healing. "The unstated goals were saving the city money, being a vehicle for the political advancement of hospital administrators, upholding the reputation of the hospital, and increasing federal funding" (p. 122).

Depression and exhaustion in the workplace are not uncommon when we have to practice the "con," the dishonesty of the organization, 40 to 50 hours a week. The con encourages collusion as a way of moving up the ladder in such organizations, and the goal becomes maintaining the organization. And of course, we must recognize the addiction to work that is touted by our society, in the illusion that we can buy it all, without recognizing the damage to our families and our relationships. There is hope in the major goal of watchdog agencies, which is to expose dishonesty in the organizations they are watching. To engender a culture of honesty or nonaddiction is another matter. Schaef

(1987) sees three essential choices in front of us as part of this culture: We can choose not to live or choose to die, including suicide or eventual death from addiction. We can choose not to die or choose not to live, which indicates an adjustment or acceptance of the system, where most Americans probably stand at this point. We can choose not to die or choose to live, which mandates that systems change. This coincides with Paulo Freire's notion of true generosity.

Choosing to live means we can no longer support the system as it is. Choosing to live means that we cannot eat much of the food in our supermarkets, breathe the air in many of our cities, allow our groundwater to be polluted by toxic wastes, or sit back and wait for the nuclear holocaust. The addictive system asks us to accept these things—and more—as inherent to being because they are inherent to the addictive, nonliving system in which we live. Addictions and trauma in the form of violence and disconnection from others are essential to the life of the system. Addictions numb us to what is going on inside us. Addictions distort how we process information. Addictions keep us from seeing things as they really are, and addictions keep us from confronting injustices that need confronting. If we love our lives, we must confront the sicknesses in our society, our cultures of origin, and in our immediate subcultures within a dominant culture. And it is only through a profound and humble love of the people, that we can enter dialogue with each other to abolish oppression (Freire, 1994).

Based on their analysis of organizations, Schaef and Fassel (1988) outline this vision: honesty, congruency, consistency, predictability, flexibility. Interestingly enough, these elements are foundational for a healthy family, a healthy community, a healthy nation. And note how these elements would support a school of social work with a mission of cultural diversity. The mission of the organization would be supported by the structure. The way of organizing work and priorities would be integral to the company's mission and must support and facilitate the work of the organization. Health organizations would require healthy staffs. Child welfare organizations would recognize the spirit of children and construct resources in this regard. International organizations would honor diversity. Organizations would be moral. Ethics would not be compromised from the top down; there would be no need for dishonesty, and the earth would not be destroyed. Organizations would develop permeable boundaries. Organizations would be open to new information, to new learning, and new ways of operating that enhance their mission. Communication in recovering organizations would be characterized as multidirectional, vertical, horizontal, and intuitive, from the inside out. Communication would enhance the effectiveness of the employees, not to maintain power bases to feed ego (Schaef and Fassel, 1988, pp. 219–220). Leadership would be diffused and situational. Power would come from employees' own honesty and be actualized in responsibility. Organizations would alter their view of change. Change would be considered normal, facilitative, and noncontrollable. Organizations would develop more flexibility, openness to information, and participation at all levels (Schaef and Fassel, 1988, p. 221).

The Iroquois practice framing their decisions based upon the consequences for the seventh generation that will certainly follow. If we pay attention to our behavior in this way, how would our decisions change? If we understood that a get-tough drug policy would focus on people of color, engender a prison industry, load these prisons to the max, and promote human rights abuses through sanctioned police violence and the death penalty, would a war on drugs be considered useful for the seventh generation? What if we acknowledged our complicity, our addictive behaviors in contributing to the addictive system, including the premise that profit is a good path and control by corporate drug dealers is tolerable?

Everything Is Connected

Everything is connected, and when we see things systemically, we cannot ignore the consequences of our actions. If we understand that everything is connected, then we understand we must critically examine our work as social workers at all levels. For example, grant applications have used the buzzwords "collaboration" and "community participation," and efforts to include community representation are sometimes supported in rich ways—like the naturally sun-dried fruits baked into pies. At other times, community voices are treated as hollow representations of the fulfillment of grant obligations. Blinded by our own ideas of expertise, the grant initiators and evaluators, even when trained as social workers, don't know how to value the expertise of the community, much less use this community expertise in solving problems. And yet, it is the community, usually people of color, who understand the wholeness of health. They understand that good sidewalks and lighted streets help people to exercise more because they can walk the streets of their own neighborhoods in safety. It is the community that understands how health is related to good social connections and the importance of visiting and watching out for their elderly neighbors. It is the community that understands that good housing and good jobs help raise good families. It is the community that recognizes that young people must be taught through strong models and that it is the spirit of the community that suffers when adults cannot do this for their children and contributes to the violence that follows. And it is the community that recognizes that some adults have been unable to grow beyond this, because positive modeling was not consistently carried out for them in the generation that came before. This is the reality that we must see, reflect upon, and act on, in concert as human beings. We must come to understand that at the point of encounter, essentially we are "only people who are trying together, to know more, than we know now" (Friere, 2000, p. 71).

Recognizing When We Oppress

We must be critically aware and recognize the times when we rely solely on our own national perspective and have failed to "travel the circle" looking at problems from multiple cultural perspectives. We must be aware that if we are only modeling ourselves after the oppressor, we, too, oppress. Tram Nguyen (2001) gives us a recent example in international women's work in the fall issue of the race, culture, and action magazine, *Colorlines*. The 1993 Vienna World Conference on Human Rights had hearings on domestic violence for the first time. The work spawned the Women's Human Rights Caucus in Geneva in 2000. In spite of the work that women are doing, there is a predictable, power-related split between women of the North and South. In December 2000, African and Afro-Latina women "forcefully called attention" to ways women from the South were marginalized in the UN Conference Against Racism process (Nguyen, 2001, p. 25). Significantly, women from the South see women from the North as the next oppressors. "Many women felt objectified by Northern women who conveyed a romanticized solidarity reminiscent of the similar constructions of class and racial struggles of the white or elite left," recalls Puerto Rican legal scholar and human rights activist Celina Romany of the troubling dynamic at the Vienna conference. "Most women were left to feel like powerless clients represented to the world by the enlightened advocates of the North" (Nguyen, 2001, p. 25).

Women from the South assert that their leadership is required for structural adjustment programs, third world debt, migrant workers, and trafficked women. A South-South (African, Asian-Pacific, Latin American, Caribbean) initiative emerged at the March 2001 meeting of the UN Committee on the Status of Women. Response from the North varied "from support to outright defensiveness to feeling left out especially among Northern immigrant and refugee women." There are women caught in the middle, living amid plenty in the U.S. and yet, under terrible conditions (Nguyen, 2001, p. 25). Cultural competence in this century requires transcultural understanding and demands a social justice framework. We must understand the historical, and sociopolitical, and economic and interplay of power and oppression.

Understanding the Extent of Oppression

Rupert Ross, a Canadian attorney, took a brave journey in the 1990s and spent a couple of years writing about the path to recovery taken by people of the First Nations, focusing on the 600 people from Hollow Water, Manitoba. In his book, *Returning to the Teachings* (1996), he offers the lessons he has learned in a cross-cultural setting, as seen through his personal and professional lens. Family group conferencing was an intervention that grabbed his attention. The basic elements of life and restoration from an indigenous view, primarily Ojibway and Maori (pre-European) that inspired the family group conferencing include the following principles:

- that consensus includes the community, not just the stakeholders;
- the desired outcome is reconciliation with a settlement that is agreeable to all parties;
- the path is to examine how things got to be this way; and
- finally, that working to restore harmony is more important than assigning blame (pp. 5–28).

Everything is connected and we must be aware. Family conferencing requires the heart to do this work and a process of healing for those who carry this out. If the "healers" are not healed, conferencing can be punishing and shaming and continues the cycle that has conditioned the very behavior that brought the conferencing together (Ross, 1996).

In examining the intersections in oppression, genocide, addiction, and sexual abuse, Ross (1996) retells the story of an Ojibway woman who told her story at a workshop on sexual abuse in a section, aptly called "Losing the Centre." This story may be familiar to those working with children, addiction, and violence. The woman was born into a small community that relied on ties to the earth, including trapping, hunting, fishing, and rice harvesting for sustenance. Like many indigenous children in the United States, she was taken from her family and community at age six or seven and placed in a residential school with all the other school-age children. Again, like many of her U.S. peers, she developed physically, mentally, and spiritually outside her community and was kept away from her family until she was sixteen. Contrary to what I expected [Ross explains], the sexual abuse did not begin at that school. While there were unquestionably many schools where the physical abuse of children, sexual and otherwise, seems to have been commonplace, she was in one where "only the children's language, spirituality, culture and world view were abused—as the priests and nuns tried to train the "Indian" out of them. This woman was not sexually abused until, at the age of 16, she was released from school and went back to her tiny village. First it was an uncle, then older cousins—her own people (Ross, 1996, p. 45).

Her response was "normal" when faced with such oppression: "the abuse of her 'Indian-ness' by the nuns and priests and the abuse of her body by her relatives." She started with alcohol and drugs and then spiraled into the shame that comes with self-abuse. She wound up on the streets of the city. "Then, to the surprise of many, she did what she called 'complete flip.' She got sober, went back to school, graduated from university, got married, and had children. She thought everything was fine" (Ross, 1996, p. 45). Then a day came when one of her daughters returned from school with a straight-A report card. She asked her daughter why there were no A plus marks on it. The daughter's tearful response was to ask why they had to be better than everyone else, and in everything they did. It was at that point that her mother understood that she was still hiding from her sexual abuse, that she had only traded alcohol and drugs for perfectionism. She began to understand that she still had not come to grips with the pain, the guilt, and the "dirtiness" of being a victim of sexual abuse. Needless to say, the fact that her own people had abused her did not help. The woman returned home in the next few years and persistently spoke out about what happened to her, in spite of hostility from community members. She sought guidance from the elders for help in dealing with the pain and healing herself and her community. "I began to learn," she said, "that the people I came back to at age sixteen were not the same people I left at age six. The change began on the day we were taken from them."

Ross acknowledges the years of wholesale attack on every aspect of aboriginal life for years in Canada's history, not unlike the attack on the American Indian by the U.S. government. Taking the children was but one act. No matter how significant the need for education, when the children were gone, the center of life was snuffed out.

Understanding the Center

For each group of peoples, there is a center, be it the children, the buffalo, the soul, the ancestors, the mother, the earth, the sun, health, or all of these. Cultural competence requires us to understand that center as the people understand this, knowing that cross-cultural influences and signs of domination abound for most. Cultural competence requires us to understand how the history of the people has influenced their understanding to date, knowing that dominant sociopolitical factors and policies have shaped responses and changed historical trajectories for many peoples. Cultural competence requires that we understand how the humanity of peoples has been undermined; how people are not marginalized or outside of society, but how they have always been inside the structure that has made them "beings for others" (Friere, 2000). Cultural competence requires us to understand new words added to old languages, and verbal plays on phrases that incorporate the dominant language, and new art forms that attempt to demonstrate old cultures. Cultural competence requires us to honestly seek the strands that weave these cultural webs, acknowledging that within cultures there are different perspectives and interpretations, different visions for different individuals handed down, told, and retold. And cultural competence requires that we understand shared power, different powers, or gifts that each of us carries to contribute to the work we do on this earth. The power to sing, the power to dance, the power to speak, the power to form relationships, the power to make the people laugh, the power to make the people pay heed. Primarily cultural competence requires that we understand how to share power and how to recognize oppressions and where we contribute and maintain. In the words of Friere (2000), it is critical that we understand how to authentically dialogue with one another, not about our own view of the world, not to attempt to impose that view on someone else, but rather to dialogue with the people about their view and ours. And to understand that it is in communion—honest communion and love—that human beings liberate each other.

Conclusion

Life is about the richness of moments. This "moment" occurred at a party for the elders at the Laguna Rainbow Center, a residential facility at Casa Blanca. The party was a Hawaiian party, but the Rainbow Center had only Country and Western music tapes that day. The recreation coordinator and staff members encouraged elders who wanted to dance to come to the floor. I looked around and one elder, who was said to have dementia, indicated he wanted to get up, so I approached. The elder stood, sounding his struggle and the stiffness of his first steps. At first, the pressure of his body weighed on the arms of the two women who stood holding him steady, anticipating the rhythm of a Country and Western song. Then, the elder began to sing in Keresan, the language of the Laguna people. "He's singin' Indian!" someone said. His body grew in strength and as his feet shuffled to the beat of his singing, his arms seemed no longer to need the women to lean on. Instead, his voice grew stronger and his song more compelling. The elder's arms moved in a dancing motion and we, the women, became partners in his dance. The Country and Western song diminished under the strength of his voice, and his singing touched the senses and sounds of my Laguna childhood. Before he would sit, he began the familiar cadence of Keresan oration. He turned to the elderly people sitting before him, some in wheelchairs, others with oxygen tubes and canisters, and he thanked them for coming. He danced for them and their health, he told them. He sang for them and their health, he told them. And he encouraged the people to have good thoughts and good feelings for one another.

Whatever time he attended, whatever place he went, the journey evoked no pity, only longing for that time and that place.

SONG

Dawahe Baba, thank you grandfather, for these moments.
Dawahe Baba, thank you grandfather, for this gift.
Dawahe Baba, thank you grandfather, for taking me with you.

References

Aristide, J. B. (2000). *Eyes of the heart: Seeking a path for the poor in the age of globalization.* Monroe, ME: Common Courage Press.

Freire, P. (1994). *Pedagogy of hope: Reliving pedagogy of the oppressed.* New York: Continuum Press.

Freire, P. (2000). *Pedagogy of the oppressed.* New York: Continuum.

Nguyen, T. (2001). North-South differences challenge women at UN, *Colorlines, 4*(3). Oakland, CA: Applied Resource Center.

Ross, R. (1996). *Returning to the teachings : Exploring aboriginal justice.* Toronto: Penguin.

Schaef, A. W. (1985). *Women's reality: An emerging female system in white male society.* San Francisco, CA: Harper & Row.

Schaef, A. W. (1987). *When society becomes an addict.* San Francisco: Harper & Row.

Schaef, A. W., & Fassel, D. (1988). *The addictive organization.* San Francisco: Harper & Row.

4

Domestic Violence, Substance Abuse, and Child Welfare

A Need for Collaborative, Culturally Competent Service Delivery

OLIVER J. WILLIAMS, LINNER W. GRIFFIN, YOLANDA DAVIS, and LARRY BENNETT

Introduction

This chapter provides an overview of the impact of substance abuse and domestic violence experiences on youngsters involved in the child welfare system through a detailed examination and synthesis of available research. The authors examine substance abuse causation from both the adult male and female roles in relationship to child welfare programs, because, according to the National Crime Victimization Survey completed by the Bureau of Justice Statistics, 2.5 million women a year are victims of violence in the United States, and alcohol and drugs are associated with up to 50% of all spousal abuse cases (Join Together, 1996). This chapter emphasizes that in order to reduce the problem of placement of children in the child welfare system we must also focus on working to stabilize parents who have substance abuse problems or are victims or perpetrators of domestic violence. There is an association with these concerns and the child welfare, domestic violence, and substance abuse systems are not clear about how to collaborate and approach these issues. That is particularly true within the African American population, which consists of women and men who frequently live in low-income, high-stress communities and who traditionally are disproportionately represented in the child welfare system.

The chapter also notes how children who are exposed to domestic violence are at higher risk for being abused. In families where women are abused, children are also six times more likely to be reported to the child welfare system. We know there is a high association between the use of drugs and alcohol and domestic violence episodes. This trend is also true in cases of child abuse and neglect. Child welfare programs are just beginning to think about the interconnectedness of this problem, but domestic violence and substance abuse programs are at even a more elementary stage of examination.

The purpose of this chapter is to describe social context influences and themes that can ultimately improve outcomes for African American men who batter and women who are victims of domestic violence but also struggle with substance abuse. There can never be too much light shed on their unique circumstances and the children who suffer in silence with them.

The Connection Between Child Welfare and Substance Abuse

In a field where difficult decisions are made every day, child welfare workers are faced with the dilemma of working with extremely troubled families whose complex and multiple problems include substance abuse, domestic violence, poverty, and child maltreatment. Services for families with multiple problems such as these are scattered across a large array of agencies, public and private, with very limited coordination among the agencies in their efforts to provide services to families.

Prevalence of Alcohol Use and Other Drug Use

Substance abuse is one of the most pervasive problems affecting the child welfare system today. Over the last half-century, the patterns of substance abuse have shown a marked increase in the incidence of female substance abusers. This is significant because a majority of families receiving child welfare services are headed by females. This is not to say that males and fathers are not involved, for, indeed, they are. However, the role of men involved with the child welfare system has long been neglected. The male's role in troubled families has not been the primary focus of child welfare agencies. Agencies look at the mother as the primary caretaker and at her ability to provide a safe haven for her children. Child welfare agencies often make recommendations for the males or fathers who are involved with the family. But the agencies do not apply pressure on the males to make contact with the helping resources, that is, it is up to the males to follow through with the recommended services. The plan for the family (mother and child) will continue regardless of the male's actions. Sometimes if he does not follow through, agency policy may dictate that women clients insist that he leave the home. This can be particularly destructive for African American families. It places more stress on Black females and can remove a significant male role model for the child from the home.

Most of the families that become involved with child welfare are considered poor and have limited financial resources. Pursuant to welfare eligibility policies, women are usually the targeted "heads of household." When substance abuse is an issue within the family, the women become the focus of treatment agencies. This supports the traditional client systems of children and their mothers. One must examine substance abuse from both the male and female roles in relationship to child welfare, because, according to the National Crime Victimization Survey completed by the Bureau of Justice Statistics, 2.5 million women annually are victims of violence in the United States, and alcohol and drugs are associated with up to 50% of all spousal abuse cases (Join Together, 1996).

The U.S. Department of Health and Human Services (1999) indicated that 11% of the nation's children (8.3 million) live with at least one parent who is either alcoholic or in need of treatment for the abuse of illicit drugs. Of those, 3.8 million live with a parent who is alcoholic, 2.1 million live with a parent whose primary problem is with illicit drugs, and 2.4 million live with a parent who abuses alcohol and illicit drugs in combination.

Child welfare workers, who work to ensure that children have a safe and nurturing environment, recognize that substance abuse is a major contributing factor to child neglect and abuse; it is also a barrier to family reunification. Children from families with substance abuse problems tend to come to the attention of child welfare agencies younger than other children, are more likely than other children to be placed in care, and once in care are likely to remain there longer. They are also more likely than other children served by child welfare agencies to have been the victims of severe and chronic neglect (Semidei, Radel, & Nolan, 2001).

Effects of Substance Abuse on Children

The use of alcohol and other drugs is a very serious risk factor for the well-being of children. Gregoire and Schultz (2001) and Lessing and Olsen (1996) cited substance abuse as one of the most common factors associated with the placement of children. It is estimated that more than 70% of all children in foster care are there because of parental abuse of alcohol or other drugs.

Children who are raised in homes where parental abuse of alcohol or other drugs is present are at higher risk and more vulnerable than those who are not. Research shows that children whose parents misuse alcohol and other drugs are almost three times more likely to be abused and four times more likely to be neglected than children of parents who don't abuse drugs (Kelleher, Chaffin, Hollenberg, & Fischer, 1994). Likewise, the National Center on Child Abuse and Neglect (1993) found that the incidence of maltreatment among children in alcohol-abusing families was 3.6 times higher than that of children in families without alcohol abuse. This is supported by other studies, which suggest a causal relationship between substance abuse and child abuse and neglect (Kelley, 1992).

A study conducted by Murphy et al. (1991) discovered that of parents referred to child protective services because of abuse of "hard" drugs such as cocaine and heroin, 90% eventually had parental rights terminated. Those who abused alcohol had parental rights terminated at 60%. These findings demonstrate the devastating affect that alcohol and other drugs have on families.

Exposure

The complexity of the problems that families face makes it difficult for child protective services workers to determine the extent to which substance abuse presents a risk to children. Child welfare workers struggle with trying to evaluate the role of substance abuse in the dynamics of a given family and what effects its exposure will have on a child.

Substance abuse has proven to have profound effects on adults and the children whom they rear. Parents who abuse alcohol and other drugs may, because of this use, make bad decisions in their disciplinary choices and child rearing behaviors. They tend to have less control over their actions and may use disciplinary methods that child welfare agencies would consider to be inappropriate. According to the National Center on Addiction and Substance Abuse at Columbia University (CASA, 2001), more women are substance abusers today than in past years. Resnik, Gardner, and Rodgers (1998) attribute the increase to the easy access to substances and the low cost of crack cocaine. As stated previously the majority of families involved with the child welfare system have females as heads of household.

According to the Alcohol and Drug Council of North Carolina (1998), nearly 700,000 people are addicted to drugs other than alcohol in North Carolina and another 700,000 have problems with alcohol. Evidence is increasing that children of substance abusers are at an elevated risk for developing substance use disorders and other difficulties attributable to their exposure. Children of alcohol- and drug-abusing parents tend to live in chaotic and often injurious environments that can cause them serious harm. They are at higher risk of being victims to physical abuse, sexual abuse, and neglect (Resnik, Gardner, & Rogers, 1998).

McMahon and Luthar (1998) report in a review of developmental issues in children of substance abusers that the two main research findings regarding such children are (1) they have poorer developmental outcomes (physical, intellectual, social, and emotional) than other children, although generally in the low-to-normal range rather than severely impaired, and (2) they are at risk of substance abuse themselves.

Evidence is increasing that children of substance abusers are at elevated risk for developing substance use disorders at young ages due to familial and genetic factors. Children of alcohol- and drug-abusing parents are at the highest risk of any children for later drug use and other adolescent behavioral health and mental health problems. It is important to note, however, that not all children of substance-abusing parents become substance abusers as adults. Little is known about "factors that promote positive development despite the presence of parental substance abuse" (McMahon & Luthar, 1998, p. 153).

Alcohol appears to have more profound and long-lasting effects on development, including serious intellectual and behavioral consequences in many children, than do cocaine and other illicit drugs. Babies whose mothers drink alcohol during pregnancy can be born with Fetal Alcohol Syndrome (FAS) or alcohol-related birth disorders. FAS is among the leading known causes of mental retardation in the United States. Infants born with FAS have difficulties with coordination, speech and hearing impairments, and heart defects. Research indicates that there is no known safe level of alcohol consumption during pregnancy, although FAS and related problems are more likely with heavy consumption of alcohol. According to CASA (1996), an estimated 12,000 infants are born with FAS annually. Consumption of illicit drugs during pregnancy also can harm the fetus and may have long-term effects on children. Babies who were prenatally exposed to cocaine or other drugs may experience a range of problems, including some that can be long-lasting and serious. However, these physical and mental deficits are not seen in infants to the extent that earlier expert warnings and media reports regarding "crack babies" had predicted (U.S. Department of Health and Human Services, 1994).

Maltreatment of Children and Substance Abuse

As mentioned above, children whose parents misuse alcohol and drugs are at greater risk of neglect (Kelleher et al., 1994). These children suffer from a variety of physical, mental, and emotional health problems. They are more likely to have low self-esteem, experience failure, and struggle with depression and anxiety (Children of Alcoholics Foundation, n.d.; McMahon & Luthar, 1998). They also tend to demonstrate more adjustment problems and conduct and attention deficit disorders than do other children.

Substance abuse impairs parents' judgment, which normally would enable parents to provide consistent supervision and guidance to their children. Determining the level of functioning of a substance-abusing parent is a difficult task when considering whether a child could be put at risk of harm. Most agencies will not jeopardize the safety of a child.

Implications for the Child Welfare System

The needs for services to families who are involved with the child welfare system are complex and forever changing. Their problems are multifaceted and require outside resources as well as those that can be provided by the child welfare program. Child welfare agencies and other professionals work to ensure that children are raised in a safe, nurturing, and loving environment, free of hazards such as domestic violence, abuse, and substance abuse, which are all closely intertwined with economic stress and neglect.

Service Delivery

In the quest to serve families with substance abuse problems, collaboration among all agencies that work with the family is critical. Unfortunately, there is a lack of a shared vision in dealing with child welfare agencies and substance abuse treatment programs. While both the substance abuse treatment and the child welfare programs have the vision of healthy, functional families, the process of moving from the family's immediate situation to the end result each agency seeks is extremely difficult. Different perspectives and philosophies sometimes impede cooperation, foster mistrust, and can cause agencies to hamper one another's efforts.

There are real and significant barriers to productive collaborations between child welfare and substance abuse agencies. But these differences can and must be accommodated in order to provide effective treatment and intervention to families. These efforts require sustained action by federal, state, and local staffs in the child welfare, substance abuse, and related fields throughout the country. There is a need for each discipline to learn about the other, to understand one another, and to establish a shared set of expectations for each of them and for their clients.

Policy Implications

Child welfare agencies are largely driven by state and federal standards and mandates. With the enactment of the Adoption and Safe Families Act of 1997, an urgency to obtain permanency for children has been created in child welfare. This is not to say that permanency was not a goal of child welfare agencies, but new mandates and initiatives place additional pressures on agencies to achieve this outcome. The Adoption Assistance and Child Welfare Act of 1980 sought to strengthen families through prevention services and to obtain reunification as quickly as possible. Agencies had the added task of showing responsible efforts to achieve family reunification. This is critical in a discussion on substance abuse because it is known that relapses occur, which can hinder the reunification process. States are required to file petitions to terminate parental rights if a child has remained in out-of-home care for at least 15 of the most recent 22 months.

Child welfare agencies expect families to be ready for reunification within a year, while not considering the tendency for substance-abusing parents to need long-term treatment for their problem and the likelihood they will relapse. This places child welfare agencies in an awkward position of taking a chance by returning a child to the home of substance-abusing caretakers without being able to guarantee the safety of the child. Service integration and collaboration are critical to work effectively with substance-abusing parents and to provide intensive, time-limited reunification services to children and families (McAlpine, Marshall, & Doran, 2001). With concurrent planning and the Adoption and Safe Family Act, agencies may move forward to obtain permanency for children, which may mean the termination of parental rights, if a parent is not successful.

Services to children are usually based on the behaviors of the parent. Child welfare agencies do not directly prescribe guidelines or treatment for substance abusers. Few child welfare workers have been trained to conduct comprehensive substance abuse assessments, and still fewer are competent to use scales or chemical screening to evaluate current substance use or abuse (Rittner & Dozier, 2000). Referrals for treatment are necessary because workers are not prepared to address the multiple problems of substance-abusing parents. The ability to cross-train substance abuse workers and child welfare workers is an obvious solution.

What are the impediments to cross-training? Several key differences in perspectives underlie the majority of misunderstandings and frustrations child welfare agencies and substance abuse treatment agencies feel toward one another. These include different definitions of who the client is, what outcomes are expected on their respective timelines, and potentially conflicting responses to setbacks. In addition, factors related to the legal and policy environments within which agencies operate set a context for joint activities and affect the willingness and ability of agencies to work together. These include state and federal laws regarding child abuse and neglect and child welfare; the sense of crisis under which many child welfare agencies operate; chronic shortages of substance abuse treatment services, particularly services appropriate for women with young children; and confidentiality requirements of both fields that are often perceived as impediments to cooperation.

The Connection Between Domestic Violence and Substance Abuse

There is a connection between domestic violence and substance abuse. Common sense, clinical experience, and practice wisdom suggest that the acute effects of alcohol and other drugs (intoxication) as well as the effects of chronic alcohol and drug use (substance abuse, addiction, or chemical dependency) increase the likelihood of both child abuse or neglect and intimate partner violence (Bennett & Williams, 2003). Data tell a similar story.

About the Children

Domestic violence and substance abuse are also risk factors for the abuse of women and children. In homes where intimate partner violence occurs, children are much more likely both to become victims of abuse and to be reported to the child welfare system. Substance abuse by one parent increases the likelihood that the substance-abusing parent will be unable to protect children if the other parent is violent (Reed, 1991). Also, parents are less able to address the needs of children in other ways. Not only do children come into the child welfare system because of abuse, they come because of neglect as well. When domestic abuse, substance abuse, and poverty occur in a family system, it increases the potential that children's needs are not being addressed by the parents. It is important to take time and consider the adult parents.

Men Who Batter and Abuse Drugs

Regarding men, researchers have found that one-fourth to one-half of men who commit acts of domestic violence also have substance abuse problems (Center for Substance Abuse Treatment [CSAT], 1996; Coleman & Straus, 1983; Gondolf, 1995; Hamilton & Collins, 1981; Kantor & Straus, 1987; Leonard & Jacob, 1987; Pernanen, 1976). Fifty percent of men who batter are believed to have an addiction problem (Faller, 1988). In the empirical literature examining substance abuse by men in batterer programs, over 50% of the participants are evaluated as substance abusers (Gondolf, 1999; Tolman & Bennett, 1990). Although less is known about domestic violence by men in substance abuse treatment programs, when agencies bother to look, they find roughly the same proportion of batterers. Chermack, Fuller, and Blow (2000) found that 53% of 126 men in substance abuse treatment had used moderate or severe partner violence in the year prior to treatment. Over a three-year period, a large westside substance abuse treatment program in Chicago screened all admissions to its substance abuse treatment program for domestic violence and reported that 70% of screened men self-reported as perpetrators of domestic abuse (Bennett & Williams, 2003). Several research groups have reported that empirically differentiating substance-abusing men from batterers is difficult. Stith, Crossman, and Bischof (1991) studied the frequency and severity of substance abuse by men in batterer programs and found it does not differ from the substance abuse of men in substance abuse treatment programs. Likewise, when researchers examine the frequency and severity of domestic violence by men in substance abuse treatment programs, it looks much the same as the domestic violence of men in batterer programs (Brown, Caplan, Werk, & Seraganian, 1999). It is easy to see, based on these data, why so many practitioners have come to think of batterers and substance abusers in treatment as the same men at different points of their lives (Bennett & Williams, 2003).

Within this theoretical framework, the societal view of substance abusers as morally weak and controlled by alcohol or other drugs actually serves some batterers; rather than taking responsibility for their actions, they can blame their violent acts on the substance(s) they are abusing (Bennett & Williams, 2003). Although drugs or alcohol may indeed be a trigger for violence, the belief that the violence will stop once the drinking or drug use stops is usually not borne out. The use of alcohol or other drugs may increase the likelihood that a batterer will commit an act of domestic violence—because it reduces inhibitions and distorts perceptions. Also, because alcohol is often used as an excuse for violence, and both alcohol abuse and domestic violence tend to follow parallel escalating patterns, it does not fully explain the behavior (CSAT, 1996; Leonard & Jacob, 1987; Steele & Josephs, 1990; Pernanen, 1976). The fact remains that nondrinking men also attack their partners, and for some individuals, alcohol actually inhibits violent behavior (Bennett, 1995; Coleman & Straus, 1983). Batterers—like survivors—often turn to substances of choice for their numbing effects. Batterers who are survivors of childhood abuse also frequently say that they use drugs and alcohol to block the pain and to avoid confronting that memory (Bennett & Williams, 2003; CSAT, 1996).

Like many phenomena, however, the link between substance use and partner abuse is not as simple as it first appears. For example, in the general population, 60% to 75% of batterers are not drinking when they batter (Kantor & Straus, 1987; Pernanen, 1976). This does not contradict previous statements, which find high levels of co-occurrence in clinical populations, because a man may not be drinking and taking drugs when he batters and still is a substance abuser. In fact, for some substance abusers, the greatest potential for violence may be when they are *not* intoxicated, either because they are unable to procure their substance of choice or because they are abstinent during early phases of recovery. In the Centers for Disease Control and Prevention's multisite study of batterer's treatment, one of the strongest predictors of reoffense is drunkenness during the batterer program (Gondolf, 1999). However, it was not possible for researchers to determine the sequence of drunkenness and violence, so it is likely that a substantial proportion of the recidivate episodes occurred when men who were frequently drunk were, at that time, not drinking. This plausible scenario suggests that a substance abuser may be at greater risk for partner violence when he is not drinking or taking drugs because alcohol or drugs act, not as a *disinhibitor*, but rather as an *inhibitor* for some substance-abusing batterers under certain circumstances. Regardless of the explanation, data suggesting minorities of batterers are intoxicated when they batter suggest that intimate partner violence cannot be well explained as a simple sequela of substance use (Bennett & Williams, 2003).

Treatment for Domestic Violence and Substance Abuse

The reality is that in the United States there are few programs that address the co-occurrence of domestic violence and substance abuse. In many batterers' treatment programs, if a batterer has a substance abuse problem he is expected to address his substance abuse problem prior to entering treatment.

In contrast, many substance abuse programs do not address the domestic violence at all. The thinking has been that once the substance abuse problem is addressed the violence will end. Practitioners in the field of domestic violence know that this is an untrue assumption. Many batterers' counselors have worked with men who are in recovery and have had years of sobriety and, still, abuse of women occurs. We must develop models of treatment that recognize and respond to the co-occurrence of such behaviors as well as respond to the needs of a diverse population.

Low-Income African American Men: Domestic Violence and Substance Abuse

Treatment paradigms for substance abuse or domestic violence that exist today come from a one-size-fits-all perspective. Men of color, such as African American men, have higher dropout rates in both batterers' treatment and substance abuse treatment than do white males. Although the traditional approaches have been successful in transforming men who batter and men who abuse drugs, many men may find that the lack of attention to diversity makes the treatment models less relevant for them. Researchers who write about minority men and violence as well as minority males who abuse drugs discuss the importance of addressing their social context in treatment. They also describe the importance of capacity building and problem solving as they relate to conflict situations.

Staples (1982) and A. N. Wilson (1991) suggest that before one can truly understand violence perpetrated by African American males, there must be a critique of the African American males' experience in the United States. Violence in the lives of African Americans is allowed and even promoted because historically their lives have been devalued in American society (Hawkins, 1987). It is, therefore, imperative to recognize the types of societal violence and oppression Black males experience. Wilson (1991) observes the following historical oppressions: slavery, wage slavery, and peonage; economic discrimination and warfare; political-economic disenfranchisement; Jim Crowism; general White hostility; Klan terrorism; lynching; injustice and "legal lynching"; the raping of Black women and the killing of Black men by Whites, which have gone unredressed by the justice system; the near-condoning and virtual approval of Black-on-Black violence, differential arrest, criminal indictments, and incarceration; segregation; job, business, professional, and labor discrimination; negative stereotyping and character assassination; housing discrimination; police brutality; addictive drug importation; poor and inadequate education; inadequate and often absent health care; inadequate family support; and so on.

Griffin and Williams (1992) note that it is imperative to address social context concerns among these men or the consequence may be abuse directed toward self, family, friends, or the community. Maladaptive behaviors among some African American men result from violent social learning environments, abusive experiences as children, societal and structural oppression, and a violent and high-stress living environment. These maladaptive behaviors can include problems such as crime, substance abuse, violence, and so forth. Although partner violence is 100% the responsibility of the perpetrator, African American men may also displace their anger toward women because of social context challenges and environmental codes of conduct that encourage such behaviors (Rich & Stone, 1996; Williams, 1999b). The traditional explanations for partner abuse by all men apply, but social context challenges are an additional explanation where low-income African American men are concerned. Again, this is not a justification for the behavior, just an additional explanation.

Substance abuse provides close similarities to the issues mentioned above. Vail and Wade (1994) and others note that it is essential to examine the social context of poor African American men before one can develop treatment approaches that are effective and congruent with their reality and life experience. He notes the importance of exploring factors that contribute to substance abuse, such as unemployment, economic deprivation, poverty, racism, discrimination, and issues pertaining to gender role and manhood, the availability and importation of alcohol and other drugs in the African American community, and the impact of criminal sanctions and incarceration. Pena and Koss-Chioino

(1992) are critical of substance abuse treatment programs that serve African American men but do not discuss the impact of the 1980s cocaine epidemic for African Americans and the resulting psychiatric comorbidity. Rasheed and Rasheed (1999) found that repeat victims of violence in emergency rooms were likely to be poor African American males who had substance abuse problems and mental health problems and who lived in neighborhoods where violence was pervasive.

Several writers who focus on the challenges of African American men suggest that such behaviors require holistic treatment. Instead of focusing on isolated behavior change with individual behavior problems, more could be accomplished through healing and teaching African American men to live a balanced life within a community of self and others (Akabar, 1985). Men who are emotionally out of balance tend to substitute one maladaptive behavior for another (Blake & Darling, 1994). Violent African American men must develop skills to negotiate racist and violent, oppressive situations and environments in adaptive ways without taking their frustration out on others (Williams, 1999a). Williams (1999b) describes a model of treatment for African American men who batter that confronts the violence and holds men accountable for behaviors, yet explores their social context challenges within culturally specific treatment groups. Taylor-Gibbs (1988) and A. N. Wilson (1991) recommend sanctions for the negative behavior, but they also suggest providing resource and developmental information for men who live in highly stressed urban communities.

Ormand (1992) proposes a model for treating substance abusers that is described as a paradigm for socialization: empowering African American male substance abusers to maximize their human potential through a continuum-of-care model. This model focuses on criminality and substance use, anxiety and depression, education/functional literacy, vocational development, therapeutic recreation, family and community psychosocial functioning, and nutrition and spirituality.

Social context challenges such as poverty and effective capacity-building skills such as problem solving are common themes for African American men and other minority males in these two fields. Researchers and practitioners who work with minority men on these issues must incorporate this content in research and treatment. The two fields must talk with each other regarding effective service delivery among this population.

Battered Women Who Abuse Drugs

Research also indicates that women who abuse alcohol and other drugs are more likely to become victims of domestic violence (Miller, Downs, & Gondoli, 1989). Further, these victims are more likely to become dependent on tranquilizers, sedatives, stimulants, and painkillers and are more likely to abuse alcohol (Stark & Flitcraft, 1988). Alcoholic women are more likely to report a history of adult or childhood physical and emotional abuse than are nonalcoholic women (Miller et al., 1989; Rodgers, McGee, Vann, Thompson, & Williams, 2003). Women in recovery tend to have a history of violent trauma and are at high risk of being diagnosed with post-traumatic stress disorder (Fullilove et al., 1993). Many in the field of domestic violence believe that battered women who have substance abuse problems use drugs and alcohol to medicate and/or numb themselves from either childhood or adult experiences with violence. Not surprisingly, some victims of rape and other violence report using alcohol and other drugs to "self-medicate" or anesthetize themselves to the pain of their situations (CSAT, 1996; Rodgers et al., 2003).

Victims of abuse who abuse drugs and alcohol experience differential attitudes by society. Societal norms indirectly excuse violence against women (tacit support for punishing unfaithful wives, for example, or stereotyped views of women as obedient or compliant) (Bennett, 1995; Kantor & Straus, 1987; Reed, 1991); this is further exacerbated if she uses alcohol or other drugs. The man who batters may use the woman's drinking or taking drugs as a rationale to label her negatively. Substance abuse treatment providers have observed that society tolerates a man's use of alcohol and other drugs more readily than it does a woman's. They also report that batterers often blame a woman they have victimized for the violence, either implicitly or explicitly, and other people, including the police, judges, and juries, often accept this argument (CSAT, 1996). It follows then that intoxicated victims are more likely to be blamed than sober ones, and that aggression toward an inebriated victim is considered more acceptable than aggression toward a sober one. And, depending on a woman's status characteristics, society may more readily accept the violence toward her, particularly if she is poor and a woman of color.

Low-Income African American Women: Domestic Violence and Substance Abuse

At this time, when domestic violence programs exist in almost every community, it is important to note that issues of access are different for African American women because (1) there are a limited number of safe places for battered women to become stabilized, (2) few programs address the dual issue of domestic violence and substance abuse, and (3) there is the perception that unless both parties address their substance abuse issues first they cannot be helped by other community resources

African American women are also more likely to experience the most severe violence compared to other groups. If she is low income and poorly educated this can increase her risk of abuse (Sullivan & Rumptz, 1994). Moss et al. (1997) note that leaving a domestic violence relationship has many similarities among women, but critical differences exist between White women and African American women. The authors conclude that for African American women, leaving is a culture-bound experience. Richie (1995) explains that the African American woman may be encouraged to subordinate her feelings, experiences, and reactions with various forms of abuse because she is encouraged to do so by her family, the abuser, and/or the community. Accordingly, the abused woman may find herself hating the abuse but supporting the abuser. Further, poverty is a major barrier for many African American battered women because it reduces their options for leaving, decreases the capacity to respond to their needs or those of their children, and increases their need for an array of services (Sullivan & Rumptz, 1994).

Janice Joseph (1995), in her study comparing African American and White women in domestic violence, found African American women more reluctant to use domestic violence shelters and other social services than White women. Although many minority women's lives are saved through shelter services, many struggle in these mainstream programs. Lynch et al. (1996) found that many African American women they surveyed were reluctant to use shelter services because of institutionalized racism; power differences among White advocates, White clients, and African American clients; the lack of African American advocates and child care staff; the lack of Black personal care products; the lack of connection associated to spirituality and the community; and the short-term nature of the services (Brice-Baker, 1994; Donnelly et al., 1995).

Low-Income African American Women: Substance Abuse and Domestic Violence

The drug use of many African American women ranges from alcohol to other prescription drugs, but among poorer women the drug of choice may also include crack cocaine. From the literature we know that younger substance-abusing women with a lower educational status will more likely receive welfare assistance. Further, their partners typically introduced them to drugs. Additionally, many low-income, drug-abusing women are often the procurers of drugs for their partners. For this reason, some of these women are often kept from drug treatment and forcibly returned to the street to deliver cash for drugs by prostitution. Women are often threatened and physically abused in the process. Typically, the woman tends to be more fearful, guarded, vigilant, and aware of potential threats and dangers in her environment than her White counterparts. She is more likely to receive opposition to entering treatment from friends and family members compared to men. Moreover, she may be cut off from social supports in families that are concerned with her divulging family secrets.

Laws and policies are punitive, particularly to minority women who use drugs. The woman may have concerns about trusting institutions such as law enforcement, drug treatment programs, and domestic violence shelters. She is also less likely to complete treatment programs or to be accepted as a referral for aftercare than are White women. Few treatment programs are designed to treat her and are able to address the dual issues of domestic violence and substance abuse (C. S. Carter, 1987; Mamis-King, 1997; Nyamathi, Bennett, & Leake, 1995).

Yet, recovery from substance abuse and domestic violence is not possible until a woman has a safe and peaceful place and an opportunity to reorder her life. Because of her distrust of institutions and programs, service organizations must be culturally competent as well. Practitioners must understand her social context experience but also her experiences as an African American battered woman and drug abuser. Where possible, programs must match an African American female with a helper who understands culturally competent approaches and, where possible, an African American helper to work with her. There is also a need to pay close attention and monitor African Americans women's physical health (Rodgers et al., 2003).

As mentioned above, there are few programs that address the intersection or nexus of domestic violence, substance abuse, and African American women. A few programs that do are identified in the last section of this chapter. The successful programs were developed by women who were challenged by these issues or practitioners who listened to the voices of the women that they served (Rodgers et al., 2003). They addressed these issues simultaneously. Similarly, the authors are not suggesting that conventional approaches to treatment be abandoned; rather, we suggest they must be expanded to address the authentic concerns of these women.

So many of these women are isolated, so helping them to connect to a functional support system is important. In the absence of support by blood relatives, extended family within the minority community can be a tremendous asset. Supportive relatives, cousins many times removed, neighbors, or church members can help. C. S. Carter (1987) and Rodgers et al. (2003) note that treatment programs often overlook these as resources first in interventions and later in ongoing efforts as support. Supportive relationship building is important with these women. There must be an emphasis on self-development programs, which emphasize coping, life management skills, and education regarding alcoholism and other substances.

Many African American women see church as a sustaining force. For some of these women, a religious orientation has been cited as a reason for the high abstinence rates among African American females, because it increases their sense of self-worth. The woman's concern over losing favor with God can be an inhibitor for drug use. African American churches may also be an alternative to many African American females who report they can't relate in 12-step groups that are not culturally specific. Also, programs need to make connections with churches and develop African American-oriented Alcoholics Anonymous (AA) or Narcotics Anonymous (NA) groups.

Conclusions and Recommendations

CONCLUSIONS

Seven points, raised by the authors in the sections above, are repeated as conclusions for this chapter.

- •One of the common characteristics among the men and women who come to the attention of the child welfare, domestic violence, substance abuse, and court systems is socioeconomic status. These individuals are consistently at or near the poverty level, which has clear implications about the difficulties they experience in accessing treatment and social services. Alcohol and drug treatment programs often require in-patient periods, which would further negatively affect an already poor financial picture. Additionally, domestic violence treatment and court-ordered services require group meetings and counseling, which can again have an impact on a bleak financial picture.

- •Another characteristic of this population is that it is disproportionately African American. We also know that African American families are disproportionately low income. As suggested in earlier sections, when poverty, substance abuse, and domestic violence occur in a family situation, out-of-home placements for children often result. The inclusion of race as an added variable places additional strains on substance abuse and domestic violence agencies. At this time, some of these agencies do not have facilities that are culturally sensitive to the needs of Black women and their children. One size fits all does not work in treatment, but there are not sufficient facilities that specifically dress the unique concerns of minority families.

- •A third persistent theme is that women still are blamed for or held responsible for the abuse of their children and the failure to protect children more than men.

- •Issues of social control are evident once an infant or child has been identified as either drug dependent or in the care of someone who is alcohol or drug dependent. Government, operating under the theory of *parens patriae*, enters the situation and exerts authority to protect the child. The women are encouraged to receive treatment, while the state assumes responsibility for their child's development and well-being. But, once identified as a substance abuser who has exposed her young to an illegal substance, the mothers become stigmatized. A. J. Carter (1996, p. 216) asserts that the stigmatization can lead to the damaging effects of labeling the women as "bad mothers," which without comprehensive assessment of the situation may lead to the child welfare system's inappropriate response to the problem.

•Current social and legal remedies lead to the destruction of families, especially African American families. Children may feel abandoned or labeled because of parental drinking or abuse of other substances. The children typically have difficulties dealing with the ensuing learning and social problems.

•Maternal substance abuse can have numerous detrimental effects on the growth and development of infants; there is a need to focus on early intervention. Ondersma et al. (2000) state that $350 million is spent annually providing special services in schools for children exposed to drugs prenatally. Belew (1996) reports that numerous studies have shown that drug use during pregnancy can cause fetal distress, stroke, seizures, and the potential for long-term deficits in learning. Furthermore, Ondersma et al. (2000) assert that drug use during pregnancy causes low birth weight and prematurity. The dual effects of a stressful, premature birth and drug exposure can cause long-term problems with the child's development, learning, attention span, and self-control. There is a need for early identification of at-risk infants and their mothers who have the potential to succeed with early intervention and treatment.

•The current out-of-home placement options are characterized by the lack of strong parental models. The state, which makes decisions and exerts control over the children's lives, shows strength, but is not a "warm, fuzzy" role model capable of exemplifying ethnic pride and caring.

RECOMMENDATIONS

Several recommendations follow that draw upon some information and ideas developed throughout this chapter.

Stabilization Sites

The authors' first recommendation is that agencies and communities begin to understand and address the uniqueness of minority experiences. There is a need for the development of sites and programs that will provide minorities with culturally sensitive support for stabilization. These efforts must necessarily support the breath of the authentic experiences of domestic violence and addicts who are poor men and women, especially African Americans. Within this social context and with the proper support, they can reconcile issues and develop strategies to negotiate life challenges of issues that have meaning for them. If such an environment is unavailable then change is less likely to occur.

Other Recommendations

In efforts to serve families with child welfare problems, collaboration among all service providers is critical. One can expect other issues, possibly substance abuse and domestic violence, to coexist within the family. Communication is a key factor in positive outcomes for families. Agency jargon and insufficient information can lead to delays, disappointing results, and fragmented service delivery. While agencies are making efforts to work together, there is still a need for increased awareness and education. Substance abuse agencies, domestic violence programs, and child welfare agencies mutually share the two goals of helping families attain self-sufficiency and of building healthier families; but they have different perspectives, additional goals, and philosophies that can impede the process, foster mistrust, and hamper each other's efforts. It is imperative that (1) the three systems communicate with each other, (2) child welfare workers gain knowledge of substance abuse and domestic violence, and (3) substance abuse agencies gain knowledge about domestic violence and child welfare.

Systems Must Begin to Talk to Each Other

Child welfare agencies are not equipped to handle the complex needs of substance-abusing parents and traditionally have used outside referrals to address parents' needs for treatment. If the parent is successful in drug treatment then reunification of the family is possible; however, if the parent does not make diligent efforts to obtain the treatment on his own, alternatives to permanence are sought by child welfare agencies. This action draws attention to the obstacles that agencies must face in the sharing of information related to a client's treatment. Child welfare agencies and substance abuse agencies have not done a good job of collaborating with each other. In fact, without a signed consent form from the client, many agencies are not at liberty to discuss a client's treatment with another agency. In addition, parents may have already been involved in some form of treatment and at the same time been involved with child welfare, with each agency having no knowledge of the other's involvement. Clients often do not freely give information about earlier contacts.

Substance abuse programs and child welfare agencies take similar actions when faced with family members who perpetrate domestic violence against one another. Again, there exists a lack of knowledge about "the specifics" of eligibility and treatment in the three helping systems that can inhibit appropriate interventions. Again, service delivery protocols impede sharing of information with staff from a different system, and, again, clients often are asked to take the initiative in securing the coordinated services they may need to maintain intact families.

Communities have been encouraged by Department of Justice initiatives to develop a "Coordinated Community Response" to incidents of violence. Their responses to the initiative have produced a variety of models. In some of the more encouraging models, local criminal justice agencies have pulled together social service agencies, health programs, domestic violence programs, and mental health agencies to develop a shared response to domestic violence episodes. The agencies, which formalized their mission and interagency relationships through memoranda of understanding, have developed community intervention protocols. Efforts, like those described above, promote real collaboration and represent what less organized communities should strive for.

Remedy the Lack of Substance Abuse Training for Child Welfare Workers

Child welfare workers receive little to no training related to substance abuse. Clients identified as having substance-related problems are referred to other agencies for treatment. Child welfare workers are not trained to assess substance abuse and its effect(s) on families. With the increased number of families identified, there is a need for child protective services workers to become knowledgeable about this area. The importance of adequate drug use and abuse screening is essential to good case planning (Rittner & Dozier, 2000). In child protective services, being able to assess the needs of a family can make or break the goals of treatment. For example, a parent who is referred to parenting classes because of inappropriate discipline, but who has a substance abuse problem that was not identified, will not achieve positive outcomes because of the failure to address a need for substance abuse treatment. This parent may complete parenting classes; however, she will more than likely come to the attention of the agency again. The cycle continues because of the first incomplete assessment, which neglected to look at substance abuse as a cause of the problem. Also, in abuse situations, agencies often do not recognize a client's need for support on multiple levels. When this happens, clients come to the attention of the agency again because of the agency's failure to assess the breadth of issues facing its female clients.

Remedy the Lack of Child Welfare Training for Substance Abuse Workers

With the continued changes occurring in the child welfare field and the new initiatives that arise, it is difficult for child welfare workers to keep abreast of updated information. For workers in other systems, staying "on top" of the never-ending procedural revisions may seem impossible. Timelines within child welfare are contradictory to treatment in most substance abuse treatment programs, which see treatment as long term and expect clients to relapse. In educating workers in substance abuse agencies about the needs of families involved with the child welfare system, it is important to address the time frames that families have to work within in order to develop realistic goals toward positive outcomes.

Remedy the Lack of Domestic Violence Training for Child Welfare and Substance Abuse Workers

Laura Feig (1998) combined the ideas of Kelley (1992) when she wrote, "Studies have shown both that substance abusers are more likely than other parents to abuse and neglect their children and that maltreating parents are more likely than other parents to abuse alcohol or other drugs" (p. 62). This one statement clearly exemplifies a need for shared learning among practitioners from the domestic violence, substance abuse, and child welfare systems. There are too many families known to the domestic violence network and the child welfare system whose predicament is exasperated by alcohol and other drug use. Meaningful communication between the three service agencies will eliminate some "game playing" by clients and uncoordinated efforts by workers. In order to communicate effectively and efficiently, workers from one system must understand the ideology and methods of the other two. This can only be accomplished through cross-training and meaningful sharing. Through cross-training, trust, which facilitates cooperation, can result.

The authors are not suggesting that any of the three social problems, domestic violence, child abuse and neglect, or substance abuse, can be easily remedied through cross-training or programming interventions. Rather, we suggest that creating "stable" individuals and reuniting children and families where possible cannot occur in a vacuum. Each system must recognize the co-occurring challenges of the other intersecting set of social problems and address them in order to maximize the potential for change and recovery.

Battered women's programs must acknowledge the fact that there are many battered women who abuse drugs and who come to the child welfare system. Although battered women's programs are always challenged because of the lack of resources for most of them and the high demand, they are also challenged because so many children have needs as well. It is difficult enough to run such a program given the competing challenges of violence and abuse, poverty, housing needs, recovery from trauma and injury, race and cultural considerations, and so on. To add substance abuse to the list can seem overwhelming. But, as has been indicated, this is the reality for so many women who are victims of violence. Rodgers et al. (2003) indicate that women can change, but they need an environment that will allow for it and support it. They note that change from domestic abuse and substance abuse will only occur for battered women who use drugs if they have a safe place to reorder their lives. Abuse and neglect of children tends to be a challenge in its own right, but is often a collateral issue for battered women who use drugs.

Batterers' treatment programs must begin to address the co-occurrence of these issues as well. In some jurisdictions batterers' programs include men who abuse children. Addressing child abuse and neglect issues should not only occur by sending men to parenting classes or anger management courses. Perhaps batterers' programs are good places to send men who abuse and neglect their children as well. Clearly, incorporating information about nonabuse of women and children is appropriate in these settings, even though much of the focus has been and should remain on battered women.

But, as Williams et al. (2001) encourage, it is important to address fathering among these men and the destructive consequences of their behaviors as well. It is equally important to address the reality of substance abuse among these men who come to the attention of multiple systems through the court, child welfare, and batterers' treatment. Substance use and abuse tends to remain a recurring theme; however, providing treatment, coeducation, and monitoring of men with these issues also is important. In the field of domestic violence more has been done to hold men accountable for their behaviors associated with abuse of women; more must be done to respond to the role of men in the abuse of children as well. Child welfare systems have to be clearer about how to address the male batterer's contribution to the victimization of women and children, and how monitoring domestic abuse and substance abuse by the mother and father or father figure influences outcomes and more stabilized living environments for children.

Substance abuse treatment programs must acknowledge the co-occurrence of child abuse and neglect within the community of the substance abuse clients they serve. As professionals in the field already understand, there are no miracle answers for change or recovery. Yet, domestic abuse and child abuse and neglect are still other ways the substance abuse field's constituent group is affected.

Glimmers of Hope

Fortunately, some programs have emerged that are glimmers of hope for African Americans with substance abuse, domestic violence, and child welfare issues. Jelani House in San Francisco provides culturally sensitive residential housing while also offering treatment for women experiencing substance abuse problems. For over five years, this organization has addressed these overlapping issues successfully. MOMs Off Meth is a political advocacy organization in Ottumwa, Iowa, that is made up of women who have experienced problems with custody and the child welfare system. These women, many of whom have histories of substance abuse and domestic violence victimization, collectively work to force the child welfare system to be more responsive to their unique situations.

Treatment groups for substance-abusing African American battered women are offered through African American Family Services (formerly the Institute for Black Chemical Abuse) in Minneapolis, Minnesota. Also in Minneapolis, Turning Point provides assistance to victims of domestic violence who also have problems with substance abuse. Similarly, Asha Family Services in Milwaukee, Wisconsin, has experienced some success in addressing the co-occurrence of domestic violence and substance abuse among Black women and men. This organization maintains a close working relationship with the local child welfare program to enhance opportunities for the women and children whom it serves. A final noteworthy program is Project Network in Portland, Oregon, which has experienced some success working with individuals and families who need domestic violence, community violence, substance abuse, and child welfare services.

These programs were started by women who were either physically abused and also abused drugs or who listened to the voices of women who were their clients and responded with programs and services (Rodgers et al., 2003). Some of these female-focused programs also developed programs for men (who were the partners of the women they were serving) because these men had problems of abusive behaviors and/or drug-abusing behaviors. Prior to the development of these unique batterers' groups, the men would sit outside in cars or in the waiting rooms waiting to pick up their partners. Some of these agencies started programs for these men and subsequently expanded their program services.

Treating these problems requires that the three systems (child welfare, substance abuse, domestic violence) think outside the box. Each field has done so in the past in order to provide needed services to its constituent group. It is time to revisit the roots of the various fields and come up with approaches that not only protect, confront, and serve these populations, but also collaboratively heal them in culturally sensitive, nurturing environments.

References

Adoption & Safe Families Act of 1997, Pub. L. No. 105-89,111 Stat. 2116 (1997).

Adoption Assistance & Child Welfare Act of 1980, Pub. L. No. 96-272, 94 Stat. 501 (1980).

Akabar, N. (1985). Our destiny: Authors of scientific revolution. In H. P. McAdoo & J. L. McAdoo (Eds.), *Black children: Social educational, and parental environments* (pp. 17–31). Beverly Hills, CA: Sage.

Alcohol and Drug Council of North Carolina (1998). North Carolina doesn't have an alcohol/drug problem or does it? Durham: Author.

Belew, K. (1996). Combating maternal drug addiction: A single system research report. Retrieved January 28, 2002, from http://hadm.sph.sc.edu/students/kbelew/SINGLESYS.HTM

Bennett, L. W. (1995). Substance abuse and the domestic assault of women. *Social Work, 40*(6), 760–772.

Bennett, L. & Williams, O. J. (2003). Substance abuse and men who batter: Issues in theory and practice. *Violence Against Women, 9*(5), 558–575.

Blake, W. M., & Darling, C. A. (1994). The dilemmas of the African American male. *Journal of Black Studies, 24*(4), 402–415.

Brice-Baker, J. R. (1994). Domestic violence in African American and Caribbean families. *Journal of Social Distress and the Homeless, 3*(1), 23–38.

Brown, T. G, Caplan, T., Werk, A., Seraganian, P. (1999). The comparability of male violent substance abusers in violence or substance abuse treatment. *Journal of Family Violence, 14*, 297–314.

Carter, A. J. (1996). Mothers in recovery: Rebuilding families in the aftermath of addiction. *Social Work, 4*(2), 214–224.

Carter, C. S. (1987) Treatment of the chemically dependent Black female: A cultural perspective. *Counselors*, 5, 16.

Center for Substance Abuse Treatment. (1996). *Substance abuse treatment and domestic violence, Treatment Improvement Protocol Series No. 25*. Washington, DC: U.S. Department of Health and Human Services, Substance Abuse and Mental Health Services Administration.

Chermack, S. T., Fuller, B. E., & Blow, F. C. (2000). Predictors of expressed partner and non-partner violence among patients in substance abuse treatment. *Drug and Alcohol Dependence, 58*, 43–54.

Children of Alcoholics Foundation. (n.d.) *Connecting child welfare and parental substance abuse.* New York: Author.

Coleman, D. H., & Straus, M. A. (1983). Alcohol abuse and family violence. In E. Gotheil, K. A. Druley, T. K. Skoloda, & H. M. Waxman (Eds.), *Alcohol, drug abuse and aggression* (pp. 104–124). Springfield, IL: Charles C. Thomas.

Donnelly, D., Cook, K., & Wilson, L.A. (1995). *The politics of exclusion: Domestic violence services in the Deep South.* Paper presented at the Summer Research Institute on family Violence, University of New Hampshire.

Faller, K. C. (1988). *Child sexual abuse: An interdisciplinary manual for diagnosis, case management, and treatment.* New York: Columbia University Press.

Feig, L. (1998). Understanding the problem: The gap between substance abuse programs and child welfare services. In R. L. Hampton, V. Senatore, & T. P. Gullotta (Eds.), *Substance abuse, family violence, and child welfare: Bridging perspectives* (pp. 62–92). Thousand Oaks, CA: Sage.

Fullilove, M. T., Fullilove, R. E., Smith, M., Winkler, K., Michael, C., Panzer, P. G., &

Wallace, R. (1993). Violence, trauma, post-traumatic stress disorder among women drug users. *Journal of Traumatic Stress*, *6*(4), 533–543.

Gondolf, E. W. (1995). Alcohol abuse, wife assault, and power needs. *Social Service Review*, *69*, 275–283.

Gondolf, E. W. (1999). A comparison of four batterer intervention systems: Do court referral, program length, and services matter? *Journal of Interpersonal Violence*, *14*, 41–61.

Gregoire, K. A., & Schultz, D. J. (2001). Substance-abusing child welfare treatment and child placement outcomes. *Child Welfare*, *80*(4), 433–453.

Griffin, L. W., & Williams, O. J. (1992). Abuse among African-American elderly. *Journal of Family Violence*, *7*(1), 19–35.

Hamilton, C. J., and Collins, J. J. (1981). The role of alcohol in wife beating and child abuse: A review of the literature. In J. J. Collins (Ed.), *Drinking and crime: Perspectives on the relationship between alcohol consumption and criminal behavior* (pp. 253–287). New York: Guilford Press.

Hawkins, D. F. (1987). Devalued lives and racial stereotypes: Ideological barriers to the prevention of family violence among Blacks. In R. L. Hampton (Ed.), *Violence in the Black family: Correlates and consequences* (pp. 189–205). Lexington, MA: Lexington Books.

Join Together (1996). *Domestic violence and substance abuse fact sheet*. Boston: Author.

Joseph, J. (1995). *Black youth, delinquency, and juvenile justice*. Westport, CT: Praeger Press.

Kantor, G. K., & Straus, M. A. (1987). The "drunken bum" theory of wife beating. *Social Problems*, *34*(3), 213–227.

Kelleher, K., Chaffin, M., Hollenberg, J., & Fisher, E. (1994). Alcohol and drug disorders among physically abusive and neglectful parents in a community based sample. *American Journal of Public Health*, *84*(10), 1586–1590.

Kelley, S. J. (1992). Parenting stress and child maltreatment in drug exposed children. *Child Abuse and Neglect*, *16*, 317–328.

Leonard, K. E., & Jacob, T. (1987). Alcohol, alcoholism, and family violence. In V. D. Van Hasselt, R. L. Morrison, A. S. Bellack, & M. Herson (Eds.), *Handbook of family violence* (pp. 383–406). New York: Plenum.

Lessing, L. A., & Olsen, L. (1996). Substance abuse—Affecting families in the child welfare system: New challenges, new alliances. *Social Work*, *41*(1), 15–23.

Lynch, A., Brewer, R., Williams, O. J., & Becker, L. (1996). *Assessment of needs for African American battered women*. Report for the Minnesota Department of Corrections, St. Paul, MN.

Mamis-King, N. (1997) Double jeopardy: Abused female drug addicts. Paper presented at the New York State Association of Alcoholism and Substance Abuse Providers. First Annual Statewide Conference.

McAlpine, C., Marshall, C. C., & Doran, N. H. (2001). Combining child welfare and substance abuse services: A blended model of intervention. *Child Welfare, 80*(2), 129–150.

McMahon, T. J., & Luthar, S. S. (1998). Bridging the gap for children as their parents enter substance abuse treatment. In R. L. Hampton, V. Senatore, & T. P. Gullotta (Eds.), *Substance abuse, family violence, and child welfare: Bridging perspectives* (pp. 143–187). Thousand Oaks, CA: Sage.

Miller, B. A., Downs, W. R., & Gondoli, D. M. (1989). Spousal violence among alcoholic women as compared to random household sample of women. *Journal of Studies on Alcoholism, 50*(6), 533–540.

Moss, Z. A., Pitula, C. R., Campbell, J. C., & Halstead, L. (1997). The experience of terminating an abusive relationship from an Anglo and African American perspective: A qualitative study. *Issues in Mental Health Nursing, 18*(5), 433–454.

Murphy, J., Jellinek, M., Quinn, D., Smith, G., Poitrast, F., & Goshko, M. (1991). Substance abuse and serious child maltreatment: Prevalence, risks, and outcomes in a court sample. *Child Abuse and Neglect, 15*, 197–211.

National Center on Addiction and Substance Abuse at Columbia University. (1996). *Substance abuse and the American woman.* New York: Author.

National Center on Addiction and Substance Abuse at Columbia University (2001). *Shoveling up: The impact of substance abuse on state budgets.* New York: Author.

National Center on Child Abuse and Neglect. (1993). *Study of child maltreatment in alcohol abusing families: A report to Congress.* Washington, DC: Author.

Nyamathi, A., Bennett, C., & Leake, B. (1995). Predictor of maintained high-risk behaviors among impoverished women. *Public Health Report, 110*, 600–606.

Ondersma, S. J., Simpson, S. M., Barestan, E. V., & Ward, M. (2000). Prenatal drug exposure and social policy: The search for an appropriate response. *Child Maltreatment, 5*(2), 93–108.

Ormand, J. (1992). A paradigm for socialization: Empowering African American substance abusers to maximize their human potential. *Journal of Health Care for the Poor and Underserved, 3*(1), 181–193.

Pena, J., & Koss-Chioino, J. D. (1992). Cultural sensitivity in drug treatment research with African American males. *Drugs and Society, 6*(1/2), 157–179.

Pernanen, K. (1976). Alcohol and crimes of violence. In: B. Kissin & Begleiter, H. (Eds.), *The biology of alcoholism*: Vol. 4. *Social aspects of alcoholism* (pp. 344–351). New York: Plenum.

Rasheed, J., & Rasheed, M. (Eds.). (1999). *Social work practice with African American men: The invisible presence.* Thousand Oaks, CA: Sage.

Reed, B. (1991). Drug misuse and dependency in women: The meaning and implications of being considered a special population or minority group. *International Journal of Addiction, 20,* 13–62.

Resnik, H., Gardner, S. E., & Rogers, C. M. (1998). Child welfare and substance abuse: Premises, programs, and policies. In R. L. Hampton, V. Senatore, & T. P. Gullotta (Eds.), *Substance abuse, family violence, and child welfare: Bridging perspectives* (pp. 96–123). Thousand Oaks, CA: Sage.

Rich, J. A., & Stone, D. A. (1996). The experience of violent injury for young African American men: The meaning of being a sucker. *Journal of General Internal Medicine, 11,* 77–82.

Richie, B. (1995). Gender entrapment: When battered women are compelled to crime. Proceedings of the National Institute on Domestic Violence in the African American Community. Washington, DC: U.S. Department of Health and Human Services. Administration for Children and Families. Office of Community Services.

Rittner, B., & Dozier, C. D. (2000). Effects of court-ordered substance abuse treatment in child protective services cases. *Social Work, 45*(2), 131–140.

Rodgers, B., McGee, G., Vann, A., Thompson, N., & Williams, O. J. (2003) Substance abuse and domestic violence: Stories of practitioners that address the co-occurrence among battered women. *Violence Against Women, 9*(5), 590–598.

Semidei, J., Radel, L. F., & Nolan, C. (2001). Substance abuse and child welfare: Clear linkages and promising responses. *Child Welfare, 80*(2), 109–129.

Staples, R. (1982). *Black masculinity: The Black male's role in American society.* San Francisco, CA: Black Scholars Press.

Stark, E., & Flitcraft, A. (1988). Women at risk: A feminist perspective on child abuse. *International Journal of Health Services, 18*(1), 97–118.

Steele, C., & Josephs, R. (1990). Alcohol myopia: Its prized and dangerous effects. *American Psychologist, 45,* 921–933.

Stith, S. M., Crossman, R. K., & Bischof, G. P. (1991). Alcoholism and marital violence: A comparative study of men in alcohol treatment programs and batterer treatment programs. *Alcoholism Treatment Quarterly, 8,* 3–20.

Sullivan, C. M., & Rumptz, M. H. (1994). Adjustments and needs of African American women who utilized domestic violence shelters. *Violence & Victims, 9*(3), 275–286.

Taylor-Gibbs, J. (1988). *Young, Black, and male: An endangered species.* Dove, MA: Auburn.

Tolman, R., & Bennett, L. (1990). A review of quantitative research on men who batter. *Journal of Interpersonal Violence, 5,* 87–118.

U.S. Department of Health and Human Services. (1994). Substance abuse among women and parents. Washington, DC: DHHS Office of the Assistant Secretary for Planning and Evaluation.

U.S. Department of Health and Human Services. (1999). Blending perspectives and building common ground: A report to Congress on substance abuse and child Protection. Washington, DC: U.S. Government Printing Office.

Vail, K. S., & Wade, J. C. (1994). Substance abuse: Implications for counseling African American men. *Journal of Mental Health Counseling, 16*(4), 415–433.

Williams, O. J. (1999a). The African American man who batters: Community response and treatment considerations. In R. Staples (Ed.), *The Black family* (pp. 229–242). Newbury Park, CA: Sage.

Williams, O. J. (1999b) Working in groups with African American men who batter. In L. D. Davis (Ed.), *A guide to working with African American men.* Thousand Oaks, CA: Sage.

Williams, O. J., Boggess, J., & Carter, J. (2001). *Fatherhood and domestic violence: Exploring the role of men who batter in the lives of their children.* Washington, DC: American Psychological Association Press.

Wilson, A. N. (1991). *Understanding Black adolescent male violence: Its remediation and prevention.* New York: Afrikan World InfoSystems.

Part 2

African Americans

5

Exploring the Intersections of Substance Use, Intimate Partner Violence, and Child Maltreatment

JAMES HERBERT WILLIAMS, GORDON LIMB, and PORTIA ADAMS

Introduction

When examining the intersections of substance use, intimate partner violence, and child maltreatment, it is important to note that the African American community is not a monolith in terms of culture or family dynamics. The African American community is consequential in ways that social science and child maltreatment literature often does not recognize. African American communities are bicultural at a minimum with the ability to interpret and appreciate the culture of the majority as well as their own. The changing demographics of the United States over the past decade have challenged many African American communities to have more multicultural context. These changes will force social scientists and child maltreatment researchers to incorporate a multidimensional view of the African American community and not operate from cultural biases or worst-case scenarios that often depict inner-city African American families as dysfunctional and fragmented. William Cross states, "If we expressed a bias, it was to be skeptical of overly pejorative or romantic interpretations of modal Black behavior, for either extreme insulted Black humanity by depicting it in simplistic terms" (1991, p. xi). A wide acceptance of such biases would perpetually relegate African Americans to the margins of society on many of the social indicators. An extensive comprehension of context and culture is critical in endeavors to understand the attitudes and behaviors of African Americans. There is a paucity of literature investigating the overlap among various social issues (e.g., substance use, intimate partner violence, child maltreatment) as related to African American families. The purpose of this chapter is to review cross-sector issues as related to substance use, intimate partner violence, and child maltreatment in African American families.

Crocker and Lawrence (1999) gave a succinct overview of the African American experience in the United States when stating: "As a group, they [African Americans] have experienced 350 years of slavery, 100 years of legal segregation, and 30 to 40 years of equality under the law" (p. 382; Sears, 1998). A look at the history of African American interaction with the child welfare system in the 20th century provides a historical perspective of how African Americans have fared in this system. Further, as social work promotes more multicultural awareness, it is instructive to note how the African American communities have evolved.

A substantial portion of research studies in the 19th and early 20th centuries claimed that African Americans were better off under a system of slavery. It was asserted that under slavery African Americans had lower rates of insanity, less immorality, and fewer health problems (Mama, 1995). Antiabolitionists then used such "facts" to posit that African Americans were constitutionally unfit for freedom, and that it was in the best interests of all that slavery should be continued (Mama, 1995). At the turn of the century the majority of social science was documenting sociological, psychological, and biological differences between African Americans and Caucasians. These studies supported some of the predominant stereotypes of African Americans (e.g., dependent, delinquent, carriers of disease, lacking self-respect), and many of these stereotypes continue to be evident in society today (Scott, 1997). From 1880 to 1920, it was commonly believed that African Americans did not have the capacity to participate in the mainstream, and that segregation and disenfranchisement were beneficial to African Americans. Progressive humanitarian interests at the time excluded African Americans. Settlement houses and charity workers, the organizations of the social work profession, excluded African Americans from their services. Settlement houses and charity organizations in the late 19th century to the 1930s, in large part, neglected and avoided providing services to African Americans (Miller & Berman-Rossi, 1994). During this time the preferred groups served by the settlements were the European immigrants and not the African American migrants (Miller & Berman-Rossi, 1994). The goal of assimilation was intended for European immigrants. During this historical period, the research on African Americans was not focused on the development of better practices and services nor did it include a strengths perspective.

It has been posited that during this period, social scientists studied the psychological and sociological aspects of African Americans and reported that African Americans were simply a lower and less developed form of Caucasians (Cross, 1991). Studies of African Americans were being conducted in order to better understand the psychological and sociological development of Caucasians (Cross, 1991). In 1986, Ralph Ellison declared:

> Since the beginning of the nations, White Americans have suffered from a deep inner uncertainty as to who they really are. One of the ways that has been used to simplify the answer has been to seize upon the presence of Black Americans and use them as a marker, a symbol of limits, a metaphor for the "outsider." Many Whites could look at the social position of Blacks and feel that color formed an easy and reliable gauge for determining to what extent one was or was not American. Perhaps that is why one of the first epithets that many European immigrants learned when they got off the boat was the term "nigger"—it made them feel instantly American. (1995, p. 582)

It is this historical and cultural context that underlies our understanding of the relationship between African Americans and social service systems such as the child welfare system. Many social service programs and policies were developed and implemented using much of this research as their basis.

Substance Use, Intimate Partner Violence, and Child Maltreatment

Human use of substances to alter mood and consciousness is ubiquitous. Drug use and drug abuse are not new problems, but rather ones that receive heightened attention at various points in time. Substance use continues to be one of the preeminent health and social problems in our nation today. The use of illicit drugs and alcohol is responsible for numerous preventable deaths each year as well as the increase in health care costs, criminal activity, and productivity loss (Harwood, Fountain, & Livermore, 1998; Institute for Health Policy, 1993). The underlying causes of alcohol and other drug use and abuse are many, varied, and not well understood. Multiple variables have been studied as predictors of the onset and use of alcohol and other illicit drugs. The research has shown a relationship between substance use and mortality rates, crime, delinquency, violence, domestic violence, child maltreatment, and job performance (Boffetta & Garfinkel, 1990; Greenfeld, 1998b; Normand, Lempert, & O'Brien, 1994; Tracy, Green, & Bremseth, 1993; White & Gorman, 2000; Zubretsky & Digirolamo, 1994).

Although alcohol and drug use are general problems in America, there is increasing recognition of the need to focus on special populations in which substance use magnifies other problems. African American families have been particularly vulnerable to the negative social and health consequences associated with substance use. For example, in comparison to Caucasians, African Americans experience an earlier onset of alcoholism and other drug problems and a greater likelihood of intersection between child maltreatment and criminal justice systems rather than treatment for legal problems caused by substance use and higher rates of drug-related homicide deaths (Harper & Dawkins, 1977; Lowe & Alston, 1973; Solomon, 1990). The surge in problems associated with crack cocaine use has compounded the substance use problem in the African American population (Carlson & Siegel, 1991).

Intimate partner violence is also not a new phenomenon. Only recently has violence in the family against children, spouses, and the elderly become recognized as a significant social problem by researchers and practitioners. Few scholars would dispute the fact that intimate partner violence is a social problem. By almost any measure, the United States is a violent country. The rates of violence in the United States are among the highest in the industrialized world (Maguire & Pastore, 1994; Siegel, 1995).

There are numerous misconceptions regarding intimate partner violence that are slowly being addressed. Providing accurate information is important for social science researchers. Misconceptions regarding the rarity of intimate partner violence, the high prevalence among poverty-stricken families, the intergenerational nature of intimate partner violence, and the causal relationship between substance use and intimate partner violence have provided oversimplifications of a very complex and serious problem.

Most of the early scholarship on intimate partner violence only gave serious attention to African American-Caucasian differences in experiences of use or responses to it (Crenshaw, 1994). These studies continued into the 1990s with survey research regularly indicating higher levels of partner violence among African Americans than among Caucasians (Anderson, 1997; Cazenave & Straus, 1990; Greenfeld, 1998b; Sorenson, 1996; Tjaden & Thoennes, 1999).

Child maltreatment researchers have identified drug use and intimate partner violence to be strong correlates of child maltreatment (Chasnoff, Anson, & Iaukea, 1998; Murphy et al., 1991; Pecora, Whittaker, Maluccio, & Barth, 2000). African American children have traditionally been and continue to be overrepresented in all areas of the child welfare system (Jenkins & Diamond, 1985). After interfacing with the child welfare system, the data indicate that African American children have longer involvement than any other racial/ethnic group (Jenkins & Diamond, 1985). Child maltreatment studies have substantiated a variety of factors contributing to the initial entry of African American children and their remaining in the child welfare system. Substance use and intimate partner violence are two of the more important factors that should be considered in understanding children's involvement with the child welfare system.

The objectives of this chapter are (1) to review the research on substance use, intimate partner violence, and child maltreatment for African Americans; (2) to address the relationship of substance use, intimate partner violence, and child maltreatment among African Americans; and, (3) to highlight the challenges for practice, research, and program and curriculum development.

Prevalence of Substance Abuse

A wide array of studies examines the prevalence and impact of substance use in our society. Many of these are summarized in the National Institute of Drug Abuse (NIDA) monographs (Gust & Walsh, 1989; Gust, Walsh, Thomas, & Crouch, 1990). Data from two large-scale surveys conducted over the past decade provide the most informative data reviewed in this chapter.

Over the past 20 years, substantial epidemiological research has been conducted on substance use. This chapter does not exhaustively review all of this work, but it does cover those studies that best allow for sound estimates of prevalence and trends of alcohol and other drug use in the population. In reviewing these studies, this chapter highlights overall prevalence, prevalence among adolescents, differences by gender, and differences by race.

This chapter is also not intended to be a comprehensive and exhaustive review of general research findings with regard to substance use in the African American population. Numerous reports provide comparison of general patterns of substance use and abuse between African Americans and other groups (Staples, 1990; Wallace & Bachman, 1991; Williams, Newby, & Kanitz, 1993). For example, the African American population continues to report lower rates of alcohol and illicit drug use than Caucasians, but more social and health problems related to substance use. The primary purpose of this review is to highlight findings concerning substance use among African Americans.

Two large-scale survey series have closely examined issues discussed in this chapter: the Monitoring the Future (MTF) surveys and the National Household Surveys on Drug Abuse (NHSDA) (Johnston, O'Malley, & Bachman, 1999, 2000; Substance Abuse and Mental Health Services Administration [SAMHSA], 1999). MTF is an ongoing study of the behaviors, attitudes, and values of American secondary school students, college students, and young adults. The NHSDA surveys offer data on drug use among the general household population. Using results from MTF and NHSDA renders a comprehensive review of substance use in the United States. Both studies provide information on current use and historical trends. MTF captures prevalence of use among youth, and NHSDA reports usage of other population age groups. Both studies are among the more highly cited substance use studies related to the onset and prevalence of substance use and abuse in United States.

ALCOHOL USE

Approximately half of Americans age 12 and older report being current drinkers of alcohol in the 1999 survey of households. This translates to an estimated 105 million individuals. Approximately one-fifth of those 12 years of age and older (45 million people) participated in binge drinking at least once in the previous 30 days (binge drinking is defined as having five or more drinks in a row on at least one occasion in the prior two weeks). Binge drinking represents approximately 43% of all drinkers (SAMHSA, 1999). Previous surveys have shown in recent years that the level of alcohol use is strongly associated with other illicit drug use. Among heavy drinkers, more than a third are current illicit drug users.

Alcohol use remains extremely high among youth in the United States, but has not changed much in the past five years (Johnston et al., 1999). The major change in alcohol use since the early 1990s has been the increased proportion of youth reporting binge drinking. In 1997, 15%, 25%, and 31% of 8th, 10th, and 12th graders indicated binge drinking, and these rates are slightly higher than they were in the early 1990s (Johnston et al., 1997).

For current alcohol use, binge drinking, and heavy alcohol use, 21 is the peak age. Unlike prevalence patterns observed for illicit drugs, alcohol use remains steady among older age groups. The highest prevalence of both binge and heavy drinking was observed for young adults (18 to 25 years). About 10.4 million persons 12 to 20 years of age reported drinking alcohol in the month prior to the 1999 survey. Males 12 to 20 years of age are more likely than their female peers to report binge drinking (22.3% compared to 16.0%). With the exception of adolescents, males are more likely than females to report past-month alcohol drinking (54.0% compared to 41.1%). For the youngest age group (12 to 17) males and females have comparable rates of current alcohol use (19.2% compared to 18.1%). Caucasians are more likely than other race/ethnicity groups to report current use of alcohol (51.0%). African Americans have a binge drinking rate of 16.5%. This rate is lower than for Hispanic/Latinos, American Indians/Alaska Natives, and Caucasians.

Among youth ages 12 to 17, Caucasians report a history of having used alcohol at a rate approximately two times that of African Americans (Johnston et al., 1999). Caucasian males consistently report the highest current use rate and Caucasian females the second highest (Johnston et al., 1999). Studies have shown that differences in alcohol use between these groups can be substantial, with African Americans consistently abstaining at higher rates than Caucasians (Peterson, Hawkins, Abbott, & Catalano, 1995; Vega, Zimmerman, Warheit, Apospori, & Gil, 1993).

ILLICIT DRUG USE

In 1999, an estimated 14.8 million Americans were current illicit drug users, meaning they had used an illicit drug during the month prior to being interviewed for the 1999 NHSDA survey (SAMHSA, 1999). This estimate represents 6.7% of the population 12 years and older.

According to the NHSDA, marijuana is the most commonly used illicit drug. It is used by 75% of current illicit drug users. About 57% of current illicit drug users consumed only marijuana. Eighteen percent used marijuana and other illicit drugs, and the remaining 25% used an illicit drug but not marijuana in the preceding month. Therefore, about 43% of current illicit drug users in 1999 (approximately 6.4 million Americans) were current users of illicit drugs other than marijuana and hashish, with or without the use of marijuana (SAMHSA, 1999).

The rate of marijuana use among most subgroups of adolescents continues to increase (Johnston et al., 1999). After six years of steady increases, marijuana use leveled off in 1997 among 8th graders, but continued to increase among 10th and 12th graders (Johnston et al., 1999). In 1997, 23%, 39%, 43% of 8th, 10th, and 12th graders, respectively, reported lifetime marijuana use (Johnston et al., 1999). These percentages represent a 13%, 16%, and 13% respective increase over a five-year period (Johnston et al., 1999).

African American adolescents have lower rates of marijuana use as compared to that of Caucasians and other ethnic groups (Johnston et al., 1999; Vega et al., 1993). In the few studies comparing marijuana use among racial subgroups, African American youth consistently have reported lower levels of use than Caucasians (Johnston et al., 1999). The differential use of marijuana by Caucasian and African American youth parallels alcohol use in national studies, indicating that overall Caucasian adolescents report a higher prevalence of marijuana use than African American adolescents (Kandel, Chen, Warner, Kessler, & Grant, 1997; Skager & Austin, 1993). Still, other race comparison studies have found prevalence rates dissimilar to these national studies. Williams, Ayers, Abbott, Hawkins, & Catalano (1996, 1999), using data from the Seattle Social Development Project, found higher prevalence rates of marijuana use for African American youth in comparison to Caucasian youth.

In 1999, an estimated 1.5 million Americans were current cocaine users. This represents 0.7% of the population age 12 and older. The estimated number of crack users was 413,000 in 1999. It is estimated that 900,000 Americans are current users of hallucinogens, and there are approximately 200,000 heroin users in the United States (SAMHSA, 1999). Surveys have shown the estimated rates of use of specific illicit drugs and alcohol did not change appreciably from 1997 to 1998. In general, rates were relatively stable from 1991 to 1998. Rates of substance use were generally much higher in the late 1970s and early 1980s than they were at the end of the 1990s (SAMHSA, 1999).

The overall rates of illicit drug use for major racial/ethnic groups were 6.6% for Caucasians and 7.7% for African Americans. Among youth age 12–17, 19.6% of the NHSDA sample, the rate of use of illicit drugs was 10.7% for African Americans and 10.9% for Caucasians (SAMHSA, 1999). Although the overall rates were similar for African American and Caucasian youth age 12–17 years, there were gender differences within these groups. Among Caucasians, males and females were about equally likely to be current illicit drug users. However among African Americans, rates were approximately 50% higher for males than females (SAMHSA, 1999).

Intimate Partner Violence

Intimate partner violence is a substantial public health problem for Americans that has serious consequences and costs for individuals, families, communities, and society (Bachman & Saltzman, 1995; Greenfeld, 1998b). Recent efforts have been made to increase resources to address gaps in knowledge and to improve services for victims, perpetrators, and child witnesses (National Research Council, 1996; Schecter, 1982; Straus & Gelles, 1990). Intimate partner violence can be defined as domestic abuse, spouse abuse, domestic violence, courtship violence, battering, marital rape, and date rape.

Many researchers consider the following prevalence data to be underestimates of family or intimate partner violence; victims may underreport family or intimate partner violence on surveys because data sources may lack information identifying victim-perpetrator relationships (Bachman & Saltzman, 1995; Straus & Gelles, 1990).

Similar to the review of the substance use data, two highly cited large-scale surveys were closely examined to determine the prevalence of intimate partner violence: the National Family Violence Surveys and the National Crime Victimization Surveys (NCVS). The two National Family Violence Surveys are the only nationally representative studies that estimate intimate partner violence (Straus, 1990). NCVS provides vastly different estimates of the rate of intimate partner violence, especially gender-specific violence. The difference in design and implementation are the two underlying explanations for the variation in estimation of incidences of intimate partner violence.

Data from both surveys between 1992 and 1996 indicate that approximately one million incidents of nonlethal intimate partner violence occurred each year from 1992 to 1996, with 85% of the victims being women (Greenfeld, 1998b). These results are consistent with findings from earlier surveys. Results from the National Family Violence Surveys indicated that approximately 16% of couples experienced one act of domestic violence during the year prior to the survey (Straus, 1990).

On average, each year during this time frame, about 8 in 1,000 women and 1 in 1,000 men age 12 or older experienced a violent victimization perpetrated by a family member or an intimate partner (Greenfeld, 1998b). Although males are more likely to experience violent crime overall, females are 5 to 8 times more likely than males to be victimized in a family or domestic environment. Between 1992 and 1996, violence victimizations in the family or domestic environment accounted for 21% of all violence experienced by women, whereas it accounted for 2% of violence victimization suffered by males (Greenfeld, 1998b).

Overall crime data are showing a decrease in intimate partner violence. The most current data from NCVS indicate that the rate of intimate partner violence declined significantly between 1993 and 2001, by approximately 49%. In 1993 the number of nonfatal violent crimes by intimate partners against females was 1.1 million as compared to 588,490 such crimes in 2001 (Rennison, 2003). A similar drop in percentage (42%) was found for males. In 1993 males were victims of about 162,870 nonfatal violent crimes by intimate partners as compared to 103,220 in 2001 (2003). Categories used to identify intimate partners in these data were spouses, former spouses, boyfriends and girlfriends, including intimate partners in same-sex relationships. On average, from 1976 to 1998, the number of murders by intimates decreased by about 4% per year for male victims and 1% per year for female victims (U.S. Department of Justice, 2003).

Results from studies exploring race and ethnicity prevalence rates have been mixed. Some studies have suggested that minority families tend to be more violent, especially when the violence is severe (Neff, Holamon, & Schluter, 1995; Straus & Smith, 1990). Other studies have questioned the intimate partner violence-race interaction, maintaining that when demographics and socioeconomic factors are controlled, there are no differences between African American and Caucasian families (Hutchison, Hirschel, & Pesackis, 1994: Straus & Smith, 1990).

Among female victims of nonfatal intimate partner violence, African Americans experienced higher rates than Caucasians. African American and Caucasian males experienced the same rates of intimate partner violence. Data from the NCVS showed that between 1992 and 1996, about 12 per 1,000 African American women experienced nonlethal violence by an intimate partner, compared with about 8 per 1,000 Caucasian women. These rates were not adjusted for socioeconomic status, which may account for the higher rates in African American women (Greenfeld, 1998b).

The number, percentages, and per capita rate of fatal violence involving spouses, ex-spouses, or other intimates have declined over the past two decades. In 1996 the number of intimate murders was 36% lower than in 1976. The number of spouse murders, the largest component of intimate murder, fell 52% (Greenfeld, 1998b). Female murder victims are more likely than male murder victims to have been killed by an intimate. During this time period murders by intimates dropped far more rapidly for African Americans than for Caucasians. In 1976 the per capita rate for murders by intimates among African

Americans was nearly 11 times (14 per 100,000) that among Caucasians (1.3 per 100,000), and in 1996 the African American rate was 4 times (4 per 100,000) higher than the Caucasian rate (0.85 per 100,000). For African Americans this represents an average intimate murder rate decrease of 6% per year (Federal Bureau of Investigation, 1996; Greenfeld, 1998b).

In exploring gender differences in fatal violence among intimates, surveys indicate that in the 20-year period between 1976 and 1996 the sharpest decrease in per capita rates of intimate murder has been among African American male victims. The rate for African American males fell from 19 times higher than that of Caucasian males in 1976, to 8 times higher in 1996. Recent data show a continued decline for African American males. The sharpest decrease in the number of intimate murders has been for Black men; there was a 74% decrease in the number of African Americans murdered by an intimate between 1976 and 1998 (U.S. Department of Justice, 2003). Among African American females the rate decreased from 7 times higher than Caucasian females to 3 times higher (Browne, Williams, & Dutton, 1999; Greenfeld, 1998b).

These patterns of incidences paint an incomplete picture, which, unto itself, is not very enlightening. To gain a clearer understanding of the problem—one helpful for prevention and intervention—the components that make up these global figures need to be brought into focus. Beyond questions of incidences, what are the various cultural and environmental correlates that contribute to the development and escalation of intimate partner violence in African American households? Our understanding of the intersectionality of substance use and intimate partner violence among African Americans is instrumental in developing appropriate prevention and intervention strategies and curriculum.

Literature on Child Maltreatment

Physical or sexual abuse, psychological or emotional abuse, and neglect are considered the dominant types of maltreatment by which children in the United States come into contact with the public child welfare system. More than 50 million people annually in the United States are victims of violence and abuse (Petr, 1998). These increases in violence and abuse are directly related to the increased rates of children being placed in out-of-home care (Kadushin & Martin, 1988; Petr, 1998). For example, in 1985, there were 276,000 children placed into foster care in the United States. By 1995, these numbers increased by more than 58% to 468,000 (Petr, 1998).

Even more alarming than the increase in the number of children being placed in out-of-home care has been the disproportionate representation of children of color, particularly African Americans, in the child welfare system. An analysis of prevalence rates in five states with large populations found that the proportion of African American children in out-of-home care ranged from 3 to more than 10 times the proportion of Caucasian children (Goerge, Wulczyn, & Harden, 1994). Goerge et al. (1994) note that in two of the country's largest states, New York and California, African American children in care accounted for more than 4% of the entire African American child population in those states. A recent study conducted in 20 states found that 46.8% of 306,914 foster children were African American. This percentage is higher than that of any other racial/ethnic group (U.S. House of Representatives, 1996).

Not only are African American children overrepresented in the child welfare system, but once in the system, they remain in care longer (Garland, Ellis-Macleod, Landsverk, Granger, & Johnson, 1998; Jenkins & Diamond, 1985; Olsen, 1982). For example, studies involving state and local-level foster care found that African American children remain in placement longer than Caucasians by an average of as much as two years (Courtney et al., 1996). Similarly, Fanshel and Shinn (1978) reported that African American children were nearly twice as likely as their Caucasian counterparts to remain in care after five years.

Both researchers and practitioners have offered many theories and explanations for the causes of African American children entering and remaining in the child welfare system. Some focus on poverty, while others see policies and laws as the main issues. Still others blame a traditional racist society for maintaining and perpetuating the destruction of African American families (Children's Services Practice Notes, 2001). In an often-cited study, Chasnoff, Landress, and Barrett (1990) conducted research on drug use during pregnancy. Urine samples from 715 pregnant women at their first prenatal visit revealed the prevalence of a positive test result to be similar among African American and Caucasian women. However, the researchers found more than 10 times as many African American women as Caucasian women were reported to health and child welfare authorities after delivery for substance use during pregnancy. To explain this difference, Chasnoff et al. (1990) suggest that physicians believed that drug use was most often likely to occur in poor, urban communities of color, so they were more likely to suspect, test, and report African American women than Caucasian women.

While there is no simple explanation why African American children are overrepresented in the child welfare system, those seeking to better understand this situation must consider two important factors affecting African American families—in addition to poverty, laws and policies, and racism—namely, substance use and intimate partner violence (Brown & Bailey-Etta, 1997; Children's Services Practice Notes, 2001).

Substance Use, Intimate Partner Violence, and Child Maltreatment Intersections

It is important to note that various research studies have focused on the prevalence and correlates of substance use, intimate partner violence, or child maltreatment independently among African Americans (Browne et al., 1999; Greenfeld, 1998b; Hutchison et al., 1994; Johnston et al., 1999; Pecora et al., 2000). Far fewer studies have investigated the intersection of substance use, intimate partner violence, and child maltreatment in African American households.

The nature of the relationship between intimate partner violence and substance use is not yet clear. Many assaults do not occur within the context of substance use, and many substance users are not violent with their partners (National Research Council, 1996). Evidence supporting this view reveals that substance use is present in many intimate partner violence situations. Estimates range from 20% to more than 80% (Leonard & Jacob, 1988). It is estimated that 60% to 70% of abusive husbands assault their wives while under the influence of alcohol and 13% to 20% do so while on other substances. When alcohol and substance use are included in the intimate partner violence equation there is an increase in the frequency and severity in comparison to intimate partner violence situations where the abusive husband was alcohol- or drug-free (Zubretsky & Digirolamo, 1994).

Similar results were found when analyzing data from the NCVS. These data indicate an association between family and intimate partner violence and alcohol and other drug use (Greenfeld, 1998b). Seventy-five percent of victims who reported alcohol or drug use by the perpetrator reported that the perpetrator was using either alcohol or drugs at the time of the crime (Greenfeld, 1998a). Other data indicate that two-thirds of the victims who suffered violence by an intimate partner reported that alcohol had been a factor. Among spouse victims, three out of four report that the offender had been drinking (U.S. Department of Justice, 2003). More than 50% of both prison and jail inmates convicted of a violent crime against an intimate partner were drinking or using drugs at the time of the offense, with less than 25% using drugs alone or in combination with alcohol. Among prisoners who had been drinking before they committed a crime against an intimate partner, about 50% of state prisoners and 33% of convicted jail inmates had been drinking for six or more hours prior to perpetrating an act of intimate partner violence. Many of these individuals (20% to 40%) had consumed the alcohol equivalent of one six-pack to two dozen or more beers prior to committing their acts of intimate partner violence (Greenfeld, 1998b).

An extensive review of the studies investigating the relationship between substance use and intimate partner violence reveals noticeable gaps. Although there is a substantial body of epidemiological research on the prevalence of both substance use and intimate partner violence as separate issues, there is a paucity of studies investigating the effects of substance use on intimate partner violence. This deficiency is more obvious when investigating these relationships in African American families. Some studies have investigated various social and psychological correlates of intimate partner violence among African Americans, including social support, poverty, sexual coercion, child maltreatment, HIV-risk practices, and patient attitudes (Hien & Bukszpan, 1999; Kalichman, Williams, Cherry, Belcher, & Nachimson, 1998; Mechem, Shofer, Reinhard, Hornig, & Datner, 1999; Rodriguez, Craig, Mooney, & Bauer, 1998; Thompson et al., 2000; Weinreb, Goldberg, Lessard, Perloff, & Bassuk, 1999). Other studies have included substance use variables in investigating domestic violence among African Americans (Gilbert, el-Bassel, Schilling, & Friedman, 1997; He, McCoy, Stevens, & Stark, 1998; Martin, Kilgallen, Dee, Dawson, & Campbell, 1998). Predictive and positive relationships were identified between many of these social and psychological correlates and intimate partner violence in African American households. Considering the limitation of these studies in the investigation of alcohol and drug use as a correlate, these studies provide a very affirmative basis for building knowledge on a very important topic.

While the nature of the relationship between intimate partner violence and substance use is not yet clear, a number of studies have found associations among substance use, intimate partner violence and child maltreatment. Interwoven into child abuse investigations are the statistics about the influence of substance use and abuse and how some children of addicted parents are no strangers to sexual abuse, physical abuse, and neglect (Crosson-Tower, 2001). According to child welfare agency managers, substance use is a major factor driving the increase in intimate partner violence reports to child protective services (CPS) (Tatara, 1989). In fact, nearly half the states report that substance use is the primary characteristic in CPS caseloads (Chasnoff et al., 1998). A number of studies support this and have found that various forms of maltreatment are associated with drug use (Murphy et al., 1991). In a study of African American children in foster care, roughly 36% were there as a result of substance use by a parent (National Black Child Development Institute, 1989). Additionally, public child welfare agencies are reporting an increase of 50% to 80% in the number of substance-abusing parents in social workers' caseloads (Solomon, 1990). While many of these children will end up in out-of-home care, Tracy (1992) reports that children of substance-abusing parents, once placed in out-of-home care, are reunified in lower numbers and after a much longer time than other children.

Research and Practice Challenges

The primary focus of this chapter is to review the literature detailing the impact of substance use, intimate partner violence, and child maltreatment on African American households. A review of the substance use, intimate partner violence, and child maltreatment literature identified many issues needing to be addressed through research and practice. Results from prevalence studies comparing racial and ethnic groups have been mixed. African Americans generally have lower rates of alcohol use as compared to other groups. Among the youth studies, some groups of African American youth report higher rates of marijuana use. Significant gender differences were identified for substance use with all types of substances.

Despite the fact that victimization data indicate significant decreases in incidences of fatal and nonfatal intimate partner violence, intimate partner violence continues to make up 20% of all nonfatal and 33% of fatal violent crime experienced by women in 2001(Rennison, 2003). For males, intimate partner violence makes up 3% of all nonfatal and 4% of fatal violent crime perpetrated against them (Rennison, 2003). The levels of intimate partner violence experienced by females and males underpin an undoubted indication that intimate partner violence continues to be a pressing social issue that calls for continued research and the continued development of effective interventions. Results from race comparison studies have been mixed with no clear sense of the extent and depth of this issue in African American households.

Studies investigating child maltreatment and child welfare are both extensive and comprehensive. Child welfare studies comparing racial and ethnic groups have well-documented issues of disparities related to prevalence, service duration, and quality of outcomes. African American children are more likely to access the child welfare system and more likely remain in the system longer than other racial and ethnic groups.

Upon disentangling the literature on substance use, intimate partner violence, and child maltreatment it is apparent how pervasive each of these social issues is in our society. Several significant areas of concern were identified as a result of this review. A limited number of studies have comprehensively examined substance use, intimate partner violence, and child maltreatment in African American households. There are no studies that have investigated the co-occurrence of substance use, intimate partner violence, and child maltreatment in African American families.

These gaps, once identified, can promote promising directions for social work research, practice, and curriculum development. Three specific areas should be addressed in the development of an agenda. First, the lack of solid prevalence data provides a strong foundation for the need for further evidence-based research. A more comprehensive analysis of data collected from current longitudinal data sets (e.g., MTF surveys, NCVS) may be instrumental in providing data on the profoundness of these problems in the African American community. If this approach proves inadequate, then new studies with national representative samples of African Americans need to be conducted to accumulate precise data on the incidences of intimate partner violence, substance use, child maltreatment, and cross-sector needs and services.

Second, a widespread issue in this literature is the lack of distinction among types and/or context of intimate partner violence and their subsequent impact on African American children entering and remaining in the child welfare system. Questions remain to be answered to provide a more complete understanding of the types of violence, types of violence resistance, types of perpetrators, intersectionality between perpetrators and types of violence, violence in different types of relationships, violence at different stages of a relationship, and underreporting in African American communities. There is a developing literature on violence in dating and cohabiting relationships. Many of these studies have been conducted on nonminority samples.

Various distinctions are key to the theory and understanding of the nature and context of intimate partner violence. A stricter definition will provide an important context for developing more sensitive and refined theories that will prevent the tendency to generalize from one racial and ethnic group to another. These theories can better inform measurement and instrument development to better capture the biopsychosocial context for intimate partner violence.

Finally, a third theme that needs to be addressed has to do with assessing the coping abilities and strategies of African American "victims" or "survivors" of family violence. What is the ability of the victim or survivor to leave the situation and be safe upon leaving? In addition to gaining a better understanding of effective strategies for coping and marshaling the situation, more research is needed on the psychological and behavioral consequences of intimate partner violence. What are the psychological consequences for the African American victim or survivor and her children? What is the extent to which there are intergenerational correlates of intimate partner violence? What are the social correlates and consequences in our society that underpin and cultivate intimate partner violence? What are the interconnections of intimate partner violence, poverty, substance use, welfare, and homelessness in African American families?

After an extensive review of the intimate partner violence and substance use in African American household literature, it has become apparent that social work researchers have not contributed substantially to this body of knowledge at the same level as other disciplines (e.g., public health, nursing, psychology, medicine, family studies). This is true despite the fact that in their profession, social workers have extensive experience in working with African Americans in the area of substance use and intimate partner violence. This lack of contribution by social work researchers and educators has had an integral effect on the totality of practice knowledge in improving this social issue.

Considering the paucity of social work literature on substance use and intimate partner violence, there is a substantial body of research literature on child welfare policies and services in the field of social work. Many of these studies have investigated the intersections of child maltreatment with school systems, juvenile justice system, community mental health, health promotion and prevention, substance use and intimate partner violence (Chasnoff et al., 1998; Crosson-Tower, 2001; Elze, Auslander, McMillen, Edmond, & Thompson, 2001; Jonson-Reid, Williams, & Webster, 2001; Stiffman et al., 2000, 2001; Tatara, 1989). In order to develop effective and evidenced-based practice guidelines to support positive outcomes and develop a more comprehensive social work curriculum, social work researchers must specifically address the intersections among substance use, intimate partner violence, and child maltreatment in African American households.

References

Anderson, K. L. (1997). Gender, status and domestic violence: An integration of feminist and family violence approaches. *Journal of Marriage and the Family, 59*, 655–669.

Bachman, R., & Saltzman, L. E. (1995). *Violence against women: Estimates from the redesigned survey*. Bureau of Justice Statistics, Special report. Washington, DC: U.S. Department of Justice.

Boffetta, P., & Garfinkel, L. (1990). Alcohol drinking and mortality among men enrolled in an American Cancer Society prospective study. *Epidemiology, 1*(5), 342–348.

Brown, A., & Bailey-Etta, B. (1997). An out-of-home care system in crisis: Implications for African American children in the child welfare system. *Child Welfare, 76*(1), 65–83.

Browne, A., Williams, K. R., & Dutton, D. G. (1999). Homicide between intimates: A 20-year review. In M. D. Smith & M. A. Zahn (Eds.), *Homicide: A sourcebook of social research* (pp. 149–164). Thousand Oaks, CA: Sage.

Carlson, R. G., & Siegal, H. A. (1991). The crack life: An ethnographic overview of crack use and sexual behavior among African-Americans in a Midwest metropolitan city. *Journal of Psychoactive Drugs, 23*(1), 11–20.

Cazenave, N. A., & Straus, M. A. (1990). Race, class, network embeddedness, and family violence: A search for potent support systems. In M. A. Straus & R. J. Gelles (Eds.), *Physical violence in American families: Risk factors and adaptions to violence in 8,145 families* (pp. 321–339). Brunswick, NJ: Transaction.

Chasnoff, I., Anson, A., & Iaukea, K. (1998). *Understanding the drug-exposed child: Approaches to behavior and learning*. Chicago: Imprint Publications.

Chasnoff, I., Landress, H., & Barrett, M. (1990). The prevalence of illicit drug and alcohol use during pregnancy and discrepancies in mandatory reporting in Pinel County, Florida. *New England Journal of Medicine, 322,* 1202–1206.

Children's Services Practice Notes. (2001, May). *African American children in foster care.* Retrieved November 18, 2001, from www.oswo.unc.edu/fcrp/cspn/cspn.html

Courtney, M., Barth, R., Berrick, J. D., Brooks, D., Needell, B., & Park, L. (1996). Race and child welfare services: Past research and future directions. *Child Welfare, 75*(2), 99–133.

Crenshaw, K. (1994). Mapping the margins: Intersectionality, identity politics, and violence against women of color. In M. A. Fineman & R. Mykitiuk (Eds.), *The public nature of private violence: The discovery of domestic abuse* (pp. 93–118). New York: Routledge.

Crocker, J., & Lawrence, J. S. (1999). Social stigma and self-esteem: The role of contingencies of worth. In D. A. Prentice & D. T. Miller (Eds.), *Cultural divides: Understanding and overcoming group conflict* (pp. 364–392). New York: Russell Sage.

Cross, W. E. (1991). *Shades of Black: Diversity in African-American identity.* Philadelphia: Temple University Press.

Crosson-Tower, C. (2001). *Exploring child welfare: A practice perspective* (2nd ed.). Boston: Allyn & Bacon.

Ellison, R. (1986). *Going to the territory.* New York: Vantage.

Ellison, R. (1995). *The collected essays of Ralph Emerson* (John F. Callahan, Ed.). New York: The Modern Library.

Elze, D. E., Auslander, W., McMillen, C., Edmond, T., & Thompson, R. (2001). Untangling the impact of sexual abuse on HIV risk behaviors among youth in foster care. *AIDS Education and Prevention, 13*(4), 377–389.

Fanshel, D., & Shinn, E. (1978). *Children in foster care.* New York: Columbia University Press.

Federal Bureau of Investigation. (1996). *Crime in the United States-1996: Uniform Crime Reports.* Washington, DC: U.S. Department of Justice.

Garland, A., Ellis-Macleod, E., Landsverk, J., Ganger, W., & Johnson, I. (1998). Minority populations in the child welfare system: The visibility hypothesis reexamined. *American Journal of Orthopsychiatry, 68*(1), 142–146.

Gilbert, L., el-Bassel, N., Schilling, R. F., & Friedman, E. (1997). Childhood abuse as a risk for partner abuse among women in methadone maintenance. *American Journal of Drug and Alcohol Abuse, 23*(4), 581–595.

Goerge, R., Wulczyn, F., & Harden, A. (1994). *Foster care dynamics: California, Illinois, Michigan, New York and Texas: A first-year report from the multi-state foster care data archive.* Chicago: Chapin Hall Center for Children, University of Chicago.

Greenfeld, L. A. (Ed.) (1998a) *Alcohol and crime: An analysis of national data on the prevalence of alcohol involvement in crime.* Prepared for the Assistant Attorney General's National Symposium on Alcohol and Crime. Washington, DC: U.S. Department of Justice.

Greenfeld, L. A. (Ed.) (1998b). *Violence by intimates: Analysis of data on crimes by current or former spouses, boyfriends, and girlfriends* (NCJ-167237). Bureau of Justice Factbook. Washington, DC: U.S. Department of Justice.

Gust, S. W., & Walsh, J. M. (Eds.). (1989). *Drugs in the workplace: Research and evaluation data* (NIDA Research Monograph No. 91). Rockville, MD: National Institute on Drug Abuse.

Gust, S. W., Walsh, J. M., Thomas, L. B., & Crouch, D. J. (Eds.). (1990). *Drugs in the workplace: Research and evaluation data, Vol. 2* (NIDA Research Monograph No. 100). Rockville, MD: National Institute of Drug Abuse.

Harper, F. D., & Dawkins, M. P. (1977). Alcohol abuse and the black community. *Black Scholar, 8,* 23–31.

Harwood, H., Fountain, D., & Livermore, G. (1998). *The economic cost of alcohol and drug abuse in the United States, 1992* (NIH Publication Number 98-4327). Retrieved December 31, 2000, from www.nida.nih.gov:80/EconomicCosts/Intro.html

He, H., McCoy, H. V., Stevens, S. J., & Stark, M. J. (1998). Violence and HIV sexual behaviors among female sex partners of male drug users. *Women and Health, 27*(1–2), 161–175.

Hien, D., & Bukszpan, C. (1999). Interpersonal violence in a "normal" low-income group. *Women and Health, 29*(4), 1–16.

Hutchison, I. W., Hirschel, J. D., & Pesackis, C. E. (1994). Family violence and police utilization. *Violence and Victims, 9,* 299–313.

Institute for Health Policy. (1993). *Substance abuse: The nation's number one health problem: Key indicators for policy.* Waltham, MA: Brandeis University, Heller Graduate School, Institute for Health Policy.

Jenkins, S., & Diamond, B. (1985). Ethnicity and foster care: Census data as predictors of placement variables. *American Journal of Orthopsychiatry, 55,* 267–276.

Johnston, L. D., O'Malley, P. M., & Bachman, J. G. (1999). *Drugs trends in 1999 are mixed.* University of Michigan News and Information Services: Ann Arbor, MI. Retrieved April 23, 2000, from www.monitoringthefuture.org

Johnston, L. D., O'Malley, P. M., & Bachman, J. G. (2000). *"Ecstasy" use rises sharply among teens in 2000; use of many other drugs steady, but significant declines are reported for some.* University of Michigan News and Information Services: Ann Arbor, MI. Retrieved December 28, 2000, from www.monitoringthefuture.org

Jonson-Reid, M., Williams, J. H., & Webster, D. (2001). Severe emotional disturbance and violent offending among incarcerated adolescents. *Social Work Research, 25*(4), 213–222.

Kadushin, A., & Martin, J. (1988). *Child welfare services* (4th ed.). New York: Macmillan.

Kalichman, S. C., Williams, E. A., Cherry, C., Belcher, L., & Nachimson, D. (1998). Sexual coercion, domestic violence, and negotiating condom use among low-income African-American women. *Journal of Women's Health, 7*(3), 371–378.

Kandel, D., Chen, K., Warner, L. A., Kessler, R. C., & Grant, B. (1997). Prevalence and demographic correlates of symptoms of last year dependence on alcohol, nicotine, marijuana and cocaine in the U.S. population. *Drug and Alcohol Dependence, 44*, 11–29.

Leonard, K. E., & Jacob, T. (1988). Alcohol, alcoholism, and family violence. In V. B. Van Hasselt, R. L. Morrison, A. S. Bellack, & M. Hersen (Eds.), *Handbook of family violence* (pp. 383–406). New York: Plenum.

Lowe, G., & Alston, J. (1973). Analysis of racial differences in services to alcoholics in a southern clinic. *Hospital Community Psychiatry, 24*, 457–541.

Maguire, R. D., & Pastore, A. L. (Eds.). (1994). *Sourcebook of criminal justice statistics—1993.* Washington, DC: U. S. Department of Justice, Bureau of Justice Statistics.

Mama, A. (1995). *Beyond the masks: Race, gender and subjectivity.* London: Routledge.

Martin, S. L., Kilgallen, B., Dee, D. L., Dawson, S., & Campbell, J. (1998). Women in a prenatal care/substance abuse treatment program: Links between domestic violence and mental health. *Maternal Child Health Journal, 2*(2), 85–94.

Mechem, C. C., Shofer, F. S., Reinhard, S. S., Hornig, S., & Datner, E. (1999). History of domestic violence among male patients presenting to an urban emergency department. *Academic Emergency Medicine, 6*(8), 786–791.

Miller, I., & Berman-Rossi, T. (1994). African-Americans and the settlements during the late nineteenth and early twentieth centuries. *Social Work with Groups, 17*, 77–95.

Murphy, J., Jellinek, M., Quinn, D., Smith, G., Poitrast, F., & Goshko, M. (1991). Substance abuse and serious child mistreatment: Prevalence, risk, and outcome in a court sample. *Child Abuse and Neglect, 15*(3), 197–211.

National Black Child Development Institute. (1989). *Who will care when parents can't? A study of black children in foster care.* Washington, DC: Author.

National Research Council. (1996). *Understanding violence against women.* Washington, DC: National Academy Press.

Neff, J. A., Holamon, B., & Schluter, T. D. (1995). Spousal violence among Anglos, Blacks, and Mexican Americans: The role of demographics variables, psychosocial predictors, and alcohol consumption. *Journal of Family Violence, 10*, 1–21.

Normand, J., Lempert, R. O., & O'Brien, C. P. (Eds.). (1994). *Under the influence? Drugs and the American work force.* Washington, DC: National Academy Press.

Olsen, L. (1982). Predicting the permanency status of children in foster care. *Social Work Research and Abstracts, 18*(1), 9–20.

Pecora, P., Whittaker, J., Maluccio, A., & Barth, R. (2000). *The child welfare challenge: Policy, practice, and research* (2nd ed.). Hawthorne, NY: Aldine de Gruyter.

Peterson, P. L., Hawkins, J. D., Abbott, R. D., & Catalano, R. F. (1995). Disentangling the effects of parental drinking, family management, and parental alcohol norms on current drinking by black and white adolescents. In G. M. Boyd, J. Howard, & R. A. Zucker (Eds.), *Alcohol problems among adolescents: Current directions in prevention research* (pp. 33–59), Hillsdale NJ: Lawrence Erlbaum.

Petr, C. (1998). *Social work with children and their families: Pragmatic foundations.* New York: Oxford University Press.

Rennison, C. M. (2003). *Intimate partner violence 1993–2001—Crime data brief.* Washington, DC: U.S. Department of Justice.

Rodriguez, M. A., Craig, A. M., Mooney, D. R., & Bauer, H. M. (1998). Patient attitudes about mandatory reporting of domestic violence. Implication for health care professionals. *Western Journal of Medicine, 169*(6), 337–341.

Schecter, S. (1982). *Women and male violence: The visions and struggles of the battered women's movement.* Boston: South End Press.

Scott, D. M. (1997). *Contempt and pity.* Chapel Hill: University of North Carolina Press.

Sears, D. (1998). Racism and politics in the United States. In J. Eberhart, & S. T. Fiske (Eds.), *Racism: The problem and the response* (pp. 76–100). Thousand Oaks, CA: Sage.

Siegel, L. J. (1995). *Criminology.* St. Paul, MN: West Publishers.

Skager, R., & Austin, G. (1993). *Fourth biennial statewide survey of drug and alcohol use among California students in grades 7, 9, and 11. Winter, 1991, 1992: Report to the Attorney-General.* Sacramento, CA: Office of Attorney-General, California, Department of Justice.

Solomon, R. (1990). Substance abusive parents: A challenge for child welfare systems. In *1990 abstract compendium for the national symposium on child victimization.* Washington, DC: Children's National Medical Center.

Sorenson, S. B. (1996). Violence against women: Examining ethnic differences and commonalities. *Evaluation Review, 20,* 123–145.

Staples, R. (1990). Substance abuse and the black family. *Western Journal of Black Studies, 14*(4), 196–204.

Stiffman, A. R., Hadley-Ives, E., Dore, P., Polgar, M., Horvath, V. E., & Elze, D. (2000). Youths' pathways to mental health services: The role of providers' training, resource connectivity, and assessment of need. *Mental Health Services Research, 2*(3), 141–154.

Stiffman, A. R., Striley, C., Horvath, V. E., Hadley-Ives, E., Polgar, M., Elze, D., Pescarino, R. (2001). Organizational context and provider perception as determinants of mental health service use. *Journal of Behavioral Health Services and Research, 28*(2), 188–204.

Straus, M. A. (1990). The National Family Violence Surveys. In M. A. Straus & R. J. Gelles (Eds.), *Physical violence in American families: Risk factors and adaptions to violence in 8,145 families* (pp. 3–16). Brunswick, NJ: Transaction.

Straus, M. A., & Gelles, R. J. (1990). *Physical violence in American families: Risk factors and adaptions to violence in 8,145 families*. New Brunswick, NJ: Transaction.

Straus, M. A., & Smith, C. (1990). Family patterns of primary prevention of family violence. In M. A. Straus & R. J. Gelles (Eds.), *Physical violence in American families: Risk factors and adaptions to violence in 8,145 families* (pp. 507–526). Brunswick, NJ: Transaction.

Substance Abuse and Mental Health Services Administration [SAMHSA]. (1999). *National household survey on drug abuse: Main findings 1999*. Washington, DC: Department of Health and Human Services.

Tatara, T. (1989). *Substitute care flow data and national estimates of children in care*. VCIS Research Notes. Washington, DC: Voluntary Cooperative Information System, American Public Welfare Association.

Thompson, M. P., Kaslow, N. J., Kingree, J. B., Rashid, A., Puett, R., Jacobs, D., & Matthews, A. (2000). Partner violence, social support, and distress among inner-city African-American women. *American Journal of Community Psychology, 28*(1), 127–143.

Tjaden, P., & Thoennes, N. (1999). *Extent, nature, and consequences of intimate partner violence: Findings from the national violence against women survey*. Washington, DC: National Institute of Justice/Centers for Disease Control and Prevention.

Tracy, E. (1992). *Substance abuse and child welfare: Protecting the child, preserving the family*. Cleveland, OH: Mandel School of Applied Social Sciences, Case Western Reserve University.

Tracy, E., Green, R., & Bremseth, M. (1993). Meeting the environmental needs of abused and neglected children: Implications from a statewide survey of supportive services. *Social Work Research & Abstracts, 29*(2), 21–26.

U.S. Department of Justice, Office of Justice Programs, Bureau of Justice Statistics. (2003). Crime statistics. Washington, DC. Retrieved July 24, 2003, from www.ojp.usdoj.gov/bjs/cvict_c.htm

U.S. House of Representatives, Committee on Ways and Means. (1996). *1996 green book: Background material and data on programs within the jurisdiction of the Committee on Ways and Means*. Washington, DC: U.S. Government Printing Office.

Vega, W. A., Zimmerman, R. S., Warheit, G. J., Apospori, E. & Gil, A. G. (1993). Risk factors for early adolescent drug use in four ethnic and racial groups. *American Journal of Public Health, 83*(2), 185–189.

Wallace, J. M., Jr., & Bachman, J. G. (1991). Explaining racial/ethnic differences in adolescent drug use: The impact of background and lifestyles. *Social Problems, 38*, 333–357.

Weinreb, L., Goldberg, R., Lessard, D., Perloff, J., & Bassuk, E. (1999). HIV-risk practices among homeless and low-income housed mothers. *Journal of Family Practice, 48*(11), 859–867.

White, H. R., & Gorman, D. M. (2000). Dynamics of the drug-crime relationship. In G. LaFree (Ed.), *The nature of crime: Continuity and change* (pp. 151–218). Washington, DC: National Institute of Justice.

Williams, J. E., Newby, R. G., & Kanitz, H. (1993). Assessing the need for alcohol abuse programs for African-American college students. *Journal of Multicultural Counseling and Development, 21*, 155–167.

Williams, J. H., Ayers, C. D., Abbott, R. D., Hawkins, J. D., & Catalano, R. F. (1996). Structural equivalence of involvement in problem behavior across racial groups using multiple group confirmatory factor analysis. *Social Work Research, 20*(3), 168–179.

Williams, J. H., Ayers C. D., Abbott, R. D. Hawkins, J. D., & Catalano, R. F. (1999). Race differences in risk factors for delinquency and substance use among adolescents. *Social Work Research, 23*(4), 227–240.

Zubretsky, T. M., & Digirolamo, K. M. (1994). Adult domestic violence: The alcohol connection. *Violence Update, 4*(7), 1–2, 4, 8.

6

A Systems Perspective

EDITH FREEMAN

Introduction

Substance abuse and family violence are co-occurring problems that affect most families at some point, either directly or indirectly. However, African American families may experience greater social, economic, health, legal, and spiritual consequences from these problems for individual and environmental reasons, such as ineffective coping and institutionalized economic oppression. Consequences include overrepresentation of African American children in foster care and other public child welfare services; higher rates of under- and unemployment for black youth and adults; and inadequate housing, health care, and education (DiNitto, 1995; Hartman, 1985; Orfield & Ashkinaze, 1991). From a systems perspective, these consequences may be both an outcome of and a contributing factor to family violence and substance abuse among African Americans (Coulton & Chow, 1995).

A new trend in the research literature attempts to clarify the intersection of these two coexisting problems among blacks, but most of the past and current literature treats the two as separate problems. This chapter briefly reviews and critiques this literature, including the demographics of African Americans affected by these coexisting problems, and then uses a systems orientation to summarize historical and present influences of oppression on substance abuse and family violence in this population. Consistent with that theoretical orientation, the chapter concludes with interrelated recommendations for culturally competent research, child welfare practice and policy, and social work education related to African Americans.

Literature Review

Much of the past research on African Americans, family violence, and substance abuse focuses either on violence or substance abuse separately. This division in research parallels a split in the two related practice fields. For instance, the child welfare literature tends to minimize or fails to explore the relationship between child abuse and substance abuse, other than to mention the latter infrequently as a mediating variable in child abuse (Wells, 1995). Similarly, the substance abuse literature has only recently began to examine violence as a co-occurring problem, often related to drug dealers and the perpetrators of spousal battering, but seldom in regard to child abuse and neglect.

The greatest proportion of literature on substance abuse and/or violence involves large-scale surveys or epidemiological research, with fewer studies presenting practice-effectiveness guidelines for addressing the intersection of these problems. Equally important, fewer of these studies focus on incidence rates *or* practice guidelines for African Americans alone. Much of this research involves cross-cultural comparison studies.

CROSS-CULTURAL COMPARISON RESEARCH: TWO SEPARATE PROBLEMS

These comparison studies analyze differences between African Americans and other cultural groups, often using Caucasians as the comparison group, and focus on either violence or substance abuse. For example, the literature indicates that African Americans have higher alcohol binge rates than Whites; however, they also have overall greater alcohol abstinence rates than Whites. A little over 7% of African American adults abuse illicit drugs compared to 6.6% of Whites. African American youths 12–17 years old have lower rates of marijuana use than White youths, but they have comparable use rates for other illicit drugs. In contrast, African American females 12–17 years of age have lower rates of overall drug use than White females of the same age (Greenfield, 1998a; Johnston, O'Malley, & Bachman, 1999; Substance Abuse and Mental Health Services Administration [SAMHSA]), 1999). While cultural differences exist, the overall high rates of illicit drug use for Americans in general remained stable or relatively unchanged from 1991 through 1998 (SAMHSA, 1999).

In terms of violence, some studies have documented that incidence rates against African American females are higher than those for White females. Rates of nonlethal violence against African American and White males are similar, therefore highlighting a common gender pattern across the two groups (Greenfield, 1998b; He, McCoy, Stevens, & Stark, 1998). Although the literature indicates that violence rates for African

Americans are decreasing, it also verifies that family violence is a continuing serious problem in this group as well as in others. For instance, rates of intimate murders by African Americans decreased 6% per year from 1976 to 1996, decreasing from 11 to 4 times those of Whites. However, while national trends confirm that intimate murder rates decreased 52% across all cultural groups, some researchers believe that this trend may soon reverse itself (Browne, Williams, & Dutton, 1999; Greenfield, 1998b).

RESEARCH ON THE INTERSECTION OF THE TWO PROBLEMS

Epidemiological studies show mixed findings on the intersection of violence and substance abuse in African Americans. Some studies conclude, for example, that the risk factors and predictors for interpersonal violence and alcoholism in African Americans are different (McCord & Ensminger, 1997; Singleton & Dale, 1996), even in long-term follow-up studies lasting up to five years. Other epidemiological studies have found that a history of violence is a predictor of substance abuse risk in African American adolescents (Kilpatrick et al., 2000), that alcohol and marijuana use is significantly related to weapons offenses by African American young adults (Friedman, Glassman, & Terras, 2001), and that sexual and combined sexual and physical assault are strongly associated with alcohol use among Black teenagers under 17 (Berenson, San Miguel, & Wilkinson, 1992). Kang, Goldstein, Spunt, Brownstein, and Lipton, (1994) warn us, however, that the intersection of these two problems is very complex, involves multiple interacting influences, and that alcohol and drug use alone do not lead to community violence.

Studies on treatment effectiveness involving the two problems have shown equally mixed results with African Americans. There is some agreement, however, that holistic approaches that address mind and body are effective, such as making racial identity and unique biological characteristics that affect African Americans' responses to medication the focus of treatment (Baker & Bell, 1999; Vontress & Epp, 1997). Strategies specific to a particular subgroup of African Americans have led to positive outcomes in some research focused on the intersection of these problems. For example, culture- and age-specific hip-hop music has been used to stimulate cooperative learning for harm reduction and substance abuse prevention among teenagers (Stephens, Braithwaite, & Taylor, 1998). Gender-specific strategies of active problem solving, religious involvement, and family support were found to be effective with African American women (Curtis-Boles & Jenkins-Monroe, 2000), while cofacilitating self-help parenting groups has improved low-income fathers' parenting and teaching skills related to violence, sexuality, substance abuse, and ethnic pride (Fagan & Stevenson, 1995).

METHODOLOGICAL AND OTHER LIMITATIONS
OF THIS LITERATURE

This analysis of the literature on African American family violence and substance abuse has highlighted a number of important limitations in the identified research. Such limitations not only point out methodological and epistemological problems in this research, but also how those problems shape the implications that can be drawn for future research, child welfare practice, policy, and education. The limitations include the following:

1. Two separate literatures on African American family violence-substance abuse: this pattern in past and current literature reinforces beliefs in child welfare, violence prevention, and substance abuse rehab services that these are two separate problems. The pattern also obscures opportunities to identify common influences on and effective interventions with these coexisting problems in African American families and other multiple factors that may influence one or both of these problems.
2. A narrow definition of family violence: these definitions often do not include child sexual, emotional, or physical abuse; suicides by adult and child family members; or the effects on children who are direct victims of or who witness family violence and substance abuse.
3. Ignoring strengths and resiliency while emphasizing problems: this literature emphasizes pathology rather than African American strengths. It often fails to explore how a majority of African Americans resist environmental triggers and risks that lead to violence and substance abuse; do not use violence against others or abuse substances although they may be victims of violence; and when they have such problems, demonstrate resilience in their recovery from violence and substance abuse.
4. Failure to identify unique African American cultural factors: much of this research simply reports inadequate demographic information on African Americans (e.g., urban poor), while ignoring cultural factors that interact with, increase, or decrease violence and substance abuse in this group. Moreover, the research, with few exceptions, does not explore the types of child welfare or other services that are needed to address these coexisting problems among African Americans.
5. Lack of focus on systemic or structural factors: this failure to consider environmental factors that contribute to or reinforce violence and substance abuse among African Americans encourages assumptions about individual deficits. It also masks how social justice barriers such as restrictive child welfare or mental health policies can interact with individual, family, community, and cultural factors in the maintenance of the two problems.

These last two limitations are perhaps the most crucial gaps in this literature because they are related to the cultural and social context of African American substance abuse and violence. Hence, this literature lacks a systems perspective in that it narrowly conceptualizes the two problems, researches them by using the same narrow lens, and then draws inadequate implications from that research. The systems perspective is useful for broadening the focus of such research and for providing information about the social and cultural context of these problems. An important part of that context includes the effects of oppression on African American violence and substance abuse.

Historical and Current Effects of Oppression: A Systems Perspective

HISTORICAL OVERVIEW: AFRICAN AMERICAN TRADITIONS AND OPPRESSIONS

The African survivals approach is one of several explanations of African Americans' efforts to cope with oppression historically (Asante, 1990; DuBois, 1969; Herskovits, 1969). This view assumes that although cultural differences existed among African tribes before the diaspora, nevertheless, they had common cultural traditions and institutions, especially the West African tribes. In America, slave owners prohibited Africans from speaking and writing their languages; engaging in their cultural rituals; learning English; and maintaining their religious or spiritual, healing, marital, agrarian, legal, and socialization institutions. Slaves were not given last names, only first names, to denote their status as property. Laws were enacted to strongly enforce these restrictions. However, the oral tradition allowed Africans to blend and maintain common aspects of the different tribes' values, traditions, rituals, and language, and, hence, to survive these oppressive measures.

In addition, Africans were confronted with other more oppressive conditions during slavery that became the foundation of their current violence and substance abuse problems. Slave masters and others in power maintained a hostile environment of physical and psychological violence. Slaves were murdered without legal consequences for their killers, beaten, raped, physically restrained, and had limbs cut off for rule violations, as well as being bred for money or forced to work long hours on meager food rations (Martin & Martin, 1985). Runaways and leaders of uprisings, in particular, were hanged as an example to others. Lesser rule violations resulted in family members, including children and spouses, being sold to other slave owners in distant localities (Gutman, 1976). Even though isolated acts of kindness occurred at times between slave owners and slaves, they occurred within a climate of continuous physical and psychological violence, in which even slaves' responses to such kindnesses were prescribed and not within their control.

These violent acts were committed while slave owners and others were under the influence of alcohol, and thus may have led to an association between violence and alcohol in the subjective experiences of slaves. Moreover, it was not uncommon for some slave owners to reward slaves with alcohol to celebrate transitions, such as the end of the planting and harvest seasons (Wright, Kail, & Creecy, 1990). Other slave owners allowed slaves to drink on weekends, although all slave-holding states prohibited or controlled the use of alcohol by slaves. Slave owners assumed alcohol would make Africans more compliant or less likely to participate in uprisings (Lender & Martin, 1982). Prior to slavery in America, Africans drank native beer as part of their religious, economic, and social life, but excessive drinking was rare (Herd, 1986).

While many African Americans believe these adaptations during slavery represent cultural strengths, some historians and researchers have often labeled them as evidence of the inferiority or absence of African culture. However, by applying a systems perspective to African Americans' preslavery and slavery experiences in this country, their adaptations are more understandable as positive coping strategies. The kidnapping of Africans and their forced Middle Passage to this country created traumatic experiences (McRoy, 1990), which placed them in a major cultural and developmental transition while also creating the disequilibrium necessary for effective adaptation and coping.

Some examples of coping and adaptation, such as using the church's support to overcome their grief and spirituals to convey information to each other about slave uprisings or runaways, helped them to transcend their oppression (Blassingame, 1970). Making unattached slaves or fictive kin part of their extended families ensured that the African clan structure survived. This survival adaptation has to be understood within the context of the owners' practice of selling slaves' family members, at times for punishment and at other times for profit (McRoy, 1990).

In contrast, other adaptations by African Americans have had long-term deleterious effects. Examples include adapting to the slave owners' practice of giving them alcohol to celebrate transitions, and to slave owners' use of violence while inebriated to make slaves more compliant. As a consequence, some African Americans continue to use alcohol and violence to cope with oppression and racial stress today. Other economic, social, and individual factors, such as hopelessness about their situations, have reinforced this coping pattern of self-medication and physical aggression.

CURRENT TRADITIONS AND EFFECTS OF OPPRESSION ON THESE PROBLEMS

A systems perspective is useful for understanding the effects of oppression on African Americans currently as well as historically. Table 1 clarifies systems concepts and assumptions that explain how individual, cultural, and environmental factors interact to decrease

TABLE 1
A Systems Framework for Knowledge Development:
Examples of African American Substance Abuse
& Violence Factors

SUBSYSTEMS	THE NURTURING ENVIRONMENT	THE TASK/INSTRUMENTAL ENVIRONMENT
Micro:		
Cultural supports:	•Bicultural or Afrocentric identity models •Cultural validation to mediate racial stress (family, other support networks) •Cultural traditions and values •Role sharing: group unity/cohesion •Cultural resistance or coping skills re: substance abuse and violence	•Limited access to basic resources and sources of personal power.
Cultural barriers:	•Violence networks (African American gangs), relationship or role triggers •Coenabling substance abuse networks	•Societal and media stereotypes, racial discrimination, color-blind perspectives, targeted marketing for alcohol/other drugs = increased racial stress
Mezzo:		
Cultural supports:	•Black economic & political development associations/organizations (structural) •Afrocentric mentoring circles (leadership) •Culture-specific treatment programs	•Self-development programs based on narrow opportunity windows without structural changes (leadership development, Head Start, job training) •Set-aside programs (e.g., small-business loans)
Cultural barriers:	•Community norms tolerant of violence & substance abuse (cultural denial) •Ethnic group exclusions (cultural secrets)	•Ghettoization maintains/reinforces economically depressed violent African American communities •Inaccuracies & failure to acknowledge African American history & contributions = racial stress
Macro:		
Cultural supports:	•Task environment buffers: informal adoptions, fictive kin, natural recovery models, religious system's social justice and advocacy roles that support recovery and nonviolence	
Cultural barriers:	•Acculturation pressures = decreased positive models for resisting violence and substance abuse.	•Biased practices and policies toward African Americans (e.g., criminal justice system: the criminalization of substance abuse discriminates against African American defendants re: harsher sentences; child welfare system: overrepresentation of African American children versus White children in out-of-home placements often results from similar substance abuse and family violence problems)

African Americans' coping with oppression and racial stress, substance abuse, and violence. These concepts and assumptions also describe how cultural factors provide supports for racial esteem, group solidarity, and leadership development among African Americans (Schiele, 1996). Some of these factors have been explored in studies on substance abuse and violence, for example, the role of African American violence networks and cultural resistance skills against substance abuse. Other factors have seldom been the focus of research, if at all, such as the effects of racial stress and positive role models on African American violence or the effects of culture-specific child welfare, substance abuse, and antiviolence programs on positive outcomes with African Americans. The systems framework illustrates how these factors may operate within different environments and subsystems for this cultural group.

The Nurturing Environment

Table 1 is organized into two related systems or environments: nurturing and task. The nurturing environment serves as a cultural resource by helping African Americans to maintain many of the historical cultural traditions identified in the previous section, along with support networks such as the Black church and community cultural centers (Chestang, 1976a). Examples of other cultural supports in the nurturing environment include opportunities for cultural validation and modeling by bicultural racial identity models. On the other hand, community norms tolerant of substance abuse and cultural triggers for violence are examples of barriers (Freeman, 2001a).

Some of these same supports and barriers may influence both substance abuse and violence by African Americans, so they require further research. For example, anecdotal information indicates that extended family members often serve as cultural role models for the children of single mothers. They may model how to negotiate conflicting demands from the two environments and how to cope with those demands without violence or substance use. In contrast, racial stress from employment discrimination often may be a trigger for both substance abuse and violence. The substance abuse is an ineffective effort to self-medicate against the stress, while the violence may heighten rather than diffuse feelings of anger and powerlessness. Unfortunately, the violence is most often directed toward other African Americans in the nurturing environment who are also oppressed and marginalized: children, spouses, the extended family, and other community members.

The nurturing environment can also serve as a cultural buffer against the effects of oppression and racial stress that are endemic to the task environment. This nurturing environment can provide reality testing, cultural validation, positive coping models, and other sources of racial esteem that can decrease the negative effects of oppression. The use of the family decision-making process in child welfare attempts to build on the cultural buffering and problem-solving qualities of the extended family within this nurturing environment (Hartman, 1985). This approach decreases the risk of biased and arbitrary placement decisions by that system through the involvement of African Americans' extended families as active participants and monitors of the process.

The Task or Instrumental Environment

The task environment is represented by dominant society, which provides or prevents access to power; basic resources such as food and shelter; employment; education; and, often, physical survival. Oppression within the task environment has been defined as the use of the European culture, norms, values, worldview, and experiences as the sole criteria for determining reality, meaning, and significance. Consequently, the values, traditions, worldviews, and experiences of African Americans and other people of color are marginalized (devalued), creating institutionalized barriers to power, basic resources, and economic, political, and social justice (Schiele, 1996).

As shown in table 1, this environment is often the source of African Americans' daily and cumulative racial stress, a result of systemic oppression. Racial stress has both psychological and physical manifestations: emotional upheaval or anxiety, survival fears, and other reactions such as nausea and shortness of breath. African Americans experience these and other symptoms when they are confronted with overt and covert signs of oppression, intolerance, or discrimination (Freeman, 2000). Racial stress and its immobilizing effects have at times been referred to as problem fatigue (Chestang, 1976b), power paralysis (Pinderhughes, 1989), and death by a thousand nicks (Comer & Pouissant, 1992).

The task environment is also a source of inequitable policies and practices that have become institutionalized within large systems, including the child welfare, health, and mental health systems. Such policies reflect the institutionalized oppression that can be a contributing factor to African American substance abuse and violence, among other individual, family, and cultural factors.

Subsystem Influences on African Americans

Table 1 includes three subsystems that can be explored to increase our understanding of current African American experiences and coping patterns, in both the task and nurturing environments. Micro, mezzo, and macro subsystems may overlap, interact, and combine their influences on supports and barriers to African American nonviolence and nonproblem use of substances. The micro subsystem includes individual factors such as African Americans' personal, ethnic, and gender identity and esteem; cultural beliefs and attitudes toward substance abuse and violence; cultural traditions; values; coping skills; and social class and related lifestyle patterns. African Americans' interpersonal roles, relationships, and interactions are also part of this subsystem in terms of nuclear and extended family members, indigenous leaders, social and cultural networks, and individual peers.

The mezzo subsystem includes organizations, for example, cultural associations, African American mentoring programs, and nontraditional or indigenous social service agencies, as well as communities in both environments. The macro subsystem involves practices and social policies of large social systems and institutions such as child welfare, health, legal, education, and the mass media. It includes formal social service agencies that are the service delivery arms of these large systems. Additional information is needed about the influence of the macro system on African American violence and substance abuse. At the same time, the macro system needs more exploration to determine how biased policies related to these problems can be reformed as one strategy for addressing the problems.

Recommendations for Future Directions

These recommendations highlight future directions that should be undertaken by the child welfare field in research, practice, policy, and social work education, based on this application of the systems perspective. Some recommendations are clearly relevant to all four areas, while others apply primarily to one of these areas.

RECOMMENDATIONS FOR CULTURALLY COMPETENT RESEARCH

An important goal is to make research on African American family violence and substance abuse more culturally competent as shown by the right side of the continuum in figure 1. Such research needs to focus on many of the cultural supports (strengths) and barriers (cultural stress and other risks) in both the nurturing and task/instrumental environments (table 1). African Americans should be included in planning and implementing studies that focus on the intersection of these problems as well as on situations in which families have been able to prevent or mitigate these problems. From this research, unique and common cultural factors that influence these and other problems can be identified and addressed, along with the important social justice issues in table 1. Social workers should be at the forefront of this research, because such a trend embodies the profession's values and cultural priorities. Other recommendations for future research flow from this overarching or umbrella goal:

1. Secondary analysis of existing epidemiological research on African American substance abuse and family violence: the focus needs to be on identifying and analyzing data about relationships, types of violence, and environmental factors that are not currently included in primary analyses of these data.

FIGURE 1

Continuum of Culturally Competent Research: African American Substance Abuse and Family Violence

Color-blind Research
Culture is invisible, not factored, not acknowledged, or research is culturally biased in focus, methods, data analysis, conclusions

Culturally aware research
Aspects of culture identified, such as some demographics, no exploration of cultural meaning, potentially biased methods and data analysis may be acknowledged

Culturally sensitive research
Broader range of demographic factors & their cultural meanings explored, common cultural factors identified, biased methods and conclusions are the focus of monitoring and revising

Culturally relevant research
Multiple unique in-depth cultural factors are explored, cultural consultation and member checking to increase relevance and challenge process, outcomes, and meaning

Culturally competent research
Focus on unique cultural factors & social justice/structural barriers to cultural adaptation and participants as partners: planning, implementing, analyzing, and disseminating

---

2. Broadening of future epidemiological research: the goal is to balance the limitations of epidemiological research by combining it with other types of quantitative and qualitative methods, or by influencing the planning process for such research to include more substantive explorations of cultural factors and common triggers for the two problem areas (e.g., broadening the national household surveys on substance abuse and violence).

3. Use of qualitative research: priority on methods that are consistent with a value of African American families as experts on their lives, the importance of their subjective realities and examples of resilience, views about how the two problems intersect and the cultural and other factors in the nurturing and task environments that influence how those problems develop, cultural priorities, and the role of the oral tradition (e.g., by using ethnographic interviews, focus groups, town meetings).

4. Treatment effectiveness or outcome research: a combination of quantitative and qualitative methods should be used to identify and document the effects of innovative treatment approaches for co-occurring violence and substance abuse problems, based on an Afrocentric or other culture-specific approach. An effort should be made to explore in particular treatment approaches that use a multidiagnosis and intervention model to bridge differences/conflicts among the child welfare, substance abuse, and antiviolence practice fields.

5. Policy analysis research: focus is required on policy impact analysis, reform, and advocacy regarding pathology-focused policies, discrimination in policy implementation, oppressive practices, and other institutionalized task environment factors that reinforce substance abuse and violence in African Americans. Relevant policies in child welfare, criminal justice, welfare to work, employment, economic and community development, health, and housing systems need to be researched.

Practice Recommendations: Substance Abuse, Violence, and Child Welfare

Some of the recommended research approaches in the previous section could be used to develop and document practice approaches that are effective in resolving and preventing African American substance abuse and family violence. Both the practice approaches and the research used to document their effectiveness should meet criteria for cultural competence. This goal requires identification of criteria for culture-specific treatment programs and examples of exemplary programs that meet those criteria.

Examples of Criteria/Guidelines for Culture-Specific Programs

Only a small number of substance abuse treatment programs actually provide culture-specific substance abuse treatment for African Americans, and even fewer programs provide such services for resolving family violence with this population. Many programs address violence issues that are common in the lifestyles of substance abusers in a general way, but often not from a cultural perspective. Some generic programs now provide user-friendly services to African Americans, such as aggressive outreach by indigenous staff, but without addressing many of the cultural and social justice issues identified in table 1.

African Americans and other people of color not only experience the typical problems encountered by all substance abusers, but also problems stemming from institutional barriers that are beyond their individual control (Freeman, 2001b). Culture-specific treatment is designed to disrupt the effects of those task environment barriers on their substance abuse (sources of powerlessness), and to help African Americans to identify and use sources of individual and cultural power (Gordon, 1993; Rogan, 1986).

Freeman's (2001b) review of literature on culture-specific treatment for African Americans identified the following criteria, some of which have been documented through research, while others have not (Amuleru-Marshall, 1991; Gordon, 1993;

Harper, 1991; Rowe & Grills, 1993). The ultimate goal in designing and analyzing programs that apply these criteria is to help them fully integrate a violence treatment component into their substance abuse services, although an initial step may be to add a violence education group to some existing programs.

1. A life-sustaining cultural belief system: includes a philosophy, beliefs, values, principles of daily living, and an ethnic identity that are consistent with the African American culture. Such a system provides a life-organizing framework for clients to center their lives as recovering people who no longer self-medicate or cope through violence. The belief system has to be taught and internalized through an intensive treatment milieu that models the application of the system to the problems that bring clients into treatment and to their interactions and relationships with peers and staff during treatment. For example, some programs use the seven principles of Kwanzaa (the Nguzo Saba) as their framework for addressing substance abuse and violence through unity, self-determination, collective work and responsibility, cooperative economics, purpose, creativity, and faith.

2. Cultural education and violence education: involves psycho-education about African American history, traditions, strengths, sources of group pride and esteem, and the role of such knowledge in recovery. The goal is to provide clients with a sense of cohesion and unity as they begin to understand how those issues are related to their addiction, use of violence, and recovery in both areas. The process also involves identifying common cultural triggers for both problems in the nurturing and task/instrumental environments as well as cultural resources or tools in table 1 that can be used to prevent relapse (in substance abuse and violence). Services may also include cultural issues counseling groups, multicultural groups, and violence prevention groups.

3. Environmental impact experiences: the goal of integrating individual and collective experiences in effectively changing the environment as needed is twofold: to practice cultural adaptive coping and problem-solving skills, and to develop identities as culturally valuable and powerful people. Clients are coached through these experiences by staff, with the former taking major responsibility for identifying issues and planning and implementing the approaches to be used. The focus is on issues that trigger substance abuse and violence. Examples of environmental impact activities include advocacy to change oppressive visitation policies for clients whose children are in foster care and peaceful participation in social action such as the Million Man March in Washington in 1996. Later, clients are helped to analyze and then record such experiences as lessons learned through oral histories or narratives, journaling, collages, videotaped reenactments of experiences, photographs, sculpture, and drawings.

4. Adapting traditional substance abuse and violence treatment components: priority is placed on examining and restructuring elements of traditional programs that are not

culturally meaningful to African Americans. For example, work is an important component of most recovery programs. Services for African American clients should include economic development, job development, and supported employment approaches to complement traditional job training and referral models. In addition, traditional anger management, antiviolence, conflict resolution, and communications training may exacerbate these clients' experiences with race and class discrimination in the workplace. Instead, they may benefit from skill training in identifying and handling racial stress and environmental triggers as well as using mediation and advocacy supports.

A CULTURE-SPECIFIC PROGRAM EXAMPLE

One program example includes substance abuse, child welfare, and antiviolence service components for its African American clients. These services are provided within a cultural context or Afrocentric milieu, including African philosophy and values and collective principles of living (the Nguzo Saba). The four main treatment components are based on Asante's (1989) teachings and on Oliver's (1989) definition of Afrocentricity:

> the internalization of values that emphasize love of self, awareness of traditional African heritage, and personal commitment to the economic and political power of African Americans and other people of African descent. (p. 16)

The program's four components include (1) traditional alcohol and drug services that have been adapted to integrate Nguzo Saba principles into the men's and women's issues groups, (2) community political and economic development to help clients make structural or task environment changes and serve as cultural and gender-related mentors, (3) wellness and health promotion that emphasize values and lifestyle changes around nutrition, exercise, traditional African healing, and other stress-prevention approaches, and (4) African rituals and traditions that focus on cultural education and history and rites of passage that facilitate recovery from violence and substance abuse. These components are consistent with many of the cultural factors and systems issues shown in table 1 and with guidelines for culture-specific practice in the previous section, with one exception.

This program also has policies for respectful communication and interactions between clients that are designed to prevent the use of profanity; culture and gender-related slurs, threats, and stereotypes; and physical violence. This zero-tolerance aggression approach and other antiviolence services provide modeling and practice experiences for coping with stress without violence. However, the program has not yet developed the more fully integrated approach recommended in the previous section.

A child welfare component helps male and female clients to develop child care plans for children in their custody; reunification plans for children in out-of-home placements; and Afrocentric parenting, disciplining, and family education skills for their current and future parenting roles. The child welfare component challenges African American parents to develop creative and nurturing ways to discipline their children without violence, and educates them about the reciprocal triggers for substance abuse and violence relapses. Child welfare, antiviolence, and substance abuse components of the program are coordinated more effectively by having staff from child welfare and harm-reduction agencies on site in the program for several days per week. While these coordination efforts have improved treatment for the intersection of these problems, this program has not yet fully integrated the three components.

Policy Recommendations

The previous practice and research guidelines emphasize the use of mechanisms for soliciting information about what is culturally meaningful to African Americans. Policy recommendations also should embrace this approach, which, according to Chapin (1995), involves (1) inclusion of people in the policy analysis and formation/reform process, and (2) strengths-based policy development that does not view people as their problems. The first guideline suggests, for example, that epidemiological research should also focus on policies and practices that African Americans believe reinforce substance abuse and violence or that impede or support their recovery from both conditions.

Policies in the three systems can conflict with each other in some circumstances. For example, substance abuse programs often encourage recovering mothers to delay reunification with their children in the child welfare system until aftercare or later, when they are far enough into recovery to take on the parenting role. The child welfare system, in contrast, often encourages reunification as soon as rehabilitation is completed, based on limited knowledge about the recovery process and biases about the parenting attitudes of African American mothers. A mother's desire to follow the policy of her rehabilitation program may place reunification in jeopardy if conflicting policies between the two systems are not reformed, coordinated, and mediated as needed.

The second guideline should encourage researchers and program developers to gather data on African American strengths as a foundation for reforming policies and programs. At the same time, existing research has documented the negative effects of policies that support economic oppression and harsher drug sentences on African Americans' violence and drug use rates (Banks, 1997; Duster, 1997; Parker & Cartmill, 1998). Social workers and other advocates should focus on helping to reform many of these punitive task environment policies and discourage blaming people for conditions and related outcomes that are the result of such policies.

Recommendations for Social Work Education

Social work education can be enhanced through changes that lead to more culturally competent curricula in research, practice, human behavior, and policy areas. First, a range of cultural diversity, including ethnicity, race, religion, gender, sexual orientation, age, disability, and location, should be integrated into the general curriculum of schools of social work. For example, in research courses the continuum of culturally competent research (figure 1) and related content areas can be integrated with information on all of the above areas of diversity. Content should be included on how some research criteria apply to all areas of diversity in similar ways, and how other criteria vary in their application to different cultural groups. Various cultural competence frameworks can be applied in practice, human behavior, and policy courses to the range of cultural diversity areas in the same way.

Second, specific content could be addressed in courses focused on particular cultural groups and problem areas. A practice course on African American families could focus on culturally competent practice across problem areas such as substance abuse, violence, and economically depressed communities with an emphasis on cultural supports and barriers. Or a policy course could use families, poverty, culture, substance abuse, violence, and child welfare as some its main exemplars for teaching policy analysis focused on culture-specific content. Such courses should emphasize strengths-based policies and a policy formation inclusion process that involves clients as experts. (Gutierrez, DeLois, & GlenMaye, 1995).

Conclusion

These recommendations for future directions, as well as the underlying philosophical and methodological criteria discussed in this chapter, are consistent with social work values and traditions, for example, the emphasis on social justice and institutional and individual change. Moreover, this chapter's literature review has documented the continuing intersection of African American substance abuse and violence and the devastating consequences. Hence, the review highlights a need to revisit and revise how we address these areas in future research, practice, and policy. A multisystems approach is essential for addressing the historical and current effects of oppression, which have been seriously underestimated as strong barriers to effectively resolving these problems. Although African Americans are and have been resilient, continuously developing adaptive coping patterns to survive, other maladaptive patterns related to violence, substance abuse, and other areas are taking their toll on the quality and ethos of their lives.

References

Amuleru-Marshall, O. (1991). African-Americans. In J. Kinney (Ed.), *Clinical manual of substance abuse* (pp. 180–196). St. Louis, MO: Mosby Year Books.

Asante, M. (1989). *Afrocentricity and knowledge*. Trenton, NJ: Africa World Press.

Asante, M. (1990). *Kemet, Afrocentricity, and knowledge*. Trenton, NJ: Africa World Press.

Baker, F. M., & Bell, C. (1999). Issues in psychiatric treatment of African Americans. *Psychiatric Services, 50,* 362–368.

Banks, R. (1997). Race, representation, and the drug policy agenda. In C. Herring (Ed.), *African Americans and the public agenda: The paradoxes of public policy* (pp. 209–223). Thousand Oaks, CA: Sage.

Berenson, A. B., San Miguel, V. V., & Wilkinson, G. S. (1992). Violence and its relationship to substance use in adolescent pregnancy. *Journal of Adolescent Health, 13,* 470–474.

Blassingame, J. W. (1970). *The slave community: Plantation life in the antebellum South*. New York: Oxford University Press.

Browne, A., Williams, K. R., & Dutton, D. G. (1999). Homicide between intimates: A 20-year review. In M. D. Smith & M. A. Zahn (Eds.), *Homicide: A sourcebook of social research* (pp. 149–164). Thousand Oaks, CA: Sage.

Chapin, R. K. (1995). Social policy development. The strengths perspective. *Social Work, 40,* 506–514.

Chestang, L. (1976a). Environmental influences on social functioning: The black experience. In P. S. Cafferty & L. Chestang (Eds.), *The diverse society: Implications for social policy* (pp. 59–74). New York: National Association of Social Workers.

Chestang, L. (1976b). The black family and black culture: A study in coping. In M. Sotomayer (Ed.), *Cross cultural perspectives in social work practice and education* (pp. 98–116). Houston, TX: University of Houston Graduate School of Social Work.

Comer, J. P., & Pouissant, A.F. (1992). *Raising Black children*. Springer: New York.

Coulton, C. J., & Chow, J. (1995). Poverty. In R. L. Edwards (Ed.), *Encyclopedia of social work* (19th ed.) (pp. 1867–1878). Washington, DC: National Association of Social Workers.

Curtis-Boles, H., & Jenkins-Monroe, V. (2000). Substance abuse in African American women. *Journal of Black Psychology, 26,* 450–469.

DiNitto, D. (1995). *Social welfare politics and public policy* (4th ed.). Boston: Allyn & Bacon.

DuBois, W. E. B. (1969). *The Negro American family*. New York: New American Library.

Duster, T. (1997). Pattern, purpose, and race in the drug war: The crisis of credibility in criminal justice. In C. Reinarman & H. G. Levin (Eds.), *Crack in America: Demon drugs and social justice* (pp. 260–287). Berkeley: Institute for the Study of Social Change, University of California Press.

Fagan, J., & Stevenson, H. (1995). Men as teachers: A self-help program on parenting for African American men. *Social Work with Groups, 17,* 29–42.

Freeman, E. M. (2000). *Moving toward cultural competence: A systems perspective. A training curriculum.* Lawrence: University of Kansas School of Social Welfare.

Freeman, E. M. (2001a). Community prevention: Empowerment, systems change, and culturally sensitive evaluation. In E. M. Freeman (Ed.), *Substance abuse intervention, prevention, rehabilitation, and systems change strategies: Helping individuals, families, and groups to empower themselves* (pp. 159–182). New York: Columbia University Press.

Freeman, E. M. (2001b). Dareisa rehab services: A culture-specific program for African American adults. In E. M. Freeman (Ed.), *Substance intervention, prevention, rehabilitation, and systems change strategies: Helping individuals, families, and groups to empower themselves* (pp. 397–429). New York: Columbia University Press.

Friedman, A. S., Glassman, K., & Terras, A. (2001). Violent behavior as related to use of marijuana and other drugs. *Journal of Addictive Diseases, 20,* 49–72.

Gordon, J. U. (1993). A culturally-specific approach to ethnic minority young adults. In E. M. Freeman (Ed.), *Substance abuse treatment: A family systems perspective* (pp. 71–99). Newbury Park, CA: Sage.

Greenfield, L. A. (Ed.). (1998a). *Alcohol and crime: An analysis of national data on the prevalence of alcohol involvement in crime.* Prepared for the Assistant Attorney General's National Symposium on Alcohol and Crime. Washington, DC: U.S. Department of Justice.

Greenfield, L. A. (Ed.) (1998b). *Violence by intimates: Analysis of data on crimes by current or former spouses, boyfriends, and girlfriends* (NCJ-167237). Bureau of Justice Factbook. Washington, DC: U.S. Department of Justice.

Gutierrez, L., DeLois, K., & GlenMaye, L. (1995). Understanding empowerment practice: Building on practitioner-based knowledge. *Families in Society, 76,* 534–542.

Gutman, H. (1976). *The black family in slavery and freedom.* New York: Pantheon.

Harper, F. D. (1991). Substance abuse and the black American family. *Urban Research Review, 13,* 1–5.

Hartman, A. (1985). Preventive child welfare services for black families and children. In A. Hartman (Ed.), *Empowering the black family* (pp. 1–6). Ann Arbor, MI: National Child Welfare Training Center.

He, H., McCoy, H. V., Stevens, S. J., & Stark, M. J. (1998). Violence and HIV sexual behaviors among female sex partners of make drug users. *Women & Health, 27,* 161–175.

Herd, D. (1986). A review of drinking patterns and alcohol problems among U.S. blacks. *Report of the secretary's task force on black and minority health* (77–132): Vol. 7. *Chemical dependency and diabetes.* Washington, DC: Department of Health and Human Services.

Herskovits, M. J. (1969). *The myth of the Negro past.* Boston: Beacon.

Johnston, L. D., O'Malley, P. M., & Bachman, J. G. (1999). *Drug trends in 1999 are mixed.* Ann Arbor: University of Michigan News and Information Services. Retrieved April 23, 2000, from www.monitoring the future.org

Kang, S. Y., Goldstein, P. J., Spunt, B., Brownstein, H. H., & Lipton, D. S. (1994). *Relationship of substance use to violent crime among homicide offenders.* New York: National Development & Research Institutes.

Kilpatrick, D. G., Acierno, R., Saunders, B., Resnick, H. S., Best, C. L., & Schnurr, P. P. (2000). Risk factors for adolescent substance abuse and dependence: Data from a national sample. *Journal of Consulting and Clinical Psychology, 68,* 19–30.

Lender, M. E., & Martin, J. K. (1982). *Drinking in America: A history.* New York: Free Press.

Martin, E., & Martin, J. (1985). *The helping tradition in the black family and community.* Silver Spring, MD: National Association of Social Workers

McCord, J., & Ensminger, M. E. (1997). Multiple risks and comorbidity in an African-American population. *Criminal Behavior and Mental Health, 7,* 339–352.

McRoy, R. G. (1990). A historical overview of black families. In S. M. L. Logan, E. M. Freeman, & R. G. McRoy (Eds.), *Social work practice with black families: A culturally specific approach* (pp. 3–17). New York: Longman.

Oliver, W. (1989). Black males and social problems: Prevention through Africentric socialization. *Journal of Black Studies, 20,* 15–39.

Orfield, G., & Ashkinaze, C. (1991). The closing door: Conservative policy and black opportunity. *Social Security Bulletin, 28,* 3–29.

Parker, R. N., & Cartmill, R. S. (1998). Alcohol and homicide in the United States 1934–1995 or one reason why U.S. rates of violence may be going down. *Journal of Criminal Law and Criminology, 88,* 1369–1398.

Pinderhughes, E. (1989). *Understanding race, ethnicity, and power: The key to efficacy in clinical practice.* New York: Free Press.

Rogan, A. (1986). Recovery from alcoholism: Issues for black and Native-American alcoholics. *Alcohol Health and Research World, 2,* 42–44.

Rowe, D., & Grills, C. (1993). African-centered drug treatment: An alternative paradigm for drug counseling with African-American clients. *Journal of Psychoactive Drugs, 25,* 21–31.

Schiele, J. H. (1996). Afrocentricity: An emerging paradigm in social work practice. *Social Work, 41,* 284–294.

Singleton, E. G., & Dale, G. A., Jr. (1996). Lack of co-occurring interpersonal violence-related emotional difficulties and alcohol and other drug use problems among African American youth with conduct disorder. *Journal of Negro Education, 65,* 445–453.

Stephens, T., Braithwaite, R. L., & Taylor, S. E. (1998). Model for using hip-hop music for small group HIV/AIDS prevention counseling with African American adolescents and young adults. *Patient Education and Counseling, 35,* 127–137.

Substance Abuse and Mental Health Services Administration [SAMHSA]. (1999). *National household survey on drug abuse: Main findings 1999.* Washington, DC: U.S. Department of Health and Human Services.

Vontress, C. E., & Epp, L. R. (1997). Historical hostility in the African American client: Implications for counseling. *Journal of Multicultural Counseling and Development, 25,* 170–184.

Wells, S. J. (1995). Child abuse and neglect overview. In R. L. Edwards (Ed.), *Encyclopedia of Social Work,* 19th ed. (pp. 346–366). Washington, DC: National Association of Social Workers.

Wright, Jr., R., Kail, B. L., & Creecy, R. F. (1990). Culturally sensitive social work practice with black alcoholics. In S. M. L. Logan, E. M. Freeman, & R. G. McRoy (Eds.), *Social work practice with black families: A culturally specific perspective* (pp. 203–222). New York: Longman.

7

Starting Early
Starting Smart Experience

An Integration of Services

**KIMBERLY BROOKS, DAVID DEERE, LORI HANSON,
IRENE JILLSON, CAROL AMUNDSON LEE, CAROLYN SEVAL,
and JOCELYN TURNER-MUSA**

Introduction

According to recent census data, about 34 million people of African descent live in the United States (U.S. Bureau of the Census, 2001), while by far most are descendants of Africans who were forced into slavery, others are immigrants from various parts of the world. In fact, 6% of all those who self-identified as African American in the 2000 census are foreign born, mostly from the Caribbean (U.S. Bureau of the Census, 2001). As with all ethnic and racial groups that make up our diverse U.S. population, African Americans are themselves diverse in terms of socioeconomic status, language, education, and, in particular, level of assimilation and acculturation. Many scholars contend the legacy of forced immigration, slavery, and racial oppression have led to the multiple health, social, and economic disparities currently existing between African Americans and European Americans (Hacker, 1992). Indeed, the 2001 report of the surgeon general of the United States, *Mental Health: Culture, Race, and Ethnicity*, suggests, "The mental health of African Americans can be appreciated only within this wider historical context" (U.S. Public Health Service, 2001, p. 53). While this by no means encompasses the totality of the African American experience, awareness of its impact on the African American family is important for an understanding of the needs and appropriate health and social services for this population. This discussion of African Americans will focus on the unique history and experiences of American-born Black children and families, since many Black immigrant groups maintain cultures and history that are distinct from the African American experience (Hacker, 1992).

Slavery and Its Impact on the African American Family

From the 1520s to the 1860s, an estimated 11 million–12 million African men, women, and children were forced onto European ships, heading for a life of slavery in the Western Hemisphere. Only 9 million–10 million are estimated to have survived the grueling Atlantic crossing (Behrendt, 1999). The systematic destruction of entire civilizations and conscious dehumanization were accomplished through this depletion of African human resources. Voluminous documentation exists on the direct and tacit ways slavery had an impact on the families of those enslaved. Among the most egregious of these was the fact that, technically, slaves were not allowed to have a family. Slave owners took clear steps to discourage slaves from marrying and forming families; in some states it was actually illegal for a clergyman to marry two slaves. Destruction of existing family relationships was pervasive; fathers were routinely sold to pay off debts, and mothers were separated from their children. However, the strong and adaptive human need for social relationships could not be eliminated.

Forced separations from blood relatives likely contributed to reinforcing tribal traditions of strong extended kinship ties among African Americans and often encouraged family groups centering around matriarchal figures. Similar family structures continue among modern-day African American families, with 51% headed by single females and less than half headed by a married couple (McLoyd, Cauce, Takeuchi, & Wilson, 2000). The phenomenon of single-parent households is counterbalanced by the historically strong and culturally rooted extended family orientation on the part of African Americans. However, recent findings indicate that succeeding generations of teen pregnancy, with added burdens of poverty and decreased social support systems, have served to "undermine [these] supportive traditions" (U.S. Department of Health and Human Services, 2000b, p. 55).

Substance Abuse, Mental Health, Family Violence, and Child Welfare

Understanding substance abuse in any population has been elusive; in the African American family it is an extraordinarily complex issue. Given the daily exposure to explicit genocide African Americans were subjected to shortly following the end of slavery through all too recent times, and extreme and insidious racism that continues through the dawn of the 21st century, it should not be surprising that African Americans have used mind-altering substances—legal alcohol and illegal drugs—as an escape from these ugly realities. At least since World War II, the choice of illegal drugs used by African Americans has generally followed the pattern of those used by the general population. During the 1950s and 1960s marijuana and heroin became drugs of choice, especially within artistic circles. Toward the end of and after the Vietnam War, heroin use increased significantly. The cocaine epidemic that began in the 1980s showed differences between African Americans and Caucasians, with cocaine used primarily by the latter and the crack derivative used primarily by African Americans.

Although it has long been reported that alcohol abuse is a much less significant issue among African Americans than among Caucasians and Hispanic Americans, the National Household Survey on Drug Abuse (NHSDA) and other data (e.g., statistics on liver cirrhosis) indicate that alcohol problems are significant for African Americans (Substance Abuse and Mental Health Services Administration [SAMHSA], 2001). According to the 2000 National Household Survey on Drug Abuse (SAMHSA, 2001), Caucasian and African Americans were equally likely to have engaged in illicit drug use in the month prior to the survey. However, pregnant African American women were much more likely to have used illegal drugs in the past month than pregnant Caucasian women: 7.1% and 2.9%, respectively, for years 1999 and 2000 combined (NHSDA, 2001). According to the NHSDA, 4% of African Americans reported heavy alcohol use in the previous month, compared with 5.6% for the general population (NHSDA, 2001).

The history of mental health, mental illness, and emotional disturbance is clouded by early racist assertions concerning both cause and incidence of psychiatric conditions among African Americans. Psychological explanations have historically been used to support and perpetuate racism, at times describing African Americans as emotionally unstable, cognitively inferior, and constitutionally compromised. For example, slaves who attempted to escape were seen as mentally ill. *The Moynihan Report, The Negro Family: The Case for National Action*, published by the U.S. Department of Labor in 1965, described the African American family as a "tangle of pathology" (Thomas & Sillen, 1979). More recently, some authors have sought to provide "scientific evidence" for the inherent cognitive inferiority of African Americans (Herrstein & Murray, 1998). Such assertions and investigations have stemmed from a deficit-based approach, resulting in a view of African Americans as not simply different in important ways from European Americans, but rather as deficient and in some cases pathological. Understandably, African Americans have been and continue to be wary of mental health services and research and commonly seek help from trusted sources in the community, such as the church or family.

The only national epidemiological study of mental health conditions was conducted in the 1980s. Although its methods and data collection instruments continue to be questioned with respect to their cultural relevance (and thus validity), it remains the only large-scale study on which to base findings. This study found that, after accounting for demographic and socioeconomic conditions, African Americans had lower lifetime prevalence of mental illness than did White Americans. However, race continues to play a role in diagnosis and treatment of mental health conditions among African Americans. For example, they are accurately diagnosed with depression less often by primary care practitioners (Borowsky et al., 2000) and when presenting for psychiatric conditions in emergency centers (Strakowski, Hawkins, & Keck, 1997). Moreover, according to the previously cited surgeon general's report on mental health, "African Americans with mental health needs are unlikely to receive treatment—even less likely than the undertreated mainstream population" (U.S. Public Health Service, 2001). This is a severe impediment to preventing family conflict and violence and to promoting and supporting healthy family structures.

Data on the incidence of family violence in general and for African American families in particular are scant—a consequence of both stigma and changing perceptions and awareness of the concept of family violence. According to a National Family Violence Survey (1985) by Straus and Gelles, African Americans are 1.58 times more likely than European Americans to report escalation of marital arguments into physical violence, even when controlling for income and social class. These findings should be viewed with caution because European American women may underreport domestic violence at higher rates than do African American and other women of color. Another potential explanation for this phenomenon may lie in the differential experiences of African American and European American women. Raj (1999) reports that although race in itself is not a significant factor relative to domestic violence incidence, it does heavily influence the contexts of women's lives. The factors related to African American women's involvement with an abusive partner might differ from those influencing White women. Specifically, the segregation of unpaid work (e.g., child care and housework) to women and inequalities in wages and educational attainment between women and men contribute to African American women's socioeconomic impoverishment and, therefore, may enhance their vulnerability to relationship abuse.

Although highly controversial, some researchers (Deater-Deckard & Dodge, 1997; Pinderhughes, Dodge, & Bales, 2000) have suggested that African American parents may use physical discipline or punishment more often than European American parents, even when controlling for socioeconomic status. Deater-Deckard and Dodge (1997) suggest the use of physical punishment by African Americans may be a vestige of often severe physical punishment received during slavery.

The child welfare system known as child protective services (CPS) is a relatively modern invention. Agencies began operating in the United States in the early 1900s, at about the same time child labor laws were enacted. Since the advent of this public responsibility for child protection, and in particular since the more recent development of adequate systems of oversight and reporting, the awareness and consequential reporting of child abuse has increased.

Data on child welfare involvement for African American children are available for only recent years, but suggest that African American children are overrepresented in the child protective system, are more likely to become wards of the state, and remain in the system longer.

It is important for service providers to know and understand this history if they are to understand, in more than a perfunctory way, the families with whom they aim to work. Subsequent sections of this chapter describe the Starting Early Starting Smart (SESS) project and the ways in which those involved in designing, implementing, and conducting the research related to this national project addressed the specific social and cultural issues that arise when working with African American children and their families.

Starting Early
Starting Smart Experience

The Starting Early Starting Smart demonstration study began four years ago as an early intervention program developed within a national, multisite initiative and evaluation funded by a partnership between SAMHSA's Office of Early Childhood—an agency of the U.S. Department of Health and Human Services—and Casey Family Programs—a private foundation. Although the demonstration phase of the project is coming to a close, the principles and lessons learned continue to be explored through additional SESS projects that seek to further examine the usefulness of SESS intervention and collaboration strategies (e.g., SESS Extended and SESS Prototypes). The major goal of SESS, as it was originally conceived and as it moves forward, is to "develop and disseminate knowledge about how to best integrate and provide behavioral health services to families of young children, increase access and utilization, and thereby improve child, caregiver, and family outcomes" (Hanson, Deere, Lee, Lewin, & Seval, 2001, p. 3). As an overall guiding principle, SESS strives to provide and evaluate services in a culturally relevant and competent context.

The original SESS sites chosen for the demonstration study (see the appendix at the end of this chapter) included five pediatric primary care and seven early childhood education settings in nine states. Ten sites provided services to some African Americans, and four served predominantly African American families; most of those served were particularly disadvantaged in terms of socioeconomic, health, and environmental factors. The sites were chosen because they represented nonstigmatizing places where parents take their children for service.

Although SESS principles and policies continue to be explored in SESS Extension and SESS Prototype programs, the information and data presented in this chapter refer to work done during the demonstration phase of SESS.

SESS programs focused on coordinating behavioral health (substance abuse and mental health) services with early childhood education, primary care, parent-child-family support, and socioeconomic services. At a minimum, SESS offered basic prevention and intervention services, ongoing screening, assessment, and referral options. In addition, direct service activities in each area of behavioral health were tailored to the specific needs of each site's population and setting. The integration of such services into easily accessible, nonthreatening settings where caregivers naturally and regularly take their young children (i.e., colocation) *was* a major step toward increasing appropriate service utilization. Indeed, integration of services is critical to reducing major barriers to accessing care and to improving behavioral health status and other outcomes. Reducing such barriers is especially important for African Americans, who often must overcome racism and their own lack of trust born out of experience.

While such integration has been elusive, through SESS, early childhood education and primary care programs and their partners have developed approaches that were applicable at the local level. Improving access to general health and social services through linkages with public and private sector agencies is a fundamental aspect of integrated services delivery strategies. Because key service personnel from other agencies were usually included in the local steering committees, SESS was able to access services from systems in ways that have not typically been possible. Even when the SESS site did not have a formal arrangement with a particular agency for services, the active involvement of the local steering committee often facilitated access to those services.

Service integration was accomplished through the efforts of a central care coordinator, family advocate, or outreach worker, who (1) provided information regarding available services and ways to access them, (2) made referrals to other agencies, (3) attended referral/intake appointments with families, (4) advocated for families with agencies and the court system, (5) provided transportation to appointments, and (6) assisted with child care while caregivers accessed needed services. Participatory family service planning was a central process that guided these activities, facilitated family empowerment, and made for individually tailored services. Reasonable staff-to-client ratios allowed a level of contact and consistency that facilitated trust and rapport building. Many sites also incorporated the use of a multidisciplinary team of staff members who were available to support care coordination efforts and provide a wider variety of services.

Approaches to Cultural Competence

African Americans have often borne the brunt of inequitable treatment as both service and research participants. Given the primary SESS goal of increasing access and utilization, a major emphasis was placed on cultural relevance for development of intervention and evaluation protocols. One task important to developing cultural competence is to recognize that within the broad structure of any culture there exists a continuum of beliefs, practices, attributes, religions, social context, and political involvement—no one individual or population sample can speak for an entire culture. SESS sites were faced with a dilemma early in the experience of this cross-site study because of the diversity of the families to be served. Specifically, what clinical interventions and research instruments would be culturally appropriate, and with which cultures? It became clear that what might be suitable for African American families might not be so for Asian American or Native American families.

Perhaps of greatest importance from the inception of SESS has been the inclusion, at the national steering committee and local advisory levels, of parent representatives whose voices echo the voices of SESS families. Parent representatives were chosen for their experience as consumers and for their awareness of families' needs and circumstances. These dedicated parents provided insight regarding the most appropriate and effective types of activities to meet families' needs, as well as the structure of activities (timing and location) to be respectful of participants and ensure greater participation. In addition, parents have actively aided in recruiting and retaining families, developing new parenting classes, identifying unmet needs, and providing input at the national level on policies for families with young children.

Services were provided from a relationship-oriented, strength-based perspective that included a focus on the entire family, which was seen as especially effective within African American families. This approach emphasizes building trust as well as assessing and valuing the unique strengths of each family and community. Among the strengths of African American families are a strong connection to the church, commitment to education, strong extended family ties, and a community worldview (Boyd-Franklin, 1989; Kernahan, Bettencourt, & Dorr, 2000; McAdoo, 1998). By understanding family assets, including informal support networks of extended family, friends, neighbors, and church, staff members can focus on positive attributes and fully use the resources available to the families, the program, and the community. Through a strength-based approach, families are able to begin addressing their own issues and become empowered to advocate for themselves and their community.

Consistency, direct communication, and investment of time in interaction with family members, as with any human relationship, prove to be important factors in developing trust between service providers and families. For example, it is imperative that providers maintain appointments as scheduled and fulfill commitments made to participants. This is always necessary in provider/client relationships, but it is particularly important when a family member has reasons to mistrust service providers. Developing a trust-based relationship with clients, and helping to ensure their access to services, often requires an extensive commitment of time. In addition, SESS staff members have found that encouraging family members to freely express their opinions and feelings (e.g., related to actual or perceived racial tension in the program) also communicated acceptance and respect.

Several strategies enabled programs to be responsive to African American families. Sites hired staff representative of the families they served. Outreach and service delivery staff members often lived in or were familiar with the community and were often from the same culture as the families. Some sites hired parents who previously participated in similar service programs and had similar backgrounds and experiences to the families recruited. Hiring staff members who share a common racial and cultural heritage with participants conveys the program's interest in understanding families' concerns and helps to ensure that they are addressed. To develop or strengthen engagement with families, some sites used existing positive relationships that non-SESS agency staff had with families. In one instance, an African American staff member from a collaborating agency agreed to cofacilitate parenting classes with the SESS parent educator, who was European American. The involvement of this individual in the classes more than doubled the level of participation.

SESS programs recognized that diversity within and across cultures made it virtually impossible to exactly match staff backgrounds to each and every family to be served. Families reflect diversity in values and beliefs and the views and expectations they have for themselves, their children, and their providers. Understanding diversity is particularly important when considering a family's perceptions of illness, wellness and health, child rearing practices, and developmental expectations for children. Because of this diversity, cultural sensitivity training is essential. This typically includes education regarding common cultural practices, norms, and beliefs as well as their origins, value, and function within various populations and subpopulations. For example, staff must be knowledgeable about both mainstream parenting practices and beliefs from other perspectives. It is imperative to move away from viewing "difference" as pathology to considering it as a reflection of cultural history and values (U.S. Department of Health and Human Services, 2000a). Another common training practice to facilitate this shift encourages self-exploration that challenges staff to become more consciously aware of their own personal values and beliefs as well as attitudes and/or potential prejudgments they may hold about others.

African American families have a long history of strong relationships with both immediate and extended family members, with the church playing a critical role as part of the extended family. Indeed, researchers from DuBois to West have pointed to the significance of the church and spirituality generally in African American sociocultural and political development. SESS programs took these important cultural factors into account in designing comprehensive service approaches. For example, several programs have specifically considered extended families when planning service delivery, recognizing that families often rely on "natural helpers," who are part of a family's informal network. Using established helping relationships or natural helper networks familiar to the family is an effective means of engaging the community generally and the families for whom services are intended specifically.

Reducing Barriers to Care

SESS programs were designed to address basic health and access issues by reducing barriers to care wherever possible. This is particularly important for African Americans, given the numerous barriers to services and the disparity in health status for both African American adults and children. Strengthening both the providers' understanding of barriers to accessing services as well as the clients' ability to overcome them is critical. Some barriers may include (1) differential or inequitable treatment of African Americans by health and social service providers, (2) the resulting lack of client trust in "the system," (3) inadequate outreach by providers, resulting in families not knowing about service availability or their eligibility to receive services, (4) service fragmentation requiring families to interact with multiple agencies, (5) lack of family economic or concrete resources (e.g., inability to pay for services, need for transportation or child care), (6) lack of the extended time required to access services, and (7) lack of respite care and support for families of young children without threats to custody.

SESS strategies to address some of these barriers have included providing transportation and "meeting families where they are" at children's health care appointments, Head Start or day care centers, homes, and other community settings, such as shelters, churches, and recreation centers. Settings within the community that families perceive as familiar and nonthreatening are specifically chosen for service delivery sites. For example, one program carried out early intervention screening in the home or during the well-child clinic visit, and others offered home-based counseling or parenting services.

When conducted appropriately and sensitively, home visits prove particularly helpful in building trust with African American families. Family members are able to be "in control" of such an exchange because it takes place in their locale, rather than at the service facility. In contrast to center-based activities, family members are more relaxed and open to developing a trusting relationship in the familiar surroundings of their own home. Home visits show respect for the family by placing the burden of time and effort on the worker, rather than on the family. Spending time in the home also allows workers to more fully understand and observe the environment in which the family lives and, therefore, better appreciate the circumstances, needs, and strengths of the family.

A hallmark of cultural competency is being responsive to the needs of the population you are working with. This involves being flexible, creative, and humble. Many SESS sites used creative opportunities to engage families and build informal networks and provide early, preventive services. Some of these creative opportunities included using social gatherings (e.g., neighborhood block parties) and cultural events (e.g., Kwanzaa celebrations), picnics, and meetings as a way for families to informally interact, sometimes in a setting where food was served (either provided by the program or through potluck meals). In these comfortable settings, parents may more readily develop informal support networks and seek casual consultation with mental health and substance abuse providers, often without recognizing any stigma related to the provider's "formal" clinical title.

Another example of the creative use of staff and circumstances occurred at one site at which the substance abuse counselor, with the consent and knowledge of the parent, attended each well-child visit for families for whom substance use had been identified as an issue. The counselor would often work directly with the medical provider and family to identify resources, conduct assessments, make referrals, and maintain contact with families. This allowed the substance abuse worker the opportunity to develop a relationship with families. Particularly for African American families, a trust-based relationship, built over time, is a necessary precursor to service provision. One young mother who had attended these medical visits and who worked regularly with the substance abuse counselor for several months announced at one visit that she was finally ready to meet with a substance abuse counselor—unaware that she had been doing so for several months.

Some sites used both informal networks and specific curricula. When curricula were used to guide services they were carefully chosen and offered with flexible scheduling. Creative group arrangements were devised to make the most effective use of the curricula selected or developed specifically for the SESS programs; in particular, grouping caregivers with similar experiences and backgrounds was an approach used to facilitate participation and peer support. For example, one site had an ongoing "Grandmothers' Support Group" composed of African American women who were all primary care-givers for their grandchildren, another offered "Wait A Minute" (WAM!) stress reduction groups for mothers, and other sites designed men's activities to involve fathers.

The "Effective Black Parenting Program" (Center for Substance Abuse Program [CSAP] and Office of Juvenile Justice and Delinquency Prevention [OJJDP], 2000) was adapted by one site and the title changed to "Pyramids to Success" when participating parents disliked the original title. The African American parents objected to "Effective Black Parenting" because they felt that the title implied that African American parents need more help with parenting than other racial groups (Sims, 2000). Such feedback from parents and staff members was critical to the ongoing process of adapting interventions to be more culturally relevant and competent. Another site used the "Strengthening Multi-Ethnic Families and Communities Program" (CSAP/OJJDP, 2000), while others have adapted or combined curricula by eliminating or incorporating particular elements. One site focusing on African American substance-using parents employed the "Engaging Moms" program, an innovative and culturally adapted approach to treatment engagement that uses family and other significant support systems to overcome barriers to treatment (Dakof et al., 2001; Quille & Dakof, 1999; Szapocznik et al., 1988).

To maintain a comfortable climate for families in service facilities, SESS used resources (i.e., books, videos, posters, pictures) and decor that were contemporary and reflected the community. Sensitive to the educational experience of some African American adults living in poverty, program literature was written using style and language that met appropriate literacy needs. Additionally, many sites had important information read to participants or read along with them to make sure everything was clearly understood and any questions or concerns addressed.

Evaluation and Research

The evaluation component of SESS emphasized the need to pilot test the data collection protocol with representative families prior to putting it in place. An even more innovative aspect has been the participation and recognition of parents in the process of developing presentations and publications regarding SESS service models and findings. In addition, some sites felt it was important to find a way to offer stipends to parent representatives to reflect the value and appreciation of their hard work and input.

The cultural relevance of data collection instruments in behavioral health research is essential to ensuring the relevance and validity of such research. Therefore, when selecting instruments for local site evaluation and cross-site research, SESS made an effort to choose culturally relevant instruments related to outcome areas of interest. This was a significant challenge, since many commonly used instruments have not been validated using a sample of the diverse racial and ethnic groups served. In addition, although some studies designed to ensure the validity of commonly used instruments include African Americans in the total study sample, the proportion of those included in the sample often reflects the national average, thereby resulting in a loss of the significant differences among subgroups. Indeed, no instrument had been validated for all of the groups represented, so instruments that had been normed for as many of the groups represented as possible, and that would yield critical information to address the SESS research questions, were selected.

The SESS steering committee has included a parent representative in review and interpretation of research findings in order to make certain that their unique perspective is taken into account and to help ensure the relevance of the findings and their interpretation. Inclusion of families in this endeavor serves as a way to keep the findings grounded in the context of the broader socioeconomic and cultural perspective of participating families.

Aware that many of the African American and other families SESS served have felt chronically undervalued, SESS sites believed that it is important to convey value and appreciation to families for their participation in the fairly extensive data collection. To that end, as compensation for participating in the research, families were offered a variety of stipends (e.g., gift certificates, clothing, museum passes, and books). In selecting these stipends, SESS staff took into account where the families lived and shopped, and sometimes engaged them in the process of deciding which were the most appropriate stipends. Finally, it should be noted that SESS programs have spent four years collecting data in a cross-site research study to evaluate the efficacy of the service integration approach, and more definitive outcome information is forthcoming. The following section provides descriptive and baseline data regarding family violence, substance abuse, child welfare, and mental health as they relate to African American families in SESS.

A Descriptive Profile of African American Participants in SESS

As discussed earlier, social problems confronting African Americans may be uniquely tied to historical antecedents of slavery and concomitant prejudice and discrimination. While neither SESS nor any other social program can erase past injustices against African Americans, nor can SESS fully address the current social-political climate that includes racism and prejudice, a major goal of the initiative was to bring together diverse systems—families, social service agencies, mental health providers, schools, medical providers, and others—to improve the well-being of children who are often the unintended victims of such past and present racially based injustices. While the previous section described the general SESS approach to intervention, this section presents descriptive baseline data for the 1,311 African American SESS caregivers and their children regarding substance, mental health, family violence, and child welfare status. It should be noted that unless indicated otherwise, the data cited here refer to the sample of African American caregivers and their children. Where possible, and available, current national data are presented.

To date, the program has reached over 3,000 children and families and is in the process of evaluating program effectiveness for 2,908 caregiver-child participants in the evaluation, 45% (n = 1,311) of whom are African American. Such representation of African Americans in studies of this nature is rare and provides an excellent opportunity to examine more fully the complex factors placing African American children and families at risk for substance abuse and mental illness. The study also enables the exploration of family and community resources available to African American families in SESS and how best to tailor programs to include these resources.

CAREGIVER SUBSTANCE ABUSE

To assess alcohol, tobacco, and other substance abuse among SESS parents, the Addiction Severity Index was administered. This commonly used assessment instrument includes questions related to past 30-day use of alcohol, tobacco, marijuana, and cocaine and multiple substance use. Overall, 7.6% of caregivers admitted having an alcohol abuse problem, and 9.6% a problem with illegal drug use. Eight percent of African American caregivers indicated they had used alcohol, 12% tobacco, 4% marijuana, 1% cocaine, and 2% multiple substances. It should be noted that these self-report methods typically result in an underestimate of actual drug use. When asked about substance abuse among other family members (i.e., biological parent and grandparents), 46% percent reported having a family history of substance abuse problems. Additionally, 11% of caregivers indicated they had a family member who had been involved in the criminal justice system in the past year (e.g., arrested, probation, or parole), and one might speculate as to how much of this involvement was drug related.

CAREGIVER MENTAL HEALTH

The importance of mental health needs in young children and their families has become heightened in recent years (U.S. Department of Health and Human Services, 2000b). The most recent surgeon general's report specifically addresses the unique relationship between and among race, culture, and mental health (U.S. Public Health Service, 2001).

Research is increasingly available to demonstrate the association between mental health problems in caregivers and child mental health outcomes (Dubowitzl et al., 2001). There is also a solid research base on the impact of family, cultural, societal, and nonfamily environmental influences on child mental health (Seccombe, 2000).

Scholars have long recognized the need to examine the environmental contingencies among African Americans that lead to poor mental health. Factors such as stress associated with racism, chronic unemployment or underemployment, and salary inequities among African Americans may not necessarily lead to a diagnosable mental disorder, but may create feelings of despair, low self-esteem, and powerlessness. Such feelings can lead to increased rates of substance abuse, mental illness, crime, child abuse, and homicide (Gullotta, Hampton, Senatore, & Eismann, 1998). Recognizing this, SESS services include assessments of caregiver mental health (e.g., emotional distress, somatic symptomatology, suicidal ideation) as well as the mental health status of other family members. Psychological symptoms were measured using the Brief Symptom Inventory (BSI) (Derogatis & Spencer, 1999), in which respondents rate the frequency of several psychological symptoms in the past week. For all SESS caregivers, about 23% had an indicated need for mental health services. Among African American caregivers, about 3% indicated they had recently been "moderately bothered" or "bothered quite a bit" by psychological symptoms. Eight percent indicated having at least one family member with a mental health problem.

FAMILY VIOLENCE

Information, albeit somewhat controversial, was presented previously in this chapter regarding family violence among African American families. In all cultures, children who witness or are subjected to varied forms of violence are forced to endure its adverse effects, which can include behavioral problems, delinquency, anxiety, depression, low self-esteem, and lower levels of social competence (Deater-Deckard & Dodge, 1997; Wolak & Finkelhor, 1998).

African American children have been found to be more likely to die as a result of child abuse when compared to European American children (McLoyd, 1990), which may be a factor related to access to early intervention and health services. To discern any differences between the African American children and their caregivers and others involved in SESS, two measurement instruments were used: (1) the Conflict Tactics Scale (CTS) (Straus, 1989), used to examine conflict in family interactions, and (2) the Parental Discipline Methods Inventory (PDMI), adapted for SESS, which detailed caregiver use of disciplinary strategies with their children.

The CTS measures the frequency of behaviors used in resolving conflict between the caregiver and a significant other in the child's environment. It includes a physical violence scale. Caregivers report the frequency of their own use of specified behaviors as well as their perception of the use of behaviors by their significant other. Fourteen percent of the African American SESS caregivers reported the presence of physical violence "20 times or more" during the past year to resolve interpartner conflict.

On the PDMI, caregivers specify the nature and frequency of disciplinary responses during the past week. The PDMI is divided into three scales, Negative Discipline (e.g., spanking), Appropriate Discipline (e.g., taking away a privilege), and Positive Reinforcement (e.g., praise child). While most caregivers endorsed Appropriate Discipline and Positive Reinforcement as their preferred strategies, approximately 15% indicated they "sometimes" or "almost always" used Negative Discipline strategies.

CHILD WELFARE

According to several reports, African Americans are disproportionately more likely to receive Temporary Assistance for Needy Families (TANF), remain on it longer, and have greater recidivism rates compared to Whites (McPhatter, 1997; Savner, 2000). Much of this is attributable to inequities in employment opportunities, limited education and work experience, and a larger number of children to support. Further complicating this is the perception by some African Americans of being differentially and unfairly treated, of receiving punitive rather than instructive services by caseworkers, which creates barriers to needed services (Keller & McDade, 2000).

Among African American SESS caregivers, 34% have not completed high school (versus 16% nationally), 55% are unemployed (versus 6% nationally), 38.4% receive public assistance, and 27% have an income per household member of less than $100 per month. Family stability patterns within the last year reveal 7.3% of respondents had been homeless, and 1% had children placed in foster care. Sixty-seven percent of the African American SESS children live in households headed by single mothers, compared to 25% nationally. These statistics are consistent with sociodemographic factors associated with poor physical, mental, and behavioral health outcomes in children (McLoyd, Cauce, Takeuchi, & Wilson, 2000).

SERVICE BARRIERS

Although low-income African American families may experience many difficulties and would likely benefit from information, counseling, or support, many do not seek aid from mental health/social service agencies or schools (Keller & McDade, 2000). Parents may not obtain available resources for their children for a number of reasons, including lack of knowledge about eligibility, lack of means to access resources, lack of trust in the system, or belief that they will be belittled and ridiculed (McPhatter, 1997). As the extant literature and these preliminary data suggest, many African American families face several social and economic disadvantages. SESS caregivers are struggling to raise their children under less than adequate circumstances, with relatively low incomes, low education levels, and many single-parent homes.

Given these multiple challenges, it is important to understand service needs and barriers from the caregivers' perspective. Over half of SESS African American caregivers (54%) reported needing at least two social services, yet not receiving them. Twenty-seven percent reported barriers to receiving physical, mental, and substance abuse services, while 46% reported barriers to other services (e.g., job training). Approximately 20% of barriers were described as internal (i.e., lack of information about resources, inaccurate information about behavioral health conditions, or reluctance to use outside help), and 13% as external (i.e., lack of resources, such as insurance or transportation, high expense for care, or dissatisfaction with available services).

FAMILY RESILIENCY

Despite statistics showing disparities in health, child welfare, and service access and utilization between African Americans and other U.S. racial and ethnic groups, many in the African American community rely upon indigenous networks of mutual aid and support (McAdoo, 1998). This support may buffer the negative consequences associated with such disparities. In an effort to examine community resources available to caregivers and children, SESS asked participants to indicate sources of support in their communities from which they sought assistance, including family members, friends, church, food banks, government agencies, and private organizations. Sixty-one percent reported having at least one other caregiver available to assist with child care needs, and 36% reported seeking help from at least one resource available to them in the past month.

As highlighted, African American SESS families are facing many challenges often associated with negative outcomes for young children, such as poor physical, mental, and behavioral health. The data presented suggest African American families have multiple needs and must negotiate various service systems to meet these needs. However, it appears that many do not have sufficient information regarding service availability or are dissatisfied with the services that are available. Often services are fragmented, not accessible to families, and lack sensitivity to cultural factors that may distinguish African American clients from others served. To address some of these challenges, a core feature of SESS is the colocation and integration of these services within community-based settings that serve young children and their families.

Starting Early Starting Smart projects have learned valuable lessons. The next section highlights some of the practices and policies that have served the African American families in SESS well. In addition, recommendations are offered based on those lessons.

Practice and Research Recommendations

SESS has found a number of keys to successfully engage African American families in prevention and intervention services for substance abuse, mental health, family violence, and child welfare. These keys, which were detailed earlier in this chapter, facilitate improved outcomes for families and are summarized below.

DEVELOPING AND MAINTAINING STRONG, SUPPORTIVE RELATIONSHIPS

Whether engaging in prevention, intervention, or research, the foundation for success is built on strong relationships with participants. As previously stated, many African Americans may be cautious about entering into such relationships, so the development of strong, supportive relationships is even more critical. To facilitate this, programs and practitioners should:

- involve family members in planning, ongoing consultation, and monitoring of services;
- hire staff members who reflect the demographics of participants, when possible;
- provide formal staff training that encourages education about the African American culture, cultural competence, and a strength-based rather than deficit-based model;
- work collaboratively with families to focus and build on family strengths;
- earn the trust of participants by keeping appointments, fulfilling commitments, and encouraging participants to express their opinions and feelings;
- select interventions and resources (e.g., books, videos, decor) that are culturally relevant to African American families;
- select evaluation outcomes and instruments that are validated for African Americans;
- select culturally relevant participation incentives that will be valued by participants;
- involve natural helpers (e.g., extended family, church members) to strengthen client-staff relationships and value those important in the lives of African American participants; and
- maintain reasonable staff-to-client ratios that allow adequate time to develop meaningful helping relationships.

REDUCING BARRIERS TO SERVICE UTILIZATION

- Programs should find ways to integrate services for African Americans. Colocating services and/or staff is one way to ensure rapid identification of needs and referral for services.
- Coordinate behavioral health, family violence, child welfare, and other services through use of full-time staff, thereby removing many barriers to service utilization.
- Effective coordination among behavioral health, family violence, child welfare, and substance abuse requires consistent contact (via conference calls, face-to-face meetings, etc.) so that relationships forged at the inception of the collaboration are maintained and supported.
- Clear, formal agreements between community collaborators are needed, with buy-in from those who are in a position to make decisions, in order to facilitate coordinated services.
- Providing services to African Americans in naturalistic situations (e.g., home visits, day care programs, primary care settings, churches) will improve service utilization and engagement.

Future Directions

SESS has identified a number of policy issues that should be addressed.

COLLABORATION AND INTEGRATION OF SERVICES: MORE THAN JUST JARGON

On the local, state, and federal levels, integration of services should become a top priority. Too often, workers in the fields of substance abuse, mental health, family violence, child welfare, and even emergency services work independently of one another. It is vital that all of these services be coordinated throughout family assessment and treatment. For example, at one site a monthly multidisciplinary team (MDT) meeting is held, where the Head Start teacher, school nurse, Head Start speech therapist and psychologist, along with the Head Start family services worker and SESS family support worker, assess and triage families. SESS sites have found that strengthening collaboration among the various agencies and staff members involved with African American children and their families is critical to ensuring improved involvement of family members in these services. Collaboration at the intervention level (e.g., in the classroom setting, the hospital unit), the program level (e.g., the school, the hospital, or the network of Head Start Centers or multi-institutional health provider), or the broad system level (e.g., the community and state in which the program is located), while not without difficulties, is possible.

Moreover, service integration should be the responsibility of all those involved in planning and providing services, not just a role assigned to a case manager. When more formal collaborations are not possible, therapists and case managers should seek out service-level workers from other agencies to coordinate approaches. Program administrators should strive to develop ongoing links with other programs to more effectively serve families through the development of coordinated care. Federal and state administrators, working in coordination with local agency directors and administrators, should initiate collaboration among substance abuse, mental health, family violence, child protection, education, and other social services. Many African Americans who need to interface with multiple systems are receiving services from only one area of these interrelated domains. Other families find they receive (sometimes duplicated) services from more than one system, but there is no coordination. Various systems may adopt strategies that unwittingly work at cross purposes with other needs of the family. Only through adequate integration of services will families receive the best possible care. Integration is not easy. Many factors work against its practice; however, SESS sites have seen it work!

Coordinated services should become line items in public budgets. This is particularly true for many African Americans who depend on public services and for whom financial barriers to care are significant impediments to treatment. Continuing to have these services dependent on public and private funding sources whose research or programmatic interests vary over time, and whose funds may not be available at critical times for the focus population, is detrimental to both those served and society at large. It is also, quite simply, not cost effective.

Flexible funding is of paramount importance—people are not square pegs and the holes are not always round. One of the most significant barriers to integrated services is the inflexibility of funding. Many SESS families required services that did not fit proscribed funding categories. For example, SESS staff identified specific funding needs that were often not available, including payment for medications and for transition from one service system to another. In some cases, because of the relationships developed with community providers through ongoing collaboration, SESS was able to arrange for agencies to pay for services not typically covered. In other instances, SESS persuaded providers to braid, rather than blend, funding and services. In this "braided services" model, each agency maintains its own responsibilities and funding stream, but weaves services with those of other agencies. The resulting pattern of services is woven like a rope, with each component distinct, but tightly interlaced with other services into a stronger unit. These integrated, braided approaches allow the development of wraparound services and fill typical service gaps.

Families in crisis often need respite or supportive family services, but may be required to relinquish custody in order to receive those services. Although the health of adult caregivers can have a direct impact on the social and emotional well-being of children, health care, including mental health services, is often available for children but not for adults in the household. Comprehensive parent education and substance abuse and mental health services that include marital and family counseling are often difficult or impossible to find for families with limited income. Funding for substance abuse and mental health programs, family violence, and child welfare should be expanded to ensure access to family therapists and other providers who, irrespective of discipline, are trained to work with families in a culturally competent framework. These providers should have the capacity to meet the needs of both children and adult family members in a variety of settings. Policy makers at all levels must engage in serious, focused deliberations to identify alternative approaches to the extant vertical and categorical funding that so severely impedes access to care.

INCREASING AVAILABILITY OF TRAINED SERVICE PROVIDERS

Several SESS sites found that there were few therapists trained in children's mental health, and fewer still in infant mental health (i.e., 0–3 years). Some SESS sites provided training for therapists and counselors who work with families of young children, thus enhancing the system's capacity to deliver services to this population. However, SESS only met the needs of certain programs in a limited number of cities. There is an urgent need to expand the pool of professionals, particularly from underrepresented populations, who are trained in early childhood issues.

Services, prevention education, and positive support must be available for staff members who work in Head Start and other early child programs as well as in primary care settings. These are the true front-line workers, staff members who most frequently bridge the gap between parents and professional, educational, health, and social service delivery personnel. They serve in demanding, high-stress positions that frequently pay little and even more frequently lack the benefits that allow workers to access behavioral health care for themselves or their families.

NEWLY NORMED INSTRUMENTS ARE NEEDED

The SESS sample was quite diverse, including not only multiple racial groups, but also subcultures within each racial/ethnic group. As noted in the introduction, 6% of self-identified African-Americans in the 2000 census are foreign born. Not surprisingly, SESS African American families were represented by those who had generations of ancestors who were U.S. citizens and by those who were themselves recent immigrants from many different nations and continents. More inquiry should be directed toward understanding nuances of culture, using both qualitative and quantitative research. Instruments, both commonly used and new, must be normed with a wide range of racial and ethnic groups and, if necessary, adapted to ensure reliability and validity. To accurately determine the cultural relevance and validity of instruments, it is necessary to conduct a separate validation study for each ethnic group for the appropriate age and gender. It is through these means, or by developing new, relevant instruments, that it will be possible to generate urgently needed information.

COST ANALYSES

While SESS posits that integration of services leads to increased utilization of services, it is important to undertake research to determine which aspects of integration of services are most efficacious and which are most cost effective. Given the limited resources available for health and social services, such studies are essential to advocating for increased funding from policy makers. In addition to studies that determine the overall cost-effectiveness of substance abuse, mental health, family violence, and child welfare services, research should evaluate, separately, the cost-effectiveness of those services for African Americans. One cannot assume that results for the general population will be the same for all groups.

Starting Early Starting Smart offers many lessons learned about how to successfully integrate services for African Americans and the positive outcomes derived from integration and collaboration; however, there is much yet to be done. Pursuing these future directions can enable us to become even more sensitive and responsive to the needs and preferences of African Americans and thus become more effective in addressing the challenges of substance abuse, mental health, family violence, and child welfare in the African American community.

References

Behrendt, S. (1999). The transatlantic slave trade. In K. A. Appiah & H. L. Gates, Jr. (Eds.), *Africana: The encyclopedia of the African and African American experience* (pp. 1865–1877). New York: Basic Civitas Books.

Borowsky, S. J., Rubenstein, L., Meredith, L., Camp, P., Jackson-Triche, M., & Wells, K. (2000). Who is at risk of nondetection of mental health problems in primary care? *Journal of General Internal Medicine, 15*(6), 381–388.

Boyd-Franklin, N. (1989). *Black families in therapy.* New York: Guilford Press.

Carter-Pokras, O., & Woo, V. (1999). Health profile of racial and ethnic minorities in the United States. *Ethnicity and Health, 4*(3), 117–121.

Center for Substance Abuse Prevention [CSAP] & Office of Juvenile Justice and Delinquency Prevention [OJJDP]. (2000). *Strengthening America's families: Model family programs for substance abuse and delinquency prevention.* Rockville, MD: U.S. Department of Health and Human Services.

Dakof, G., Quille, T. J., Tejeda, M. J., Bandstra, E. S., & Szapocznik, J., (2000). *Engaging cocaine dependent mothers into drug abuse treatment.* Unpublished manuscript, submitted to *Journal of Consulting and Clinical Psychology.*

Deater-Deckard, K. & Dodge, K. (1997). Externalizing behavior problems and discipline revisited: Nonlinear effects and variation by culture, context and gender. *Psychological Inquiry, 8,* 161-175.

Derogatis, L., & Spencer, P. (1999). *The Brief Symptom Inventory: Administration, scoring, and procedures manual.* Baltimore, MD: Clinical Psychometric Research.

Dubowitz, H., Black, M., Kerr, M., Morrell, T., Hussey, J., Everson, M., Starr, R., Jr., (2001). Type and timing of mothers' victimization: Effects on mothers and children. *Pediatrics, 107*(4), 728–736.

Gullotta, T., Hampton, R., Senatore, V., & Eismann, M. (1998). When pap gets too handy with his hick'ry: A selected literary and social history of substance abuse and child abuse. In R. Hampton (Ed.), *Substance abuse, family violence, and child welfare: Bridging perspectives* (pp. 1–17). Thousand Oaks, CA: Sage.

Hacker, A. (1992). *Two nations: Black and white separate, hostile, unequal.* New York: Scribner's.

Hanson, L., Deere, D., Lee, C., Lewin, A., & Seval, C. (2000). *Key principles in providing integrated behavioral health services for young children and their families: The Starting Early Starting Smart experience.* Washington: DC: Casey Family Programs and the U.S. Department of Health and Human Services, Substance Abuse and Mental Services Administration.

Herrstein, R. J., & Murray, C. (1998) *The bell curve: Intelligence and class structure in American life.* New York: Free Press.

Keller, J., & McDade, K. (2000). Attitudes of low-income parents toward seeking help with parenting: Implications for practice. *Child Welfare, 79*(3), 285–302.

Kernahan, C., Bettencourt, A., & Dorr, N. (2000). Benefits of allocentrism for the subjective well-being of African-Americans. *Journal of Black Psychology, 26*(2), 181–193.

McAdoo, H. P. (1998). African American families: Strengths and realities. In H. McCubbin, E. Thompson, A. Thompson, & J. Futrell (Eds.), *Resiliency in African American families* (pp. 17–30). Thousand Oaks, CA: Sage.

McLoyd, V. (1990). The impact of economic hardship on Black families and children: Psychological distress, parenting, and socioemotional development. *Child Development, 61,*311–346.

McLoyd, V., Cauce, A., Takeuchi, D., & Wilson, L. (2000). Marital processes and parental socialization in families of color: A decade review of research. *Journal of Marriage and the Family, 62*(4), 1070–1093.

McPhatter, A. (1997). Cultural competence in child welfare: What is it? How do we achieve it? What appears without it? *Child Welfare, 76*(1), 255–278.

National Family Violence Survey. (1985). Durham: University of New Hampshire, Family Research Laboratory.

National Household Survey on Drug Abuse [NHSDA]. (2001). Washington, DC: Substance Abuse and Mental Health Services Administration.

Pinderhughes, E., Dodge, K., & Bales, J. (2000). Discipline responses: Influences of parents' socioeconomic status, ethnicity, beliefs about parenting, stress, and cognitive-emotional processes. *Journal of Family Psychology, 14*, 380-400.

Quille, T., & Dakof, G. (1999). *Helping drug addicted mothers enter and remain in treatment: An intervention manual.* Unpublished manual, University of Miami School of Medicine.

Raj, A. (1999). Prevalence and correlates of relationship abuse among a community-based sample of low-income African American women. *Violence Against Women, 5*, 272–292.

Savner, S. (2000). Welfare reform and racial/ethnic minorities: The question to ask. *Poverty and Race, 9*(4). Retrieved July 18, 2005, from http:www.prrac.org/display-newsletter-php

Seccombe, K. (2000). Families in poverty in the 1990s: Trends, causes, consequences, and lessons learned. *Journal of Marriage and the Family, 62*(4), 1094–1113.

Sims, B. E. (2000). Fostering positive parent-child interaction through family support. *Zero to Three 20*(3), 37–40.

Strakowski, S., Hawkins, J., & Keck, P. (1997). The effects of race and information variance on disagreement between psychiatric emergency service and research diagnoses in first-episode psychosis. *Journal of Clinical Psychiatry. 58*(10), 457–463.

Straus, M. (1989). *Conflict Tactics Scale.* Durban: Family Research Laboratory, University of New Hampshire.

Substance Abuse and Mental Health Services Administration [SAMHSA]. (2001). 2000 National Household Survey on Drug Abuse. Retrieved July 17, 2000, from http://www.samsha.gov/oas/NHSDA/2001/chapter2. and chapter3.htm

Szapocznik, J., Perez-Vidal, A., Brickman, A. L., Foote, F. H., Santisteban, D., Hervis, O., & Kurtines, W. M. (1988). Engaging adolescent drug abusers and their families in treatment: A strategic structural systems approach. *Journal of Consulting and Clinical Psychology, 56*(4), 552–557.

Thomas, A., & Sillen, S. (1979). *Racism and psychiatry.* Secaucus, NJ: Citadel Press.

U.S. Bureau of the Census. (2001). Selected social characteristics of the population, by region and race. Retrieved July 23, 2001, from http://www.census.gov.htm

U.S. Department of Health and Human Services. (1999). *Substance abuse a national challenge: Prevention, treatment and research at DHHS.* Washington, DC: Author.

U.S. Department of Health and Human Services. (2000a). *Substance Abuse: Healthy People 2010: Understanding and Improving Health*, 2nd ed. Washington, DC: U.S. Government Printing Office, 32–33.

U.S. Department of Health and Human Services. (2000b). Report of the surgeon general's conference on children's mental health: A national action agenda. Retrieved July 17, 2001, from http://www.surgeongeneral.gov/cmh/chi/dreport.htm

U.S. Public Health Service. (2001). *Mental health: Culture, race, and ethnicity a supplement to mental health: A report of the surgeon general.* Rockville, MD: U.S. Department of Health and Human Services, Substance Abuse and Mental Health Services Administration, Center for Mental Health Services.

Wolak, J., & Finkelhor, D. (1998). Children exposed to partner violence. In J. Jasinski & L. Williams (Eds.), *Partner violence: A comprehensive review of 20 years of research* (pp. 73–112). Thousand Oaks, CA: Sage.

Appendix
Starting Early Starting Smart Grant Sites

STUDY SITE	PRINCIPAL INVESTIGATOR	PROJECT DIRECTOR	LOCAL RESEARCHER
Data coordinating center			
EMT Associates, Inc. Folsom, CA	Joel Phillips	J. Fred Springer, PhD	J. Fred Springer, PhD
Primary care sites:			
Boston Medical	Carol Seval, RN, LMHC	Carol Seval, RN, LMHC	Ruth Rose-Jacobs, ScD
Casey Family Partners Spokane, WA	Christopher Blodgett, PhD	Mary Ann Murphy, MS	Christopher Blodgett, PhD
University of Miami Miami, FL	Connie E. Morrow, PhD	K. Lori Hanson, PhD	Emmalee S. Bandstra, MD April L. Vogel, PhD
University of Missouri- Columbia, MO	Carol J. Evans, PhD	Robyn S. Boustead, MPA	Carol J. Evans, PhD
University of New Mexico, Albuquerque, NM	Andy Hsi, MD, MPH	Bebeann Bourchard, MEd	Richard Boyle, PhD
Early childhood sites:			
Asian American Recovery Services, Inc., San Francisco, CA	Davis Y. Ja, PhD	Elizabeth E. Iida, Dr. PH	Elizabeth E. Iida, Dr. PH
Child Development Inc., Russellville, AR	JoAnn Williams, MEd	Carol Amundson Lee, MA, LPC, MCC	Mark C. Edwards, PhD University of Arkansas for Medical Sciences
Children's National Medical Center, Washington, DC	Jill G. Joseph, MD, PhD	Amy Lewin, PhD	Michelle J. C. New, PhD
Johns Hopkins University Baltimore, MD	Philip J. Leaf, PhD	Jocelyn, Turner-Musa, PhD	Philip J. Leaf, PhD
State of Nevada Div. Child & Family Services, Las Vegas, NV	Christa R. Peterson, PhD	Laurel L. Swetnam, MA, MS	Margaret P. Freese, PhD, MPH
The Tulalip Tribes Beda Chalh, Marysville, WA	Linda L. Jones, BA	Linda L. Jones, BA	Claudia Long, PhD University of New Mexico
The Women's Treatment Center, Chicago, IL	Jewell Oates, PhD	Dianne Stansberry, BA, CSADP	Victor J. Bernstein, PhD University of Chicago

Part 3

Latin Americans

8

The Changing Latino Family

ROBERT ORTEGA

Introduction

Across the United States, as indicated by the 2000 decennial census, the Latino or Hispanic American population exceeded census growth rate estimates by over 3 million people, which may be conservative when one considers the strong likelihood that a number of Latinos were not counted in the 2000 census. Coinciding with the rapid growth in the Latino population is the number of Latinos who are either born into or (im)migrate into the United States. (Enchautigui, 1995; "Hispanic Households," 1997). Perhaps most troubling is the relatively slow emergence of studies reflecting upon the health, mental health, and social problems among Latinos that are often associated with conditions of poverty (Alaniz, Cartmill, & Parker, 1998; Gutierrez, Yeakley, & Ortega, 2001). The dramatic increase in the Latino population, the large and growing number of Latino families living in poverty, and clinical evidence that a greater number of Latino families are in need of victim and social services underscore the urgent need to closely monitor family safety and security in Latino communities.

Numerous concerns are raised about conceptualizing the problems, identifying the population, and distinguishing cultural contexts to better understand the dynamic interplay of risk, protection, and resiliency processes in Latino culture. In this chapter, we review these concerns relevant to substance/alcohol use and family violence and consider implications for treatment, policy, and future research.

Countability and Accountability

Understanding family violence among Latinos begins with the challenge of "countability," or our ability to count the number of Latino families affected by violence. A primary barrier to this lack of countability is locating Latino or Hispanic membership in race-reported studies. Latinos typically find themselves aggregated in "White/not Hispanic," "Black/not Hispanic," or "Other" racial categories when victim data are reported because of their ethnic rather than race status (Dugan & Apel, 2003; Ortega, Guillean, & Gutierrez-Najera, 1996). Hence, knowledge about the prevalence and incidence of family violence among Latinos is essentially poorly understood.

The terms "Latino" and "Hispanic" are usually based on physical appearance, and the term "Hispanic," although coined by the government for census purposes, has taken on a life of its own. The use of the term "Latino" is problematic since most studies fail to differentiate Latinos based on ancestry or diverse historical, economic, political, religious, language, geographic region, immigrant status, generation, and other important social characteristics. Studies instead give the impression that Latinos are a monolithic ethnic group. Typically, the generic term "Latino" refers to individuals of Mexican, Puerto Rican, Cuban, Dominican, and Central and South American ancestries.

Latinos or Hispanics are heavily concentrated in certain areas of the Southwest, West Coast, East Coast, Midwest, and South. Some states, such as North Carolina, Georgia, Iowa, and Utah, have witnessed significant growth in areas where Latinos were once relatively obscure. A national focus, which aggregates data from all 50 states, dilutes the numbers as well as the attention that must be drawn to those states and areas within states where the vast majority of Latino victims of family violence reside.

The lack of clarity and relative diffusion poses a serious challenge to our ability to accurately count and account for Latino victimization in family violence. As families move from their home to various types of protective custody, this limitation presents a serious roadblock to understanding the extensiveness of the problems and in developing and implementing needed support. For example, in a 1995 study focusing on domestic violence among Latinas in New York City, race- and ethnic-specific domestic violence statistics were not accessible. At the same time, information from the New York State Spanish Domestic Violence Hotline indicated a more than doubling of calls to report domestic violence between 1994 and 1995 (from 192 to 425) (Rivera, 1997–1998). Without accessible data, the Latino community remains invisible, and cultural- and language-consistent services will remain absent.

Inaccessible data also have implications for policy development and enactment. Rivera (1995), for example, argues that the domestic violence movement and the adoption of the Violence Against Women Act (VAWA) in 1994 did not reflect the views and priorities of the Latino community—the population that has been historically absent or excluded from the legislative process. Consequently, not taking their voices into account may actually place Latinas in danger since current policy has had minimal impact on institutional racism and patriarchal structures that await Latina victims. Their absence (and the absence of data on Latinos) challenges fundamental assumptions about appropriate levels of funding, target populations and eligibility requirements, types of services to provide, training requirements for workers, and direct service practices through which effective services can be delivered. It suggests that current policy considerations may be ignoring the complexity of needs necessary for an effective and culturally relevant system of care.

Incidence and Prevalence

Current evidence reflecting upon substance/alcohol use and family violence among Latinos has produced mixed results. Some evidence suggests that Latinos are affected in great numbers, exhibit some of the highest rates of violent behavior toward their spouses, and bear a disproportionate share of violence-related morbidity and mortality, although Latino subgroups are found to vary markedly (Champion, 1996; Jasinski, 1998; O'Keefe, 1994; Rodriguez & Brindis, 1995). Straus and Smith (1990), for example, found that the rate of spousal abuse was 54% greater than for non-Hispanic Whites. When controlling for ethnic differences, Puerto Ricans who drank were five times more likely to hit their wives than their nondrinking counterparts (Kaufman Kantor 1997). There is also some evidence that frequency of intoxication of the male partner is a strong predictor of wife battering among immigrant Latinos (Perilla, Bakeman, & Norris, 1994; Repack, 1997). Among the Latino migrant population, one of every four Latina farmworkers participating in a nationwide study reported having been physically or sexually abused by a husband, boyfriend, or companion. The strongest predictors of domestic violence among this population were drug/alcohol use by the respondent's partner, pregnancy, and migrant status (Van Hightower, Gorton, & DeMoss, 2000).

For the most part, incidence and prevalence rates of family violence among Latinos are reportedly similar to Whites, or else results are inconclusive. This is generally the case despite the high number of risk factors for relationship abuse among Latinos (Caetano, Schafer, Clark, Curandi, & Rasberry, 2000; Dugan & Apel, 2003; Hamby, 2000; Perilla, 1999; Rivera, 1994). It is worth repeating here that the data used to report these findings typically do not do well in distinguishing Latinos from non-Hispanic racial categories. In addition, researchers focusing on Latinos call for making a clear distinction among Latino subgroups since differences do appear among the various risk and protective processes that either exacerbate or buffer family violence (Kaufman Kantor, 1997; Kaufman Kantor, Jasinski, & Aldarondo, 1994; Rivera, 1994).

Conceptual Challenges

A review of the literature produces a multidimensional understanding of substance/ alcohol use and family violence among Latinos. Sophisticated analyses have been called for, to explore the complicated interaction of variables such as race/ethnicity, social class, culture, social networks, and communitywide variables such as resource deprivation, neighborhood effects, family disruption, and other socioeconomic factors. The lingering effects of family violence are also explained in the historical oppression and violence that Latinos and Latinas experienced in their own country, during the process of (im)migration, and as part of their acculturation to mainstream society.

Cultural explanations linking substance/alcohol use and family violence have been explored, although such explanations risk the possibility of rationalizing violence against women where cultural norms and values may be used to deny, minimize, rename, or normalize violence against women (Beasley & Thomas, 1994; Marcus, 1994). This approach also misrepresents differing worldviews expressed among Latino subgroups as if suggesting that they are uniform and undifferentiated (Hampton, Carillo, & Kim, 1998).

What follows is a discussion of current linkages between alcohol/substance use and family violence, which examines Latino cultural scripts, acculturation, the family experience, and systemic issues described as barriers to help seeking and treatment of victims and batterers. This review is not intended to ignore the risks and overgeneralizations but serves to draw on current conceptualizations as a summary understanding of a complex interaction between alcohol/substance use and family violence, from a Latino cultural perspective.

Latino Acculturation and Cultural Scripts

Conceptualizations and research methods that reflect upon diverse cultural socialization and acculturative experiences essentially suggest that Latino family life not only offers order and consistency but may increase tension and hostility especially when juxtaposed onto mainstream U.S. culture. For example, male dominance, husband dominance, and father dominance in family relationships are suggested to reflect cultural scripts of machismo, *respeto*, *marianismo*, and gender role identification based on traditional values, beliefs, and family organization (Carrol, 1980; Dimmitt, 1995; Perilla, 1999).

Mirande (1977; see also Coltrane & Valdez, 1993; Marin & Marin, 1991) characterizes the machismo ethos as two opposing views of masculinity. The first view emphasizes internal attributes such as honor, respect, responsibility, and courage. Abalos (1986) writes about the manner in which he, like other Latino males, inherited and from his culture "the drama of possessive love" (p. 72). This aspect potential for a lack of distinction between love and power in which Latino expected to exercise power whereas females are taught to use love.

The second perspective stresses external characteristics such as physical str aggressiveness, sexual prowess, heavy drinking, and power. Mirande (1977) argu at for many Latino men, the very definition of maleness includes the notion of heavy alcohol consumption.

When Latino batterers are confronted about their use of sexual violence as a separate and serious form of abuse, many of them confess to using sex as a form of power and control. Delving deeper into the issue, it becomes clear that overt and covert messages are received from their fathers, male relatives, and friends regarding their sexual rights over their women. According to Rouse (1988), men and women are equally likely to have witnessed violence in their family of origin, and Latinos have experienced more father-only violence as children. In many parts of the world, especially where women's status is lower than that of males, the issue of power over a wife is a cultural norm. Vestiges of these expectations can be found in many Latino subpopulations, regardless of country of origin, level of acculturation, and socioeconomic status (Coltrane & Valdez, 1993; Fernandez-Kelly & Garcia, 1997).

Another cultural script relevant to the dynamics of family violence is that of *respeto*. Latino children are socialized early on to show deference and respect for their elders—parents, older siblings, older relatives, and people in power (such as physicians, teachers, clergy, police, and members of the court). The father in traditional Latino families is accorded utmost respect, regardless of his actions. Feelings of respect and fear are closely associated, in both abused Latinas and Latino batterers, with memories of their parents' demands for respect, especially their father.

Power, in the form of family violence is also suggested to be a manifestation of the lack of social power at work, which leads Latino males to become even more authoritarian in their relationship with their partner at home (Gutmann, 1996; Martin-Baro, 1994). Data from urban U.S. husbands showed that there was a higher association between work stressors and increased levels of drinking and violence among Latinos than among workers of other ethnic groups (Jasinski, Asdigian, & Kantor, 1997). Family violence, then, reflects both the privilege Latino men perceive as the natural order of things that their gender socialization provides, and the imposition of social, economic, and cultural disparities experienced outside the home.

The concept underlying *marianismo* is that women are spiritually superior to men and therefore can endure all suffering inflicted by men. The term is derived from Maria (the Virgin Mary), whose attributes are self-sacrifice, abnegation, passivity, and sexual purity.

raditionally, a Latina would derive her sense of identity and self-esteem from fulfilling specific cultural mandates. Some of the most important mandates are putting others' needs before her own, standing by and supporting her husband regardless of his behavior, being a good mother, remembering her place as a woman, being responsible for passing on cultural traditions, and keeping the family together. Traditional Latina women are suggested to acquiesce to family violence as a form of mediation over male frustrations that allow them to continue in their roles as economic providers (Perilla, Bakeman, & Norris, 1994). Even when mothers have authority over daily activities, there is still a facade of patriarchy in the respect and honor given to the man as head of the household (Coltrane & Valdez, 1993). Traditionally, Latina mothers are the principal figures in the home, providing resources and services while patriarchy continues to be the axle the family revolves around, although this perspective of the self-sacrificing mother has been recently challenged (Marsiglia & Holleran, 1999).

One other cultural script relevant to the discussion of family violence focuses on the role of the church in the socialization of many Latinas (Carillo & Tello, 1998; Perilla, Bakeman, & Norris, 1994). The emphasis placed on the family and the indissolubility of marriage, at whatever cost, is found in the Catholic faith as well as in many fundamentalist religions. It is the unconditional acceptance of marriage as a sacrament and vocation that presents a "tie that binds." Today, it is this spiritual strength of Latinos, typically perceived as the bedrock in the healing processes, which appears to be eroding as a consequence of their experiences, many of which have historical roots. This erosion may further unleash prior restraints and inhibitions relevant to personal (as in alcohol/substance use) and relationship abuse. Such examples of breakdown in traditional cultural domains are worthy of additional research. The work of Gil, Vega, and Biafora (1998), for example, presents evidence to suggest that changes in family environments are strong predictors of the initiation of drug use among Hispanic immigrants compared to nonimmigrants. Changes in religious precepts are hypothesized to have predictive potential as well.

The Changing Latino Family

Despite the heterogeneity among Latinos, and perhaps because of their shared mestizo identity, certain basic cultural values are held in common and have a strong impact on this population. As suggested earlier, the centrality of the family and distinct gender roles are two aspects of Latino culture that find consistency among Latino subgroup cultural descriptions. Related themes that emerge in the literature, and are thought to distinguish Latino families, center around a strong commitment to family interaction, maintenance of values of interdependence, and flexibility when handling familial and extrafamilial stressors (Amey & Albrecht, 1998; Mirande, 1977; Szapocznik & Kurtines, 1980; Williams, 1990). The absence of these qualities is associated with family conflict and disintegration (Adler, Ovando, & Hocevar, 1984; Rio, Santisteban, & Szapocznik, 1991).

Latino families are affected differently according to other factors such as acculturation and relationship characteristics associated with familism (Gil, Vega, & Biafora, 1998). The importance of family and parenting variables is repeated throughout the literature, although Latino subgroup and gender differences offer additional elaboration on these cultural themes (Gorman-Smith, Tolan, Henry, & Florsheim, 2000; Marsiglia & Holleran, 1999;. Szapocznick & Kurtines, 1980; Vega, 1995).

Within contemporary society, traditional Latino family composition and family functioning are challenged by social stratification shifts, fertility, changing gender role status, intermarriage, and cultural diffusion (Jiobu, 1988; Ortiz, 1995; Williams, 1990; Vega, 1995). Compounding these shifts are family conflicts associated with exposure to drugs, alcohol, and domestic violence and other risk factors present in a significant number of family violence incidents (Buriel, Calzada, & Vasquez, 1982; Rio, Santisteban, & Szapocznik, 1991).

Both empirical and theoretical bases for conceptualizing the problem of family violence assume a Western, traditional family type, which overlooks, misperceives, and pathologizes different family types. Even assumptions about the family as a homeostatic group fail to take into account differences within families in terms of social experiences, differing family interests, and access to resources. Conceptualizing the needs and experiences of the Latino family requires a focus on intra- and interpersonal family events embedded within their diverse social, cultural, and historical contexts. This extends conceptualization of family violence beyond systemic formulations that have been criticized, because such approaches tend to describe incidents in mechanistic terms while relegating responsibility of family violence to both partners. This perspective diminishes both the imbalance of power and the severe trauma caused by family violence. Additional criticism suggests that systemic approaches do not extend their analysis of battering to include the larger context of the social, economic, political, and cultural environments in which the battering takes place (Bograd, 1984).

There are no studies of the effects of family violence on Latino children, although it would appear that the centrality of family and strict family roles found in this culture may play an important role in Latino children's understanding of domestic abuse as well as in their coping strategies. The closeness and interdependency that characterize most Latino families may in some cases provide fertile ground for a dynamic that may be quite detrimental to children. Anecdotal data suggest that in many cases, Latino children and adolescents of families affected by domestic violence take on adult roles, especially as it relates to the physical defense and emotional support of their mothers.

Systemic Issues

A review of the literature published over the past decade highlights discrepancies in considering the role of ethnicity in family violence assessment and intervention, research, and policy enactment. In general, Latino victims of family violence are largely disadvantaged in terms of system responsiveness and access to ancillary services and safe havens. Considerable concern has been raised about the system's capacity to adequately serve Latino families.

For Latinos, service considerations must be given to value differences, bilingualism/biculturalism, community-based resources, and pathways to help seeking and service utilization (Cortés & Rogler, 1993; Wist & McFarlane, 1998; Zambrana, 1995). Personal welfare, rather than "family welfare," has historically led to individual-based policies and practices that consistently threaten Latino familistic values of interdependence, mutual aid, collectivism, and so on (Ortega, 2000; Triandis, 1995). These clashes have placed a long-standing wedge between social institutions and Latino family needs.

Awareness of policies, sanctions, and services also pose threats to effectiveness in meeting the needs of victims. Immigrant Latinos and Latinas are often surprised that laws exist in the United States specifically to protect women from violence in their own homes. Many Latino batterers claim ignorance as a defense for their behavior that went unnoticed and/or unpunished in their countries of origin but landed them in jail in the United States. Many stumbling blocks make it difficult for any abused woman to seek help and make the most of services available to her. Abused Latinas seldom know their rights regarding protection against domestic violence, often have little knowledge of existing services, and lack English fluency. Even when awareness exists, Latinas are often reluctant to use programs that, although directed toward their safety, do not take into account the cultural mandates regarding their responsibilities as wives and mothers. Latinas must take the very difficult first steps into totally unknown circumstances. Their vulnerability in terms of language, documentation, education level, knowledge of laws and services, and work skills is often used by their abusers as ammunition in their abusive practices (Bauer, Rodriguez, Quiroga, & Flores-Ortiz, 2000; Perilla, 1999; Rodriguez, Szkupinski, & Bauer, 1996).

Implications

The previous discussion encourages an analysis of assumptions about alcohol/substance use and family violence from a multicultural perspective. Such an approach advocates for a more comprehensive understanding of the etiology of family violence, grounded in personal, interpersonal, structural, cultural, and historical contexts (Belsky, 1980;

Bronfenbrenner, 1979; Garbarino & Ebata, 1983; Hay & Jones, 1994). In this regard, both culture (i.e., cultural difference) and the experience of being culturally different must also be taken into account. This perspective confronts the complexity involved in understanding family violence and suggests domains of influence necessary to consider in developing relevant programs and practices, research, and policies (Belsky, 1980; Gelles, 1992; Gil, 1970; Pelton, 1994).

A growing number of Latino families will carry with them the burdens of acculturative stress and related problems from poverty, exposure to neighborhood violence, drugs, disease and environmental hazards, high rates of mobility, and barriers to accessing resources and services because of language and cultural differences. Many Latino families will experience segregation, social marginalization, discrimination, and oppression—all of which are manifested in high rates of depression, suicide, social withdrawal, and family conflict. Currently there is no indication that services as a whole recognize these unique aspects of the Latino experience. Without question, Latino families present multiple and complex needs. Clearly the call is for diversity in methods and contexts of service delivery. Training and technical assistance must be offered to improve awareness of and sensitivity to language and cultural differences.

Latinos are fairly heterogeneous in terms of racial and ethnic composition, level and extent of segregation, immigrant status, and language preference (Massey, Zambrana, & Bell, 1995). Generalizing services without recognizing differences among and between Latinos will add nothing to improving their current status nor in understanding their needs. Such an effort, again, calls for active participation by the Latino community, particularly among grassroots organizations, as the call for help in addressing family violence extends beyond the responsibility of any one system of care.

Perilla (1999) calls for a "conscientization" among Latinos to bring about an awareness of the false roles and expectations derived from cultural norms and values imposed on Latino men, women, and children. For example, for men it requires a cultural redefinition of what it is to be a real man based on the positive attributes of the machismo ethos and a dismantling of the negative and extreme attitudes. It involves the knowledge of individual physiological markers that signal to a man that he is about to commit an act of violence. It is an awareness of attitudes, beliefs, and expectations that creates a climate in which unmet demands for services from the man's partner and children are used as an excuse or rationalization for violent behavior. It is also knowledge about alternative behaviors and situations that require accountability and respect on the road to nonviolence.

Conscientization, according to Perilla, requires Latino men to recognize and accept the fundamental human rights of their partners and children to a life free of terror, violence, and abuse. It is also an awareness of and respect for their integrity and individuality as separate human beings who have a right to self-determination. A critical consciousness for Latino men who batter must also include a clear understanding that domestic abuse will not be tolerated under any circumstances and that the entire community—including the church and courts—will hold them responsible for violent behavior.

In terms of abused women, conscientization has to do with the acquisition of knowledge regarding resources, laws, and options available in this country. It is also a realization and acceptance of the fact that a woman's plight is not an individual issue but rather one that belongs to the entire community. Critical consciousness for Latinas also has to do with awareness of the right to have their decisions respected, regardless of the attitudes or beliefs of others. It includes a redefinition of their identities as partners rather than victims and the use of their individual and collective voices to speak against what had been silenced.

Conscientization also requires a careful examination of cultural traditions and values so that the most positive and effective ones can be passed on to the next generation while discarding the most negative and/or destructive ones.

Grassroots Latino organizations, made up of knowledgeable and concerned indigenous individuals, have been underused in policy, practice, and research decisions. Their absence from the decision-making table represents another gap in understanding Latino family needs and in promoting effective change. The evidence thus far suggests that the most successful programs designed to meet the needs of Latinos are those in which Latino participation is obvious, unique Latino cultural perspectives are accommodated, Latino family strengths are valued, and their perspective on interests and needs is validated (Shartrand, 1996).

Community participation and development in relation to Latino family well-being is the larger challenge. Included in this effort is the need to build linkages between and among the various programs, organizations, and agencies that have been charged with nurturing the healthy development of all families: school, child welfare, health, mental health, the courts, religious affiliations, and so on (Ortega, 2000; Ortega, Guillean, & Gutierrez-Najera, 1996).

A policy perspective depends, to a great extent, on decision making based on valid and reliable data. While it is difficult to imagine how understanding the experiences of Latinos can occur without accurate identification and tracking of Latino victims and batterers, assumptions about their treatment needs and service requirements prevail. The literature presents example after example of differential treatment based on race and ethnicity; yet, without accurate data, very little can be discerned about the effectiveness of services in meeting the needs of Latino families and their children. Such an absence of knowledge has serious implications for the growing number of Latino families living in situations where alcohol/substance use and family violence pose a constant threat to their welfare, and for appropriations directed at improving their quality of life.

Future Directions

It is clear that more focus on diversity is necessary to meet the needs of the growing number of families and children affected by the serious, complex interaction of social problems. As the goals of service effectiveness, efficiency, and expediency become bolstered by fiscal incentives, the Latino child and family experience supports the need for research on family violence and healthy family development grounded in a multicultural context. Such research must challenge previous assumptions about what makes for well-being, positive family functioning, and a "good" system. The policy goals of services can not be seriously pursued without evidencing an appreciation for the complex interaction between the Latino family (and its familial experiences) and the influences thought to define the family at a particular moment in time. Further effort must be made to relate the experience with a system of care that maximizes a respect for difference while at the same time ensures the safety and security for a growing number of the nation's Latino families in need.

References

Abalos, D. T. (1986). *Latinos in the United States: The sacred and the political.* Notre Dame, IN: University of Notre Dame Press.

Adler, P., Ovando, C., & Hocevar, D. (1984). Familiar correlates of gang membership: An exploratory study of Mexican-American youth. *Hispanic Journal of Behavioral Science, 6*(1), 65–76.

Alaniz, M. L., Cartmill, R. S., & Parker, R. N. (1998). Immigrants and violence: The importance of neighborhood context. *Hispanic Journal of Behavioral Sciences, 20*(2), 155–174.

Amey, C. H., & Albrecht, S. L. (1998) Race and ethnic differences in adolescent drug use: The impact of family structure and the quantity and quality of parental interaction. *Journal of Drug Issues, 28*(2), 282–298.

Bauer, H. M., Rodriguez, M. A., Quiroga, S. S., & Flores-Ortiz, Y. G. (2000). Barriers to health care for abused Latina and Asian immigrant women. *Journal of Health Care for the Poor and Underserved, 11*(1), 33–44.

Beasley, M. E., & Thomas, D. Q. (1994). Domestic violence as a human rights issue. In M. A. Fineman & R. Mykitiuk (Eds.), *The public nature of private violence: The discovery of domestic abuse* (pp. 323–346). New York: Routledge.

Belsky, J. (1980). Child maltreatment: An ecological integration. *American Psychologist, 35,* 320–350.

Bograd, M. (1984). Family systems approaches to wife battering: A feminist critique. *American Journal of Orthopsychiatry, 54*(4), 558–568.

Bronfenbrenner, U. (1979). *The ecology of human development: Experiments by nature and design.* Cambridge, MA: Harvard University Press.

Buriel, R., Calzado, S., & Vasquez, R. (1982). The relationship of traditional Mexican-American culture to the adjustment and delinquency among three generations of Mexican-American male adolescents. *Hispanic Journal of Behavioral Sciences, 1,* 45–55.

Caetano, R., Schafer, J., Clark, C. L., Curandi, C. B., & Rasberry, K. (2000). Interpersonal partner violence, acculturation and alcohol consumption among Hispanic couples in the United States. *Journal of Interpersonal Violence, 15*(1), 30–45.

Carillo, R., & Tello, J. (1998). *Family violence and men of color: Healing the wounded male spirit.* New York: Springer Publishing.

Carrol, J. C. (1980). A cultural consistency theory of family violence in Mexican American and Jewish ethnic groups. In M. A. Straus & G. T. Hotaling (Eds.), *The social causes of husband-wife violence* (pp. 68–81). Minneapolis: University of Minnesota Press, 1980.

Champion, J. D. (1996). Women abuse, assimilation and self-concept in a rural Mexican American community. *Hispanic Journal of Behavioral Sciences, 18,* 508–521.

Coltrane, S., & Valdez, E. O. (1993). Reluctance compliance: Work-family role deallocation in dual earner Chicano families. In J. C. Wood (Ed.), *Men, work and family* (pp. 151–175). Newbury Park, CA: Sage.

Cortés, D. E., & Rogler, L. H. (1993). Help-seeking pathways: A unifying concept in mental health care. *American Journal of Psychiatry, 150,* 554–61.

Dimmit, J. (1995) Rural Mexican American and non-Hispanic white women: Effects of abuse on self-concept. *Journal of Cultural Diversity, 2*(2), 54–63.

Dugan L., & Apel, R. (2003). An exploratory study of the violent victimization of women: Race/ethnicity, situational context. *Criminology, 4*(3), 959–980.

Enchautegui, M. E. (1995). *Policy implications of Latino poverty.* Population Studies Center. Washington DC: Urban Institute.

Fernandez-Kelly, M. P., & Garcia, A. M. (1997). Power surrendered, power restored: The politics of work and family among Hispanic garment workers in California and Florida. In M. Romero, P. Hondagneu-Sotelo, & V. Ortiz (Eds.), *Challenging fronteras: Structuring Latina and Latino lives in the U.S.* (pp. 215–228). New York: Routledge.

Garbarino, J., & Ebata, A. (1983). The significance of ethnic and cultural differences in child maltreatment. *Journal of Marriage and the Family, 45,* 773–783.

Gelles, R. J. (1992). Poverty and violence toward children. *American Behavioral Scientist, 35,* 258–274.

Gil, D. G. (1970). *Violence against children: Physical abuse in the United States.* Cambridge, MA: Harvard University Press.

Gil, D. G., Vega, W., & Biafora, F. (1998). Temporal influences of family structure and family risk factors on drug use initiation in a multiethnic sample of adolescent boys. *Journal of Youth and Adolescence, 27*(3), 373–393.

Gorman-Smith, D., Tolan, P. H., Henry, D. B., & Florsheim, P. (2000). Patterns of family functioning and adolescent outcomes among African American and Mexican American families. *Journal of Family Psychology, 14*(3), 436–457.

Gutierrez, L. M., Yeakley, A., & Ortega, R. M. (2001). Education for social work with Latinos in the 21st century. *Social Work in Education, 36*(3), 541–557.

Gutmann, M. C. (1996). *The meaning of macho: Being a man in Mexico City*. Berkeley, CA: University of California Press.

Hamby, S. L. (2000). Labeling partner violence: When do victims differentiate among acts? *Violence and Victims, 15*(2), 173–182.

Hampton, R., Carillo, R. A., & Kim, J. (1998). Violence in communities of color. In R. Carillo & J. Tello (Eds.), *Family violence and men of color: Healing the wounded male spirit* (pp. 1–30). New York: Springer Publishing.

Hay, T., & Jones, L. (1994) Societal interventions to prevent child abuse and neglect. *Child Welfare, 73*(5), 379–403.

Hispanic households struggle as poorest of the poor in the U.S. (1997, January 30). *New York Times*, pp. A1, A12.

Jasinski J. L. (1998). The role of acculturation in wife assault. *Hispanic Journal of Behavioral Sciences, 20*(2), 175–191.

Jasinski, J. L., Asdigian, N. L., & Kaufman Kantor, G. (1997). Ethnic adaptation to occupational strain: Work-related stress, drinking and wife assault among and Hispanic husbands. *Journal of Interpersonal Violence, 12*(6), 814–831.

Jiobu, R. (1988). *Ethnicity and assimilation*. Albany, NY: SUNY Press.

Kaufman Kantor, G. (1997). Alcohol and spouse abuse: Ethnic differences. In M. Galenter (Ed.), *Recent developments in alcoholism* (pp. 57–59). New York: Plenum Press.

Kaufman Kantor, G., Jasinski, J. L., & Aldarondo, E. (1994). Sociocultural status and incidence of marital violence in Hispanic families. *Violence and victims, 9*(3), 207–222.

Marcus, I. (1994). Reframing "domestic violence": Terrorism in the home. In M. A. Fineman & R. Mykituik (Eds.), *The public nature of private violence: The discovery of domestic abuse* (pp. 11–35). New York: Routledge.

Marin, G., & Marin, B. V. (1991). *Research with Hispanic populations*. Newbury Park, CA: Sage.

Marsiglia, F., & Holleran, L. (1999). I've learned so much from my mother: An ethnography of a group of Chicana high school students. *Social Work in Education, 21*(4), 220–237.

Martin-Baro, I. (1994). The Lazy latino: The ideological nature of Latin American fatalism (P. Berryman, Trans.). In A. Aron & S. Come (Eds.), *Writings for a liberation psychology* (pp. 198–220). Cambridge, MA: Harvard University Press.

Massey, D. S., Zambrana, R. E., & Bell, S. A. (1995). Contemporary issues in Latino families: Future directions for research, policy and practice. In R. Zambrana (Ed.), *Understanding Latino Families* (pp. 190–204). Thousand Oaks, CA: Sage.

Mirande, A. (1977). The Chicano family: A reanalysis of conflicting views. *Journal of Marriage and the Family, 39*(4), 747–755.

O'Keefe, M. (1994). Racial/ethnic differences among battered women and their children. *Journal of Child and Family Studies, 3*, 283–305.

Ortega, R. M. (2000). Child welfare and Latino adolescents. In M. Montenero-Sieburth & F. Villaruel (Eds.), *Making invisible Latino adolescents visible: A critical approach to Latino diversity* (pp. 309–331). New York: Falmer Press.

Ortega, R. M., Guillean, C., & Gutierrez-Najera, L.(1996). *Latinos and child welfare/Latinos y el beinestar del niño: Voces de la comunidad.* Ann Arbor, MI: University of Michigan School of Social Work.

Ortiz, V. (1995). The diversity of Latino families. In R. Zambrana (Ed.), *Understanding Latino families* (pp. 18–39). Thousand Oaks, CA: Sage.

Pelton, L. H. (1994). Is poverty a key contributor to child maltreatment? In E. Gambrill & J. Stein (Eds.), *Controversial issues in child welfare* (pp. 16–21). Needham Heights, MA: Allyn & Bacon.

Perilla, J. L. (1999). Domestic violence as a human rights issue: The case of immigrant Latinos. *Hispanic Journal of Behavioral Sciences, 21*(2), 107–133.

Perilla, J. L., Bakeman, R., & Norris, F. H. (1994). Culture and domestic violence: The ecology of abused Latinas. *Violence and Victims, 9*(4), 325–338.

Repack, T. A. (1997). New roles in a new landscape. In M. Romero, P. Hondagneu-Sotelo, & V. Ortiz (Eds.), *Challenging fronteras: Structuring Latina and Latino lives in the U.S.* (pp. 247–257). New York: Routledge.

Rio, A. T., Santisteban, D. A., & Szapocznik, J. (1991). Juvenile delinquency among Hispanics: The role of family in prevention and treatment. In M. Sotomayor (Ed.), *Empowering Hispanic families: A critical issue for the 90's* (pp. 191–214). Milwaukee WI: Family Services America.

Rivera, J. (1994). Domestic violence against Latinas by Latino males: An analysis of race, national origin and gender differentials. *Boston College Third World Journal, 14*, 231.

Rivera, J. (1995). The politics of invisibility. *Georgetown Journal on Fighting Poverty, 3*(1), 61–65.

Rivera, J. (1997–1998). Preliminary report: Availability of domestic violence services for Latina survivors in New York State. *In the Public Interest, 16*, 1–32.

Rodriguez, M. A., & Brindis, C. D. (1995). Violence and Latino youth: Prevention and methodological issues. *Public Health Reports, 110*(3), 260–267.

Rodriguez, M., Szkupinski, S., & Bauer, H. (1996). Breaking the silence: Battered women's perspectives on medical care. *Archives of Family Medicine, 5*, 153–160.

Rouse, L. P. (1988). Abuse in dating relationships: A comparison of Blacks, Whites and Hispanics. *Journal of College Student Development, 29*, 312–319.

Shartrand, A. (1996). *Supporting Latino families: Lessons from exemplary programs (Resumen en español).* Vol. 1. Harvard Family Research Project.

Straus, M. A., & Smith, C. (1990). Violence in Hispanic families in the United States: Incidence rates and structural interpretations. In M. A. Straus & R. J. Gelles (Eds.), *Physical violence in American families: Risk factors and adaptations to violence in 8,145 families* (pp. 341–367). New Brunswick, NJ: Transaction.

Szapocznik, J., & Kurtines, W. (1980). Acculturation, biculturalism and adjustment among Cuban Americans. In A. M. Padilla (Ed.), *Acculturation: Theory, models and some new findings* (pp. 139–158). Boulder, CO: American Association for Advancement of Science.

Triandis, H. C. (1995). *Individualism and collectivism.* Boulder, CO: Westview Press.

Van Hightower, N. R., Gorton, J., & DeMoss, C. L. (2000). Predictive models of domestic violence and fear of intimate partners among migrant and seasonal farm worker women. *Journal of Family Violence, 15*(2), 137–154.

Vega, W. (1995). The study of Latino families; A point of departure. In R. Zambrana (Ed.), *Understanding Latino families* (pp. 3–17). Thousand Oaks, CA: Sage.

Williams, N. (1990). *The Mexican American family: Tradition and change.* Dix Hill, NY: General Hall.

Wist, W. H., & McFarlane, J. (1998). Severity of spousal and intimate partner abuse to pregnant Hispanic women. *Journal of Health Care for the Poor and Underserved, 9*(3), 248–261.

Zambrana, R. (Ed.). (1995). *Understanding Latino families.* Thousand Oaks, CA: Sage.

9

Latino Families

The Use of Culture as an Informative Perspective

CLAUDIA L. MORENO

Introduction

Latinos are the largest and fastest-growing ethnic group in the United States, with more than a third of their population under the age of 18. The growth and youth of this population represents enormous challenges for social work practitioners, researchers, and policy makers. The literature widely discusses the importance of acquiring cultural competence in working with Latino families in today's times. Latino families are complex and live in complex environments and require a range of skills, programs, and interventions. This complexity is enlarged by the cultural differences of families. Culture is a central focus that serves as a frame of reference to define the problem, the manifestation of the problem, the treatment provider, and the treatment approach (Pinderhughes, 1989).

With the growing number of Latino families, child welfare agencies are seeing an increase in the presence of Latino clients. Many children who enter the child welfare system come from families and neighborhoods faced with enormous challenges and limitations. A body of evidence suggests that the majority of children referred to child welfare agencies come from families exposed to violence and substance abuse in their households and neighborhoods. These elements are reciprocal in nature and intersecting, which makes the cases entering the child welfare system very complicated. Furthermore, when we deal with the element of cultural differences and cultural meanings, the difficulties confronting child welfare workers are greater. These complexities compel workers to look at cases as multidimensional in nature requiring an understanding of the sociocultural context, a need to develop and enhance cultural awareness and competence with a refinement of practice skills, and an appreciation of how all these factors have an impact on agencies, research, education, and policies.

This chapter dissects the intersection of child welfare, substance abuse, and family violence in Latino families by providing a historical context and current aspects of these factors among Latino families.

Sociocultural Context

SOCIODEMOGRAPHIC OVERVIEW

Latinos have always been in the United States, and their history of territorial eradication and colonization has made an impact on Latinos at different levels. During the last century, many Latinos started to emigrate from about 20 different countries in larger numbers, at different times and for different reasons, with great diversity in immigration patterns. Many Latinos come from countries with similar histories of colonization. They share many traditions and cultural patterns connected by similar histories and influences such as the Catholic Church, the Spanish language, and Spanish and indigenous traditions. Many people use the terms "Latino" and "Hispanic" without knowing that both have sociopolitical connotations and that, according to the region, sociopolitical identity, and acculturation, one is preferred over the other. Both terms are relatively new and did not exist 50 years ago (Suarez-Orozco & Paez, 2002). The term "Hispanic" was first used during the Nixon administration to identify people who come from Spanish-speaking countries. The term links individuals from Latin America to Spain and, therefore, the colonizers. It is a term that reminds many of us of our histories of colonization and genocide and does not acknowledge our indigenous history. The term "Latino," although not inclusive either, is preferred by many in this country because it embraces indigenous, African, Spanish, and other influences that Latinos historically have had. For this chapter Latino is used mostly because it embraces the cultural and indigenous survival for over 500 years.

In the last decade, the U.S. Latino population increased 58%, achieving the status of the largest minority population in the nation. Currently, one of nine people in the United States is of Hispanic origin. The 2000 Census estimates there are 35.3 million Latinos in the United States representing 12.5% of the total population (Therrien & Ramirez, 2000), with 58% of Hispanics concentrated in three states, California, Texas, and New York.

Latinos in the United States are a diverse and heterogeneous group in terms of socioeconomic factors such as income, education, marital and family composition, and employment, along with histories of colonization and politics. However, there has been a tendency to view Latinos collectively and as a homogeneous group, which masked differences and vulnerabilities of certain groups (Zambrana & Dorrington, 1998).

Hispanics are primarily foreign born, representing 39.1%, or 12.8 million, of all Hispanics (Therrien & Ramirez, 2000). Hispanics of Mexican origin are the largest ethnic group and represent two-thirds, or 66%, of all Latinos in the United States. This is followed by 15% of people from Central America (the largest groups are Salvadoran, 43%, and Guatemalan, 20%) and South America (the largest groups are Colombian, 37%; Ecuadorian, 18.5%; and Peruvian, 17%). Finally, 9% of Latinos are from Puerto Rico, 6% from the Caribbean, and 4% from Cuba (Ramirez, 2000).

Their histories of migration and immigration have had an impact on many Latinos. A large number of Latinos live in poverty and have low educational skills, and a large majority have low-skill jobs, which perpetuates their poverty. Latinos are three times more likely to live in poverty (21.4%) than non-Hispanic Whites (7.8%) (Ramirez & de la Cruz, 2002). Puerto Ricans and Mexicans have the highest rates of poverty among Hispanic groups, 31%, compared to 14% for Cubans. Thirty-four percent of Hispanic children live in poverty, compared to 11% of non-Hispanic White children. Among the Latino children who live in poverty, 44% are Puerto Ricans; 35%, Mexicans; 32%, other Hispanics; 27%, Central and South Americans; and 16% Cubans (Ramirez, 2000). Education is lower among Latinos, with only 56% earning a high school degree, compared to 88% of non-Hispanic Whites. Latinos are also less likely to be married and more likely to have female-headed households, with about 24% of Latinos coming from families headed by a female, compared to 13% of non-Hispanic Whites. Puerto Ricans are the largest group to have female-headed households (36%), compared to 21% for Mexicans, 25% for Central and South Americans, and 18% for Cubans (Ramirez, 2000).

Most of the population of Puerto Ricans and Dominicans lives in the Northeast and is economically disadvantaged in comparison to other Hispanic subgroups. New York City has the largest group of Dominicans (495,000) outside of the Dominican Republic: 36% of the Dominican population. They constitute the second-largest group of Hispanics in New York City after Puerto Ricans, and it is estimated that eventually Dominicans will constitute the largest Latino group in New York City. Currently, Dominicans constitute the largest Latino group in Manhattan. In addition, Dominicans are relatively new immigrants in comparison to other Hispanic subgroups, and about 45% of Dominicans in New York City live below the poverty line (Hernandez & Rivera-Batiz, 1997).

Detailed information on Latino subgroups is slowing emerging. It is imperative to acknowledge the diversity among Latino subgroups, the sociodemographic differences, the population increase of certain groups, and the specific needs of each community. The continuous shifts and changes within Latino groups have a direct impact on service delivery. For example, during the 1970s, Cuban refugees were among the three largest Latino subgroups, but today they only represent 4.6% of the Latino population. Today's third-largest subgroup consists of South Americans, according to recent census estimates (Ramirez, 2000). South Americans constitute the largest Latino group in Queens, New York (Ramirez, 2000).

Oppression

Latinos have diverse histories of oppression and cultural identities. Spaniards, "the *conquistadores*," colonized Latin America and left religious, cultural, and language influences that have merged in various degrees with indigenous populations. This merger implies a unique adaptation of different codes of ethics and moral principles (Fortes de Leff & Espejel, 2000). Historically, other groups migrated to Latin America and left the imprint of their African, Asian, Arabic, and European influences on the culture. Different social classes and color lines emerged through the effects of colonization (Fortes de Leff & Espejel, 2000). The conquistadors were mostly White Europeans who used their power to discriminate and oppress the indigenous *criollos* or *mestizos* (mixed blood) as well as the imported slaves. Their power structures are still prevalent and have created class and color divisions in Latin American societies that have resulted in economic and social differences across social classes (Fortes de Leff & Espejel, 2000). In the United States, there also exists oppression by color, class, and socioeconomic status, which has extended to new immigrant Latino groups. Within the mainstream, this oppression has been translated into allocation of services and opportunities to certain groups and not others.

The conquest of Latin American countries has been perceived as an act of sociocultural violence through genocide, imposition of customs and beliefs systems, and sexual violence toward women (Fortes de Leff & Espejel, 2000). It is believed that the historical trauma of colonization resulting in violence, discrimination, and oppression has contributed to perpetuating violence and substance abuse among many Latin American groups.

Cultural Strengths

In spite of this violent history of colonization, Latinos have survived centuries of brutal colonizers, oppression, and genocide. This survival is manifested in the resistance to abandoning culture, language, customs, and belief systems. The Latino presence has deep sociohistorical roots that have influenced its relationships with and trust of institutions of power because of the legacy with racism (Larkey, Hecht, Millers, & Alatorre, 2001). Racism and oppression have defined Latinos from a cultural deficit perspective without taking into consideration the social and economic disadvantages of many Latino groups. Socioeconomic disadvantages cannot be confused with "cultural disadvantages"; rather, social and economic injustices contribute to such risk factors as violence, substance abuse, and entering the child welfare system for many Latino families (Zambrana & Dorrington, 1998).

Latinos have a rich culture; a rich religious, spiritual, and value system; and traditions that have been transmitted for many generations and still prevail. Many cultural values, such as familialism, personalism, *confianza* (trust), *respeto* (respect), and fatalism, guide and influence attitudes, behaviors, and belief systems. Familialism (*familialismo*) is one of the most important factors that influences the lives of Latinos. Familialism emphasizes the importance of the family over individual needs and the importance of maintaining a strong kinship network (Marin, 1993). Strong familialism has been implicated as a protective factor against child abuse (Coohey, 2001), substance abuse (Catalano, Morrison, Wells, Gilmore, Iritani, & Hawkins,1992), and family violence among Latinos (Gorman-Smith, Tolan, Zelli, & Huesmann, 1996).

Substance Abuse

Substance abuse, like family violence, cannot be separated from contextual micro and macrosystemic factors. Researchers and practitioners knowledgeable about substance abuse have identified a plethora of systemic factors. These include demographic variables, family variables, peer influences, educational variables, adjustment attitudes and behaviors, personality variables, and environmental variables (Amey & Albrecht, 1998; Farrell, 1993). The literature points out family characteristics that seem to have the strongest correlation with substance abuse. The weakness of some of these studies is that they have focused mostly on family structure rather than on family quality and family patterns. Some researchers suggest that later studies can draw different results (Dawson, 1991).

Most researchers agree that there is no single pathway or direct causation of substance abuse, but, rather, there are different pathways and risk factors. On the other hand, initiation into substance abuse creates a sequence of events that evolves into other risk factors, and very few studies discuss the reciprocity between substance abuse and risk factors (Farrell, 1993). Substance abuse initiation patterns seem to be different for different ethnic groups. However, these differences have been attributed to family structure characteristics. New evidence has suggested that economic deprivation, along with family disruption, is a more important factor than family structure (Amey & Albrecht, 1998).

The National Survey on Drug Use and Health (Substance Abuse and Mental Health

Services Administration [SAMHSA], 2004) reports that drug use is lower among Latinos (8.0%) compared to non-Hispanic Whites (8.3%). It is argued that part of the reason for the lower rates among Latinos is low substance abuse among Hispanic women. About 13% of Latino men use any kind of illicit drug, compared to 8% of Latinas. Although addiction has been considered a "male disease," recent research methodologies have criticized this assumption because some studies have not investigated gender differences in the nature and course of addiction (Amaro, Nieves, Wolde, & Labault, 1999). Few studies of drug addiction among Latinas appear in the literature (Amaro et al., 1999), and when those studies compared alcohol use to illicit drugs, it shows a different picture (Amaro et al., 1999). Gender differences in substance abuse among Latino subgroups seem to vary. Latino men are reported to use more drugs and alcohol than women. Of those women who drink, Mora (1998) reports that Mexican Americans report heavier drinking (14%) than Cuban (7%) or Puerto Rican women (5%).

Latinos in general are overrepresented in cases of alcohol, heroin, and cocaine use when compared with non-Hispanic Whites. Latinos, for instance, account for 21% of binge drinking and are the highest among all groups (SAMHSA, 2004). Binge drinking is defined as drinking five or more alcoholic beverages on the same occasion on at least one day in the past 30 days.

Latino subgroups vary markedly in the prevalence of substance abuse, alcohol dependence, and illicit drug dependence. Two Latino groups, Mexicans and Puerto Ricans, have a high prevalence of illicit drug use (marijuana, cocaine, and other illicit drugs), heavy alcohol use, alcohol dependence, and the need for illicit drug use treatment (Amaro et al., 1999; SAMHSA, 2004). High rates of substance abuse among Latinos have been attributed to acculturation and subgroup differences.

Very few studies have been conducted on Latino subgroup differences, and few studies have discerned prevalence rates, drug of choice, and patterns of use among Latino subgroups. In addition, there are few studies of Latino subgroups that are just emerging in U.S. society today, such as Dominicans and other growing Latino subgroups (Nielsen, 2000; Zayas, Rojas & Magaldy, 1998). One major study of the growing Latino subgroups was conducted by Zayas et al. in 1998. The authors interviewed 288 Puerto Rican, Dominican, and Colombian men and found differences in drinking patterns and drug of choice. Puerto Ricans, for instance, were more likely to use drugs, Colombians were more likely to drink heavily and have more alcohol-related problems, while Dominicans drank less and used fewer drugs. A larger study conducted by Nielsen (2000) used a national probability sample ($n=4,462$) and compared the drinking patterns of major Latino subgroups (Cubans, Mexican Americans, Puerto Ricans, and other Hispanics). This study found significant differences among subgroups. For instance, Mexican Americans reported the most frequent and heaviest drinking patterns and the greatest prevalence of drunkenness, compared to Cubans who reported the lowest prevalence of alcohol abuse. Puerto Ricans and other Hispanics were in between. For women, the Nielsen study found that among Latinas, Puerto Ricans and Mexican Americans drank more often and heavily than the other groups and experienced more problems related to drinking. In addition, research studying gender differences has shown that Latino males drink more than females. Current evidence shows that this gap is narrowing (Rodriguez-Andrew, 1998).

Child Welfare

Children occupy a special place in many Latino families. Being a parent is highly valued in the Latino culture (Falicov, 1998; Fontes, 2002), and Latino children are prized and often indulged in Latino families (Falicov, 1998). However, the presence of children in the child welfare system connotes the fragility of families and how structural factors such as poverty, stress, substance abuse, psychopathology, trauma, and violence influence child rearing practices.

There are multiple causes of child abuse. Several researchers agree that the causes seem to be a multitude of factors that increase the possibility of child abuse and neglect. These factors do not operate in isolation from each other (Straus & Smith, 1990a).

Parents are for the most part the abusers. In about 80% of the cases of child abuse and neglect, the perpetrator is one of the parents. Females are 60.4% of the perpetrators and 87.1% of those who were maltreated by their own parents (U.S. Department of Health and Human Services [DHHS], 1998). Of the children who were maltreated by their parents, 72% were maltreated by their mothers. In contrast, children who were maltreated by other parents or parent substitutes were primarily maltreated by males (80%) (Sedlack & Broadhurst, 1996). A study conducted by McCloskey and Bailey (2000) found that a history of maternal sexual abuse placed girls at 3.6 times the risk for sexual abuse. Studies controlling for ethnicity have found that there were ethnic differences in childhood victimization rates. A large study conducted in Los Angeles found that Latinas were less likely to report sexual abuse than Anglo-Americans (Sorenson, Siegel, Golding, & Stein, 1992).

Considering that Latinos represent 13.5% of the total population, about 15% of the cases of maltreatment are Latino children (DHHS, 2003a). Latino children in foster care represent 17%, and 12% are waiting to be adopted (DHHS, 2003b).

Poverty is a generally accepted risk factor for child abuse and neglect. Among the risk factors for child abuse and maltreatment are poverty and related conditions, for example, substandard housing, overcrowding, hunger, inadequate schools, and dangerous neighborhoods (Fontes, 2002); substance abuse (Kumpfer, 1999); parental stress; and social isolation (Whipple, 1999). It is estimated that families with an income below $15,000 were over 22 times more likely to inflict maltreatment on their children (Sedlack & Broadhurst, 1996). According to Straus and Smith (1990b), the combination of living in poverty and a parent's prior history of witnessing violence increase the potential for child abuse by 400%.

The literature about Latino child maltreatment research is slim compared to that of other ethnic groups. Although Latino children are overrepresented in child welfare statistics, only 7% of research studies have been specific to them in the last 19 years (Behl, Crouch, May, Valente, & Conyngham, 2001). The literature has also been biased because it has failed to distinguish among culture and poverty (Zayas, 1992), subgroup differences, acculturation, and language (Behl et al., 2001). Fontes (2002) argues that family stress, among other socioeconomic factors, contributes to physical abuse, but the literature is unclear about which stressors are most important for Latino families. In addition, researchers cannot determine whether rates of child maltreatment are higher for Latinos compared to other groups when comparing socioeconomic status (Fontes, 2002). It is strongly recommended that before looking at child maltreatment as an individualistic problem, we must focus attention on the interactive effects of social stress, poverty, individual psychology, and culture (Fontes, 2002; Zayas, 1992) and the levels of familialism. A study conducted by Coohey (2001) compared the levels of familialism among Latina and Anglo mothers who were abusing and not abusing their children. The Latina sample included 35 Latinas who were abusing their children and 35 Latinas who were not. Coohey (2001) found that higher levels of familialism were found among those Latinas and Anglo mothers who were not abusing their children. The study articulates that higher levels of familialism can be a protective factor for child maltreatment across ethnic groups.

Family Violence

In reference to prevalence rates of family violence, studies have found increased rates of partner abuse among Latinos (Champion, 1996). The National Family Violence Survey (Straus & Smith, 1990a) found that the rate of spousal abuse was 54% greater for Latinos than for non-Latino Whites. Other studies support this finding of increased rates of spousal abuse among Hispanics compared to non-Hispanic Whites (Champion, 1996). Few studies have compared partner abuse among Latino subgroups (Jasinski 1998; Straus & Smith, 1990a). Jasinski used a probability sample of 1,970 respondents (Puerto Rican, Mexican, and Cuban) from a national study on alcohol/family violence relationships and found that Cubans were the group least likely to abuse their spouses, and Puerto Ricans were the group most likely to abuse their spouses. In controlling for age and acculturation, the study found that recent immigrants who were young were more likely to abuse their spouses, and surprisingly those Latinos who were more acculturated or had lived longer in the United States, such as third-generation Hispanics, were potential abusers.

There are gender differences in the occurrence of family violence and victimization. For instance, in partner abuse women are five times more likely to be the victims than males (U.S. Department of Justice, 2000). In child abuse, girls are three times more likely to be abused than boys, and being born female is the most universal risk factor (McCloskey & Bailey, 2000). Statistics implicate women as the majority of the abusers; contextually, females are more likely to be at risk for being abused in all forms, then they become abusers and a cycle of violence starts. This is often called the cycle of revictimization (McCloskey & Bailey, 2000).

Family violence cannot be separated from context since it is so embedded in other interactions. Several predictors of violence have been identified by the literature to explain the development of violent and nonviolent behaviors. However, the most prominent factors are familial variables that include family history of criminal behavior, abusive parental discipline, and parental social isolation (Jackson, Thompson, Christiansen, & Colman, 1999). Conflicted parenting and family relationship are important variables in the risk for the development of violent behavior (Gorman-Smith, Tolan, Henry, & Florsheim, 1996; Loeber & Dishion, 1983). Alternative perspectives argue that the disinhibitory effects of alcohol and other substances make those who use them more apt to engage in violent or neglectful behaviors because of the sedating effects of substances (Mitchel & Savage, 1991). Difficult behaviors of children born to substance-abusing mothers place children at risk for abuse and neglect (Nair et al., 1997).

Changes in family environments have been stronger predictors of the initiation of drug use among Latino immigrants than among nonimmigrants (Gil, Vega, & Biafora, 1998). Family risk factors have been stronger contributors of drug use among multiethnic adolescents. However, among Latino adolescents, low familialism or lack of strong family connections is a stronger predictor of drug use among adolescents, and family variables are implicated in protective factors for Latino adolescents (Catalano et al., 1992; Gil et al., 1998).

Families have been found to be influential in risk and protective factors for Latino adolescents. Minority status has been a predictor of family violence; however, Latino families have been underresearched and most often misunderstood. Generalizations about Latino families ignore important factors such as differences in socioeconomic status, the heterogeneity of Latino subgroups (Guerra, Huesmann, Tolan, VanAcker, & Eron, 1995), the conditions of the neighborhoods where Latino families live (Alaniz, Cartmill, & Parker, 1998), availability of resources and social supports, and acculturation.

The evaluation of causation of family violence and substance abuse must consider each of these factors at one point in time because families are different and change over time (Gorman-Smith et al., 2000). Latino families are affected differently according to other factors: family resettlement, family relationship characteristics such as familialism (Gil et al., 1998), and the importance of family and parenting variables (Gorman-Smith et al., 1996). Few studies reveal that minority groups are different from each other in reference to beliefs about the importance of the family. Gorman-Smith et al. (1996) found strong beliefs about the importance of the family were related to decreased risk of involvement for African American families in both violent and nonviolent behaviors. The opposite was found for Latino families, where strong beliefs in the importance of the family were related to increased risk for violent and nonviolent delinquency.

The social context of Latino families is pivotal, and research does not seem to reflect these realities. For instance, most Latino families live in urban environments and are economically disadvantaged. Latino children are exposed to high rates of community violence and social disorder, discrimination, and oppression. All these factors bring additional stressors to families, and parenting becomes increasingly difficult under these conditions (Gorman-Smith et al., 2000).

The concept of family varies among ethnic groups. For Latinos the concept of family is not limited to the nuclear family but includes the extended family. *La familia* includes different generations of the extended family that can be traced on both sides of the family (Amey & Albrech, 1998). On the other hand, family violence needs to be defined multidimensionally and contextually. Families are exposed to microforms of violence that include partner abuse, child abuse and neglect, and elder abuse. And macroforms of violence affect families directly and indirectly through such things as interpersonal violence, community violence, and delinquency and media violence.

The Intersection of Substance Abuse, Child Welfare, and Intimate Partner Violence

Substance abuse is an emerging and difficult problem in child welfare. In 1999, 88% of U.S. states surveyed mentioned that in child welfare, dealing with substance abuse was one of the top priorities, along with dealing with poverty (Child Welfare League of America [CWLA], 2002). It has been estimated that about 80% of the families involved in the child welfare system have problems with alcohol and/or other substances (CWLA,

2002; Ondersma, 1999). Children whose families have a history of alcohol and substance abuse are almost three times more likely to be abused and four times more likely to be neglected (Ondersma, 1999). It is evident that the relationship of substance abuse to child abuse and neglect is plaguing child welfare services. On one hand, of those parents who are in the system and need substance abuse treatment, less than one-third receive treatment through child welfare agencies (CWLA, 2002). On the other hand, all states report having long waiting lists for substance abuse services and about 62% of those who are in need of treatment do not receive it (CWLA, 2002). In the majority of cases, the parent's substance abuse is a long-standing problem that will require at least five years of treatment on average (CWLA, 2002). Children whose parents do not receive appropriate substance abuse treatment are more likely to find themselves in foster care, remain in foster care longer, or reenter the child welfare system more frequently than those whose parents have received treatment. This situation becomes a catch-22 for effective child welfare services.

The literature indicates that substance abuse is implicated in many events of family violence. For instance, Caetano, Schafer, and Cunradi (2001) analyzed results from a national study that included 1,440 couples where 38% were White, 25% were Black, and 37% were Hispanic. They found that in 30% to 40% of the men and 27% to 34% of the women who perpetrated violence against their partners, drinking alcohol was involved at the time of the violent event. However, in controlling for ethnic differences the study found that alcohol-related problems were associated with interpersonal partner violence (IPV) among White, Black, and Latino couples. This study compared the results with neighborhood characteristics by ethnicity and found that Blacks who resided in impoverished neighborhoods were three times more likely to abuse their partners, Whites living in impoverished neighborhoods were four times more likely, and Latinos were two times more likely to abuse their partners while living in impoverished neighborhoods. This is one of the few studies that take into consideration structural factors such as impoverished neighborhoods, where most people with lower socioeconomic status and lower educational levels reside.

Substance abuse can be directly related to family violence as a predictive factor, but it can also be a consequence factor for family violence. Furthermore, different studies indicate that parental abuse may be associated with the physical and/or sexual abuse of children (Widom & Hiller-Sturmhofel, 2001), and people who have been abused as children may be have an increased likelihood for abusing alcohol as adults (Widom & Hiller-Sturmhofel, 2001). Few studies have identified the relationship between child neglect and alcohol abuse and how this relationship can be a predictor or a consequence of family violence needing further investigation that includes different methodologies such as longitudinal, cross-sectional, and in-depth interviews.

The family as a unit of analysis has been documented by many researchers as being an important predictor of the presence, severity, and maintenance of child and youth violence, sexual abuse, maltreatment, and substance abuse (Dakof, 1996; Patterson, 1986). Substance abuse and family violence have been studied separately, but new evidence is emerging to see them as intersecting and interacting (Besinger, Garland, & Litrownick, 1999; El-Bassel et al., 1998; Ondersma, 1999).

National rates of partner abuse are two or three times higher for women who are substance abusers (Straus, Gelles, Steinmetz, 1980). Studies using the National Family Violence Survey have correlated partner abuse among Latinas with binge-drinking husbands at 10 times the rate of assault as those with moderate-drinking husbands (Kaufman Kantor, 1990). When controlling for ethnic differences, Puerto Ricans who abuse alcohol were five times more likely to hit their wives than their nondrinking counterparts (Kaufman Kantor, 1990). Epidemiological studies indicate that sexually abused women have a higher risk of substance abuse or dependence than nonabused women (Jarvis, Copeland, & Walton, 1998; Paone, Chavkjn, Willets, Firedman, & Des Jars, 1992). About 47% to 74% of women attending drug and alcohol treatment programs have reported histories of sexual abuse (Ondersma, 1999). Similar figures suggest that about 60% to 70% of women attending substance abuse treatment programs have been victims of partner abuse (El-Bassel et al., 1998). Evidence suggests that partner violence leads to substance abuse. Burnam et al. (1988) found that after a traumatic event occurred, participants were more likely to abuse alcohol or drugs. Research has also found associations between women's drug use and partner violence (Kessler et al., 1996; Kilpatrick, Acierno, Resnick, Saunders, & Beest, 1991) and between male partner's drug use and partner violence (Miller, Downs, Gondoli, & Keil, 1987; Miller et al., 1993). Most studies are cross-sectional, providing only noncausal associations between substance use and partner abuse. Very few studies have demonstrated that substance abuse and violence are reciprocal in nature. For instance, Kilpatrick et al. (1991) found that as substance abuse increases, sexual and physical violence increase, making the relationship cyclical. A study conducted by Cottler, Compton, Mager, Spitznagel, & Janca (1992) showed that men who reported cocaine and marijuana use were 5.06 and 1.46 times more likely to abuse their partners than their counterparts. Other studies have demonstrated that the incidence of intimate partner violence among drug-involved women is higher than among non-drug-involved women (Amaro, Fried, Cabral, & Zukerman, 1990; Fischbach & Herbert, 1997; Miller et al., 1993). The extent of this relationship is still under research and is not clearly delineated.

Family violence and substance abuse have been linked to socioeconomic variables (Johnston, O'Malley, & Bachman, 1995; Alaniz et al., 1998), and Latinos are overrepresented in both areas in high numbers. Poverty continues to be a high-risk factor in different forms of violence. The executive summary of the Third National Incidence of Child

Abuse argues that children in families with incomes below the poverty line are 22 times more likely to be abused and neglected and 18 times more likely to be sexually abused than those with incomes of $30,000 (Sedlack & Broadhurst, 1996). The Bureau of Justice Statistics (1995) reported that women between the ages of 19 and 29 with incomes below $10,000 are more likely to be victims of partner abuse by an intimate. It is evident that research and prevalence reports demonstrate that demographic variables such as socioeconomic factors and minority status have been identified as risk factors for family violence. However, it is not clear what magnitude of risk is attributable to minority status, socioeconomic status, or community context (Guerra et al., 1995). Few studies have examined how risk variables vary by socioeconomic status and ethnic group (Gorman-Smith et al., 1996), and it becomes erroneous to attribute risk just to minority status without taking into consideration other variables. As Lyles and Carter (1982) pointed out, researchers continue to eulogize the superiority of the traditional nuclear family, discounting the complexity of the structure and characteristics of minority families and the complex family networks that characterize many families of color. If substance abuse and family violence intersect with child welfare, it is imperative to conduct more studies on Latino groups to see how these three factors might differ in terms of manifestation, incidence, and progress. With the results of these studies, practitioners are in a better position to develop meaningful ways of approaching practice, policies, and services for families that are culturally different.

Conclusion

Latino families constitute the fastest-growing ethnic group in the United States and are overrepresented in cases of child welfare, family violence, and substance abuse. Child welfare, family violence, and substance abuse are emerging as intersecting problems that cannot be seen independent from each other because each constitutes similar risk factors and is interrelated. Research as the foundation for practice, curriculum, service development, and policy making often minimizes the diversity and changing face of the Latino community, and generalizations are made without accounting for this diversity. Some Latino groups have been identified as riskier than others. This risk is usually associated with socioeconomic status, race, and the lack of acceptance in mainstream society. Research has documented that drug of choice, prevalence rates, child maltreatment rates, and perception of family violence vary among Latino groups. The following recommendations must be included in the knowledge base of child welfare, family violence and substance abuse among Latinos:

1. Sampling selection and research methodologies need to improve in order to understand the Latino context. Sampling selection needs to include emerging and larger

Latino groups, including adequate numbers of specific Latino subgroups, in order to make inferences and comparisons. Often studies have ignored the diversity of family functioning and substance abuse development among economically underprivileged families (Gorman-Smith et al., 2000). Research methodologies have to include longitudinal studies in order to understand the path and the intersection of family violence and substance abuse. Qualitative studies must include in-depth specific and contextual forms of violence and substance abuse. Intervention research needs to address this complexity and relationship, which will lead to appropriate forms of prevention and intervention.

2. Prevention and practice approaches should be targeted to different parts of the system in order to assist members of a family who have different needs and developmental courses. For instance, it is imperative to develop interventions and practice approaches with families that are at risk. Prevention efforts should address the intersection between family violence and substance abuse, looking not only at the individual level but also within the nested structures of family, community, and culture. Attention to ecological factors such as poverty, neighborhood crime, alcohol availability, and advertisement in Latino neighborhoods (Alaniz et al., 1998) and the conditions that many Latino families live under cannot be overlooked. Latino communities need revitalization with new allocation of resources, identification of role models, and an effort to improve neighborhoods by reducing alcohol outlets, drug availability, and violence.

3. Identification of risk factors is imperative. The risk factors for child maltreatment and substance abuse are very similar to the risk factors for family violence. Risk factors for Latino adolescents include single-parent homes, low socioeconomic status, having peers who use alcohol and drugs, higher acculturation, parental unemployment, family psychopathology, parental substance abuse, poor parental supervision, inadequate housing, insufficient or nonexistent recreational and cultural activities, dropping out of school, and living in high-crime neighborhoods with high drug use and prostitution (Dakof, 1996; Guerra et al., 1995). Feelings of discrimination and poor self-esteem have also been associated as risk factors for substance abuse (Gil et al., 1998). For Latino adults there are similar environmental and socioeconomic risks in addition to high-stress levels, unemployment, marital conflict and stress, lack or minimal child care, low income, history of child abuse, violence, and parental substance abuse. Having a substance-addicted partner has been identified as a risk factor for family violence and substance abuse.

4. Research needs to examine the ecological correlates of child maltreatment, family violence, and substance abuse such as the family's social context, poverty, high-crime neighborhoods, social supports, and availability of resources. These factors are implicated in the incidence of child maltreatment, family violence, and substance

abuse among Latino families. For example, extensive advertisement of alcohol in the media seems to be influential in the acceptance of alcohol and drug use. These are aspects that affect Latino adolescents and adults and Latino communities at large. Poor communities have limited child care and other resources, which are also related to violence.

5. Practice, research, and policy should be tailored specifically for Latino communities, taking culture as a frame of reference and informed by existing studies in child welfare, family violence, and substance abuse. For instance, Puerto Ricans seem to use more drugs than Mexicans. Mexicans have lower levels of alcohol abstention and, like Colombians and other South Americans, seem to be more alcohol drinkers and binge drinkers than other groups. Prevention strategies should be informed by culturally effective models that use culture as an informative perspective and that acknowledge the value placed on Latino history, familialism, and collectivism, which often contrast with American values of individualism, competition, and materialism. Treatment strategies should also include cultural models, along with a comprehensive therapeutic approach that treats mental health issues in addition to family violence and substance abuse. The strategies should work on micro-, macro-, mezzo-, and exosystem issues that include the use of cultural supports and nontraditional resources available in the community, such as places of worship, bodegas, botanicas, large supermarkets, and beauty parlors (Delgado, 1998). Individuals working in these places can be trained to identify family violence and substance abuse and serve as the initial contact source for referrals to appropriate resources and services.

6. Advocacy efforts, empowerment, and allocation of resources in Latino communities are essential. Latino communities are often neglected, and more prevention efforts and attention is necessary. Activities such as workshops and outreach efforts that include recreational, cultural, spiritual, and networking events can help revitalize and empower stronger communities. It becomes problematic to focus all of the attention on the family without taking into consideration micro-, macro-, mezzo-, and exosystemic issues involved in substance abuse, family violence, and the Latino culture. This systemic view surrounds the context of family violence and substance abuse and creates opportunities for culturally competent practice, research, curriculum development, and policy.

7. Special attention is necessary to improve curriculum development in social work education that includes practice, research, and policy issues that relate to family violence and substance abuse. The curriculum in social work education should have more diverse topics about Latinos and the diversity of Latino subgroups, including risk and protective factors, cultural values, linguistic issues, religion, and historical and belief

systems. Specific courses about practice, research, and policy issues are necessary as well as infusion throughout the entire curriculum with practice, human behavior, research, policy, and field education. Students in social work education need to develop the skills to understand the scope of the problem, identify risk factors, apply theories in relation to family violence and substance abuse, human behavior, and cultural competence models. Practice skills and advocacy efforts need to be strengthened when working with specific Latino populations.

8. Special attention should be given to Latina women, who are at a greater risk for being victims of family violence and substance abuse than Latino men, although prevention and intervention efforts should address both men and women (Mora, 1998). Statistics implicate women as the majority of child abusers (DHHS, 1998); however, in social work practice and policy it is imperative to understand the contextual factors of both substance abuse and family violence. Women in general are more at risk than males for both. Latina women carry a double burden: their minority status within the Latino culture compounded by the status of many minorities in this country and the lack of power that many Latina women encounter in this society (Amaro et al., 1999; Falicov, 1998).

References

Alaniz, M. L., Cartmill, R. S., & Parker, R. N. (1998). Immigrants and violence: The importance of neighborhood context. *Hispanic Journal of Behavioral Sciences*, *20*(2), 155–174.

Amaro, H., Fried, L., Cabral, H., & Zuckerman, B. (1990). Violence during pregnancy and substance abuse. *American Journal of Public Health*, *80*, 575-579.

Amaro, H., Nieves, R., Wolde, S., & Labault, N. (1999). Substance abuse treatment: Critical issues and challenges in treatment of Latina women. *Hispanic Journal of Behavioral Sciences*, *21*(3), 266–282.

Amey, C. H., & Albrecht, S. L. (1998). Race and ethnic differences in adolescent drug use: The impact of family structure and the quantity and quality of parental interaction. *Journal of Drugs Issues*, *28*(2), 282–298.

Behl, L. E., Crouch, J. L., May, P. F., Valente, A. L., & Conyngham, H. A. (2001). Ethnicity in child maltreatment: A content analysis. *Child Maltreatment*, *6*(2), 143–147.

Besinger, B. A., Garland, A. F., & Litrownick, A. J. (1999). Caregiver substance abuse among maltreated children placed in out-of-home care. *Child Welfare*, *78*(2), 221–239.

Bureau of Justice Statistics. (1995). Violence against women: Estimates from the redesigned survey. *Bureau of Justice Statistics: Special Report, NCJ-154348*, Washington, DC: U.S. Government Printing Office, pp. 1–7.

Burnam, M. A., Star, J. A., Golding, J. M., Siegel, J. M., Sorenson, S. B., Forsythe, A. B., & Telles, C. A. (1988). Sexual assault and mental disorders in a community population. *Journal of Consulting and Clinical Psychology, 56*, 843–850.

Caetano, R., Schafer, J., & Cunradi, C. (2001). Alcohol-related intimate violence among White, Black, and Hispanic couples in the United States. *Alcohol Research & Health, 25*(1), 58–65.

Catalano, R. F., Morrison, D. M., Wells, E. A., Gillmore, M. R., Iritani, B., & Hawkins, J. A. (1992). Ethnic differences in family factors related to early drug use initiation. *Journal of Studies in Alcohol, 53*, 208–217.

Champion, J. D. (1996). Women abuse, assimilation, and self-concept in a rural Mexican American community. *Hispanic Journal of Behavioral Science, 18*, 508–521.

Child Welfare League of America [CWLA]. (2002). National fact sheet 2002: Making children a national priority. Retrieved April 24, 2002, from http://www.cwla.org/advocacy/nationalfactssheet02.htm

Coohey, C. (2001). The relationship between familialism and child maltreatment in Latino and Anglo families. *Child Maltreatment, 6*(2), 130–142.

Cottler, L. B., Compton, W. M., Mager, D., Spitznagel, E. L., & Janca, A. (1992). Post-traumatic stress disorder among substance users from the general population. *American Journal of Psychiatry, 149* (5), 664–670.

Dakof, G. A. (1996). Meaning and measurement of family: Comment on Gorman-Smith et al. *Journal of Family Psychology, 10*(2), 142–146.

Dawson, D. A. (1991). Family structure and children's health and well-being: Data from the 1988 National Health Survey on Child Health. *Journal of Marriage and the Family, 53*, 573–584.

Delgado, M. (1998). *Social services in Latino communities: Research and strategies.* Binghamton, NY: Haworth Press.

El-Bassel, N., Gilbert, L., Krishman, S., Schilling, R. F., Gaetha, T., & Purpura, S. (1998). Partner violence and HIV-risk behaviors among women in inner-city emergency departments. *Violence and Victims, 13*(4), 377–393.

Falicov, C. J. (1998). *Latino families in therapy: A guide to multicultural practice.* New York: Guilford Press.

Farrell, A. D. (1993). Risk factors for drug use in urban adolescents: A three-wave longitudinal study. *Journal of Drug Issues, 23*(3), 443–462.

Fischbach, R. L., & Herbert, B. (1997). Domestic violence and mental health: Correlates and conundrums within and across cultures. *Social Science and Medicine, 45*(8), 1161–1176.

Fontes, L. A. (2002). Child discipline and physical abuse in immigrant Latino families: Reducing violence and misunderstandings. *Journal of Counseling and Development, 80,* 31–40.

Fortes de Leff, J., & Espejel, A. (2000). Cultural myths and social relationships in Mexico: A context for therapy. *Journal of Family Psychotherapy, 11*(4), 79–92.

Gil, A. G., Vega, W. A., & Biafora, F. (1998). Temporal influences of family structure and family risk factors on drug use initiation in a multiethnic sample of adolescent boys. *Journal of Youth and Adolescence, 27*(3), 373–393.

Gorman-Smith, D., Tolan, P. H., Henry, D. B., & Florsheim, P. (2000). Patterns of family functioning and adolescent outcomes among urban African American and Mexican American families. *Journal of Family Psychology, 14*(3), 436–457.

Gorman-Smith, D., Tolan, P. H., Zelli, A., & Huesmann, L. R. (1996). The relation of family functioning to violence among inner-city minority youths. *Journal of Family Psychology, 10*(2), 115–129.

Guerra, N. G., Huesmann, L. R., Tolan, P. H., VanAcker, R., & Eron, L. D. (1995). Stressful events and individual beliefs as correlates of economic disadvantage and aggression among urban children. *Journal of Consulting and Clinical Psychology, 63,* 518–528.

Hernandez, R., & Rivera-Batiz, F. (1997). *Dominican New Yorkers: A socioeconomic profile, 1997.* New York: Dominican Research Monograms, CUNY Dominican Studies Institute.

Jackson, S., Thompson, R. A., Christiansen, E. H., & Colman, R. A. (1999). Predicting abuse-prone and discipline in a nationally representative sample. *Child Abuse and Neglect, 23*(1), 15–29.

Jarvis, T. J., Copeland, J., & Walton, L. (1998). Exploring the nature of the relationship between child sexual abuse and substance use among women. *Addiction, 93*(6), 865–875.

Jasinski, J. J. (1998). The role of acculturation in wife assault. *Hispanic Journal of Behavioral Science, 20*(2), 175–191.

Johnston, L. D., O'Malley, P. M., & Bachman, J. G. (1995). *National survey results on drug use from the Monitoring the Future Study, 1975–1994*: Vol. 1. Secondary School Students. Rockville, MD: National Institute on Drug Abuse.

Kaufman Kantor, G. (1990). Alcohol and spouse abuse: Ethnic differences. In M. Galanter (Ed.), *Recent developments in alcoholism* (pp. 57–79). New York: Plenum.

Kessler, R. C., Nelson, C. B., McGonagle, K. A., Edlund, M. J., Frank, R. G., & Leaf, P. J. (1996). The epidemiology of co-occurring mental disorders and substance use disorders in the National Comorbidity Survey: Implications for prevention and service utilization. *American Journal of Orthopsychiatry, 66,* 17–31.

Kilpatrick, D., Acierno, R., Resnick, H., Saunders, B., & Beest, C. (1991). A 2-year longitudinal analysis of the relationship between violent assault and substance use in women. *Journal of Consultant Clinical Psychology, 5,* 834–847.

Kumpfer, K. L. (1999). Outcome measures of interventions in the study of children of substance-abusing parents. *Pediatrics, 103*(5), 1128–1144.

Larkey, L. K., Hecht, M. L., Millers, K., & Alatorre, C. (2001). Hispanic cultural norms for health-seeking behaviors in the face of symptoms. *Health Education and Behavior, 28*(1), 65–80.

Loeber, R., & Dishion, T. (1983). Early predictors of male delinquency: A review. *Psychological Bulletin, 94,* 68–99.

Lyles, M. R., & Carter, J. H. (1982). Myths and strategies of the Black family: A historical and sociological contribution to family therapy. *Journal of the National Medical Association, 74,* 1119–1123.

Marin, G. (1993). Influence of acculturation on familialism and self-identification among Hispanics. In M. E. Bernal & G. P. Knight (Eds.), *Ethnic identity: Formation and transmission among Hispanics and other minorities* (pp. 181–196). SUNY Series United States Hispanic Studies. Albany, NY: SUNY Press.

McCloskey, L. A., Bailey, J. A. (2000). The intergenerational transmission of risk for child sexual abuse. *Journal of Interpersonal Violence, 15*(10), 1019–1035.

Miller, B., Downs, W., Gondoli, D., & Keil, A. (1987). The role of childhood sexual abuse in the development of alcoholism in women. *Violence and Victimization, 2,* 157–211.

Miller, B., Downs, W., & Testa, M. (1993). Interrelationships between victimization experiences and women's alcohol use. *Journal of Studies in Alcohol, 11,* 109–117.

Mitchel, L., & Savage, C. (1991). *The relationship between substance abuse and child abuse.* Working paper no. 854. Chicago: National Committee for Prevention of Child Abuse.

Mora, J. (1998). The treatment of alcohol dependency among Latinas: A feminist, cultural and community perspective. *Alcohol Treatment Quarterly, 16*(1–2), 163-177.

Nair, P., Black, M. M., Schuler, M., Keane, V., Snow, L., Rigney, B., & Magdes, L. (1997). Risk factors for disruption in primary caregiving among infants of substance abusing women. *Child Abuse & Neglect, 21*(11), 1039-1051.

Nielsen, A. L. (2000). Examining drinking patterns and problems among Hispanic groups: Results from a national survey. *Journal of Studies on Alcohol, 61*(2), 310–310.

Ondersma, S. J. (1999). Substance abuse, family violence, and child welfare: Bridging perspectives. In R. L. Hampton (Ed.), *Child maltreatment* (pp. 264–265). Thousand Oaks, CA: Sage.

Paone, D., Chavkjn, W., Willets, I., Firedman, P., & Des Jars, D. (1992). The impact of sexual abuse: Implications for drug treatment. *Journal of Women's Health, 1,* 149–153.

Patterson, G. R. (1986). Performance models for antisocial boys. *American Psychologist, 41*, 432–444.

Pinderhughes, E. (1989). *Understanding race, ethnicity, and power: The key to efficacy in clinical practice*. New York: Free Press.

Ramirez, R. (2000). *Hispanic population in the United States: Population characteristics; March*. Current Population Report. Washington, DC: U.S. Census Bureau, pp. 20–527.

Rodriguez-Andrew, A. (1998). Alcohol use and abuse among Latinos: Issues and examples of culturally competent services. *Alcoholism Treatment Quarterly, 16*(1/2), 55–70.

Sedlack, A. J., & Broadhurst, D. D. (1996). *Executive summary of the third National Incidence Study of Child Abuse and Neglect*. U.S. Department of Health and Human Services Administration for Children and Families, Administration on Children, Youth and Families, National Center on Child Abuse and Neglect. Retrieved July 19, 2005, from http://www.calib.com/nccanch/pubs/factsheets/canstats.htm

Sorenson, S. B., Siegel, J. M., Golding, J. M., & Stein, J. A. (1992). Gender, ethnicity and sexual assault: Findings from a Los Angeles study. *Journal of Social Issues, 48*, 93–104.

Straus, M, A., Gelles, R. J., & Steinmetz, S. (1980*). Behind closed doors: Violence in the American family*. Garden City, NY: Anchor Press.

Straus, M. A., & Smith, C. (1990a). Violence in Hispanic families in the United States: Incidence rates and structural interpretations. In M. A. Straus & R. J. Gelles (Eds.), *Physical violence in American families: Risk factors and adaptations to violence in 8,145 families* (pp. 341–367). New Brunswick, NJ: Transaction.

Straus, M. A., & Smith, C. (1990b). Family patterns and child abuse. In M. A. Straus & R. J. Gelles (Eds.), *Physical violence in American families: Risk factors and adaptations to violence in 8,145 families* (pp. 245–261). New Brunswick, NJ: Transaction.

Suarez-Orozco, M., & Paez, M. M. (2002). The research agenda. In M. Suarez-Orozco & M. M. Paez, (Eds.). *Latinos: Remaking America* (pp. 1–37). Berkeley, CA: University of California Press.

Suarez-Orozco, M. & Paez, M. (Eds.). (2002). *Latinos: Remaking America*. Berkeley, CA: University of California Press.

Substance Abuse and Mental Health Services Administration [SAMHSA]. (2004). Overview of findings from the 2003 National Survey of Drug Use and Health. (Office of Applied Studies, NSDUH Series H-24, DHHS Publication No. SMA 04-3963). Rockville, MD. Retrieved July 18, 2005, from: http://oas.samhsa.gov/nhsda/2k3nsduh/ 2k3overview.htm#ch2

U.S. Department of Health and Human Services [DHHS]. (1998). *Child maltreatment 1998: Report from the States of the National Child Abuse and Neglect Data System*. Washington, DC: U.S. Government Printing Office.

U.S. Department of Health and Human Services [DHHS], Administration on Children, Youth and Families. (2003a). *Child maltreatment 2001.* Washington, DC: U.S. Government Printing Office.

U.S. Department of Health and Human Services [DHHS]. (2003b). *The adoption and foster care analysis and reporting system report: Preliminary FY 2001 estimates as of March 2003.* Washington, DC: U.S. Government Printing Office. Retrieved July 17, 2005, from http://www.acf.hhs.gov/programs/cb/publications/afcars/report8.htm

U.S. Department of Justice. Bureau of Justice Statistics. (2000, May). *Intimate partner violence.* Washington, DC: Author.

Whipple, E. E. (1999). Researching families with preschoolers at risk of physical child abuse: What works? *Families in Society, 80*(2), 148–160.

Widom, C. S., & Hiller-Sturmhofel, S. (2001). Alcohol abuse as a risk factor for and consequence of child abuse. *Alcohol Research & Health, 25*(1), 52–57.

Zambrana, R. E., & Dorrington, C. (1998). Economic and social vulnerability of Latino children and families subgroups: Implications for child welfare. *Child Welfare, 77*(1), 5–27.

Zayas, L. (1992). Childrearing, social stress, and child abuse: Clinical considerations with Hispanic families. *Journal of Social Distress and the Homeless, 1,* 291–309.

Zayas, L. H., Rojas, M., & Malgady, R. G. (1998). Alcohol and drug use, and depression among Hispanic men in early adulthood. *American Journal of Community Psychology, 26*(3), 425–438.

10

Processes of Resiliency and Vulnerability Among Latinos

FLAVIO MARSIGLIA

Introduction

This chapter explores possible associations between drug use and family violence, focusing on the experiences of Latino communities with an emphasis on Mexican and Mexican American families. The inquiry relies on existing literature on the phenomenon and hypothesizes a reciprocal association between drug use and family violence. The ecological risk and resiliency approach provides the theoretical framework for this research. The main emerging protective and risk processes identified in this work are family support, the child welfare system, polarized gender roles, immigration/migration and internal colonization, socioeconomic status, and acculturation. Recommendations for future research, social work education, and policy and practice implications are discussed.

Existing research has demonstrated that Latinos and Latinas bear a disproportionate share of violence-related morbidity and mortality (Rodriguez & Brindis, 1995), and as a group they exhibit some of the highest rates of violent behavior toward their spouses (Jasinski, 1998). Hispanic and African American couples have been found to be at a higher risk for intimate partner violence than White couples; however, interrelationships among intimate partner violence, alcohol consumption, and ethnicity have been inconclusive (Caetano, Cunradi, Clark, & Schafer, 2000).

Alcohol consumption has been frequently associated with violent behavior, and family violence in particular (Athanasiadis, 1999; Brown, Caplan, Werk, & Serganian, 1999; Markowitz, 2000). In the general population, alcohol intoxication, rather than mere alcohol consumption, has been associated with aggression, and it has been more strongly associated with physical aggression than with verbal aggression (Wells, Graham, & West, 2000).

Researchers have argued for a causal role of alcohol in exacerbating relationship conflict (MacDonald, Zamma, & Holmes, 2000). Among middle school students in rural and semirural communities alcohol use was identified as an independent risk factor for delinquent and violent behavior (Komro et al., 1999). Some have concluded that the relationship between husband alcohol use and marital violence is not spurious nor the result of conflict and violence promoting alcohol use (Quigley & Leonard, 2000).

Heavy drinking on the part of male marital partners was found to double the risk of violence against wives, but when the effects of proxy measures of negative attitudes toward female partners are factored out, the effect of alcohol abuse becomes nonsignificant. It was suggested that the link between alcohol and violence, after all, may be a spurious one in which masculinity is acted out through both heavy drinking and attacks on and degradation of female partners (Johnson, 2000). That's is our question: *Es culpa de la botella?* (Is it the bottle's fault?) There is a risk of exaggerating the power of alcohol and, by doing so, transferring the responsibility for the act of aggression from the perpetrator to the bottle.

Another common assumption is that men are more aggressive than women; therefore, when intoxicated, they cannot control their natural instincts toward violent behavior. In an experiment conducted with a group of men and women in a competitive aggression paradigm either sober or intoxicated women manifested aggression comparable to the intoxicated men. The study suggests that women can be as aggressive as men, and that alcohol intoxication does not seem to be as important a determining factor (Hoaken & Pihl, 2000).

Participants in another experiment shared their perceptions about vignettes depicting a domestic violence incident. Domestic violence victims who drink alcohol were ascribed more blame and derogation in comparison to abstinent domestic violence victims (Harrison & Esqueda, 2000). Testosterone level, demographic characteristics, and alcohol consumption were also identified as contributing factors in explaining the variance in self-reported verbal and physical abuse in a study of low-income, multiethnic males (Soler, Vinayak, & Quadagno, 2000).

A study based on answers from both romantic partners reported that the discrepant drinking partners were strongly predictive of relational distress and the incidence of physical violence (Leadley, Clark, & Caetano, 2000). Research with female victims of male offenders concluded that the quantity and frequency of alcohol use was less predictive of threatening or physical battering than was male drunkenness. Frequent drunkenness was highly correlated with both threats and battering (Hutchison, 1999).

A major longitudinal study with young adolescents concluded that there was a reciprocal rather than a unidirectional association between substance use and violence (White, Loeber, Stouthamer-Loeber, & Farrington, 1999). The reciprocal or mutual effects of alcohol and violence appear to better explain the phenomenon without falling into causality traps. The reciprocal hypothesis studies the association among alcohol intoxication before, during, and after acts of violence.

A family history of alcoholism and violence affects both men and women but it appears to have a greater impact on women's adult problems with alcohol, other drugs, and violence (Chermack, Stoltenberg, Fuller, & Blow, 2000). Research has documented the relationships between women's experiences of violent victimization and their use of alcohol and other drugs, and it has explored the etiologic nature of these relationships (Miller, Wilsnack, & Curandi, 2000). Existing research has also consistently supported the hypothesis that intimate partner violence increases risk for mental health problems (Golding, 1999).

Specifically, women in shelters who experienced both sexual and physical abuse report high use rates of marijuana and alcohol and identify such behaviors as a coping mechanism (Wingood, DiClemente, & Raj, 2000). An ethnographic study conducted with a large sample of pregnant women concluded that for this population drug use is both a survival strategy and a source of vulnerability to violence (Sales & Murphy, 2000).

Exposure to violence and alcohol use at home also may lead to violent behavior and to multiple substance use among adolescents and adults (DuRant et al., 2000; Easton, Swan, & Sinha, 2000; Simantov, Schoen, & Klein, 2000). Family conflict may or may not involve the child but will affect the child eventually. Adolescents who use drugs often report their family environment to be hostile, lacking understanding, lacking in love, lacking in cohesiveness, lacking cooperation, and highly alienating (Seydita & Jenkins, 1998). A study conducted with polytoxic drug abuse patients found that 70% of the females and 56% of the males had been sexually abused as children (Schafer, Schmack, & Soyka, 2000). Adolescents who were physically assaulted, sexually assaulted, witnessed violence, or had family members with alcohol or drug problems are at an increased risk of marijuana and hard drug abuse/dependence (Kilpatrick et al., 2000). Mothers with current or past alcohol or other drug problems are more punitive toward their children. Mothers' histories of partner violence and parental violence also predicted higher levels of mother-to-child punitiveness (Miller, Smyth, & Mudar, 1999). Specific research on substance abuse and child welfare has concluded that parental substance abuse is a factor in much abuse and neglect suffered by children (Semidei, Radel, & Nolan, 2001, p. 125).

Child Welfare

Childbearing by itself can be an effective way in which women who use alcohol, tobacco, and/or other drugs (ATOD) move toward recovery and secession (Linares, 1998). The child welfare system has been described as having the potential of reinforcing the power-lessness of or providing empathy and support to parents recovering from addiction (Akin & Gregire, 1997). Involvement with the child welfare system is an important predictor of program completion for women going through substance abuse treatment in residential settings (Knight, Logan, & Simpson, 2001). Child welfare mothers in recovery from substance abuse seem to long for a life very much like any other mother, aiming at a better life for themselves and their children, meaningful relationships, and self-actualization (Sun, 2000). Family reunification is a tangible reward for complying with treatment. Family-centered interventions seem to provide the best results in supporting mothers to achieve their individual treatment and family goals. These services provide a continuing of care toward substance abuse recovery and support substance-abusing parents with recovering their role with their families (Gruber, Fleetwood, & Herring, 2001). Due to the documented overlap between substance abuse and family violence, the child welfare system appears to be an ideal setting to intervene and address both issues, as they often affect the child's and the parents' well-being.

An Approximation to the Ethnicity Paradigm

Connecting the child welfare, substance abuse treatment, and family violence services presents challenges that only are augmented when the ethnic variable is introduced. Cultural variables and issues of access and equity seem to make this integration particularly difficult when serving vulnerable Mexican American clients. One of every four Mexican/Mexican American farmworkers participating in a nationwide study reported having been physically or sexually abused by a husband, boyfriend, or companion. The strongest predictors of domestic violence among this population were drug/alcohol use by the respondent's partner, pregnancy, and migrant status (Van Hightower, Gorton, & DeMoss, 2000). Related research determined that alcohol abuse is an important predictor of intimate partner violence, and that the exact association between alcohol abuse and violence seems to be ethnic-specific (Cunradi, Caetano, Clark, & Schafer, 1999). Research conducted with children from families with varying levels of domestic violence provides further evidence about possible culturally based, learned norms associated with violent behavior. Family role stereotyping and beliefs regarding the acceptability of family violence were found to differ by gender and ethnicity minority status and to vary by age and income (Graham-Bermann & Brescoll, 2000). Such findings invite further exploration and point to the need to conduct more culturally specific studies.

Specific research with ethnic minorities in general and with Mexican Americans in particular has not been as extensive as investigators might expect. In addition, the limited existing research generally has overlooked the great diversity that lies beneath umbrella labels such as Latino/Latina or Hispanic. Findings from some of these research efforts may mislead researchers and practitioners because the results artificially create a supra group from singularly diverse individuals and communities (Phinney, 1996). Also, there is a real risk of exaggerating the incidence of behaviors such as drug use and family violence when samples are not representative and their findings are generalized to artificially created groups. This myopic approach often overlooks culturally based and environmental strengths, but also misunderstands or exaggerates risks. Much remains to be done in advancing an ethnicity paradigm to the study of drug use and family violence.

In social work and related disciplines there has been a broad acceptance of the ethnicity paradigm recognizing the importance of culture over phenotypical (racial) differences (Wallace, Bachman, O'Malley & Johnson, 1995). However, the tendency to overgeneralize persists. Generalizations about Latinos/Latinas in the United States fall into what has been called *ethnic glossing*. Ethnic glosses (Collins, 1995; Trimble, 1995), or conceptualizations of ethnicity as homogenous categories, have been shown to be problematic for several reasons. The one-dimensional Latino or Hispanic ethnic labels may obfuscate differences within groups and create overinclusive categories that are meaningless for understanding behavior (Beauvais, 1998; Cheung, 1993; Longshore, 1998). In 1996, Phinney cited a variety of authors, such as Jones (1991), Reid (1994), and Zuckerman (1990), who have found that the variation within ethnic groups on such factors as educational level, family structure, and socioeconomic status (SES) made predicting behaviors by ethnic group membership alone untenable. Ethnic labels tend to obscure variables (e.g., SES) that may have a more potent effect on behavior (Cheung, 1990–1991, p. 591).

Variations in health status among ethnic groups is a result of differential exposure and vulnerability to behavioral, psychological, social, material, and environmental risk factors and resources rather than some intrinsic ethnic characteristic (Williams, Lavizzo-Mourey, & Warren, 1994). Ethnicity affects health status through intermediaries such as risk factors in the environment, community violence, and exposure to toxins that affect well-being more directly. Failure to identify these proximal factors can reinforce ethnic prejudices and perpetuate racist stereotypes. For example, when compared to Whites and Blacks, arrested California Latinos were found to have a significantly lower prevalence of drug use at the time of arrest but were more likely to use dangerous drugs such as cocaine, heroine, and PCP than any other ethnic group (Gil-Rivas, Anglin, & Annon,

1997). Thus, different measures of drug use and nonrepresentative samples make generalizations difficult. In the California example, the question becomes: Are Latinos at a higher risk or lower risk than other groups? On the one hand, those arrested had a lower prevalence of drug use. From another perspective, when they did use, they used more dangerous drugs. What is protecting those who are not using or who are using less? Are some protective processes related to culture/ethnicity?

While considerable empirical evidence exists on risk factors for substance use and family violence, much less is known about protective processes (Garmezy, 1985; Wills, Vaccaro, & McNamara, 1992). There is little empirical research about drug- and violence-free Latino families (Gold, Thomas, & Davis, 1987; O. Rodriguez, 1995). Even less is known about the cultural processes that buffer Latino families against drug use and family violence.

Individual characteristics and collective identity factors, particularly peers and family, have long been associated with drug-resisting and violence-free families (Hansen, 1991; Newcomb & Bentler, 1986). Numerous studies have identified a relationship between drug use and social identities (Anderson & Henry, 1994; Bartle & Sabatelli, 1989; Jones & Hartmann, 1988; Jones, Hartmann, Grochowski, & Glider, 1989; Marsiglia, Kulis & Hecht, 2001). Ethnicity has also been explored in relationship to drug-related attitudes and behaviors (Hecht, Trost, Bator, & MacKinnon, 1999; Korzenny, McClure, & Rzyttki, 1990) and drug resistance skills (Hecht et al., 1999; Hecht, Anderson, & Ribeau, 1989; Hecht, Ribeau, & Alberts, 1989; Hecht, Ribeau, & Sedano; 1990; Kochman, 1982).

Several researchers have found that the direct effects of ethnic affiliation and ethnic identity on drug use and family violence behaviors were equivocal, but that the mediating effects on more proximal factors were significant. Nevertheless, when taken together, ethnicity, income, and family structure provided only limited understanding of risk behaviors (Blum et al., 2000). For example, ethnic identity did not emerge as a predictor of attitudes toward violence for a Latino/Latina sample of Texan adolescents (Arbona, Jackson, McCoy, & Blakely, 1999). A drug use study with Puerto Rican subjects found that only two of five measures of ethnic identity used—language preference and native/migrant status—were related to drug use (Brook, Whiteman, Balka, Win, & Guersen, 1998). Ethnic identity, while not directly related to treatment motivation, increased motivation when combined with problem recognition (Longshore, 1997). Similarly, ethnic identity— measured by media preferences, sociopolitical awareness, endogamy, and social networks—influenced drinking behavior among African Americans both directly and indirectly. Finally, ethnic identity was found to mediate effects on drinking norms and religiosity that, in turn, influenced drinking behavior (Herd & Grube, 1996).

Although the association of ethnicity with drugs and violence may be mediated by other factors, its importance in combination with environmental elements such as culture cannot be ignored. As a result, the ecological risk and resiliency approach is a useful theoretical framework to advance a more comprehensive understanding of these issues.

The Ecological Risk and Resiliency Approach

The resiliency processes approach moves beyond the focus on static risk or protective factors and attends to cultural processes that facilitate positive adaptational outcomes (Bogenschneider, 1996). From this perspective, prevention efforts and interventions concentrate on bolstering protective processes. To accomplish such a goal, it becomes important to better understand the protective processes that are present in the lives of Latino families and children. In other words: What protects these families and children against drug use and family violence?

There is also a need to support Latino youth and families negotiating risky environments and stressors. Risks must be identified and researched, but not used to label or stereotype individuals and families. On the contrary, a better understanding of the environmental stressors would permit more efficient support of community members in their efforts to successfully transform the conditions that are generating the risks.

The ecological culturally grounded risk and resiliency approach focuses on learning or relearning attitudes, behaviors, and strategies that foster strengths rather than undermine social competencies. Drug use and family violence may harm the individual physically and mentally but may also interfere often with family growth, educational progress, attainment of job skills, holding a job, supporting a family, and contributing to a safe community.

Moreover, practitioners and researchers agree that just as drug use, choice, and involvement differ by age, gender, SES, ethnicity, and culture, so do incidences of family violence (Kulis, Marsiglia, & Hecht, 2002). Communities also vary in their competencies to lower the prevalence of drug use and family violence. Correspondingly, we need to consider how program designs can capitalize on community strengths and might be adapted to fit diverse communities in such a fashion that program effectiveness is improved. By applying the ecological risk and resiliency approach in our work with Latino communities, researchers and practitioners strive to develop a common understanding across disciplines of the meaning of culturally grounded drug use and family violence prevention and services.

If we are to craft effective interventions that prevent drug use and family violence, individually based risk factors need to be contextualized by examining what puts people at risk. Social factors such as SES and social support are relevant to disease prevention/ treatment because they influence access to important resources and affect multiple outcomes, including drug abuse and family violence. Ethnicity and culture are also important social contexts that influence SES and shape social support for Latinos (Patterson & Marsiglia, 2000). Although membership in particular ethnic or geographic communities is not in itself a risk factor, it may influence access or lack of access to both prevention resources and effective service delivery systems.

Research has delved into the intriguing question of how, even in the midst of multiple risks, some individuals exhibit remarkable resilience against negative social and health outcomes (Bernard, 1994). Resilience has been defined as "a manifested competence in the context of significant challenges to adaptation or development" (Matsen & Coatsworth, 1998, p. 206). Resilience is marked by positive adaptational outcomes in spite of exposure to significant adversity. Adversity is typically indexed by two categories of risk factors: (1) challenging life circumstances, for example, financial stress in the family, parental drug use, and (2) trauma, for example, war, death of a parent, or family violence (Matsen & Coatsworth, 1998).

Resilience comprises a range of protective factors that "modify, ameliorate, or alter a person's response to some environmental hazard" (Rutter, 1985 p. 60). It appears that the same factors that protect against negative outcomes in general, protect against negative outcomes related to drug use and family violence in particular. Some protective individual attributes associated with resistance to drug use and family violence include self-esteem, a realistic view of what is in a person's control, personal competence and goal setting, problem-solving skills, faith in a higher power, or a religious philosophy of life (Anthony & Cohler, 1987). What is not known is if these individual protective attributes apply equally to Latino individuals and communities with a higher degree of collectivism and *familismo* (Méndez-Negrete, 2000).

Rutter (1985) argues that the proper focus of attention in studies of resiliency for all ethnic groups should be on protective *processes* rather than on protective factors or variables, because the word "processes" better captures the complex relational and contextual aspects of resilience and moves perspective away from the linear, reductionistic idea that certain individuals, families, communities, and environments have intrinsic protective attributes. The term "processes" more accurately reflects the dynamic and interactive nature of the human response to life stressors.

Protective processes are not fixed attributes of individuals, families, communities, and environments (Rutter, 1985). Rather, they are dynamic and their effect is evident only in the context of their interaction, the circumstances in which this interaction occurs, and the meaning of a particular factor to an individual. The current challenge for resiliency researchers and practitioners is to discover the processes by which anyone might rebound or regenerate from adversity (Bernard, 1994; Garmezy, 1994) and to identify the environmental conditions that are most conducive to these regenerative processes.

Similarly, it is important to maintain an ecosystemic perspective that attends not only to the relationship between the individual and the stressor but also to the context in which this relationship takes place. By considering the relational and ecosystemic context of drug resistance and violence-free environments further, both researchers and practitioners enhance understanding of why some individuals use drugs or become perpetrators and others do not (Saleebey, 1997).

Interdisciplinary research has confirmed the role of three categories of protective processes at three different ecosystemic levels. These include individual processes, family support, and community and environmental support (Garmezy, Masten, & Tellegen, 1984). Efforts need to focus on these three interconnected levels simultaneously. This interconnection may be even more pronounced among Latino communities (Patterson & Marsiglia, 2000). The following section examines the possible overlapping impact of individual processes, family support, and community and environmental support on resilience and vulnerability toward drug use and family violence among Latinos.

Processes of Resilience/Vulnerability Among Mexican Americans

A comprehensive review of the most recent literature about drug use, family violence, and Mexican Americans reveals an imbalance: a much broader set of studies emphasizing vulnerability processes and far fewer examining resiliency processes. Despite this limitation, emerging themes can contribute to our discussion and, one hopes, to our future research endeavors. In fact, the identified resiliency/vulnerability processes tend to overlap at the individual, family, and community levels.

FAMILY SUPPORT

The devotion and loyalty that Latinos/Latinas feel toward *la casa* and *la familia* have been identified as a protective process against family violence (Marsiglia & Zorita, 1996). Also known as *familismo*, the centrality of family in the social life of Latinos/Latinas may act as a buffer against family violence. Epidemiological evidence is tentatively supportive of such a premise. For example, in a multiethnic study of child homicide cases in Los Angeles, Latino victims had the lowest proportion of within-family suspects (Sorenson, Peterson, & Richardson, 1997). Ethnicity-based differences were also found among adults of both genders. When compared with U.S.-born, non-Latino Whites, Mexican immigrants were half as likely to report having experienced a traumatic event (Holman, Silver, & Waitzkin,

2000). It appears that children and males tend to benefit more than women from *familismo* as a protective process against family violence. These gender differences need to be explored further.

GENDER ROLES

Many of the severe socioeconomic, health, and mental health unmet needs of Hispanic women in the United States have often been attributed to machismo. Machismo has been described as a belief in male superiority and dominance that is legitimized by patriarchal social systems (Mayo & Resnick, 1996). This kind of perspective often presents acculturation as a process nonmajority individuals need to go through as a means to achieve equality between the sexes. Subliminally, the message is that once Latinas/Latinos become less Latina/Latino, machismo decreases and, therefore, drinking and violence against women also decrease. This line of thinking appears to reflect a lack of understanding of Latino cultures and of the traditional meaning of precolonial machismo.

Gangotena (1997) notes that in the rhetorical vision of *la familia*, women are never considered weak or passive. She states, "women are important because they are women." (p. 28). Women hold the family together through the family's values and beliefs. Thus the proverb, *la mujer es el centro del hogar* (a woman is the central player in the home).

The literature about Latinas also points to *marianismo* as a traditional source of strength. *Marianismo*, identified by Stevens (1973), takes its name from Mary, mother of God. The concept underlying *marianismo* is that women are spiritually superior to men, and therefore can endure all suffering inflicted by men. This concept traces back to the Spanish-Catholic colonial experience and not necessarily to the indigenous cultures' conceptions of womanhood before the Spanish Conquest. Thus, contradictory ideals about gender roles may coexist, mixing different cultural traditions and contemporary feminist thought.

A longitudinal study conducted in rural Mexico puts machismo and *marianismo* into context by explaining that the perpetuation of binge drinking and violence has been part of a historic cycle of male dominance that dates to the introduction of alcohol distillation during colonization by the Spaniards, compounded today by frustration over the males' inability to control the economic and political aspects of their households and communities. The acquiescence of women to the resultant violence has been described as a form of mediation over male frustrations that allows women to continue in their roles as economic providers (Pérez, 2000).

Some of these dynamics appear to continue in some communities. In fact, symbolic violence was found to be associated with physical violence in a study conducted with pregnant, physically abused Hispanic women (McFarlane, Wiist, & Watson, 1998). The status of being an internally colonized population (Blauner, 1972) is a shared condition for many Latinos/Latinas in the United States. The postcolonial form of machismo appears to be perpetuated by the lower socioeconomic status of Latino males in the United States (Gutmann, 1996).

Although there is a trend toward more equality regarding decision making because of more women being in the labor force, women still do the bulk of domestic work in Latino families (Coltrane, 1996; Coltrane & Valdez, 1993; Williams, 1990). Research has shown a perpetuation of the division of labor within the home along traditional gender lines (Flores-Ortíz, 1996). In addition, the mothering practices of Latinas have been found to include differential consequences for the development of group identity as compared with mothering practices of the White European American middle class (Segura & Pierce, 1993).

Marianismo influences the identity formation of young Latinas when it is part of the identity of their closest female role models: mothers, grandmothers, and aunts (Marsiglia & Holleran, 2000). Research suggests a greater inclination among Latina than Anglo adolescents to adopt their parents' polarized sex roles (Griggs & Dunn, 1996). On the other hand, Latinas' collective approach to identity development makes them prone to listen to other voices. Researchers have shown an interdependence of schooling, work, and family influences in the development of identity of Latinas (Ortiz, 1996). A high-school-based study of Latinas found that on the surface mothers promoted a *marianista* code while at the same time they were sharing with their daughters a feminist ideal for their future, speaking of self-reliance, family planning, independence, and plans for attaining a college degree (Marsiglia & Holleran, 2000).

The legacy of colonialism and internal colonialism may weaken as women learn to negotiate their urban experience by successfully integrating traditional women's roles and expected behavior patterns (Zimm, 1982). In the process, urban Hispanic women experience an additional challenge of balancing majority culture values with a more family-oriented ethnic identity. In a multiethnic survey of professional women, masculinity scores were significantly higher for Hispanic professional women, and self-acceptance scores were significantly lower than for other women professionals (Long & Martinez, 1994).

Data from a national household survey showed a higher association between work stressors and increased levels of drinking and violence among Latino than among Anglo husbands (Jasinski, Asdigian, & Kantor, 1997). The process of integration into consumer society appears to bring with it new stressors and conditions that put Latinos and Latinas at risk for violence, while drinking appears to increase their vulnerability. Hispanic women, as complainants in domestic disputes, were more likely to be injured than non-Hispanic women by the time the police arrived, but few of them consented to medical care (Duncan, Stayto, & Hall, 1999). Another study, conducted in New York among Latina and African American women seeking care from a New York City hospital emergency department, found that nearly half of the patients had experienced physical, sexual, or life-threatening abuse by a boyfriend or spouse in the past (El-Bassel, Gilbert, Krishnan, & Schilling, 1998).

Research findings have shown a higher prevalence of depression among Latinos/Latinas, with females showing even higher rates than males (Roberts, Roberts, & Chen, 1997). Depression and need for social support were associated significantly with partner abuse among a sample of African American and Hispanic women who were patients in methadone clinics in Harlem and South Bronx (Gilbert, El-Bassel, Schilling, & Friedman, 1997). When compared to women from other ethnic groups, Latinas suffering from depression were more likely to report physical violence during the past year and were more likely to be treated in primary care settings (Van-Hook, 1999).

There is a need to recognize the resiliency of Latinas without falling into the Superwoman syndrome. For example, the fact that Hispanic women who have been abused experienced a lower prevalence of psychological distress than White women (Torres & Han, 2000) needs to be contextualized in such a manner that these more resilient women receive the needed services without falling into the *marianista* role. A higher level of resiliency does *not* imply a lack of needs.

A constant flow of new immigrants makes interpreting some of the cited epidemiological data a difficult task. The trauma of immigration and acculturation adds stressors to the lives of many Latino communities around the nation. Gender roles appear to be important, but simplistic interpretations of machismo and *marianismo* as disconnected behaviors from environmental and historical factors may lead to simplistic research conclusions. For example, a study conducted with Latino/Latina adolescents in the Southwest found that a certain type of masculinity-linked gender identity (dominant masculinity) was associated with more frequent drug use by boys and some girls. Machismo was identified as a risk factor for alcohol use, while another type of masculinity (confident masculinity) was identified as a protective factor against alcohol use for boys and girls (Kulis et al., 2002). These findings may be pointing at important generational differences and at a different conceptualizations of masculinity and machismo.

Gender roles, drug use, and violence need to be studied in the context of the complex stressors Latino communities cope with as they migrate, immigrate, become internally colonized, or go through the acculturation process. Generational differences need to be better understood as young people attempt to reconcile often contradictory sets of norms as they become acculturated.

Immigration/Migration and Internal Colonialism

Most Latinos in the United States are citizens, 62% by birth and an additional 7% by naturalization (Kilty & de Haymes, 2000). However, as a group they are often victims of anti-immigration sentiments and xenophobia. A group of abused Latina immigrant women in the San Francisco Bay Area identified sociopolitical barriers to seeking help and patient-provider communication. Those barriers included social isolation, language problems, discrimination, and fears of deportation. Furthermore, sociocultural barriers also identified by the participants included dedication to the children and family unity, shame related to the abuse, and the cultural stigma of divorce (Bauer, Rodriguez, Quiroga, & Flores-Ortíz, 2000).

Recent immigration and border legislation, welfare reform, English-only policy, and discriminatory educational programs are making it even more difficult for Latinos/Latinas to access needed resources (Kilty & de Haymes, 2000). A multiethnic study concluded that Central American immigrants, a highly disenfranchised Latino sub-group, were more likely than any other Latino group to have been arrested for violent and domestic violence crimes (Gil-Rivas et al., 1997).

Great numbers of Latinos/Latinas have been excluded from the remarkable advances in drug use and family violence intervention and prevention. Also, they lack the awareness other sectors of society have acquired in the last few decades. Denying access to vital resources or not providing culturally relevant services is an infringement on the human potential of many poor Latino communities. Based on the described historical, social, political, and cultural realities of Latinos in the United States, some authors are examining domestic violence from a human rights perspective (Perilla, 1999). They have suggested using the works of Paulo Freire (1995) as a means to conduct consciousness-raising campaigns about drug use and family violence among disenfranchised Latino communities (Perilla, 1999).

Socioeconomic Status and Social Support

Poverty affects Latinos disproportionately in the United States, and their comparative high poverty rate has been identified as affecting their overall well-being (de la Rosa, 2000). A recent study assessed the contribution of neighborhood poverty to the risk of male-to-female and female-to-male partner violence (MFPV, FMPV) among White, Black, and Hispanic alcohol-using couples. The association between residence in an impoverished neighborhood and MFPV was statistically significant for Black couples, and FMPV was statistically significant for Black and White couples (Cunradi, Caetano, Clark, & Schafer, 2000).

Nearly one out of three Latinos of working age does not have health insurance, and poor Latinos are three times more likely than upper-income Latinos to lack health insurance (Cornelius, 2000). Financial conditions (income, employment status, amount of insurance premiums) as well as nonfinancial factors (type of usual source of medical care, citizenship status) play a role in seeing a physician and seeking other help (Cornelius, 2000). These factors clearly influence access to needed services and make it more difficult to reach early diagnosis and implement early interventions.

Contradictory evidence exists concerning the association among SES, drug use, and family violence. Low SES can be seen as a risk factor for communities more likely to be affected by policy changes. Poor women are more vulnerable to policy changes than poor men. For example, welfare reform is likely to have a profound effect on the lives of poor women who are being abused. The backlash hypothesis predicts that violence will increase as men attempt to compensate for women's enhanced state of independence (Riger & Krieglstein, 2000), and Latinas continue to be overrepresented among poor women. Regardless of the presence or lack of an association among SES, drug use, and family violence, the effects of SES in terms of access and equity issues cannot be ignored.

Acculturation

Acculturation appears to play an important role in predicting alcohol use and family violence. A commonly used proxy measure for acculturation among Latinos/Latinas is language use (Sabogal, Marin, Otero-Sabogal, Martin, & Pérez-Stable, 1987). English language use has been identified as a risk factor for substance use (Finch, 2001; Marsiglia & Waller, 2002). A common theme in this kind of research is that more traditional or conservative cultural norms have a buffer or protective effect on Latinos/Latinas against substance abuse. The ethnic loyalty component of cultural orientation of a group of Mexican American college students was the most consistent predictor of adherence to traditional beliefs, including gender roles (Niemann, Romero, & Arbona, 2000). As long as ethnic loyalty is maintained, the assumption is that the protective effect will be in place. This buffer or protective effect, however, does not necessarily transfer to violence against women. A study conducted with pregnant Hispanic women found that the victims of violence were mostly Spanish monolingual (Wist & McFarlane, 1998).

A study based on a national sample of Hispanic households found that the rates of male-to-female and female-to-male partner violence were highest in the moderately acculturated group, followed by the high acculturation group and the low acculturation group. It was hypothesized that intimate partner violence among moderately acculturated individuals may be the result of the difficulties of negotiating between cultures without the support of a strong social network (Caetano, Schaefer, Clark, Cunradi, & Raspberry, 2000). Differences were also found between rural Anglo and Hispanic victims of domestic violence. Study findings indicated differences in terms of the typology of domestic violence experienced and in the violence during in childhood and in previous intimate relationships (Krishnan, Hilbert, VanLeeuween, & Kolia, 1997).

Discussion

These emerging themes do not provide a separate set of competing protective and risk processes related to drug use and family violence. Instead, they identify key contextual or environmental issues influencing the phenomenon. A particular process may have a protective effect in one community and may become a source of vulnerability in another. The review of the existing literature, although not conclusive, tends to support the reciprocal association hypothesis between alcohol intoxication and family violence. Once ethnicity was considered, ethnic identity was identified as a protective process. At the same time, in some Latino communities evidence was found to advance a symbolic/cultural vulnerability that attaches to alcohol and violence against women as part of a legacy of colonialism.

The reciprocal hypothesis is expanded by adding ethnicity as a protective process for some or as a vulnerability process for others within the spectrum of the Latino experience. One possible explanation of these differences could rest in the intensity of the colonial or internal colonization legacy in the communities of origin or host communities. Even those individuals who come from more culturally intact backgrounds may become more vulnerable as they go through the acculturation process, through immigration or migration, into uncaring and xenophobic political environments.

Women seem to be carrying the burden and suffering the consequences of much of this trauma. Family violence emerges as a strong indicator of cultural breakdown, and alcohol appears to be hiding deeply held negative conceptions about women. Alcohol is connected in some men to their postcolonial machismo, allowing them to act out their feelings and insecurities about their role in a postindustrial economy that does not seem to be able to accommodate many of them. These women and their male partners are in need of much support as they navigate through complex adaptational challenges.

Recommendations for Future Directions

Social worker practitioners and researchers are called on to play a main role in supporting Latino families as they identify and effectively employ their existing competencies to overcome the described challenges. By addressing drug use, practitioners may help some men take off their disguise and start working on changing perceptions about themselves and changing perceptions about their female partners that put them at risk of violent behavior. In the process, these perceptions need to be understood by researchers and practitioners and worked on within their proper political, historical, economic, and social contexts.

PRACTICE

Based on the described reciprocal hypothesis, assessment becomes a vital tool to identify possible associations between clients' alcohol use and family violence and to design the appropriate interventions. Regardless of which of the two is the presenting problem (drug use or family violence), we must always assess for the other. It is also important to consider drug use in children, adolescents, and women as a form of medicating/coping with their own abuse or the abuse inflicted against other family members. In addition, social work practitioners and researchers need to address family violence and drug use in connection to safer sex among heterosexual and homosexual partners (El-Bassel et al., 1998).

Norms and behaviors related to gender roles need to be explored in their proper social, historical, and political contexts, such as the postcolonial historical cycle of male dominance (Pérez, 2000). We must avoid labeling men and women by superficially using concepts such as machismo and *marianismo* outside of their proper cultural and historical contexts. Instead, we must aim at opening communicating channels that would allow for true consciousness raising on issues related to gender roles and oppression within a cultural context (Freire, 1995).

Alcohol, drug use, and family violence cannot be approached in isolation and just with the single client. Whole families and whole communities need to be part of regenerative efforts by embracing culturally grounded interventions that build upon the communities' existing strengths and resiliency. The child welfare system appears to be an ideal setting where comprehensive service delivery models can be implemented and evaluated. Positive culturally based gender roles need to be rediscovered and embraced, and norms associated with colonialism and internal colonialism need to be identified, questioned, and dismissed. Communities need help in conducting a critical review of their own practices and beliefs from within the culture. Practitioners must avoid the trappings of neo-colonial discourses and practices.

Coalitions need to be forged among mainstream social service providers, indigenous community-based providers, and informal providers such as healers (*curanderas/curanderos*) in order to facilitate early diagnosis and the development and implementation of culturally relevant interventions.

Special emphasis must be placed on youth and their strengths and challenges as they go through the acculturation process and often live in two different worlds—inside the home and outside the home—with different cosmologies, values, and expectations. Prevention messages need to be coined by youths themselves, based on their own experiences and underlying their own strengths and indigenous resistance strategies.

POLICY

Social workers through their institutions and expert professional opinion need to inform the appropriate national, state, and local government bodies about the effects of xenophobic legislation and regulations and lobby them for just and equal policies. Issues of inequality and inequity must be denounced and resisted by the communities themselves through organizing, mobilizing, and formulating alternative proposals.

Policies enacted at the social services agency level need to be critically reviewed, checking for a possible replication of xenophobic and exclusionary practices against Latinos/Latinas. Social workers through their continuing education activities especially need to be current about immigrant clients' rights under federal and state law. In addition, continuing education must approach professional ethics, assisting practitioners with frequent ethical dilemmas that emerged as they work with immigrant communities and with cases related to drug use and domestic violence.

RESEARCH

Much research is needed to better understand the reciprocal relationship between drug use and family violence within the spectrum of the Latino experience. Epidemiological research needs to be complemented by quasi-experimental designs testing innovative interventions based on culturally grounded, resiliency-based models. Ethnographies are needed in order to explore the meaning attached to Latino symbolic/cultural behaviors connected to drug use and family violence. Some of the additional variables that should be part of future research endeavors are acculturation status, gender roles, rural versus urban settings, SES, migration/immigration status, educational level, and employment history.

EDUCATION

Social work students need to be exposed to culturally grounded content about the Latino experience. The historical, cultural, political, and economic contexts in which Latino communities live have to be addressed in class. Teaching about diversity involves teaching about oppression and its consequences. Drug use and family violence need to be understood within those contexts. Students should be familiar with systems—such as the child welfare system—that Mexican American and other Latino families use. It is within the child welfare system and related services that the greatest impact can be obtained in preventing family violence and drug abuse.

Curricula must assist students to learn how to identify and effectively implement individual, family, and community strengths and competencies. Students will also acquire the needed skills to screen prevention and intervention strategies for cultural competency and appropriateness.

Schools of social work need to make available to their students community-based practicum experiences where innovation is encouraged and where science-based applied research is produced and disseminated. Drug use and family violence prevention and intervention will be addressed as an essential part of the community's well-being.

References

Akin, B. A., & Gregire, T. K. (1997). Parents' views on child welfare's response to addiction. *Families in Society, 78,* 4, 393–404.

Anderson, A. R., & Henry, C. S. (1994). Family system characteristics and parental behavior as predictors of adolescent substance use. *Adolescence, 29,* 114, 405–20.

Anthony, E. J., & Cohler, B. J. (Eds.). (1987). *The invulnerable child.* New York: Free Press.

Arbona, C., Jackson, R. H., McCoy, A., & Blakely, C. (1999). Ethnic identity as a predictor of attitudes of adolescents toward fighting. *Journal of Early Adolescence, 19*(3), 323–340.

Athanasiadis, L. (1999). Drugs, alcohol and violence. *Current Opinion in Psychiatry, 12*(3), 281–286.

Bartle, S. E., & Sabatelli, R. M. (1989). Family system dynamics, identity development, and adolescent use: Implications for family treatment. *Family Relations, 38*(3), 258–265.

Bauer, H. M., Rodriguez, M. A., Quiroga, S. S., & Flores-Ortíz, Y. G. (2000). Barriers to health care for abused: Latina and Asian immigrant women. *Journal of Health Care for the Poor and Underserved, 11*(1), 33–44.

Beauvais, F. (1998). Cultural identification and substance use in North America: An annotated bibliography. *Substance Use & Misuse, 32*(14), 2013–1336.

Bernard, B. (1994, December 5–6). Applications of resilience. Paper presented at The Role of Resilience in Drug Abuse, Alcohol Abuse and Mental Illness. Substance Abuse and Mental Health Services Administration. Washington, DC.

Blauner, R. (1972). *Racial oppression in America.* New York: Harper & Row.

Blum, R. W., Beuhring, T., Shew, M. L., Bearinger, L. H., Sieving, R. E., & Resnick, M. D. (2000). The effects of race/ethnicity, income, and family structure on adolescent risk behaviors. *American Journal of Public Health, 90*(12), 1879–1884.

Bogenschneider, K. (1996). An ecological risk protective theory for building prevention programs, policies, and community capacity to support youth. *Family Relations, 45*(2), 127–138.

Brook, J. S., Whiteman, M., Balka, E. B., Win, P. T., & Guersen, M. D. (1998). Drug use among Puerto Ricans: Ethnic identity as a protective factor. *Hispanic Journal of Behavioral Sciences, 20*(2), 241–254.

Brown, T. G., Caplan, T., Werk, A., & Serganian, P. (1999). The comparability of male violent abusers in violence or substance abuse treatment. *Journal of Family Violence, 14*(3), 297–314.

Caetano, R., Cunradi, C. B., Clark, C. L., & Schafer, J. (2000). Intimate partner violence and drinking patterns among white, black and Hispanic couples in the U.S. *Journal of Substance Abuse, 11*(2), 123–138.

Caetano, R., Schafer, J., Clark, C. L., Cunradi, C. B., & Raspberry, K. (2000). Intimate partner violence, acculturation and alcohol consumption among Hispanic couples in the United States. *Journal of Interpersonal Violence, 15*(1), 30–45.

Chermack, S. T., Stoltenberg, S. F., Fuller, B. E., & Blow, F. C. (2000). Gender differences in the development of substance-related problems: The impact of family history of alcoholism, family history of violence and childhood conduct problems. *Journal of Studies on Alcohol, 61*(6), 845–852.

Cheung, Y. W. (1990–1991). Ethnicity and alcohol/drug use revisited: A framework for future research. *International Journal of Addictions, 25*, 581–605.

Cheung, Y. W. (1993). Approaches to ethnicity: Clearing roadblocks in the study of ethnicity and substance use. *International Journal of the Addictions, 28*(12), 1209–1226.

Collins, R. L. (1995). Issues of ethnicity in research on prevention of substance abuse. In G. J. Botvin, S., Schinke, & M. A. Orlandi (Eds.), *Drug abuse prevention with multiethnic youth* (pp. 28–45). Thousand Oaks, CA: Sage.

Coltrane, S. (1996). *Family man: Fatherhood, housework and gender equality.* New York: Oxford University Press.

Coltrane, S., & Valdez, E. O. (1993). Reluctance compliance: Work-family role deallocation in dual earner Chicano families. In J. C. Wood (Ed.), *Men, work and family* (pp. 151–175). Newbury Park, CA: Sage.

Cornelius, L. J. (2000). Financial barriers to health care for Latinos: Poverty and beyond. *Journal of Poverty, 4*(2), 63–83.

Cunradi, C. B., Caetano, R., Clark, C. L., & Schafer, J. (1999). Alcohol-related problems and intimate partner violence among white, black, and Hispanic couples in the U.S. *Alcoholism-Clinical and Experimental Research, 23*(9), 1492–1501.

Cunradi, C. B., Caetano, R., Clark, C. L., & Schafer, J. (2000). Neighborhood poverty as a predictor of intimate partner violence among white, black, and Hispanic couples in the United States. *Annals of Epidemiology, 10*(5), 297–308.

de la Rosa, M. R. (2000). An analysis of Latino poverty and a plan of action. *Journal of Poverty, 4*(2), 27–62.

Duncan, M. M., Stayto, C. D., & Hall, C. B. (1999). Police reports on domestic incidents involving intimate partners: Injuries and medical help-seeking. *Women and Health, 30*(1), 1–13.

DuRant, R. H., Altman, D., Wolfson, M., Barkin, S., Kreiter, S., & Krowchuck, D. (2000). Exposure to violence and victimization, depression, substance use, and the use of violence by young adolescents. *Journal of Pediatrics, 137*(5), 707–713.

Easton, C. J., Swan, S., & Sinha, R. (2000). Prevalence of family violence in clients entering substance abuse treatment. *Journal of Substance Abuse Treatment, 18*(1), 23–28.

El-Bassel, N., Gilbert, L., Krishnan, S., & Schilling, R. F (1998). Partner violence and sexual HIV-risk behaviors among women in an inner-city emergency department. *Violence and Victims, 13*(4), 377–393.

Finch, B. K. (2001). Nation of origin, gender, and neighborhood differences in past-year substance use among Hispanics and non-Hispanic Whites. *Hispanic Journal of Behavioral Sciences, 23*(1), 88–101.

Flores-Ortíz, I. (1996). Levels of acculturation, marital satisfaction, and depression among Chicana workers: A psychological perspective. *Aztlan, 20*(1/2), 151–175.

Freire, P. (1995). *Pedagogy of the oppressed.* New York: Continuum.

Gangotena, M. (1997). The rhetoric of la familia among Mexican Americans. In A. Gonzalez, M. Houston, & V. Chen (Eds.), *Our voices: Essays in culture, ethnicity, and communication* (pp. 28–32). Los Angeles: Roxbury Publishing.

Garmezy, N. (1985). Stress resistant children: The search for protective factors. In J. Stevenson, Jr. (Ed.), *Recent research on developmental psychopathology* (pp. 213–233). Oxford, U.K.: Pergamon Press.

Garmezy, N. (1994). Reflections and commentary on risk, resiliency, and development. In R. J. Haggarty, L. R. Sherod, N. Garmezy, & M. Rutter, (Eds.), *Stress, risk and resiliency in children and adolescents: Processes, mechanisms, and interventions* (pp. 1–18). Cambridge, MA: Harvard University Press.

Garmezy, N., Masten, A. S., & Tellegen, A. (1984). The study of stress and competence in children: A building block for developmental psychopathology. *Child Development*, *55*, 97–111.

Gilbert, L., El-Bassel, N., Schilling, R. F., & Friedman, E. (1997). Childhood abuse as a risk for partner abuse among women in methadone maintenance. *American Journal of Drug and Alcohol Abuse*, *23*(4), 581–595.

Gil-Rivas, V., Anglin, M. D., & Annon, J. J. (1997). Patterns of drug use and criminal activities among Latino arrestees in California: Treatment and policy implications. *Journal of Psychopatholgy and Behavioral Assessment*, *19*(2), 161–174.

Gold, R. S., Thomas, S. B., & Davis, D. (1987). *The literature on prevention in minority communities: Some lessons to be learned*. Minority Health Research Laboratory. Washington, DC: Office of Minority Health.

Golding, J. M. (1999). Intimate partner violence as a risk factor for mental disorders: A meta-analysis. *Journal of Family Violence*, *14*(2), 99–132.

Graham-Bermann, S. A., & Brescoll, V. (2000). Gender, power, and violence: Assessing the family stereotypes of the children of the batterers. *Journal of Family Psychology*, *14*(4), 600–612.

Griggs, S., & Dunn, R. (1996). *Hispanic American students and learning style*. Urbana, IL: ERIC Clearinghouse on Elementary and Early Childhood Education. ERIC Document Reproduction Service No. ED393607.

Gruber, K. J., Fleetwood, T. W., & Herring, M. W. (2001). In-home continuing care services for substance-affected families: The Brides Program. *Social Work*, *46*(3), 267–277.

Gutmann, M. C. (1996). *The meaning of macho: Being a man in Mexico City*. Berkeley, CA: University of California Press.

Hansen, W. B. (1991). School-based substance abuse prevention: A review of the state of art curriculum, 1980–1990. *Health Education Research*, *7*(3), 403–430.

Harrison, L. A., & Esqueda, C. W. (2000). Effects of race and victim drinking on domestic violence attributions. *Sex Roles*, *42*(11/12), 1043–1057.

Hecht, M. L., Anderson, P. A., & Ribeau, S. (1989). The cultural dimensions of nonverbal communication. In M. K. Asanti & W. B. Gudykunst (Eds.), *Handbook of intercultural communication* (pp. 163–185). Beverly Hills, CA: Sage.

Hecht, M. L., Ribeau, S. & Alberts, J. K. (1989). An Afro-American perspective on interethnic communication. *Communication Monographs*, *54*, 385–410.

Hecht, M. L., Ribeau, S., & Sedano, M. V. (1990). A Mexican-American perspective on interethnic communication. *International Journal of Intercultural Relations*, *14*, 31–55.

Hecht, M. L., Trost, M., Bator, R, & McKinnon, D. (1999) Ethnicity and gender similarities and differences in drug resistance. *Journal of Applied Communication Research*, *25*, 75–97.

Herd, D., & Grube, J. (1996). Black identity and drinking in the U.S.: A national study. *Addiction*, *91*(6), 845–862.

Hoaken, P. N. S., & Pihl, R. O. (2000). The effects of alcohol intoxication on aggressive responses in men and women. *Alcohol and Alcoholism, 35*(5), 471–477.

Holman, E. A., Silver, R. C., & Waitzkin, H. (2000). Traumatic life events in primary care patients: A study in an ethnically diverse sample. *Achieves of Family Medicine, 9*(9), 802–810.

Hutchison, I. W. (1999). Alcohol, fear, and woman abuse. *Sex Roles, 40*(11/12), 893–920.

Jasinski, J. L. (1998). The role of acculturation in wife assault. *Hispanic Journal of Behavioral Sciences, 20*(2), 175–191.

Jasinski, J. L., Asdigian, N. L., & Kantor, G. K. (1997). Ethnic adaptation to occupational strain: Work-related stress, drinking, and wife assault among Anglo and Hispanic husbands. *Journal of Interpersonal Violence, 12*(6), 814–831.

Johnson, H. (2000). The role of alcohol in male partners' assaults on wives. *Journal of Drug Issues, 30*(4), 725–740.

Jones, J. (1991). Psychological models of race: What have they been and what should they be? In J. Goodchilds (Ed.), *Psychological perspectives on human diversity in America* (pp. 3–46). Washington, DC: American Psychological Association.

Jones, R. M., & Hartmann, B. R. (1988). Ego identity: Developmental differences and experimental substance use among adolescents. *Journal of Adolescence, 11*(4), 347–360.

Jones, R. M., Hartmann, B. R., Grochowski, G. O., & Glider, P. (1989). Ego identity and substance abuse: A comparison of adolescents in residential treatment with adolescents in school. *Personality and Individual Differences, 10*(6), 625–631.

Kilpatrick, D. G., Acierno, R. Saunders, B., Resnick, H. S., Best, C. L., & Schnurr, P. P. (2000). Risk factors for adolescent substance abuse and dependence: Data from a national sample. *Journal of Consulting and Clinical Psychology, 68*(1), 19–30.

Kilty, K. M., & de Haymes, M. V. (2000). Racism, nativism, and exclusion: Public policy, immigration, and the Latino experience in the United States. *Journal of Poverty, 4*(2), 1–25.

Knight, D. K., Logan, S. M., & Simpson, D. D. (2001). Predictors of program completion for women in residential substance abuse treatment. *American Journal of Drug and Alcohol Abuse, 27*(1), 18.

Kochman, T. (1982). Urban danger: Life in a neighborhood of strangers. *American Ethnologist, 9*, 616–619.

Komro, K. A., Williams, C. L., Forster, J. L., Perry, C. L., Farbakhsh, K., & Stigler, M. H. (1999). The relationship between adolescent alcohol use and delinquent and violent behaviors. *Journal of Child and Adolescent Substance Abuse, 9*, 13–28.

Korzenny, F., McClure, J., & Rzyttki, B. (1990). Ethnicity, communication, and drugs. *Journal of Drug Issues, 20*, 87–98.

Krishnan, S. P., Hilbert, J. C., VanLeeuween, D., & Kolia, R. (1997). Documenting domestic violence among ethnically diverse populations: Results from a preliminary study. *Family and Community Health, 20*(3), 32–48.

Kulis, S., Marsiglia, F. F., & Hecht, M. L. (2002). Gender labels and gender identity as predictors of drug use among ethnically diverse middle school students. *Youth and Society, 33*(3), 442–475.

Leadley, K., Clark, C. L., & Caetano, R. (2000). Couples' drinking patterns, intimate partner violence, and alcohol-related partnership problems. *Journal of Substance Abuse, 11*(3), 253–263.

Linares, L. (1998). Substance-abusing mothers in the child welfare system. *Women's Health Issues.* 8 (4): 254-60.

Long, V. O., & Martinez, E. A. (1994). Masculinity, femininity, and Hispanic professional women's self-esteem and self-acceptance. *Journal of Counseling and Development, 73*(2), 183–186.

Longshore, D. (1997). Treatment motivation among Mexican-American drug-using arrestees. *Hispanic Journal of Behavioral Sciences, 19*(2), 214–229.

Longshore, D. (1998). Desire for help among drug-using Mexican American arrestees. *Substance Use & Misuse, 33*(6), 1387–1406.

MacDonald, G., Zamma, M. P., & Holmes, J. G. (2000). An experimental test of the role of alcohol in relationship conflict. *Journal of Experimental Social Psychology, 36*(2), 182–193.

Markowitz, S. (2000). The price of alcohol, wife abuse, and husband abuse. *Southern Economic Journal, 67*(2), 279–303.

Marsiglia, F. F., & Holleran, L. (2000). I've learned so much from my mother: An ethnography of a group of Chicana high school students. *Social Work in Education, 21*(4), 220–237.

Marsiglia, F. F., Kulis, S., & Hecht, M. L. (2001). Ethnic labels and ethnic identity as predictors of drug use among middle school students in the Southwest. *Journal of Research on Adolescence, 11*(1), 21–48.

Marsiglia, F. F., & Waller, M. (2002). Language preference and drug use among Southwestern Mexican American middle school students. *Social Work in Education.*

Marsiglia, F., & Zorita, P. (1996). Narratives as a means to support Latino/a students in higher education. *Reflections, 2,* 54–62.

Matsen, A. S., & Coatsworth, J. D. (1998, February). The development of competence in favorable and unfavorable environments. *American Psychologist, 53*(2), 205–220.

Mayo, Y. Q., & Resnick, R. P. (1996). The impact of machismo on Hispanic women. *Affilia, 11*(3), 257–77.

McFarlane, J., Wiist, W., & Watson, M. (1998). Predicting physical abuse against pregnant Hispanic women. *American Journal Preventive Medicine, 15*(2), 134–138.

Méndez-Negrete, J. (2000). "Dime con quien andas": Notions of Chicano and Mexican American families. *Families in Society, 81*(1), 42–48.

Miller, B. A., Smyth, N. J., & Mudar, P. J. (1999). Mothers' alcohol and other drug problem and their punitiveness toward their children. *Journal of Studies on Alcohol, 60*(5), 632–642.

Miller, B. A., Wilsnack, S. C., & Curandi, C. B. (2000). Family violence and victimization: Treatment issues for women with alcohol problems. *Alcoholism-Clinical and Experimental Research, 24*(8), 1287–1297.

Newcomb, M. D., & Bentler, P. (1986). Substance use and ethnicity: Differential impact of peer and adult models. *Journal of Psychology, 120*(1), 83–95.

Niemann, Y. F., Romero, A., & Arbona, C. (2000). Effects of cultural orientation on the perception of conflict between relationship and education goals for Mexican American college students. *Hispanic Journal of Behavioral Sciences, 22*(1), 46–63.

Ortiz, A. (1996). *Puerto Rican women and work: Bridges and transnational labor*. Philadelphia: Temple University Press.

Patterson, S. L., & Marsiglia, F. F. (2000). "Mi casa es sus casa": Beginning exploration of Mexican American natural helping. *Families in Society, 81*(1), 22–31.

Pérez, R. L. (2000). Fiesta as tradition, fiesta as change: Ritual, alcohol and violence in a Mexican community. *Addiction, 95*(3), 365–373.

Perilla, J. L. (1999). Domestic violence as a human right issue: The case of immigrant Latinos. *Hispanic Journal of Behavioral Sciences, 21*(2), 107–133.

Phinney, J. S. (1996). Understanding ethnic diversity: The role of ethnic identity. *American Behavioral Scientist, 40*(2), 143–152.

Quigley, B. M., & Leonard, K. E. (2000). Alcohol and the continuation of early marital aggression. *Alcoholism-Clinical and Experimental Research, 24*(7), 1003–1010.

Reid, P. (1994). *Gender and class identities: African Americans in context*. Paper presented at the American Psychological Association Annual Convention, Los Angeles. August 12–16

Riger, S., & Krieglstein, M. (2000). The impact of welfare reform on men's violence against women. *American Journal of Community Psychology, 28*(5), 631–647.

Roberts, R. E., Roberts, C., & Chen, Y. R. (1997). Ethnocultural differences in prevalence of adolescent depression. *American Journal of Community Psychology, 25*(1), 95–110.

Rodriguez, M. A., & Brindis, C. D. (1995). Violence and Latino youth: Prevention and methodological issues. *Public Health Reports, 110*(3), 260–267.

Rodriguez, O. (1995). Causal models of substance abuse among Puerto Rican adolescents: Implications for prevention. In G. Botvin, S. Schinke, & M. Orelandi (Eds.), *Drug abuse prevention with multiethnic youth* (pp. 130–146). London: Sage.

Rutter, M. (1985). Resilient children. *Psychology Today, 18*(3), 57–65.

Sabogal, F., Marin, G., Otero-Sabogal, R., Marin, B. V., & Pérez-Stable, E. J. (1987).

Hispanic familism and acculturation: What changes and what doesn't. *Hispanic Journal of Behavioral Sciences. 9*(4), 397-412.

Saleebey, D. (1997). *The strengths perspective in social work practice* (2nd ed.). New York: Longman.

Sales, P., & Murphy, S. (2000). Surviving violence: Pregnancy and drug use. *Journal of Drug Issues, 30*(4), 695–723.

Schafer, M., Schmack, B., & Soyka, M. (2000). Sexual and physical abuse in early childhood and later drug addiction. *Psychotherapie Psychosomatik Medizinische Pysychologie, 50*(2), 38–50.

Segura, D. A., & Pierce, J. L. (1993). Chicana/o family structure and gender personality: Chodorow, familism, and psychoanalytic sociology revisited. *Signs, 19*(1), 62–91.

Semidei, J., Radel, L. F., & Nolan, C. (2001). Substance abuse and child welfare: Clear linkages and promising responses. *Child Welfare, 80*(2), 109–128.

Seydita, R., & Jenkins, P. (1998). The influences of families, friends, schools, and community on delinquent behavior. In T. P. Gullotta, G. R. Adams, & R. Montemayor (Eds.), *Delinquent violent youth: Theory and interventions* (pp. 53–97). Thousand Oaks, CA: Sage.

Simantov, E., Schoen, C., & Klein, J. D. (2000). Health-compromising behaviors: Why do adolescents smoke or drink? Identifying underlying risk and protective factors. *Archives of Pediatrics & Adolescent Medicine, 154*(10), 1025–1033.

Soler, H., Vinayak, P., & Quadagno, D. (2000). Biosocial aspects of domestic violence. *Psychoneuroendocrinology, 25*(7), 721–739.

Sorenson, S. B., Peterson, J. G., & Richardson, B. A. (1997). Child homicide in the city of Los Angeles: An epidemiologic examination of a decade of deaths. *Journal of Aggression, Maltreatment and Trauma, 1*(1), 189–205.

Stevens, E. (1973). Machismo and marianismo. *Transition-Society, 10,* 57–63.

Sun, A. P. (2000). Helping substance-abusing mothers in the child welfare system: Turning crisis into opportunity. *Families in Society, 81*(2), 142–151.

Torres, S., & Han, H. R. (2000). Psychological distress in non-Hispanic White and Hispanic abused women. *Archives of Psychiatric Nursing, 14*(1), 19–29.

Trimble, J. E. (1995). Toward an understanding of ethnicity and ethnic identity, and their relationship with drug use research. In G. J. Botvin, S. Schinke, & M. A. Orlandi (Eds.), *Drug and prevention with multiethnic youth* (pp. 3–27). Thousand Oaks, CA: Sage.

Van Hightower, N. R., Gorton, J., & DeMoss, C. L. (2000). Predictive models of domestic violence and fear of intimate partners among migrant and seasonal farm worker women. *Journal of Family Violence, 15*(2), 137–154.

Van-Hook, M. P. (1999). Women's help-seeking patterns for depression. *Social Work in Health Care, 29*(1), 15–34.

Wallace, J. M., Jr., Bachman, J. G., O'Malley, P. M., & Johnson, L. D. (1995). Racial/ethnic differences in adolescent drug use: Exploring possible explanations. In G. J. Botvin, S. Schinke, & M. A. Orlandi (Eds.), *Drug abuse prevention with multiethnic youth* (pp. 81–104). Thousand Oaks, CA: Sage.

Wells, S., Graham, K., & West, P. (2000). Alcohol-related aggression in the general population. *Journal of Studies on Alcohol, 61*(4), 626–632.

White, H. R., Loeber, R., Stouthamer-Loeber, M., Farrington, D. P. (1999). Development associations between substance use and violence. *Development and Psychopathology, 11*(4), 785–803.

Williams, D. R., Lavizzo-Mourey, R., & Warren, R. C. (1994). The concept of race and health-status in America. *Public Health Reports, 109*(1), 26–41.

Williams, N. (1990). *The Mexican-American family*. New York: General Hall.

Wills, T. A., Vaccaro, D., & McNamara, G. (1992). The role of life events, family support, and competence in adolescent substance use: A test of vulnerability and protective factors. *American Journal of Community Psychology, 20*(3), 350–373.

Wingood, G. M., DiClemente, R. J., & Raj, A. (2000). Adverse consequences of intimate partner abuse among women in non-urban domestic violence shelters. *American Journal of Preventive Medicine, 19*(4), 270–275.

Wist, W. H., & McFarlane, J. (1998). Severity of spousal and intimate partner abuse to pregnant Hispanic women. *Journal of Health Care for the Poor and Underserved, 9*(3), 248–261.

Zimm, M. B. (1982). Chicano men and masculinity. *Journal of Ethnic Studies, 10*(2), 28–42.

Zuckerman, M. (1990). Some dubious premises in research and theory on racial differences: Scientific, social and ethnic issues. *American Psychologist, 45*(12), 1297–1303.

Part 4

First Nations Peoples

11

Cumulative Effects of Federal Policy on American Indian Families

KATHLEEN EARLE FOX and TERRY L. CROSS

Introduction

Policy making in the United States is an incremental, evolutionary process based largely on the values of society rather than on major, discrete decisions (Shotland & Mark, 1985). American Indian policy in the United States is further entwined with issues of identity, culture, and state/federal/tribal relationships. The intertwining came about through centuries of changes in status and interaction among the U.S. government, state governments, and the original inhabitants of North America. Policies of the American government toward Native people have been characterized in general as shifting among three major initiatives: destruction, segregation, and assimilation (Nabokov, 1991).

The effects of policy shifts on American Indian families are severe. As the dominant society has attempted to eradicate American Indian tribes and assimilate American Indian people, the values of mainstream society such as dominance and patriarchy, competitiveness, and dominance over nature have gradually been assimilated by some American Indian people, frequently with disastrous results. These factors have been implicated in family violence in tribal communities (Hagen & House, 1995; Hamby, 2000). The underlying reasons for violence in Native communities include both misguided federal policies toward Native children (Cross, Earle, & Simmons, 2000) and the trauma associated with contact with the dominant society through the past three centuries (Weaver & Yellow Horse Brave Heart, 1996).

There have been various studies of the interdependence and interactive effects of child abuse/neglect, domestic violence, and alcohol abuse in the general population (Maker, Kemmelmeier, & Peterson, 1998; Mills, 2000; Stanley, 1997). For American Indian people, a study among the Navajo concluded that physical abuse is a risk factor for both alcohol dependence and domestic violence, and that alcohol dependence is a risk factor for family violence in general in this population as well (Kunitz, Levy, McCloskey, & Gabriel, 1998).

More than 2 million American Indian people and 442,000 American Indian families live in the United States today. The integrity of the Indian family has been threatened for many years. Although the federal government of the 1960s recognized the need for a uniform national policy to address child welfare, family, and substance abuse issues and began creating funding strategies to back up the policies, tribal governments were over-looked or not considered viable service providers.

Issues of Abuse/Neglect, Domestic Violence, and Alcoholism

Statistics on abuse/neglect of American Indian children are grim. Although high rates of abuse/neglect of American Indian children reported nationally are suspect (Earle, 2000), it is clear that children from American Indian families are more likely to be labeled as neglected and more likely to be removed from their homes than children of other races. In 1986, there were over 9,000 Indian children in out-of-home placements, an increase of 25% over the number in care in 1980. This constitutes 3.1% of the total number of children in placement, but since Indian children in the United States represent only 0.9% of the total child population in the United States, they are being placed at a rate 3.6 times greater than the rate for non-Indian children.

The reasons for this are many and include the reaction of child protective workers to widespread alcohol use in American Indian communities. A University of Iowa study that looked at the factors contributing to child abuse and neglect in Indian and non-Indian families reported that 57% of abuse cases and 85% of neglect cases in the study involving Indian children were alcohol- or substance-abuse-related (Saunders, Nelson, & Landsman, 1993). American Indian families come under additional scrutiny and concern in the area of domestic violence. The U.S. Department of Justice (DOJ, 2000) reports, "Among violence victims of all races, about 11% of intimate victims and 5% of family victims report the offender to have been of a different race; however, among American Indian victims of violence, 75% of the intimate victimizations and 25% of the family victimizations involved an offender of a different race" (p. 8). Alcohol is a factor in these statistics as well. American Indian victims of violence are the most likely of any race to report that alcohol was involved in the violent offense.

Native communities have long been grappling with the devastating effects of alcoholism, with few or no resources to effectively prevent or treat victims of this disease. Thirty-five percent of all Indian deaths are alcohol-related. The Indian Health Service reports that rates for Native American FAS (fetal alcohol syndrome) and FARC (fetal alcohol-related conditions) victims in some areas of the country are well above the rates for the general population. These children require comprehensive and expensive care. They are vulnerable to abuse, and they enter the child welfare system at alarmingly high rates. The National Indian Child Welfare Association has estimated that between 75% and 90% of all Indian child welfare cases in the nation are alcohol-related. Supporting this estimate were numbers on the Yakama reservation in Washington state, which indicated that 60% of children placed in foster care exhibited the effects of FAS or FARC.

There is widespread experimentation with alcohol among Native youth. Among young Native people, May (1988) reported that by 12th grade 60% to 90% of Native youth report using alcohol. Beauvais (1998) found that in 1993 71% of Native youth from grades 7 to 12 reported having used alcohol, and 55% reported having been drunk. According to Beauvais, although about the same percentage of Native and non-Native youth have tried alcohol, Native youth appear to engage in heavier drinking with more negative consequences.

Among Natives who have been arrested, the rate of arrest for alcohol-related violations (liquor law violations, public drunkenness), is double the national rate. Half of Native inmates in local jails were consuming alcohol at the time of their offense, and an estimated 70% of Natives in local jails convicted of a violent crime had been drinking when they committed the offense (DOJ, 2000). In 1988, May reported that from 1986 to 1988, 17% to 19% of all Native deaths were probably alcohol-related, compared to the general U.S. average of 4.7%.

It is important to note, however, that "not all American Indians drink and not all who drink do so excessively" (Gill, Eagle Elk, & Deitrich, 1997, p. 41). There are wide variations in rates among and within different Native tribes/nations (Mail & Johnson, 1993; May, 1988).

As previously stated, the link between the abuse and/or neglect of children and later violent behavior has been made by various authors. While Bowers (1990); Senn, Desmarais, Verberg, & Wood (2000); and Widom (1989) present research regarding the link between early abuse and later delinquency and/or crime among the general population,

Fry (1993) deals specifically with an indigenous group. Fry's study of the intergenerational transfer of violence among the Zapotec of Oaxaca, Mexico, revealed that differences in level of aggression were directly attributable to differences in parent-child interaction. In the community with lower levels of violence, parents expressed views that children are naturally well behaved, are capable of responsibility, and will naturally learn what is expected of them. The people in the more violent community expressed the opinion that children are naturally mischievous, somewhat uncontrollable, and not yet responsible. The value of respect for children, associated with lower levels of violence, has been commonly found among Native communities in the past (Cross, 1986; Red Horse, 1997; Red Horse et al., 2000).

Traditional American Indian societies valued and protected children. This was the foremost concern of elders, chiefs, clan mothers, and other members of the extended families and communities. There were customs and traditions for regulating civil matters such as child custody and what is now called child welfare. Tribal elders acted as judges. Traditional chiefs governed as the protectors of family well-being. Clan and kinship systems functioned as social service providers. There were no words in American Indian languages for "orphans" because children in need were the responsibility of everyone in the tribe. Federal policy over the past few centuries worked to diminish the tribal capacities and resources that allow full exercise of sovereignty and related governmental functions by forced dependence and destruction of traditional governmental structures.

Interestingly, centuries of oppression and restriction did not diminish tribal sovereignty and responsibility to the children in the eyes of tribal leaders. The concept of tribal sovereignty is based in international law, the U.S. Constitution, treaty law, and numerous federal laws and policies (Nighthorse Campbell, 2000). Whether a government can fulfill its obligations to its citizens, sovereign governments are responsible for the safety and well-being of those citizens. Tribes, like states, have sovereign authority over and responsibility for the protection of children and families.

Early American-Indigenous Relations

When the first Europeans came to the Western Hemisphere, they found families and societies that were strong, thriving, and powerful. Very early relations between Native people and the early U.S. government were tinged with begrudging respect on the part of American leaders. At that time Indian nations were the superior military force, controlling trade routes and most natural resources and often playing key roles in international alliances and diplomacy. Because the Indian nations of the time had well-established government-to-government relations with European powers, the Constitution of the fledgling United States specifically placed the responsibility for relationships with Indian nations with the federal government. Further, this course was taken, ostensibly, in order to prevent Indian land wars with individual states (Canby, 1998). But as the balance of power shifted in the early 19th century, and as more and more immigrants demanded a place to live, American Indians were allotted a smaller and smaller portion of their once endless territories, and the U.S. government increasingly took on the role of overseer of those territories.

Some of the early activities of the federal government regarding Native people had an effect on long traditions crucial to the health and welfare of American Indian children and families. Early establishment of trading houses through the Trade and Intercourse Acts from 1790 to 1834 (Prucha, 1990) became a means to provide indirect supervision of Indian people through the use of agents appointed by the federal government (Nabokov, 1991). A pattern of exchanging lands for services developed, and treaties with Indian tribes specifically provided federal services and care (Prucha, 1990). The creation of the Civilization Fund in 1819 financed church efforts to "save and civilize the Indian" (Bremner, 1970). The establishment of the Bureau of Indian Affairs in 1824 under the War Department led to the use of army medical personnel to oversee the health care of Indians on reservations (Attneave, 1984).

The *Cherokee v. Georgia* (1831) and *Worcester v. Georgia Supreme Court* (1832) decisions reaffirmed he concept of federal, not state, oversight of Indian affairs, but also defined Indian nations as separate but "dependent" nations for which the federal government was responsible (Canby, 1998). These decisions, although affirming the lack of state jurisdiction over Indian affairs, led to further erosion of autonomy among Native people. The Bureau of Indian Affairs was transferred from the War Department to the Department of the Interior in 1849, indicating a possible change in philosophy from Indian-as-enemy to Indian-as-dependent.

Period of Removal

A period of Indian removal began officially with the Indian Removal Act of 1830 (Canby, 1998). During the next decades many Native people were forcibly removed from lands desired for White settlement to less desirable areas, most notably to the state of Oklahoma. The suffering of Native people during this period is illustrated by the story of the Trail of Tears traveled by the Cherokee, Choctaw, Creek, Chickasaw, and Seminole. Strikingly, these peoples were not the unsophisticated Natives depicted in the popular media. For example, the Cherokee of that time had the highest literacy rate in the world and were merchants, traders, and farmers (Weatherford, 1991) But they were in the way, and "ethnic cleansing" became the policy of the day, with the passage of the Indian Removal Act. By the mid 1880s isolating Indians and teaching them mainstream ways of living was considered the easiest and cheapest way to deal with the proud and persistent Indian nations, as wars had been found to be prohibitively expensive (Nabokov, 1991). This task was undertaken by, among others, well-meaning missionaries who lived among the Native people on federally established reservation lands.

Off-reservation boarding schools were established in 1878 where Native children were taken by force. Once there they were forbidden to use their Native language or customs. In 1883 the Courts of Indian Offenses were authorized, and rules of Indian Courts were drawn up. As part of the civilizing mission of these courts, certain religious dances and the practices of medicine men were outlawed to encourage Indians to abandon "their barbarous rites and customs" (Prucha, 1990, pp. 186–187).

Period of Allotment/Assimilation

Enforcement of the federal policy of assimilation of Native people dates officially from the Dawes Act of 1887, which attempted to force the division of Western Indian lands into farmable acreage, ostensibly to make the Indians more like White people. The provisions of this act gave Native people land allotments and conferred U.S. citizenship on them to become farmers, but grantees were allowed to sell the land, thus breaking up tribal monopolies on community-owned property. It was anticipated that many Indian people would either become assimilated or would sell their land to hungry White settlers waiting in the wings (Canby, 1998; Prucha, 1990). Meanwhile, in New York state, the Lake Mohonk Conferences of the Friends of Indians, held between 1883 and 1916, produced a report favoring and encouraging the assimilation of Indians.

The Indian Citizenship Act passed by Congress in 1924 further encouraged assimilation by conferring national and state citizenship on all Indians born in the United States who had not already been declared citizens through other means, such as allotment or veteran status (Canby, 1998).

A Sort of Return to Sovereignty

The Indian Reorganization Act of 1934 was an admission that total assimilation of Indian tribes had not worked. Instead, it authorized the establishment of tribal governments and courts on Indian reservations following the U.S. model. Tribes were instructed to adopt constitutions similar to that of the United States and required the approval of the secretary of the interior (Canby, 1998). Many tribes declined to create governments in the U.S. image, however, and many of those that did elect new leaders set up years of rancor and conflict between elected and traditional tribal factions that continue today. Tragically, the idea of assimilation did not die either. The wholesale removal of Indian children into White society, homes, and institutions continued and was about to increase to even greater numbers.

Termination and Urbanization

The era of termination and urbanization was characterized by attempts to make Indians disappear, either by assimilation into urban neighborhoods or through legislated endings to federal oversight. In 1953 Public Law (P.L.) 280 extended state jurisdiction over civil and criminal American Indian matters. This opened the doors to state jurisdiction over Indian affairs. From 1953 to 1968 the U.S. government tried to end its relationship with Indian people through policies such as P.L. 280; through House Resolution 108, which terminated the tribal status of specific Indian nations; and through policies of urbanization (Canby, 1998). Although the policies were unsuccessful, many Native people left the reservations during this time to find jobs; many ended up in urban areas.

P.L 280 eroded tribal authority and capacity to protect children. This set the stage for pervasive attempts to assimilate American Indian children. In the 1950s and '60s, adoptions of American Indian children into non-Indian families were widespread. Children were removed from their homes and placed in non-Indian homes, foster homes, or boarding schools operated by the Bureau of Indian Affairs or private organizations. The tragic, long-range effects of the placement of thousands of children away from their homes included not only effects on individuals (Fanshel, 1972; Robin, Rasmussen, & Gonzalez-Santin, 1999), but also consequences for the well-being of entire communities of American Indian people.

Self-Determination

In 1968 the Indian Civil Rights Act authorized tribes to either deny or approve the transfer from federal to state jurisdiction specified in P.L. 280. This allowed states to return jurisdiction to tribes through retrocession of P.L. 280. Although few tribes took advantage of the legislation, the Indian Civil Rights Act ended further transfers of tribal jurisdiction to the states (Bloom, Manson, & Neligh, 1980). The Indian Civil Rights Act also gave American Indian people the protections of the American Bill of Rights that had been extended to the rest of the U.S. populace for the previous 150 years.

In 1975 the Indian Self-Determination and Education Assistance Act (P.L. 93-638) was passed to allow Indian nations/tribes to manage their own mental health, health, child welfare, and alcoholism programs formerly operated by the federal government. This was usually done by assuming responsibility for programs already created by the Indian Health Service. According to Churchill and Morris (1992), this act, although outwardly supportive of tribal interests, continues the tradition of "preeminent authority" of the federal government over Indian affairs. Not all American Indian nations elected to run their federal programs, and some tribes elected to run some but not all of the programs formerly operated by the federal government.

In response to two years of testimony regarding the widespread removal of Indian children, Congress passed the Indian Child Welfare Act (ICWA) of 1978 (P.L. 95-6087). This act sets up requirements and standards for child-placing agencies to follow in the placement of Indian children, including providing remedial, culturally appropriate services for Indian families before a placement occurs; notifying tribes regarding the placement of Indian children; and making the first placement of a child in an Indian home, rather than the home of another ethnic/racial group. The ICWA was a huge step in the right direction, but the funding, desire, or know-how did not necessarily follow. Program development "has been hampered by lack of funding, jurisdictional barriers, lack of trained personnel, lack of information about the extent of the problem, lack of culturally appropriate service models and community denial" (Cross, Earle, & Simmons, 2000, p. 53).

Current Status of American Indian Policy

Indian families today are still reeling from centuries of misguided federal policy. The results include not only identity confusion, but widespread negative factors that have led to conditions ripe for abuse, domestic violence, and alcoholism. Many of the elements identified by Shepherd (2001) were found to be related to domestic violence in rural Alaskan villages. These were:

Isolated communities

Lack of adequate law enforcement

Prevalence of alcohol or drugs

Absence of many basic public services, such as affordable housing and transportation

Lack of jobs and dependence on public assistance

Infrequent visits by mental health professionals

Lack of treatment programs for abusers (p. 496)

Although recent federal policies have attempted to meet the needs of Indian families, these attempts have been, to date, too little too late. Most of the legislation that affects the lives of Indian people has been designed for all Americans, and most funding has been allocated to states, not tribes. In order to benefit from these funds, tribes must maintain a healthy relationship with the states where they are located. This is in conflict with the government-to-government tribal-federal relationship defined in the U.S. Constitution and has led in many states to additional tribal-state difficulties.

Tribal-friendly legislation such as the ICWA is not the norm and is constantly being bombarded by those who do not have a vested interest in individual Indian children. In 1996 a serious attack on the ICWA was mounted by adoption advocates following the adoption of two Indian children in direct violation of the ICWA and a lower court ruling, later overturned, to return the children to their tribe. Although the effort to overturn the ICWA was defeated eventually, it became clear that this important policy was vulnerable to attack. Further, courts in at least four states have diminished the effectiveness of the ICWA via case law and the adoption of the "existing Indian family" doctrine. The doctrine basically takes the preamble of the ICWA that states its purpose is "to prevent the breakup of the existing Indian family" (ICWA, 1978) and that if a family is assimilated, it is not an "Indian" family. Courts in these few states have used the doctrine to subvert tribal authority and to apply the ICWA when and how they wish. Some decisions have gone so far as to say that infants relinquished at birth were never part of the Indian family and thus the ICWA does not apply because the adoption did not break up "a family." These arguments are based purely in racist, class-oriented interpretations meant to further erode the sovereign power of tribes when those powers get in the way of non-Indians getting what they want, namely Indian children.

The Personal Responsibility and Work Opportunity Reconciliation Act (PRWORA) of 1996 (Kaiser Family Foundation, 2002) included provisions to allow tribal governments to operate their own Temporary Assistance to Needy Families (TANF) programs for tribal families. Although this provision has been embraced by tribal leaders as a step in the right direction, the funding to set up the administrative structure to operate these programs was not included in the legislation. As of October 2001, 34 tribes had federal approval to operate TANF programs. However, this represents only about 16,900 tribal families; the majority of Indian families (about 40,000) continued to obtain benefits from the states rather than the tribes (Kaiser Family Foundation, 2002). According to Brown et al. (2001), current welfare policies in Indian country are bound to fail because of the lack of an economic growth strategy. The authors recommend tribal institutional capacity building and greater tribal control over programs as a way to address this deficiency.

Much of the funding available to tribes is from grants or contracts with the federal government. For example, in response to U.S. Department of Justice (DOJ) statistics indicating that American Indian rates of violence are much higher than among any other group (DOJ, 2000), the DOJ has allocated grant funds to support various programs in Indian country. An example is the STOP (Services Training Officers Prosecutors)

Violence Against Indian Women Discretionary Grant Program, which has provided funding to develop or implement 273 tribal programs since 1995 to combat violence against Indian women. Money has also been allocated to tribes from the Substance Abuse and Mental Health Services Administration to address problems of mental illness and substance abuse. These grant-funded programs have been successful when they use as a cornerstone of treatment the return to traditional indigenous forms of care (Cross, Earle, Echo-Hawk Solie, & Manness, 2000).

Child welfare, violence, and substance abuse issues are being addressed, incrementally, in Indian country today. Communities have been able to protect and nurture children and families even without funding. Cultural competency is a cornerstone of prevention and treatment projects. Addressing alcohol abuse and poverty also reduces domestic violence and child abuse and the subsequent removal of Indian children from their homes and communities. Policy makers need to understand that, given the resources, Indian people can and will engage in prevention and intervention efforts. Butterfield, Boyer, and Reddish (1992), among others, provide examples of how returning to traditional Native ways has changed the lives of tribes for the better. In the communities described by these authors, alcoholism was ignored and untreated. This has been changing, as individual members of a Native tribe or nation make conscious interventions. The authors cite an example from the Shuswap Tribe of Alkali Lake in Canada in which the rate of alcoholism went from 95% to 2% over a 15-year period largely because of the efforts of one tribal member (Butterfield et al., 1992).

However, in most instances changes cannot be made without support. States, tribes, social service agencies, and the federal system must work together to undo centuries of misguided policy that has led to the dysfunctional system operating today on tribal lands.

Policy Reform Efforts

American Indian advocacy, professional, and political organizations have increasingly taken leadership roles in defining and pressing for needed reforms. The National Indian Child Welfare Association, a membership organization of tribal child welfare programs and Indian child welfare professionals, has published numerous reports and position papers in recent years. The National Congress of American Indians, an organization of tribal governments, has picked up many of these policy recommendations and helped move forward a national agenda of policy reform. As a beginning step, changes in current federal-tribal relationships are needed to encourage and support tribal initiatives. To that end, Indian advocates are pressing for the following reforms:

   •Federal agencies should provide greater tribal access to social service treatment and prevention funds. This could include expanding tribal access to grant funds and making tribes eligible for the Social Services Block Grant program under Title 20 of the Social Security Act.

•Increased funding is needed for evaluation and dissemination of knowledge regarding successful programs. This could be supported with funds from foundations interested in outcome evaluation.

•Laws specifically addressing social service needs in Indian county, such as P.L. 95-608, the Indian Child Welfare Act, P.L. 101-630, and the Indian Child Protection and Family Violence Prevention Act, should be funded at the level originally authorized.

•Promotion and support of service methods that are culturally based and that look at clients' strengths rather than deficits should be made a priority at all government levels.

•Indian tribes must be provided with training, technical assistance, and resources that are fully funded and Indian-specific.

•Federal agencies funding child welfare, violence prevention, or substance abuse treatment programs (Health and Human Services, Bureau of Indian Affairs, and Indian Health Service) on American Indian reservations need to allocate adequate resources for evaluation and technical assistance.

•Greater dissemination of information about models that work in Indian country is necessary, through Indian publications and Web pages as well as Indian colleges and libraries.

•Federal agencies must adopt a needs-based budgeting process that deals with the real needs of Indian people. Needs-based funding for tribal governments must take into account not only the level of need in the target population (beyond just raw population numbers), but also the level of funding necessary to establish effective programs and services (Cross, Earle, & Simmons, 2000).

Other recommendations from Indian country to address the myriad needs of American Indian people include the following:

•A tribal locus of responsibility, in which tribal members own and operate their own programs. An expansion of resources equivalent to those given to states will be needed to accomplish this goal.

•A coordinated, community-based system of care, in which smaller tribes can combine with larger tribes or groups of tribes to provide services tailored to the unique elements of their tribal community for their members. The system may also include state, local, or private organizations dedicated to serving the same clients.

•Good working relationships with state and local agencies that work with tribes to provide social welfare services in a culturally appropriate manner.

Summary

Policy for American Indians is the result of changing attitudes toward Indian people as reflected in decisions of law and in federal regulations and statutes. The issue is complicated by other issues of identity and tribal allegiance. The involvement of Indian people in Indian policy, issues, and treatment is a current trend on a national and local level, as illustrated above. This is a positive development. However, as the national mood slips once more into a period of conservative ideology, old goals of assimilation, termination, and dispersal may once more come to the fore, leading to the possible reversal of recent gains in the encouragement and return to traditional belief and healing among indigenous people.

References

Attneave, C. L. (1984). Themes striving for harmony: Conventional mental health services and American Indian traditions. In S. Sue & T. Moore (Eds.), *The pluralistic society: A community mental health perspective* (pp. 149–161). New York: Human Sciences Press.

Beauvais, F. (1998). American Indians and alcohol. *Alcohol Health and Research World, 22*(4), 253–259

Bloom, J. D., Manson, S. M., & Neligh, G. (1980). Civil commitment of American Indians. *The Bulletin of the American Academy of Psychiatry and the Law, 8*, 1–10.

Bowers, L. B. (1990). Traumas precipitating female delinquency: Implications for assessment, practice, and policy. *Child and Adolescent Social Work Journal, 7*, 389–402.

Bremner, R. H. (Ed.). (1970). *Children and youth in America: A documentary history*, Vol. 1. Cambridge, MA: Harvard University Press.

Brown, E. F., Whitaker, L. S., Springwater, M., Cornell, S., Jorgenson, M., Hale, M., & Nagle, A. (2001). *Welfare, work and American Indians: The impact of welfare reform—A report to the National Congress of American Indians*. St. Louis, MO: Kathryn M. Buder Center for American Indian Studies, George Warren Brown School of Social Work, Washington University.

Butterfield, N., Boyer, P., & Reddish, J. G. (1992). Cultures in recovery. *Tribal Colleges Journal of American Indian Higher Education, 4*(1), 8–11.

Canby, W. C. (1998). *American Indian law*. St. Paul, MN: West Publishing.

Churchill, W., & Morris, G. T. (1992). Key Indian laws and cases. In M. A. Jaimes (Ed.), *The State of Native America* (pp. 13–22). Boston: South End Press.

Cross, T. L. (1986). Drawing on cultural tradition in Indian child welfare practices. *Social Casework, 67*, 283–298.

Cross, T. L., Earle, K. A., Echo-Hawk Solie, H., & Manness, K. (2000) *Promising practices: Cultural strengths and challenges in implementing a system of care model in American Indian communities.* Washington DC: Child, Adolescent and Family Branch/Center for Mental Health Services, Substance Abuse and Mental Health Services Administration.

Cross, T. L., Earle, K. A., & Simmons, D. (2000). Child abuse and neglect in Indian country: Policy issues. *Families in Society, 81,* 49–58.

Earle, K. (2000). *Child abuse and Neglect: An examination of American Indian data.* Seattle, WA: The Casey Family Programs.

Fanshell, D. (1972). *Far from the reservation: The transracial adoption of American Indian children.* Metuchen, NJ: The Scarecrow Press.

Fry, D. P. (1993). The intergenerational transmission of disciplinary practices and approaches to conflict. *Human Organization, 52,* 156-185.

Gill, K., Eagle Elk, M., & Deitrich, R. A. (1997). A description of alcohol/drug use and family history of alcoholism among urban American Indians. American Indian and Alaska Mental Health Research. *Journal of the National Center, 8,* 41–52.

Hagen. J. W., & House, T. (1995). Kanuhkwene: An empowering concept by and for Oneida women. *Journal of Humanistic Counseling, 33,* 123–131.

Hamby, S. L. (2000). The importance of community in a feminist analysis of domestic violence among American Indians. *American Journal of Community Psychology, 28,* 649–669.

Indian Child Welfare Act [ISWA]. (1978). United States Code, Title 25. Washington, DC.

Kaiser Family Foundation. (2002). *American Indian families and tribes: Key issues in welfare reform reauthorization.* Retrieved March 15, 2003, from: http://www.kff.org/minority health/loader.ftm?url=commonspot/security/getfile.cfm+pageid=14161

Kunitz, S. J., Levy, J. E., McCloskey, J., & Gabriel, K. R. (1998). Alcohol dependence and domestic violence as sequelae of abuse and conduct disorder in childhood. *Child Abuse and Neglect, 22,* 1079–1091.

Mail, P., & Johnson, S. (1993). Boozing, sniffing, and toking: An overview of the past, present and the future of substance abuse by American Indians. American Indian and Alaska native mental health research. *Journal of the National Center, 5,* 1–33.

Maker, A. H., Kemmelmeier, M., & Peterson, C. (1998). Long-term psychological consequences in women of witnessing parental physical conflict and experiencing abuse in childhood. *Journal of Interpersonal Violence, 13,* 574–589.

May, P. (1988). The health status of Indian children: Problems and prevention in early life. In S. P. Menson & N. G. Dinges (Eds.), *Behavioral issues among American Indians and Alaska Natives: Explorations on the frontiers of bio-behavioral sciences. American Indian and Alaska Native Mental Health Research*, Monograph No. 1, p. 244–289.

Mills, L. G. (2000) Woman abuse and child protection: A tumultuous marriage. *Children and Youth Services Review, 22*, 199–205.

Nabokov, P. (1991). *Native American testimony: A chronicle of Indian–White relations from prophecy to the present, 1492–1992*. New York: Viking Penguin.

Nighthorse Campbell, B. (2000). Challenges facing American Indian youth: On the front lines with Senator Ben Nighthorse Campbell. *Juvenile Justice, VII*, 3–8.

Prucha, F. P. (1990). *Documents of United States Indian policy*. Lincoln: University of Nebraska Press.

Red Horse, J. G. (1997). Traditional American Indian family systems. *Families, Systems, and Health, 3*, 242–250.

Red Horse, J. G., Martinez, C., Day, P., Day, D., Poupart, J., & Scharnberg, D. (2000). *Family preservation: Concepts in American Indian communities*. Seattle, WA: Casey Family Programs.

Robin, R. W., Rasmussen, J. K., & Gonzalez-Santin, E. (1999). Impact of out-of-home placement on a Southwestern American Indian tribe. *Journal of Human Behavior in the Social Environment, 2*, 69–89.

Saunders, E., Nelson, K., & Landsman, M. (1993. Racial inequality and child neglect. *Child Welfare, 72*, 341–354.

Senn, C. Y., Desmarais, S., Verberg, N., & Wood, E. (2000). Predicting coercive behavior across the lifespan in a random sample of Canadian men. *Journal of Social and Personal Relationships, 17*, 95–113.

Shepherd, J. (2001). Where do you go when it's 40 below? Domestic violence among rural Alaska Native women. *Affilia, 16*, 488–510.

Shotland, R. L., & Mark, M. M. (1985). *Social science and social policy*. Beverly Hills, CA: Sage.

Stanley, N. (1997). Domestic violence and child abuse: Developing social work practice. *Child and Family Social Work, 2*, 135–146.

U.S. Department of Justice [DOJ]. (2000). Promising practices and strategies to reduce alcohol and substance abuse among American Indians and Alaska natives. Washington DC: Office of Justice Programs, Department of Justice.

Weatherford, J. M. (1991). *Native roots: How the Indians enriched America*. New York: Crown.

Weaver, H., & Yellow Horse Brave Heart, M. (1996). Examining two facets of American identity: Exposure to other cultures and the historical trauma. *Journal of Human Behavior in the Social Environment, 2*, 19–34.

Widom, C. S. (1989) Child abuse, neglect, and adult behavior: research design and findings on criminality, violence, and child abuse. *American Journal of Orthopsychiatry, 59*(3), 355–367.

12

The Continuing Effects of American Colonialism

MICHAEL YELLOW BIRD

Introduction

This chapter focuses on the intersections among substance abuse, family violence, and child welfare within First Nations populations in the lower 48 United States and Alaska. The chapter begins by discussing how American colonialism is at the center of these intersections and how most Americans, including social workers, know very little about the effects of American colonialism on Indigenous Peoples. To illustrate this connection, I share a personal narrative that tells how this system of oppression has affected, and continues to affect, my tribal community. This section is followed by a political and cultural demography of Indigenous Peoples; an overview of substance abuse, family violence, and child welfare statistics; a discussion of stereotypes of indigenous peoples' substance abuse and violence; and an overview of practice, policy, and research innovations. The chapter concludes with a discussion of what social workers can do to address American colonialism, substance abuse, family violence, and child welfare problems in First Nations communities. It is important to remember that since there are more than 550 First Nations groups, with distinct histories and cultures, what is presented in this chapter often provides only a generalized overview.

American Colonialism:
The Center of Intersection

It is comfortable for us to believe that colonialism is something which happened two hundred or more years ago, and which involved injustices which never could happen today. Yet, colonialism is a continuing process.   —Carmel Tapping, *Other Wisdoms, Other Worlds*, 1993

In my capacity as an Indigenous person and social work professor, I have been invited to visit, consult, and work with numerous tribal communities, leaders, and academics in the United States and Canada. These experiences have thoroughly persuaded me that a considerable proportion of substance abuse, family violence, and child welfare problems number First Nations Peoples are a result of American colonialism. Indeed, a significant amount of excessive rates of premature death, depression, poverty, unemployment, poor health, loss of personal and cultural identity, family and community conflicts, and lack of tribal unity also can be attributed to this oppressive system. However, I do not believe that Indigenous Peoples are hapless victims devoid of the intelligence and strengths necessary to transform their present exigent circumstances. On the contrary, for more than 500 years, First Nations have survived, and thrived, in spite of U.S. colonial, federal, and state-sponsored campaigns of physical, bureaucratic, and cultural genocide. Indigenous Peoples will not go away so easily and will remain vigilant and vocal about the contracts (treaties) they made with this nation in order to guarantee and maintain their sovereign rights, freedom, and respect for their beliefs and cultures.

Over the years, I have come to realize that most Americans, including social workers, do not associate the United States with the activities of colonization and, therefore, very few know how the special strain of American colonialism subjugates, dominates, bullies, kills, and festers within and beyond the borders of the Americas. Until the events of September 11, 2001, few Americans were knowledgeable about the resentment that was directed at the United States by other nations that have been victimized by U.S. colonization policies.

In *Blowback: The Costs and Consequences of American Empire* (2000), Chalmers Johnson argues, "Most Americans are probably unaware of how Washington exercises its global hegemony, since so much of this activity takes place either in relative secrecy or under comforting rubrics" (p. 7). Similarly, Sardar and Davies in their international bestseller, *Why Do People Hate America?* (2002), conclude, "Most Americans are simply not aware of the impact of their culture and their government's policies on the rest of the world. But more important, a vast majority simply do not believe that America has done, or can do, anything wrong" (p. 9). To back their claims, these authors cite an international survey as evidence:

A poll of world "opinion leaders" in politics, media, business, culture and government, commissioned by the Paris-based *International Herald Tribune*, revealed that a majority of non-US respondents—58%—felt that Washington's policies were a "major cause" in fuelling resentment and anger against the United States. In contrast, only 18% of US respondents blamed their government's policies. Moreover, 90% of Americans listed their country's power and wealth as the chief reason why they are disliked, while the non-Americans overwhelmingly thought that the US bears responsibility for the gap between the rich and poor. (pp. 9–10)

People within the United States possess the privilege of remaining uninformed of the actions of their government, "America has the power and resources to refuse self-reflection. More pointedly, it is a nation that has developed a tradition of being oblivious to self-reflection" (Sardar and Davies, 2002, p. 13). While there are many examples of America's lack of introspection that can be drawn from the past and present, one that has greatly disturbed me over the years came from the highest level of American leadership—former President George H. W. Bush. On July 3, 1988, the USS *Vincennes*, a missile cruiser stationed in the Persian Gulf, illegally shot down an Iranian commercial air jet that was on a routine flight in a commercial corridor in Iranian airspace. All 290 passengers on board—civilian elders, children, babies, and adults—were killed. One hundred seventy bodies were recovered from the sea, 40 were unidentified, and many were mutilated beyond recognition. *Newsweek* bureau chief in Paris Christopher Dickey reported that during the funerals for the deceased many families pinned cards on the bodies with the words "Death to America" (http://72.14.207.104/search?q=cache: vu0eF8DpZ-AJ:www.geocities.com/CapitolHill/5260/vince.html+christopher+dickey+ +iran+uss+vincennes&hl=en). Following this shameful and tragic event, the Pentagon attempted to cover it up while the U.S. Navy lied about what had happened. When he was asked about the incident, George H. W. Bush replied: "I never apologize for the United States—I don't care what the facts are."

America's long history of refusing to engage in self-reflection has created a vast degree of arrogance and ignorance that has blunted its ability to understand and remedy the pain and oppression it causes others. Another horrific example was the first U.S.-led Gulf War of 1991, where massive bombing killed tens of thousands of innocent Iraqi citizens and destroyed major water, communication, and electric power systems. Following the war, 10 years of U.S.-led sanctions against Iraq killed over 500,000 Iraqi toddlers and about 1.5 million older children and adults, who died from starvation, lack of medicine, trauma, and drinking contaminated water. In an interview on May 11, 1996, news reporter Lesley Stahl of CBS asked U.S. Secretary of State Madeleine Albright whether the more than half a million children killed by the sanctions was "worth it." Albright's response was, "It's a hard choice, but I think, we think, it's worth it" (Mahajan, 2001). After listening to the response, I have often wondered if Ms.

Albright knows what it feels like to personally suffer at this level and to watch her children suffer and die from starvation, lack of medicine, or the bloody diarrhea that results from drinking contaminated water, because someone else thought it was worth it.

Likewise, in the United States very few Americans are aware of, or interested in, the pain and oppression that this nation has caused, and continues to cause, Indigenous Peoples through its long and continuing history of colonization activities. In the past when Indigenous Peoples defended themselves and their lands against American colonial invasion, they were killed, jailed, and/or confined to reservations. When they protested their inhumane treatment, theft of their lands, and destruction of their culture, they were often met with twisted, racist logic that places the blame on them for their problems. For instance, the famous Hollywood actor and American icon John Wayne, who was awarded the Congressional Medal of Honor in 1979 for being an "American," once arrogantly asserted, "I don't feel we did wrong in taking this great country away from [the Indians]. There were great numbers of people who needed new land, and they were selfishly trying to keep it for themselves" (Riggin, 1992, pp. 43–44).

When Indigenous Peoples protest or attempt to educate non-Indigenous peoples about the historical and contemporary forms of oppression caused by this nation, they often receive a variety of responses. For example, *compassionate colonizers* will react with a sense of helplessness and guilt perhaps accompanied by phases such as, "That's terrible," or "I didn't know that." *Callous colonizers*, on the other hand, reply with anger and sentiments such as, "That was in the past," "Get over it," "Don't blame me, I wasn't here when that happened," or "Get a life." Yet, there are non-Indigenous individuals, such as former U.S. Attorney General Ramsey Clark, historian Howard Zinn, and human rights attorney Jennifer Harbury, who respond with neither helplessness nor denial, but are committed to actively countering the effects of American colonialism and injustice through their writing, public speaking, and activism.[1]

Aspects of American Colonialism

Social workers have an obligation to understand that colonialism is a brutal, exploitive, and violent experience and institution; depending upon the relationships between the colonizers and colonized, its effects can resonate for generations. Colonialism refers to when alien peoples invade the territories inhabited by peoples of a different race and culture and force their political, social, intellectual, psychological, and economic ideas and rules on the territory and people. Invasion is motivated by many factors, but greed, self-interests, and expansion of the invading colonial society appear to be the primary motives. Colonialism is a despotic regime that brings death, pain, and humiliation to its victims and denies them rights to self-determination until they bend to the will of the colonizer.

One of the most recent examples of American colonialism is the United States' current military invasion and subjugation of Iraq, which began on March 20, 2003. To date, American military forces have killed ten of thousands of innocent civilians—including elders, women, babies, and children—and imprisoned, abused, and tortured to death numerous Iraqi people, including children under the age of 18, who may or may not have been military combatants. The United States military has continued rounding up and jailing suspected "insurgents" and killing dozens each day with no clear proof that they are military participants. It has bombed, and continues to bomb, and destroy the communities and homes of Iraqi citizens, has created shortages of food, water, and medical supplies, and has damaged electrical services to the point where many people suffer daily from the lack "power." In some instances, many of the most vulnerable succumb to temperatures that reach triple digits. The American invasion has helped create numerous daily suicide bombing campaigns by insurgents that have taken the lives or brutally maimed hundreds of innocent Iraqi people. Finally, the U.S. government lied to the American public and the rest of the world when it accused Iraq of having weapons of mass destruction, which was cited as the chief reason for its invasion of this nation. Almost everything the United States has done in Iraq can be considered classic American colonialism.

In the founding of the United States of America, the history of colonialism has included the enslavement of Indigenous Peoples, countless deaths from oppression or neglect, enforced migrations, appropriation of territories and of land, the institutionalization of racism, the destruction of entire groups, and the superimposition of the laws, beliefs, and values of the colonizer (Young, 2001). Under colonial rule, the colonizer appropriates, often through force or deception, the territories, resources, wealth, and power of the Indigenous Peoples while Indigenous Peoples simultaneously experience significant loss of life, wealth, culture, lands, and inherent sovereign rights (Yellow Bird, 2001).

To subjugate Indigenous Peoples in the United States, colonization activities were aimed at discrediting and destroying the social, political, and economic institutions of these groups. For example, the traditional rites of passage used to socialize young Indigenous men and women into healthy adulthood, create stable communities, and build societal allegiance to tribal ways of life are now almost nonexistent among most reservation and urban natives. Most tribes no longer practice such rites because, during some of the harsh years of American colonization, Christian missionaries and government "Indian" agents encouraged individuals and communities to abandon these practices and ridiculed and punished them whenever they did not. Today, the loss of these organized, meaningful rituals has resulted in disproportionately high rates of suicide, depression, crimes, low self-esteem, obesity, substance abuse, despondency, homicide, and nihilism among Indigenous youth. To help resolve these problems Indigenous communities must revive or recreate formal tribal rites of passage that teach young males and females how to move into healthy adulthood.

Long before this country's promotion of English-only language laws, tribal languages, which are critical to the social and cultural expression and identity of Indigenous Peoples, were outlawed by the United States. The ban against indigenous languages was enforced for such a long period of time that many are now rarely spoken while others have become extinct or are in rapid decline. In the early 1990s, about 155 First Nations languages were spoken in the United States. However, of this number 138 were classified as dying, and most indigenous children were growing up speaking English and only a few words of their Native language (Krauss, 1992). Over the years, racist government "Indian" boarding schools, Christian organizations, and Hollywood films engendered an overwhelming prejudice toward Indigenous languages when they stereotyped them as primitive, guttural, and backward.

Most of the traditional systems of social and political mediation that provided peace keeping and built cooperation within and between people in indigenous societies were destroyed, while many tribal society groups made up of outstanding men and women who provided healthy leadership and role modeling for their communities no longer exist. Among the Arikara (Sahnish) of the northern plains, the *Piraskani*, were an important class of women and men who were an integral part of the ruling political body that guided the conscience and well-being of the tribe. However, missionaries and government agents seeking to convert and destroy the tribal customs of the Arikara undermined this group until it became nonfunctional.

Not so long ago, government and Christian boarding schools removed Native children from their homes to be "civilized" in the image of their oppressor; these schools were instrumental in mentally colonizing many Indigenous Peoples to believe they were inferior to Whites. Such educational systems taught children to be passive against White rule, to doubt and devalue Native culture, to accept their second-class citizenship and status, and to accept the distorted images, words, and stories that White society used to describe them.

The Indian mascots and names of professional and amateur sports teams are, perhaps, the most obvious evidence of the mental colonization of Indigenous and non-Indigenous Peoples in this country. A telephone opinion poll conducted by *Sports Illustrated* magazine in 2002 helps support this claim (Price, 2002). The survey asked a sample of First Nations Peoples and sports "fans" whether the "Indian" mascots or names used by sports teams contributed to discrimination toward indigenous peoples. A total of "88 percent of the fans," "81 percent off reservation and 53 percent on reservation" Native Peoples said they did not (p. 69). The results are disturbing since names such as "Savages" or "Redskins" are racist, "offensive" labels (*Merriam-Webster's Collegiate Dictionary*, 2000), while "official" team logos depict Indigenous Peoples in stereotypical, derogatory, or dehumanized ways. One of the most striking examples comes from the professional baseball team, "Cleveland Indians," whose emblem portrays Native Peoples as ugly, red-faced, big-nosed, grotesquely grinning caricatures. To view this image, go to the official site of the Cleveland Indians at http://www.cleveland.indians.mlb.com.

In his online article "Crimes Against Humanity," Ward Churchill, an Indigenous professor in the Department of Ethnic Studies at the University of Colorado, fiercely interrogates and analyzes the racist use of Indian names and images by amateur and professional sports teams (Churchill, 2005). To help readers understand this situation in a larger context, he demonstrates that there would be many disparaging names for various ethnic groups if sports organizations employed team names that are equivalent to the racist ones used to describe Indigenous Peoples. For instance, he says that "as a counterpart to the 'Redskins' we need an NFL team called the 'Niggers' to honor Afro-Americans," and there would be teams called the "Spics," "Wetbacks," and "Beaners" to represent Hispanic Americans; there would be teams called the "Dinks," "Gooks," and "Zipperheads" to represent Asian Americans; and there would be teams called the "Kikes," "Honkies," "Shylocks," "Dagos," and "Polacks" to represent various European American groups.

It should not be difficult to understand Professor Churchill's point, and it is reasonable to assume that few, if any, African, Hispanic, Asian, or European Americans would put up with these racist, hateful names. In fact, it is very likely that if sports teams tried to use such names, the various affected ethnic and racial groups would quickly look past their racial and ethnic differences and mobilize to form human "rainbow" coalitions to file lawsuits and launch protests and boycotts against the teams who used these horrible labels. I imagine that once they were successful at squelching this "free hate speech," to prevent this from ever happening again, they would begin a massive campaign to educate their children, youth, and young adults about how these names promote racism and hatred toward their groups and must never be used.

Why are this nation's sports teams allowed to continue using racist names and images of Indigenous Peoples despite all of the protests, lawsuits, and educational campaigns launched by these groups against labels? What makes Indigenous Peoples so different from other racial and ethnic groups that this practice can be tolerated? If such names as Redskins are regarded as racist, why did the Indigenous Peoples and sports fans who participated in the *Sports Illustrated* magazine poll believe they did not contribute to discrimination? I hope that you, the reader, will discuss these questions with your colleagues and contemplate what may be at the root of this particular form of racism. Is colonialism at the center of this phenomenon? Sports culture is but one example where colonial encounters occur within the United States. Indigenous Peoples find that these encounters are part of the everyday routine, occurring within a broad array of ordinary activities. For example, one day when I was walking on my university campus to a meeting, I came face-to-face with a young White man who was wearing a colorful Washington Redskins sports jersey. He appeared to be the age of my youngest son and had the same thin stature and relaxed, smooth gait. As we approached each other I noticed the racist wording on his shirt, which caused me to begin looking at his face and at his jersey several times before our opposing worldviews collided on the sidewalk. When he noticed me looking, he looked back and smiled and said hello and continued walking without breaking stride. As for me, I continued to feel the sting of racist American colonialism for several blocks. I later wondered what would have happened if he walked across campus wearing a Washington Niggers, Beaners, Zipperheads, or Kikes sports shirt.

A few years earlier, when I was on the social work faculty at another university, I was asked to be a marshal for our school's graduating undergraduate class. As we waited in the hot sun for the procession to begin, a young man from another academic discipline who was standing with his graduating class in front of us turned around and looked past our group. From the right side of me two older people quickly approached him with outstretched arms and bright, beaming smiles. The woman gave him a big, long, loving hug and gazed into his face with the biggest smile possible. The man gave him an equally big smile and firm handshake and said, "We're very proud of you son." As I looked on at this tender, wonderful moment, the ugly, red-faced, big-nosed, grotesquely grinning Cleveland Indians team logo on the baseball cap that the young man wore began laughing at me. I looked around to see if anyone else could hear him, but it seemed no one could.

The contemporary colonization of First Nations in the United States goes far beyond the racist Indian mascots and names used by sports teams. Tribal governments and individuals are continually forced to resist, litigate, and negotiate with powerful non-Indigenous governments and private and corporate interests as concerning their tribal lands, water, subsistence, and other resource rights. For instance, in 2003, the Forest County Potawatomi and Sokaogan band of Chippewa of northern Wisconsin won a hard fought, 27-year legal and public relations battle against Exxon Minerals, a subsidiary of Exxon Oil that prevented the creation of a Crandon mine. The mine would have extracted zinc and copper ore—two minerals strongly associated with sulfide mining, which causes ecological risks. The Cradon mine would have compromised the air, soil, and water quality and the health of the people and destroyed the traditional wild rice beds that are culturally and nutritionally important to the tribes. The Potawatomi and Chippewa were able to end any further attempts at opening this mine by spending $16.5 million to purchase the acreage where the zinc and copper mine would have been located (Buege, 2004).

Carrie and Mary Dann, elder members of the Western Shoshone Nation, are two individuals who exemplify Indigenous Peoples' struggle to reclaim tribal lands from non-Indigenous governments. For more than a quarter of a century, the Dann sisters have fought a courageous battle against the U.S. Bureau of Land Management (BLM) to get back millions of acres of tribal lands seized by the United States under the 1863 Treaty of Ruby Valley. In 1974, the United States brought trespass charges against the Dunn sisters for grazing their livestock without a BLM permit, and in 2002 the United States confiscated and auctioned off 232 head of cattle belonging to the Danns. The Dann sisters argued that the United States used "illegitimate means" to gain control of Western Shoshone ancestral lands and that the tribe still holds title to this ancestral territory. In the late 1970s the United States attempted to give a $26 million payoff to the tribe as compensation for past illegal intrusions of White settlers. Traditional members of the tribe rejected that and subsequent settlement offers, preferring the return of their stolen lands.

The Dann case has gained international attention, which helped the sisters take it to an international legal body, the Inter-American Commission on Human Rights (IACHR). On July 29, 2002, the IACHR, a body of the Organization of American States (OAS), ruled that the U. S. government is violating international human rights in its treatment of Western Shoshone elders Carrie and Mary Dann. The Commission recommended that the "U.S. government provide a fair legal process to determine the Danns' and other Western Shoshone land rights, which includes adopting legislative or other measures necessary to ensure respect for their right to property...." It was further recommended that the United States "review its procedures and practices to ensure that Indigenous Peoples' property rights are determined in accordance with the rights established in the American Constitution" (Sansani, n.d.). The response of the United States has been that the OAS has no jurisdiction over this case and that the Dann sisters cannot bring their case before the Commission because they have not "exhausted domestic remedies" (Sansani, n.d.). (Mary died in April of 2005 in a vehicle accident.)

Some of the economic enterprises owned by various tribes, such as casinos and smoke shops (cigarette stores), which are operated to generate revenue for the tribal membership, are raided and shut down by federal marshals or state police whenever these bodies believe the tribes are not in compliance with their laws. The fight for jurisdiction on tribal lands is a constant battle between tribal and the state and federal governments; who has authority on these territories has shifted back and forth among these three bodies for many years. When a disagreement of jurisdiction exists and the state and federal authorities feel that the stakes are high enough, and the tribes refuse to back down because of their sovereign nation status, federal and state authorities will often assert their power and force using aggressive military tactics, weapons, and manpower. For instance, on July 14, 2003, the State of Rhode Island made a "violent raid" on a Narragansett tribal smoke (cigarette) shop, brutally arresting Chief Sachem Matthew Thomas and other tribal members because "the state felt it had a right to seek taxes on the sale of tobacco products to non-Indians" (http:www.indianz.com/news/2005/008171.asp). The tribe had just begun operating the new tax-free tobacco shop in order to work toward becoming economically self-sufficient.

The economies, social relations, and political lives of Indigenous Peoples are still infringed upon by local and state governments and paternalistic bureaucratic agencies, including the Bureau of Indian Affairs and the U.S. Department of the Interior. Historical concerns such as past wrongs, treaty rights violations, and trust responsibilities are still trivialized, denied, ignored, or unknown. One of the most egregious present-day federal government failures has been the mismanagement of "Individual Indian Trust" accounts, which has taken place over a period of many years. The timeline of activities relating to this case (*Cobell v. Norton*) can be viewed at http://www.indiantrust.com/.

Dating back to 1887, the U.S. Congress decided that Indigenous Peoples were not competent to manage their own money or resources and took, without consent of most tribes, control of the task. Individual Indian Trust accounts get their money from the leasing of tribal gas and oil interests and land and timber sales, to name only a few. The control of these monies and the leasing process are considered a legal trust responsibility of the federal government. In a current lawsuit against the United States, plaintiff Eloise Cobell (Blackfeet) has sued the interior and treasury departments for the mismanagement, diversion, embezzlement, and loss of billions of dollars that were supposed to have been placed in the trust accounts of more than 500,000 individual tribal members. Widespread fraud and deception by the United States is evident in this case. The records of these monies have been lost and/or deliberately destroyed by the federal government, which has yet to take responsibility for almost 120 years of this particular deceit and theft of tribal monies.

Tribal health care, educational needs, and social services are also poorly, if at all, funded by the federal government, even though Indigenous Peoples ceded huge portions of their territories for guarantees of these rights and services from the United States. The Indian Health Service says, "American Indians" have a life expectancy six years less than the rest of the U.S. population, a 500 percent higher rate of tuberculosis, 390 percent higher rate of diabetes, and 740 percent higher rate of alcoholism (http://www.crihb.org/campaign/FactSheet.pdf). Despite these figures for 2003, per capita health care spending for federal prisoners is $3,803, compared to $1,914 for Native Americans (http://www.tribalconnections.org/health_news/health_briefs/oct2003.html). Quality education is critical to survival for many Indigenous nations, yet the National Indian Education Association reported that proposed federal 2006 funding for Native education programs is inadequate and remains at $119 million, the same level as fiscal year 2005, down from FY 2004 and 2003 levels (http://www.niea.org.issues/tracking_detail. php?id=10).

There are numerous other areas and situations where America has failed to live up to its agreements made with Indigenous Peoples. Rarely has the United States taken its legal responsibilities to Native Peoples seriously and rarely has it reflected on the myriad injustices it has and continues to perpetuate against these groups. For instance, in his 2003 national address to the U.S. Congress and the Bush administration, regarding this U.S. trust responsibility to Indigenous Peoples, tribal leader Tex Hall, president of the National Congress of American Indians, the largest and oldest Native organization in the United States, discussed America's continued failure to live up to its promises:

> When you consider that every acre of this country once was under care of the tribes and provided for our people, it is easy to understand what is called the "trust responsibility." When these lands were taken from tribes, the U.S. gave its solemn promise to protect the rights of tribes to govern themselves, and to provide for the health, education, and well being of tribes. That commitment, the "trust responsibility"—is *not* a hand-out, but a *contract*—and that contract has been broken time and again by the federal government. It is time for the U.S. to honor those promises." (National Congress of American Indians, 2003, p. 10)

American colonialism has many vile faces which continue to assault Indigenous Peoples in numerous ways. American colonialism contributes greatly to the intersections among substance abuse, family violence, and child welfare in Native communities and is a major cause of the poverty, unemployment, racism, family disintegration, and poor parenting found in many First Nations communities.

The Processes of Colonialism

The only human rights we [First Nations] have is the right to remain silent . . . but that's not good enough anymore and we can't afford to let that continue.

—Chief Louis Stevenson, Peguis First Nations, 2001

I am Sahnish and Hidatsa First Nations, a child of the hereditary chiefs of the Awahu village of the Sahnish and I believe that a great deal of the excessive rates of substance abuse, family violence, and child welfare problems in our community is the direct result of our subjugation under American colonialism. I know that my people did not suddenly wake up one day and decide, en masse, to abuse their children and spouses, commit suicide, kill one another, drink themselves to death, act like fools, become addicts, go to prison, or lose our languages, beliefs, and values. Rather, a disproportionate number of the past and present struggles of my community are the result of the oppressive policies of our colonizer: the United States of America.

I grew up in a small, tribal community that was, and in many ways, continues to be, traumatized by substance abuse,[2] family violence, and child welfare problems. From my earliest years, I recall the cultural, spiritual, and physical carnage spawned by the use of substances in our small community. Shootings, stabbings, drownings, car accidents, hangings, beatings, and freezing to death were the more common ways that people died under the influence. For those who did not die by these means, alcohol poisoning, mostly in the form of cirrhosis, waited impatiently for them. The latter deaths were, perhaps, the most traumatic for our community because we would experience, on a daily and nightly basis, the slow and drawn-out deaths of our relatives. I became so accustomed and desensitized to the stream of deaths of people from my community that long after I had left the reservation, one of the first things I would ask my mother whenever I called home was, "Who died?" It would be years later when I finally realized that my "don't feel" response was one way that I, and many people from my community, coped with all the death we experienced.

Death was not the only form of misery that we experienced because of substance abuse. Family breakups, accidents, injuries, arrests, jail terms, fires, sexual abuse, child abuse and neglect, poor health, child apprehension by social workers, unemployment, and welfare dependency were also common (Maracle, 1993). On the rez (reservation), keeping track of family members who were actively using substances was an ongoing struggle for many families. When those family members who had been drinking didn't come home when they were expected, other family members would often go looking for them. Sometimes we would find our relatives passed out, quivering in their urine-soaked nightmares, exuding the heavy smell of death in a house where people regularly "partied." At other times, we would see our family member's wasted, intoxicated frame walking slowly down the road attempting to hitch a ride to the nearest rez bar to get a drink to quiet the demons and tremors that had made a home in his or her soul. Still other times, we would embarrassingly encounter our relatives on the streets of some off-rez White border town begging White people for change for their next drink.

There were many times when the traumas of violence, substance abuse, and child welfare problems were personalized and embedded deep within the psychological structure of our people. I recall when it happened to me. When I was a little boy, one of my earliest and most vivid memories was not getting a beautiful pony for my birthday or my mother reading me my favorite bedtime story. It was being picked up and held by an intoxicated uncle whose face was badly beaten and bloodied by his drinking "buddies," and whose pores, clothes, and breath radiated with the sickening smell of many days of drinking cheap wine. It was late one night when he came pounding and crying at the door of my parents' house. When my mother opened the door and saw her brother, she cried out, cupped her hand over her mouth, and her face and body fell into a brief, but profound, state of shock. My father, having much more experience with such things, reacted with silence and an odd smile.

I remember all the blood, and the grotesque, lumpy shape of his face reminded me of a monster. Yet, this monster was crying like a child who had lost his mother, so many of the sounds he made were soft and pitiful. I was terrified by how he looked and the cries he made. When I cried out in fear to my mother, my uncle stopped crying and looked and smiled at me through all the blood. He walked over, picked me up, and gently hugged me and patted my back to comfort me. However, I frantically screamed and cried as I made contact with the blood on his face and shirt. Even though I screamed and pushed to get away from him, he didn't let me go until one of the drunken ladies he was with scolded him and took me and set me back on the couch where I had been sleeping. As I trembled with uncontrollable shock and tried to suck back my deep sobs of fear and confusion, my mother made my uncle and the other late-night visitors sit down at our kitchen table. As she prepared a meal for them, she quietly reminded them they shouldn't be drinking. This uncle died about 10 years later from having his head run over by the rear wheel of a car he had passed out under. Shortly after my uncle's death all his children were taken from their mother and placed for adoption or sent to government boarding schools.

These kinds of events happened repeatedly in our community, yet our people were not always this way. According to my mother, alcoholism, child abuse and neglect, and family violence were nearly nonexistent in our villages when she grew up during the 1920s to the early 1940s. However, during the late 1940s and the early 1950s the federal government finally succeeded in forcing us out of our villages and off of our aboriginal homelands, which were located alongside the "mysterious river" (what Whites call the Missouri River). Before this forced removal, our people worked closely together and cared for one another. We understood that our health and survival depended on performing our most sacred ceremonies—these ceremonies renewed our lives, assisted our communion with our Creator, and helped our children through various rites of passage to become responsible members of our society.

Before the United States of America "civilized" us, the entire village took responsibility in caring for our children. It is said that before the American invasion, "protecting, nurturing, and teaching children were shared between parents and clan membership" (Yellow Bird, 1999b, p. 231). Our elders said that to neglect the children, to be lazy, intoxicated, or abusive was taboo and strongly discouraged. Our very survival depended upon our people being industrious, generous, kind, compassionate, courageous, intelligent, and lucid. However, after the illegal seizure and flooding of our lands and the destruction of our villages by the United States of America, our lives changed drastically for the worse. As our people's way of life was increasingly condemned and controlled by Christian missionaries and the federal and state government, we were forced to begin abandoning our cultural beliefs and values.

Under past colonial rule, our Chiefs were routinely threatened that the village would lose its food rations if they asserted leadership that was in conflict with the White missionaries and bureaucrats. Our spiritual leaders were jailed for conducting traditional religious and spiritual practices. The socialization, welfare, and teaching of our children was stripped from our peoples and taken over by White ministers, priests, social workers, teachers, and bureaucrats, who believed we were primitive, dirty, savage, ignorant heathens whose beliefs, values, and knowledge had few or no redeeming qualities (Napoleon, 1993; Yellow Bird, 2001). Until the passage of the Indian Child Welfare Act of 1978, children from our community were "legally abducted" from their parents by social workers and placed into White homes that cared little about our culture. Those who did not end up in these environments were sent to government and Christian boarding schools, where our culture was ignored or ridiculed, and they were severely punished for speaking their language or acting like an Indian (Yellow Bird & Chenault, 1999).

Aside from the fact that our colonizers took our children because they felt that our people's beliefs and values would contaminate them and keep them in perpetual savagery, other reasons for removal were poverty, abuse and neglect, alcoholism, and violence in the home. While removing our children from these latter conditions was a "noble attempt" to look out for the "best interests of the child," I believe that much of American colonial society does not realize that it contributed a great deal to the creation of these problems among our peoples. For many years, our colonizer minimized the control we had over our own lives in our community. As this treatment of our people continued throughout the years, our rates of homicide, suicide, child abuse and neglect, family and community disintegration, violence, and alcoholism continued to increase. Today, the rates of homicide and suicide have slowed somewhat while substance abuse and child abuse and neglect continue unabated. The epidemics of diabetes, depression, obesity, tribal factionalism, unemployment, poor health care, and substandard education and housing continue to swirl within many tribal communities, each a testament to the continuing effects of American colonialism.

Indigenous Peoples: A Political and Cultural Demography

Indigenous Peoples are not simply minorities or people of color. A large majority belong to tribal nations that are recognized by the U.S. Congress as having a special, legal "government-to-government" relationship with the United States. These groups form distinct political communities possessing the necessary conditions for sovereignty, nationhood, and self-determination. No other racial group in the United States can claim a similar political and legal standing. Yet, First Nations tribal governments possess only a quasi-sovereign status since their political, social, and economic lives are closely regulated, and often administratively dominated, by the plenary (unlimited) power of the U.S. government.

There are 557 "federally recognized" Indigenous nations and another 150 petitioning for recognition. Federal recognition is perhaps one of the most oppressive colonial policies of this nation. Under this policy the U.S. government decides, using its own rules, which tribal groups are Indigenous. No other people in this nation have to go through such a humiliating process of having to prove who they are; many Indigenous scholars, elders, tribal leaders, and activists maintain that this U.S. policy has forced U.S. First Nations Peoples to become "the only pedigreed race of people in the world." (First Nations in Canada also face the same situation under the 1876 Indian Act.) Although it is a subjugating regulation, especially for those groups that the United States refuses to acknowledge, "recognition" means those that are acknowledged are regarded as "distinct, independent political communities possessing and exercising the power of self government" (U.S. Congress, 1986, p. 46). Federal recognition is based upon a principle, called "trust responsibility," which grew out of treaty making between the United States and Indigenous Peoples that lasted from 1787 to 1871. In most treaties, Indigenous Peoples gave up land in exchange for promises that the United States "would protect the safety and well-being of tribal members. The Supreme Court has held that such promises create a trust relationship" (Pevar, 1992, p. 26). However, the United States has rarely lived up to its trust responsibility or its treaties' promises made with Indigenous Peoples.

Culturally, First Nations Peoples are diverse groups that reside on ancestral lands and share a lineage with the original residents, possess distinct cultures and languages, and regard themselves as different from those who have colonized and control their lands (Stamatopoulou, 1994). Differences among these groups can be significant with respect to history, language, land, dress, food, sacred and secular ceremonies, worldviews, and social and political organization. Most identify themselves according to their membership in a clan, band, nation, pueblo, rancheria, confederacy, tribe, or village. Defining who is Indigenous is difficult because each nation has its own requirements for recognition. Most identify their members according to language, residence, cultural affiliation, recognition by an Indigenous community, degree of blood, genealogical lines of descent, and self-identification (Thornton, 1996).

The population of Indigenous Peoples continues to grow. Census 2000 showed that there are 4.1 million Indigenous Peoples (those referred to as American Indians and Alaska Natives) in the United States, or 1.5 percent of the total U.S. population. This number includes 2.5 million who reported only being Indigenous (American Indian/Alaska Native) and 1.6 million who said they were First Nations as well as one or more other races (Ogunwole, 2002, p. 1). Because most were forced off their aboriginal homelands because of poverty; racism; lack of services, opportunities, and housing; and federal government forced-relocation policies, the majority now reside in rural or urban areas off the reservation. About 37% reside on 279 reservations, in 223 Alaskan native villages, and on historic areas in Oklahoma (Snipp, 1996).

Statistics on Substance Abuse, Family Violence, and Child Welfare

American colonialism contributes immeasurably to the overwhelming substance abuse, family violence, and child welfare problems among Indigenous communities. Alcohol, the main substance abused by Indigenous Peoples, has had a catastrophic outcome for many groups. During early periods of American colonization, when First Nations communities were intact and independent, most viewed alcohol as disruptive and destructive and pro- hibited its use in their nations. For instance, when Lewis and Clark were on their way to the Pacific Ocean in 1804, they met the Arikara (Sahnish) and attempted to give them alcohol and quickly discovered that this nation viewed it, and the traders who brought it, with disgust. The Arikara expressed their surprise that it was offered to them and stated that no man could be their friend who tried to induce them into such foolishness (Moulton, 1988; Will, 1934).

It is crucial to note that while alcohol abuse among Indigenous Peoples is a major health concern, not all Native Peoples are passive victims of this colonial affliction. Many tribal governments, grassroots organizations, and resolute individuals, despite the gross lack of support from the U.S. government, are taking measures to combat the abuse of alcohol and substances in their communities. It is also crucial to note that the rates of use vary among tribes, subgroups within tribes, and individuals, as do the problems that are associated with it (Mancall, 1995; Watts & Lewis, 1988; Westermeyer, 1974). Several studies show that there is no single response to alcohol use by Native Peoples (May, 1996; Watts & Lewis, 1988), and, in fact, the vast majority of indigenous peoples do not drink alcohol or use other substances. For many who do, they do not suffer as a result (Mancall, 1995).

The outcome has been devastating for those who do abuse alcohol. The U.S. Department of Justice reported, "in 1997, the arrest rate among Indigenous Peoples for alcohol-related offenses (driving under the influence, liquor law violations, and public drunkenness) was more than double that was found among all races. Drug arrest rates for American Indians were lower than average" (Greenfeld & Smith, 1999, p. vii). In some age categories and communities the abuse of alcohol has reached epidemic proportions (U.S. Department of Health and Human Services, 1996), and alcoholism is considered by some to be the number one health problem for Indigenous Peoples (Office of Substance Abuse Prevention, 1991).

For instance, in 1986, the U.S. Congress passed P.L. 99–570, the Indian Alcohol and Substance Abuse Prevention and Treatment Act. "The act was based upon findings that alcohol and substance abuse are the most severe health and social problems facing Indian tribes and people today and nothing is more costly to Indian people than the consequences of alcohol and substance abuse measured in physical, mental, social, and economic terms" (U.S. Department of Justice, 2000, p. ix). Deconstructing the language in this government act reveals that it is only superficially correct: alcohol *is* costly to Indigenous Peoples. But, alcohol and substance abuse are only symptoms of the root cause—American colonialism—which has, and continues to have, devastating effects on all aspects of Indigenous Peoples' lives, making it far more costly and damaging. Such shortsighted "official" language provides an excellent example of the nonreflective thinking of U.S. policy makers.

In a review of health promotional efforts among Indigenous Peoples, May and Moran (1995) found that "alcohol takes disproportionate toll" on these groups (Moran, 1999, p. 52). For instance, between 1991 and 1993, the Indian Health Service (IHS) statistics report that deaths related to alcoholism were five and a half times higher for Indigenous Peoples than for the general population in the United States (U. S. Department of Health and Human Services, 1996). In addition, chronic liver disease and cirrhosis, commonly associated with excessive alcohol abuse, were almost four times higher and were the fifth leading overall cause of death. Hospital discharge rates for alcohol psychosis were three times higher in Indian Health Service and Tribal Hospitals than they were in U.S. general short-stay hospitals, whose rates are considered representative of the overall U.S. population.

The intersection between substance abuse and family violence is well documented among all racial groups in the United States. In a national study of Indigenous Peoples and crime, Greenfeld and Smith (1999, p. 8) reported that "intimate and family violence each account for 9 percent of all violent victimizations experienced by American Indian victims, about the same percentage as found among all victims of violence." However, First Nations Peoples who are victimized by someone who is using alcohol or drugs are "more likely than others to be injured and need hospital care" (p. 8). While this statistic does not identify whether the perpetrator is Native or non-Native, what it does suggest is that it is more acceptable to do greater injurious violence to Indigenous Peoples than others, which further suggests that American colonialism has succeeded in making these groups among the least valued members of society.

Alcohol is also closely connected to the high rates of injuries, accidental poisonings, and car and firearms accidents among Indigenous Peoples. It is thought to be responsible for most suicides and accidental injury deaths, and some researchers claim that alcohol causes up to 90% of all homicides among these groups (Bachman, 1991, 1992). In 1997, 70% of all the Indigenous Peoples who were in jail for violent crimes, committed them while they were drinking (Greenfeld & Smith, 1999). This figure is almost double that of the general population.

Alcohol abuse is also closely connected to the abuse and neglect of Indigenous children and is a serious problem in several tribal communities. However, it is important to be aware that the historical record clearly shows that before Indigenous Peoples were subjugated under American colonialism, the abuse and neglect of Native children was a very rare event. Most tribal groups considered their children to be the future of the nation and, thus, they were highly revered, protected, and respected. U.S. government policy, a major element of American colonialism, subverted this relationship and caused many of the child welfare problems now present among First Nations Peoples. Today many Native children have become targets of the rage, frustration, and hopelessness that is felt by many Indigenous parents and caretakers who suffer the ravages of colonialism.

In 1997 the Bureau of Indian Affairs reported that there were 9,040 incidents of abuse and 19,200 incidents of neglect of Indigenous children on federal "Indian" lands (National Indian Child Welfare Association, n.d.). Included in these numbers were 4,567 incidents of child sexual abuse. From 1992 to 1995, when the national average of child abuse and neglect cases dropped by 8%, there was an 18% increase in the number of reports of abuse and neglect for Indigenous children (Greenfeld & Smith, 1999). In 2001, 1.1 million children in the United States were victims of abuse and/or neglect. Indigenous children constituted 2% of this total, despite the fact that they account for only 1% of the U.S. population (About Child Abuse, National Exchange Club Foundation, n.d.).

Child abuse and neglect, related to alcohol abuse, is more likely to be reported for American Indian/Alaska Native families than for White families (Earle & Cross, 2001). Data from the National Child Abuse and Neglect Data System at Cornell University show that Indigenous children are more than twice as likely (14.6% compared to 6.9%) to have a caretaker who has a problem with alcohol abuse than are White children (Earle & Cross, 2001). "Violence and victimization," two products of alcohol abuse, "are present in the lives of many Native children in rural, urban, and reservation settings" (Goodluck & Willeto, 2000, p. 56). Indeed, the victimization rate for Indigenous children is twice that of White children: Native children are victimized at the rate of 20.1 per 1,000 compared to 10.6 per 1,000 for White children (U.S. Department of Health and Human Services, 2001). Violence and victimization are often a fatal experience for children, and this is especially true for Native children. In 1999, the Child Welfare League of

America reported that Indigenous children represented 1.8% of all children who died as a result of child abuse and/or neglect, yet they comprise only 1.1% of the U.S. population (Earle & Cross, 2001).

While the above figures provide important indicators of the incidence of child abuse and neglect among Indigenous Peoples, it is difficult to know the extent to which alcohol abuse influences these rates. The National Indian Child Welfare Association (NICWA) stresses there are no accurate national data to determine the full extent of Indigenous child abuse and neglect due to the separate reporting jurisdictions of the federal, state, and tribal agencies that collect such statistics (Jody Becker Green, personnel communication, June 30, 2003). The NICWA also maintains that the rates and causes of child abuse and neglect vary among tribal communities due to their diverse circumstances. Alcohol-related child abuse and neglect also varies. For instance, a Pulitzer Prize-winning newspaper series, titled "Alcohol: Cradle to Grave," reported Bureau of Indian Affairs statistics for child abuse and neglect cases that were alcohol-related on four Montana reservations. The data confirm differences in the number of cases and the percentages: on the Blackfeet reservation, 38% of its 51 reported cases were alcohol-related; on the Northern Cheyenne reservation, 40% of the 314 cases were alcohol-related; on the Crow reservation, 51% of 210 cases were alcohol-related; and on the Fort Peck reservation, 55% of 544 cases were alcohol-related (Newhouse, 1999). While these statistics are compelling, what is equally important is asking how these families from beautiful, proud Indigenous nations, who once revered their children and despised alcohol, ended up in this condition.

The intersection between alcohol abuse and child welfare also occurs frequently with the condition know as fetal alcohol syndrome (FAS), which victimizes many Indigenous children and is caused by a mother's consumption of alcohol during pregnancy. Children born with FAS suffer from mental health problems, disrupted school experiences, homelessness, trouble with the law, alcohol and drug problems, inappropriate sexual behavior, and difficulty caring for themselves and their children (Streissguth & Kanter, 1997). While rates of FAS vary widely among Indigenous communities, some studies show that the incidence of this condition can be 33 times higher than what is found in the general population (Stratton, Howe, & Battaglia, 1996). Three important questions that must be asked and answered, considering these horrific realities are: What factors made these Indigenous women so hopeless, frustrated, indifferent, and depressed that they would drink poison (alcohol) while they are pregnant? What feeds and nurtures these factors? And what will make Indigenous women stop this abusive practice?

Suicide and alcohol abuse have a strong intersection. Suicide is an act of violence, desperation, self-hatred, and hopelessness and is one of the leading causes of death among Indigenous peoples, despite the fact that almost every tribe, prior to American colonization, considered it highly taboo and a form of spiritual desecration. Suicide rates for Indigenous Peoples are significantly higher than the rates are for all other races in the United States and have been for some time. In 1996, the U.S. Department of Health and Human Services reported suicide was 46% higher among First Nations Peoples than for the general population. Overall, suicide rates are higher for men than they are for women; this is also true for Indigenous Peoples. Suicide is the fifth leading cause of death for Indigenous men. Indian Health Service statistics show that the highest rates of suicide among Indigenous men occurs between the ages of 15 and 24 years, when there are 51.7 deaths per 100,000 population. Comparatively, there are 10.9 suicide deaths per 100,000 among Indigenous women in this same age group. Among the general U.S. population ages 15–24, there are 21.9 suicide deaths per 100,000 population. Again, important questions remain: What factors make Indigenous Peoples so hopeless and distressed that they take their own lives at these unprecedented rates? What feeds these factors? And what will take to make Indigenous Peoples stop committing suicide?

Stereotypes of Indigenous People's Substance Abuse and Violence

Indian-hating still exists; and, no doubt, will continue to exist so long as Indians do.
—Herman Melville, 1857

For many years the racist stereotype of the "drunken Indian" assumed, among other things, that most Indigenous Peoples had genetic traits that led to abusive drinking and metabolized alcohol more slowly than non-Indigenous Peoples. Studies conducted among some Indigenous populations show that neither of these assumptions is correct (May 1996). Goldman, et al. (1993) argue that there is no identifiable genetic trait that prompts abusive drinking among Indigenous Peoples, while others agree there is no firm evidence that Indigenous Peoples metabolize alcohol more slowly than non-Indigenous Peoples (Bennion & Li, 1976; May, 1994). In fact, some studies show that Indigenous Peoples in North America have enough aldehyde dehydrogenase isozyme (ALDH) to prevent the flushing process unlike some groups, such as Asians, whose livers contain less ALDH[3] (Chan, 1986; Dyck, 1993). In addition, Indigenous Peoples' liver structures and phenotypes are not unusual, but are similar to those of other ethnic groups, especially Europeans (Rex, Bosron, Smialek, & Ting-kai, 1985). While the statistics clearly show that, proportionally speaking, Indigenous Peoples do abuse alcohol at higher levels than the general U.S. population and get into more serious problems when they drink, the current studies demonstrate that, for many, biology is not the problem.

Since the time of Christopher Columbus, European American society has perpetuated the belief that Indigenous Peoples are a violent race. While violence does exist among

First Nations peoples, family and intimate violence overall is not a bigger problem among these groups than it is in the rest of the population (Greenfeld & Smith, 1999). Statistics do show, however, that the family and intimate violence experienced by Indigenous Peoples is more likely to be perpetrated by someone from a different race. The most recent national data show that "among violence victims of all races, about 11 percent of intimate victims and 5 percent of family victims report the offender to have been of a different race; however, among American Indians victims of violence, 75 percent of the intimate victimizations and 25 percent of the family victimizations involved an offender of a different race" (Greenfeld & Smith, 1999, p. 8).

Statistics from a 1999 U.S. Department of Justice report show that Indigenous Peoples are victims of violent crimes at a rate more than double the rest of the population and are more likely than a member of another racial group to be the victim of a murder, assault, robbery, or rape (Greenfeld & Smith, 1999). Offenders from a different race—usually White—commit approximately 70% of all violent episodes against First Nations Peoples (1999). Only 19% of crimes committed against Blacks and 31% of crimes against Whites are interracial. An important question is: Why do Whites commit so many violent acts against Indigenous Peoples?

Practice, Policy, and Research Implications

Overall, there are well-developed practice approaches used for addressing American colonialism, the treatment of substance abuse, family violence, and child welfare problems among Indigenous Peoples. Generally, program development is based upon many of the current approaches. Practice approaches and program development are closely interfaced with one another within First Nations Peoples' communities and incorporate two paradigmatic slants. The first approach uses generic contemporary mainstream methods such as individual, family, and group counseling and therapy, along with support groups to address issues related to substance abuse, violence, grief, depression, parenting, child abuse and neglect, and suicide (LaFromboise & Lowe,1989).

The second approach focuses on the use of traditional Indigenous cultural and spiritual practices within the therapeutic process and has become a strong and important strategy used to counter the many devastating effects of American colonialism. Certain factors have been identified as being important to practice and program development with First Nations Peoples. These include, but are not limited to, "strengths" (Yellow Bird & Chenault, 1999; Waller & Yellow Bird, 2002), "historical trauma" (Brave Heart Yellow Horse, 2001), "post-traumatic stress" (Napoleon, 1993), "spirituality" (Morrisette, McKenzie, & Morrisette, 1993; Yellow Bird, 2001), "consciousness raising" (Yellow Bird,

2001), and "colonialism" (Duran & Duran, 1995; Lewis, 1995; Morrisette, McKenzie, & Morrisette, 1993; Yellow Bird, 1996, 1998, 1999a, 1999b, 1999c, 2000, 2001).

However, these approaches do not have a long history of theoretical development and supporting research (LaFromboise, Berman, & Sohi, 1994). Thus, success must be measured carefully. What is known about practice approaches in use with Indigenous Peoples is that they are compatible with various aspects of "culturally competent practice" (Devore & Schlesinger, 1999; Lum, 1999; Fong & Furuto, 2001). Culturally competent practice with First Nations includes, but is not limited to, knowledge of their histories, worldviews, values and beliefs, understanding of communication patterns, appropriate interviewing techniques, strengths, differences among and within groups, behavioral expectations, cultural knowledge, and help-seeking behavior (Lum, 1999).

SUBSTANCE ABUSE

Today there are many programs on reservations and in urban settings that specifically target substance abuse and family violence. However, not all Indigenous Peoples have access to such programs, and for those that do, the effectiveness and appropriateness of such programs can vary because of lack of funding, resources, cultural competency, and skilled personnel. Practice approaches in many programs and communities may also vary because of the diversity of the population and the extent to which they may be affected by substance abuse and violence. Many programs have worked closely with their service populations and have developed a sense of what works and what doesn't with respect to integrated "mainstream" and "nonmainstream approaches. An excellent example of the combined approach comes from a national study of model Indigenous Peoples' substance abuse programs conducted by the U.S. Department of Justice.

In 1991, the U.S. attorney general ordered a U.S. Department of Justice working committee to examine the current efforts of Indigenous Nations to reduce alcohol and substance abuse among their people (U.S. Department of Justice, 2000). The working group consisted of representatives from the offices of the Associate Attorney General, the Office of Tribal Justice, the Office of Policy Development, and the Office of Justice Programs, American Indian and Alaskan Native Affairs Office. In March 2000, the consultant to this group, American Indian Development Associates, began collecting information from several identified programs throughout the United States to create a document that examined the alcohol and substance abuse problems that were being addressed. The document also highlighted the best practice approaches that were used, concentrating on those that met with the most success.

In total, nine model projects from across the country were reported on: (1) Poarch (Muskogee) Creek Indian Nation Drug Court Program, Artmore, Alabama; (2) Cheyenne River Sioux Alcohol Legislation and Taxation Initiative program, Eagle Butte,

South Dakota; (3) Turtle Mountain Safe Communities Program, Belcourt, North Dakota; (4) Southern Ute Peaceful Spirit Youth Services Program, Ignacio, Colorado; (5) Boys & Girls Club of the Northern Cheyenne Nation Smart Moves Programs, Lame Deer, Montana; (6) Na'Nizhoozhi Center Incorporated, Gallup, New Mexico; (7) Pueblo of Zuni Recovery Center, Pueblo, New Mexico; (8) Southeast Alaska Regional Health Consortium, Sitka, Alaska; (9) Medicine Wheel Treatment Program, Montana State Prison, Deer Lodge, Montana. Several of these projects shared similar approaches when addressing alcohol and substance abuse problems in their respective communities. It is important to note that these projects, along with their specific approaches, represent model programs and should not be generalized to the rest of the substance abuse programs used by Indigenous Peoples across the country. Nonetheless, the following "cutting edge" practices that were vital to the success of these programs are summarized below in three areas: community development, organizational initiatives, and direct practice.

COMMUNITY DEVELOPMENT

For some programs the tragic deaths of tribal members in the community inspired "a review of the impact of alcohol use and abuse in the community" (U.S. Department of Justice, 2000, p. 13), which further inspired the development of their programs and prompted greater community involvement. Several programs found that coordinating and enlisting the support of different reservation and off-reservation agencies was essential to adequately address substance abuse in their communities. Often such groups consisted of tribal councils, courts, elder groups, faith communities, private citizens, public schools, law enforcement, social services, and health care providers. Partnerships were built with these groups to identify and incorporate strategies that could be used to prevent and treat substance abuse. One of the most consistent and effective actions for these programs was getting tribal councils to take aggressive measures, which included passing tribal legislation, to control and restrict the use of alcohol and other substances in the community. Success also depended upon different agencies understanding the grave effects of substance abuse and then committing themselves to specific cooperative roles to address its causes.

While several communities took very active stances against substance abuse, the Cheyenne River Program was perhaps most aggressive in dealing with this issue. The tribal council took the position that it is a sovereign government and, thus, believed it held the final authority to restrict and control the use of substances in its nation. Acting upon this conviction, the Council

> requested all reservation liquor establishments to voluntarily comply with the tribal liquor laws regarding introduction, sale, use and distribution of alcoholic beverages. Several of these were white-owned establishments who refused, alleging that the Tribe

lacked authority to regulate their businesses because they were non-Indian operators on fee patented lands in towns within the reservation. In response, the Tribe filed lawsuits in the Tribal Court and obtained closure orders for the liquor establishments in non-compliance . . . the liquor establishments fought against tribal regulation of liquor sales in tribal and federal courts for over six years. But the tribe took its battle for control over the alcohol industry all the way to the U.S. Supreme Court and ultimately won recognition of its authority to regulate and control alcoholic beverages on the reservation. (U.S. Department of Justice, 2000, p. 5)

ORGANIZATIONAL INITIATIVES

Several of the programs found that implementing successful services meant that they needed to collect data from many sources: the police, courts, corrections departments, and behavioral, health, and social service agencies. Analysis of these data was undertaken to understand the extent of the problem of alcohol and its effects on the lives of people in the community. Many programs used this information for creating public awareness campaigns to improve the organizational operation and effectiveness of their programs and to educate tribal members about the diverse effects that alcohol has on the community. Through this process greater community understanding of the problem was achieved, which gave way to increased community support and involvement.

Several of the programs included prevention, intervention, and aftercare services, along with teaching and reinforcing healthy skills and practices. In addition, they focused on changing community norms about substance abuse. Other programs found that using a team approach, which involved agency staff, community representatives, and workers from other agencies, was important to help coordinate services. Finally, some programs incorporated continuum of care models. For instance, the Na'Nizhoozhi Center used: (1) intake and assessment; (2) medical intervention; (3) residential treatment; (4) halfway house programs; and (5) outpatient and recovery support. This program employs an intensive 23-day inpatient and outpatient program that cultivates self-sufficiency and teaches skills to maintain sobriety.

DIRECT PRACTICE

All programs employed culturally appropriate counseling and treatment services. For example, use of elders who instructed in traditional teachings, values, and beliefs was a priority for service provision for many of the programs. Spiritual ceremonies such as the sweat lodge, talking circles, and smudging were also incorporated as part of the practice approach in many of the programs. For instance, in the Southern Ute Peaceful Spirit Youth Services Program, an essential part of youth counseling "is the use of indigenous beliefs, values, and approaches to help youth value and view their culture as a source of knowledge and guidance to deal with their challenges. For example, Talking Circles are utilized" (U.S. Department of Justice, 2000, p. 15). Most of the programs stress the importance of a holistic approach for treatment, based on the philosophy "that each person is a part of the whole, and an individual action affects the balance of everyone and everything within the whole" (p. 14). Some used the concept of the Medicine Wheel, which stresses that balance of the emotional, physical, mental, and spiritual bodies is essential for successful treatment. In the Southeast Alaska Regional Health Consortium (SEARC), the Gunaanasti Bill Brady Healing Center uses "a holistic model that combines biological, psychological, social, and internal spiritual elements . . . for treatment . . . allowing the center to address other major problems clients may have such as depression, low self-esteem, victimization issues and family problems" (p. 32).

"The holistic philosophy that life is sacred guides the activities of each component of the Turtle Mountain Safe Communities Program. The activities integrate the values and the morals passed down through the generations by Chippewa elders that define the relationship of the Chippewa people to their environment, society and the universe" (U.S. Department of Justice, 2000, p. 11). The Pueblo of Zuni Recovery Center focuses on the use of Pueblo philosophies and the strengths of its culture. "Zuni-specific knowledge and techniques regarding child and adolescent development, family systems, gender relationships, spiritual beliefs and communal principles guide counseling and therapy sessions" (p. 28).

FAMILY VIOLENCE

In many reservation communities and urban areas, Indigenous women have been at the forefront of developing and operating programs related to preventing family violence in their communities. These women have also defined what practice approaches are necessary to employ in their work with their people. In northern New Mexico, women from the Tewa-speaking pueblos have turned to their cultural roots to address the rape and sexual violence in their communities (Papin, 2000). Tewa Women United, an activist group, created one of the first antiviolence programs in North America controlled by the Indigenous women it serves. This group's main project is called V.O.I.C.E.S. (Valuing Our Integrity with Courage, Empowerment, and Support). The volunteers who work with this program "encourage healing by working closely with sexual assault victims' families and the communities to make offenses publicly known despite resistance from mostly male tribal councils" (p. 37). The entire pueblo (community) is encouraged to take responsibility for the violence and come together to create healing and peace among all members. This inclusion of all stakeholders to address the problem is critical when working within a "relational culture" (Cheatham, Ivey, Ivey, & Morgan, 1993, p. 116). This practice approach is a form of "Network Therapy," that was created by Carol Atteneave (1969) in her work with First Nations communities (LaFromboise & Lowe, 1989). The Network Therapy approach brings together the individual(s) experiencing problem(s) with family and community networks, such as the nuclear and extended family, important neighbors, and key people in the community, such as religious leaders, teachers, law enforcement, and even the local bartender, if the issue is alcoholism (Cheatham, et al., 1993). Membes of this group work at informing each other of the extent of the problem and then decide how to collectively resolve it.

Similar to many mainstream programs that address violence, V.O.I.C.E.S. assists women and children from their pueblo find safe shelters, medical help, and emergency interventions. The program also operates a halfway house for the perpetrators and runs a hotline for those in need of services. Beyond this, the program has volunteers who provide culturally sensitive services to those it helps, and provides counseling and cross-cultural training to outside community medical and legal agencies that are used. The V.O.I.C.E.S. program helps to instruct those it serves to regain their inner strength by using the spiritual rituals of their ancestors. Kathy Sanchez, director of Tewa Women United, says that each morning all people involved with the program say prayers of thanks to acknowledge the people, animals, plant life, wind, and water that sustain them, and they present themselves to the sun to receive its healing powers. Sanchez says, "once you claim these connections, you recognize the sacred energy of the universe and gain strength from it to make choices that empower you" (Papin, 2000, p. 37).

The White Buffalo Calf Women's Society, the oldest shelter in the United States for Indigenous women, and women of color, who are victims of rape and domestic violence, was opened on the Rosebud reservation in Mission, South Dakota, by Lakota women in 1978. The program is a grassroots, nonprofit organization staffed and managed entirely by women of the Lakota Nation who are survivors of violence. Tillie Black Bear states that to inform community members about family violence, the organization uses community development strategies that include public service announcements on local radio stations and in local newspapers (personal communication, January 26, 2001). The program also works closely with the Rosebud Sioux Tribal Council to address the problem of violence in the community.

Traditional Indigenous spiritual practices are incorporated into practice approaches, and attending to the spiritual needs of the women is a priority of this program (Tillie Black Bear, personal communication, January 26, 2001). "Smudging," the use of the smoke from a bit of burning sage wiped over one's body to purify one's thoughts and prayer, is used to help clients. A "sweat lodge," which is also used, is a dome-like structure that people enter to pray. It is made with strong slender willow poles, which are tied together and covered by tarps and blankets. In the center of the lodge is a pit where hot rocks are placed. Water is poured over the stones while special prayers and songs are recited to assist in helping the participants. The White Buffalo Calf Women's Society sweat lodge ceremonies are conducted for women by women. Talking circles and traditional medicine people are used in this program (Tillie Black Bear, personal communication, January 26, 2001). A "talking circle" incorporates a circular group process where participants express their views and feelings on an issue, one at a time, until all have shared. The circle often begins and ends with a prayer and sometimes includes smudging. This program requires that the perpetrators of the violence (mostly men) are mandated by the tribal court to attend men's violence re-education classes that are sponsored by the White Buffalo Calf Women's Society.

Not unlike the reservation-based programs, urban Indigenous Peoples' family violence projects incorporate the use of spirituality and cultural traditions, along with mainstream individual and group counseling. The "Healing the Sacred Hoop" (2001) project in Lawrence, Kansas, which was founded and directed by Theresa Chief Eagle, focuses on healing the "sacred hoop" (the individual, family, and Indigenous nations) by stressing that family violence is not a tradition within Indigenous cultures. This project has provided parent education and support groups for Indigenous parents in Kansas City, Kansas, Minneapolis, and Lawrence since 1987. Mainstream practice approaches used in this program include weekly individual in-home sessions and support group for families. Cultural activities include educating clients about tribally based child and family development matters and providing activities to strengthen the family and the extended family system. Contemporary and traditional arts, such as beadwork and making star quilts, are incorporated into the program, while spiritual practices, such as smudging, talking circles, use of eagle feathers, and sweat lodge and pipe ceremonies, are offered.

CHILD WELFARE

There exist several initiatives that address child abuse and neglect in tribal communities. First, attitudes are changing about the worth of Native children. To protect this vulnerable population, many different First Nations groups now advance the traditional cultural teaching that children are sacred gifts from the Creator and must be respected and lovingly cared for. For instance, national Native child advocate Terry Cross states, "In traditional Indian spiritual belief systems, all things had a spiritual nature that demanded respect. Children were not seen as their parent's property, but were considered gifts from the Creator, endowed with an intrinsic value based upon their relationship to the Creator. Thus respect was extended to children as well as to the earth and creatures from the land, sea, and sky" (Cross, Earle, & Simmons, 2000, p. 149). Many tribal child welfare programs now employ this message in their work with clients and prospective clients.

Second, communities are developing and using parenting skills and child care curriculum that are based upon traditional, tribal cultural methods of child rearing and caring for children. These materials are used in treatment and prevention situations and are aimed at several different groups: prospective parents, parents or caretakers who want to learn how to parent more effectively, and parents who have abused or neglected their children. Much of the material focuses on parent and extended family roles, tribal values and customs, and strategies for successful nurturing.

Third, tribal governments are encouraging greater protection for their children by developing tribal child welfare legal codes that focus specifically on Native child well-being and safeguarding against abuse, neglect, and exploitation. Individuals who violate these codes are remanded to tribal child parenting and caretaker classes that use tribal parenting skills and child care curriculum. Fourth, former abusers of Native children, especially Indigenous women whose drinking during their pregnancy resulted in their child developing fetal alcohol syndrome (FAS), have been retained by alcohol and child welfare programs to talk about their experiences as a means of prevention. While the number of speakers is small, their message to Native youth, prospective parents, and caretakers can be very powerful, moving, and effective.

Countering the Effects of American Colonialism

The conquest has not yet ended, and neither has resistance to the conquest.
— Juan Adolfo Vasquez, 1982

Social workers can do a lot to help counter the effects that America colonialism, substance abuse, family violence, and child welfare have on First Nations Peoples. First, it is imperative that social workers acknowledge that American colonialism is a system of oppression that festers within Indigenous communities and is at the root of many of the social, economic, and political problems experienced by these groups. The disturbingly high incidence of substance abuse, violence, and child welfare problems among First Nations presented in this chapter is evidence of the continuing effects of this system. The absence of shock, outrage, and action to correct this oppression by mainstream society is also symptomatic of colonialism.

Second, the United States has major problems with recognizing, reflecting upon, and resolving the pain and oppression its actions causes others. Social workers must refuse to be complicit with this shortsighted, indifferent mind-set. Colonialism is a system that has caused a great deal of mistrust of and dislike for Americans, both here and abroad; social workers can help to counter this oppressive system by aggressively educating others about its injurious and racist consequences. Social workers can gain a better perspective by examining colonialism on a global level—by paying special attention to the views of other peoples (and nations) throughout the world. There are numerous Web sites, magazines, books, news programs, and videos that can be helpful in this process.[4]

Third, the narrative I shared about my community's American colonialism experience is only one example of the destructive effects of this system. For generations, the U.S. system has taken little responsibility for what it has done to Indigenous Peoples and, instead, has oftem ignored them and/or blamed them for their dismal circumstances by suggesting the excessive social and economic problems in their communities were/are due to their inability to adapt to the demands of modern White society. However, Indigenous Peoples have their own side to this story, and social workers can learn more about it by working with tribal communities to gather first-person and community stories that offer such insights. With permission from the storytellers, the narratives can be shared with the general public, policy makers, service providers, and political representatives to create greater knowledge of past and present injustices.

Fourth, there are many oppressive aspects of American colonialism that need to be addressed. However, social workers are especially well suited to counter the racist stereotypes of Indigenous Peoples and the excessive violence directed at them. Social workers can join groups that organize protests against racist sports team names and images. They can also write letters of protest to the editors of local newspapers, to sports team owners, to the players, and to school boards. On the university campus, social work students can organize protests against any clothing and other merchandise that depicts racist and stereotypical images of Indigenous Peoples. They can work with their university student government and administration to enforce a ban or creatively put on trial all such racist names and images.

Social workers can address the violence directed at First Nations by working closely with tribal communities to push for stronger laws and surveillance to protect potential Indigenous crime victims. Social workers can work to expand the definition of hate crimes against Indigenous Peoples and then develop a database to identify victims of hate crimes. Social workers can help sponsor relevant workshops and conferences in tribal communities, petition the U.S. government to provide more resources and money to address violence against Indigenous Peoples, and help victims and perpetrators understand how American colonialism contributes to the excessive violence.

Fifth, the sovereignty of First Nations must be acknowledged and legally and morally supported by social workers and the U.S. government. The affairs of tribal governments continue to be dominated by U.S. colonial policies, and Indigenous Peoples must be free from this control and have the ability to determine what is best for them. They must be treated with respect and regarded as legitimate governments that can legally deal with the United States on a government-to-government basis. When Indigenous Peoples' land, treaty, human, and civil rights are violated by this nation and they cannot get relief in its courts due to the subjective colonial relationship, they must be accorded the opportunity to take their grievances to international courts of justice for remedy.

Sixth, social workers must remember that Indigenous Peoples are very resilient. They are not passive victims of substance abuse, family violence, and child abuse and neglect. Many have done a great deal to address these and other problems. For instance, they have created innovative practice approaches and programs with limited resources and have employed strategies to get their communities to understand the scope of these problems and work together to resolve them. They use whatever mainstream methods work, with cultural teachings, values, beliefs, ceremonies, and resources. They train outside providers about their traditions and what they need to know to be effective. They educate their own people about the destructive nature of substance abuse, family violence, and child abuse and neglect and that these problems are not traditional practices within Indigenous culture.

Seventh, it is important that social workers concentrate their efforts on getting more Indigenous men involved in addressing the problems associated with substance abuse, family violence, and child welfare. In many communities Native women are doing the greater part of the work, especially since men are much more likely to be the perpetrators. Native men who are healthy or have successfully recovered from these problems can be especially helpful in working with other men in the areas of prevention and treatment. Every tribal community should have healthy men's groups to keep watch over the behavior of its men, set codes of conduct and morality for them, and serve as the major source for socializing its men into healthy manhood according to its tribal traditions.

Eighth, language in official government acts that are intended to help Indigenous Peoples address substance abuse, family violence, and child abuse and neglect consistently focus on the symptoms instead of the root causes. Social workers can help correct this situation by including language in such policies that describes how colonialism has negatively affected these groups. It is important that policy makers/writers understand the difference between the symptoms and root causes as they concern the social challenges faced by Indigenous Peoples.

American colonialism has chronically ignored, trivialized, and superficially responded to the needs of Indigenous Peoples in the United States, despite the fact that these groups gave up billions of acres of land and countless other natural resources in exchange for promises that the United States would protect their safety and well-being. This nation has abused Indigenous Peoples, denied that it has a colonizer/colonized relationship with them, and has deprived them of the resources and support they need to recover from the grasp and effects of this oppressive system. The United States has failed to be accountable for its oppressive activities and attitudes and appears to chronically suffer from a condition know as "hypegiaphobia," (a strong fear of, dislike of, or aversion to responsibility). Social workers can help the United States recover from this deficit if they intelligently, courageously, and continuously demand that this nation provide the necessary resources and opportunities that First Nations need to address the effects of American colonialism. Many Indigenous Peoples are doing more than their part to recover from this historical trauma; it's time that social workers joined this effort.

Notes

1. Ramsey Clark was the U.S. attorney general under President Lyndon B. Johnson. He is the author of *The Fire This Time: U.S. War Crimes in the Gulf* (2002) and is one of the attorneys for Leonard Peltier, an Indigenous activist who is considered to be a political prisoner of the United States. Howard Zinn, the author of several books, including the brilliant *A People's History of the United States* (1997), is a professor emeritus of political science at Boston University. Jennifer Harbury, the author of *Searching for Everardo: A Story of Love, War, and the CIA in Guatemala* (1997), is a human rights lawyer who has dedicated her life to the rights of Indigenous Peoples in Latin America and was also an attorney for Leonard Peltier.

2. In this chapter, when I refer to substance abuse I am generally referring to the use of alcohol.

3. Aldehyde dehydrogenase isozyme (ALDH) is an enzyme that helps break down alcohol in the body. "ALDH inactivity results in the accumulation of acetaldehyde in the body, which leads to the so-called flushing reaction. This reaction is characterized by facial flushing, nausea, headache, dizziness, and rapid heart beat" (Makimoto, 1998, p. 274).

4. Web sites
   - Center for World Indigenous Studies, Fourth World Documentation Project (www.cwis.org)
   - Third World Traveler, Progressive Media Links, Speaking Truth to Power (www.thirdworldtraveler.com/General/Prog_Media_Links.html)
   - Global Exchange (www.globalexchange.org)
   - The Independent Media Center (www.indymedia.org)

   Journals:
   - *Z Magazine*
   - *Dissent Magazine*
   - *The Progressive*

- *The Nation*
- *The New Internationalist*
- *Cultural Survival Quarterly*

Radio news programs
- *Democracy Now* (www.democracynow.org)
- *AIROS/Native America Calling* (www.nativetelecom.org/)
- *Native America Public Telecommunication* (www.nativecalling.org)

Books
- *Rethinking Globalization: Teaching for Justice in an Unjust World* edited by Bill Bigelow and Bob Peterson, Rethinking Schools Press, 2002
- *The Gaia Atlas of First Peoples: A Future for the Indigenous World* by Julian Burger, New York: Anchor Books, 1990
- *The State of Native America: Genocide, Colonization, and Resistance* edited by M. Annette Jaimes, Boston: South End Press, 1992
- *Indians Are Us? Culture and Genocide in Native North America* by Ward Churchill, Monroe, ME: Common Courage Press, 1994.

Newspapers
- *Indian Country Today*
- *News From Indian Country*
- *The Independent Native Journal.*

Videos
- *Teaching Indians to Be White* (1993), available from Films for Humanities and Sciences, P.O. Box 2053, Princeton, NJ, 08543, (800) 257-5726, Cataloging 306.08'97, Indians of North America-Government relations, Print Entry #: 4:1221
- *Healing the Hurts* (1989), distributed by Phil Lucas Productions, P.O. Box 1274, Issaquah, WA, 98027, (206) 979-9819
- *Global Village or Global Pillage*, Jeremy Brecher, 1999
- *What I've Learned about U.S. Foreign Policy* by Frank Dorrel.

References

About Child Abuse, National Exchange Club Foundation, Preventing Child Abuse . . . Serving America, Frequently Asked Questions. (n.d.). Retrieved August 19, 2005, from www.preventchildabuse.com/abuse.htm

Atteneave, C. (1969). Therapy in tribal settings and urban network interventions. *Family Process, 8*, 192–210.

Bachman, R. (1991). The social causes of American Indian homicide as revealed by the life experiences of thirty offenders. *American Indian Quarterly, 15*, 469–492.

Bachman, R. (1992). *Death and violence on the reservation: Homicide, family violence, and suicide in American Indian populations*. Westport, CT: Auburn House.

Bennion, L., & Li, T. K. (1976). Alcohol metabolism in American Indians and whites: Lack of racial differences in metabolic rate and liver alcohol dehydrogenase. *New England Journal of Medicine, 294*, 9–13.

Brave Heart Yellow Horse, M. (1999). Culturally and historically congruent clinical social work interventions with Native clients. In Rowena Fong & Sharlene Furuto (Eds.), *Culturally competent practice: Skills, interventions, and evaluations* (pp. 285–298). Needham Heights, MA: Allyn & Bacon.

Buege, D. J. (2004). Resource Wars: The Crandon Mine Saga. Retrieved August 5, 2005, from: http://zmagazine.zmag.org/Feb2004/bueger0204.html

Chan, A. W. K. (1986). Racial differences in alcohol sensitivity. *Alcohol and Alcoholism, 21*, 93–104.

Cheatham, H. E., Ivey, A. E., Ivey, M. B., & Morgan, L. S. (1993). Multicultural counseling and therapy: Changing the foundations of the field. In Allen E. Ivey, Mary Bradford Ivey, & Lynn Simek-Morgan (Eds.), *Counseling and psychotherapy: A multicultural perspective*, 3rd ed. (pp. 93–123). Needham Heights, MA: Allyn & Bacon.

Churchill, W. (2005). Crimes against humanity. Retrieved August 19, 2005, from http://www.dickshovel.com/crimes.html

Clark, R. (2002). *The fire this time: U.S. War Crimes in the Persian Gulf*. International Action Center: New York, NY.

Cross, T. A., Earle, K. A., & Simmons, D. (2000). Child abuse and neglect in Indian country policy issues. *Families in Society: The Journal of Contemporary Human Services, 81*, 149–158.

Devore, W., & Schlesinger, E. G. (1999). *Ethnic-sensitive social work practice*, 5th ed. Needham Heights, MA: Allyn & Bacon.

Duran, E., & Duran, B. (1995). *Native American postcolonial society*. Albany, NY: SUNY Press.

Dyck, L. E. (1993). Absence of the atypical mitochondrial aldehyde dehydrogenase (ALDH) isozyme in Saskatchewan Cree Indians. *Human Heredity, 43*, 116–120.

Earle, K. A., & Cross, A. (2001). *Child abuse and neglect among American Indian/Alaska Native children: An analysis of the existing data*. Oregon, CA: Casey Family Programs, National Indian Child Welfare Association.

Fong, R., & Furuto, S. (2001). *Culturally competent practice: Skills, interventions, and evaluations*. Boston, MA: Allyn & Bacon.

Goldman, D., Brown, G., Albaugh, B., Robin, R., Goodson, S., Trunzo, M., Akhtar, L., Lucas-Derse, J., Linnoila, M., & Dean, M. (1993). DRD dopamine receptor genotype, linkage disequilibrium, and alcoholism in American Indians and other populations. *Alcoholism: Clinical & Experimental Research*, *17*(2), 199–204.

Goodluck, C., & Willeto, A. A. A. (2000). *Native American kids 2000: Indian child well-being indicators*. Oregon, CA: Casey Family Programs. National Indian Child Welfare Association.

Greenfeld, L. A., & Smith, S. K. (1999). *American Indians and crime*. Washington, DC: U.S. Department of Justice, Office of Justice Programs, Bureau of Justice Statistics, NCJ 173386.

Harbury, J. (1997). *Searching for Everardo: A story of love, war, and the CIA in Guatemala*. New York: Warner Books.

Healing the sacred hoop: Parent education and support program. (2001). Resident services, Lawrence-Douglas County Housing Authority, Lawrence, KS.

Johnson, C. (2000). *Blowback: The costs and consequences of American empire*. New York: Henry Holt.

Krauss, M. (1992). Statement of Mr. Michael Krauss, representing the Linguistic Society of America. In U.S. Senate, *Native American Languages Act of 1991: Hearing before the Select Committee on Indian Affairs* (pp.18-22). Washington, DC: U.S. Government Printing Office.

LaFromboise, T., Berman, J. S., & Sohi, B. K. (1994). American Indian women. In Lillian Comas-Diaz & Beverly Greene (Eds.), *Women of color: Integrating ethnic and gender identities in psychotherapy* (pp. 30–71). New York: Guilford Press.

LaFromboise, T., & Lowe, K. G. (1989). American Indian children and adolescents. In J. Gibbs, & L. Hwang (Eds.), *Children of color* (pp. 114–147). San Francisco: Jossey-Bass.

Lewis, R. G. (1995). American Indians. *Encyclopedia of social work*, 19th ed. (pp. 216–225). Washington, DC: National Association of Social Workers.

Lum, D. (1999). *Culturally competent practice: A framework for growth and action*. Pacific Grove, CA: Brooks/Cole.

Mahajan, R. (November/December 2001). We think the price is worth it: Media uncurious about Iraq policy's effects—there or here. FAIR: Fairness and Accuracy in Reporting. Retrieved August 17, 2005, from http://fair.org/index.php?page=1084

Makimoto, K. (1998). Drinking patterns and drinking problems among Asian-Americans and Pacific Islanders. *Alcohol Health & Research World*, *22*, 4, 270–275.

Mancall, P. C. (1995). *Deadly medicine: Indians and alcohol in early America*. Ithaca, NY: Cornell University Press.

Maracle, B. (1993). *Crazywater: Native Voice on Addiction and Recovery*. Toronto: Penguin Books Canada.

May, P. A. (1994). The epidemiology of alcohol abuse among American Indians: The mythical and real properties. *American Indian Culture and Research Journal, 18*(2):121–143.

May, P. A. (1996). Overview of alcohol abuse epidemiology for American Indian populations. In G. Sandefur, R. Rindfuss., & B. Cohen (Eds.), *Changing numbers, changing needs: American Indian demography and public health* (pp. 235–261). Washington, DC: National Academy Press.

May, P. A., & Moran, J. R. (1995). Prevention of alcohol misuse: A review of health promotion efforts among American Indians. *American Journal of Health Promotion, 9*(4), 288–299.

Merriam-Webster's Collegiate Dictionary (10th ed.). (2000). Springfield, MA: Merriam-Webster.

Morrisette, V., McKenzie, B., & Morrisette, L. (1993). Towards an aboriginal model of social work practice. *Canadian Social Work Review, 10*(1), 92–108.

Moran, J. R. (1999). Preventing alcohol use among urban American Indian youth: The seventh generation program. In H. Weaver (Ed.), *Voices of First Nations People: Human service considerations* (pp. 51–67). New York: The Haworth Press.

Moultan, G. E. (1988). *The journals of the Lewis and Clark expedition, August 25, 1804 to April 6, 1805*, (Vol. 3). Lincoln: University of Nebraska Press.

Napoleon, H. (1993). *Yuuyaraq: The way of the human being.* Publications Center, Center for Cross-Cultural Studies, College of Rural Alaska, University of Alaska Fairbanks.National Congress of American Indians. *2003 Annual Report.*

National Congress of American Indians. (2003). Retrieved March 20, 2006, from www.ncai.org/ncai/resurce/documents/2003_AnnualReport.pdf

National Indian Child Welfare Association. (n.d.). Retrieved May 31, 2003, from www.nicwa.org/involved/membership.index.asp

Newhouse, E. (1999). Making reservation "dry" is no guarantee. Alcohol: Cradle to grave. *Great Falls Tribune.* Retrieved June 30, 2003, from www.gannett.com/go/difference/greatfalls/pages/part8/dry.html

Office for Substance Abuse Prevention. (1991). *Prevention resource guide: American Indians and Native Alaskans.* Washington, DC: Center for Substance Abuse Prevention. p. 1.

Ogunwole, S. U. (2002). *The American Indian and Alaska Native population: 2000.* Washington, DC: U.S. Department of Commerce, Economics and Statistics Administration, U.S. Census Bureau.

Papin, L. (2000, October/November). *Healing voices* (p. 37). Ms. News: Women Organizing Worldwide.

Pevar, Stephan L. (1992). *The rights of Indians and tribes: The basic ACLU guide to Indian and tribal rights*, 2nd ed. Carbondale: Southern Illinois University Press.

Price, S. L. (2002, October). The Indian wars. *Sports Illustrated, 96*(10), 66–72.

Rex, D., Bosron, W. F., Smialek, J. E., & Ting-kai, L. (1985). Alcohol and aldehyde dehydrogenase isoenzymes in North American Indians. *Alcoholism: Clinical & Experimental Research, 9*(2), 147–152.

Riggin, J. M. (1992). *John Wayne: A bio-bibliography.* New York: Greenwood Press.

Sansani, I. (n.d.) *American Indian lands rights in the inter-American system: Dann v. United States.* Retrieved June 30, 2003, from http:www.wcl.American.edu/hrbrief/102indian.cfm

Sardar, Z., & Davies, M. W. (2002). *Why do people hate America?* New York: Disinformation Company.

Snipp, C. M. (1996). The size and distribution of the American Indian population: Fertility, mortality, and residence. In G. D. Sandefur, R. Rindfuss, & B. Cohen (Eds.), *Changing numbers, changing needs: American Indian demography and public health* (pp. 17–52). Washington, DC: National Academy Press.

Stamatopoulou, E. (1994). Indigenous peoples and the United Nations: Human rights as a developing dynamic. *Human Rights Quarterly, 16,* 58–81.

Stratton, K., Howe, C., & Battaglia, F. (Eds.). 1996. *Fetal alcohol syndrome: Diagnosis, epidemiology, prevention, and treatment.* Washington, DC: Institute of Medicine, National Academy Press.

Streissguth, A., & Kanter, J. (Eds.). 1997. *The challenge of fetal alcohol syndrome.* Seattle: University of Washington.

Tapping, C. (1993). Colonialism: Then and now. In Carmel Tapping (Ed.), *Other wisdoms, other worlds: Colonisation & family therapy* (pp. 4–8). Dulwich Centre Newsletter, 1: 3-37.

Thornton, R. (1996). Tribal membership requirements and the demography of "old" and "new" Native Americans. In G. Sandefur, R. Rindfuss, & B. Cohen (Eds.), *Changing numbers, changing needs: American Indian demography and public health* (pp. 79–102). Washington, DC: National Academy Press.

U.S. Congress, Office of Technological Assessment. (1986). *Indian health care.* OTA-H-290. Washington, DC: U.S. Government Printing Office.

U.S. Department of Health and Human Services. (1996). *Trends in Indian health, 1996.* Rockville, MD: Office of Planning, Evaluation, and Legislation, Division of Program Statistics.

U.S. Department of Health and Human Services, Administration for Children and Families. (2001). *Child maltreatment, 1999.* Washington, DC: U.S. Government Printing Office.

U.S. Department of Justice. (2000). *Promising practices and strategies to reduce alcohol and substance abuse among American Indians and Alaska Natives.* Report prepared by American Indian Development Associates for the Office of Justice Programs.

Vasquez, J. A. (1982). In R. Wright, *Stolen continents: The "New World" through Indian eyes.* Toronto: Penguin Books.

Waller, M., & Yellow Bird, M. (2002). Strengths of First Nations Peoples. In Dennis Saleebey (Ed.), *The strengths perspective in social work practice.* New York: Longman.

Watts, T. D., & Lewis, R. G. (1988). Alcoholism and Native American youth: An overview. Alcohol problems and minority youth. *Journal of Drug Issues, 18*(1), 69–86.

Westermeyer, J. (1974). "The drunken Indian": Myths and realties. *Psychiatric Annals, 4*(11), 29–36.

Will, G. (1934). *Notes on the Arikara Indians and their ceremonies.* Denver, CO: John VanMale.

Yellow Bird, M. (1996). *A model of the effects of colonialism on First Nations Peoples.* Unpublished manuscript.

Yellow Bird, M. (1998). *Deconstructing colonialism: A First Nations social work perspective.* Unpublished manuscript.

Yellow Bird, M. (1999a). Indian, American Indian, and Native Americans: Counterfeit identities. *Winds of Change: A Magazine for American Indian Education and Opportunity, 14*(1).

Yellow Bird, M. (1999b). Indigenous peoples parenting. In Charles A. Smith (Ed.), *Encyclopedia of Parenting Theory and Research* (pp. 231–233). Westport, CT: Greenwood Press.

Yellow Bird, M. (1999c). *Treating and preventing violence in First Nations families and communities.* Horton, KS: Kickapoo Nation.

Yellow Bird, M. J., & Chenault. V. (1999). The role of social work in advancing the practice of indigenous education: Obstacles and promises in empowerment-oriented social work practice. In K. Gayton Swisher & J. W. Tippeconnic (Eds.), *Next steps: Research and practice to advance Indian education* (pp. 201–236). Charleston, WV: ERIC Clearinghouse on Rural Education and Small Schools.

Yellow Bird, M. (2000, February). *Disarming colonialism: A First Nations social worker's manifesto.* Paper presented at the 4th Annual American Indian Social Work Educator's Meeting in conjunction with the Council on Social Work Education, Annual Program Meeting, New York City.

Yellow Bird, M. (2001). Critical values and First Nations Peoples. In Rowena Fong & Sharlene Furuto, (Eds.), *Culturally competent practice: Skills, interventions, and evaluations* (pp. 61–74). Needham Heights, MA: Allyn & Bacon.

Young, R. J. C. (2001). *Postcolonialism: An historical introduction.* Oxford, UK: Blackwell Publishers.

Zinn, H. (1997). *A people's history of the United States.* New York: New Press.

13

Catching Our Breath

A Decolonization Framework for Healing Indigenous Families

TERESA EVANS-CAMPBELL and KARINA L. WALTERS

I went to boarding school when I was five and I got really sick—I almost died—I couldn't breathe. I had pneumonia . . . I think I was really sick from a broken heart. [Talking about the trauma] before, with the [emotional] pain, my breath would stop . . . for a long time my life was really like that from all the trauma I'd been though. A lot of it stopped my breath.

—Lakota boarding school survivor

Not only the animals possessed *iinruq* [a spirit, the essence, the soul of the object or being] humans also possessed them. But human spirits . . . are called *anerneq*—literally, "breath"—and as in animals, a human being could not live without its breath. Death came when the *anerneq* left the body due to injury, illness, or by the will of the person.

—Yup'ik elder

Introduction

American Indians, Alaska Natives, and other First Nations Peoples of North America (hereafter referred to as Natives or AIAN) have endured a succession of traumatic and systematic assaults by foreign governments on their nations, communities, and families. From Columbus's horrific enslavement and dismemberment of Caribe indigenous peoples to the plundering of southeastern indigenous populations for the "triangle" slave trade, indigenous peoples have had unique experiences directly related to surviving colonization. Such experiences also include genocide, massacre, sterilization of Native women without their consent, health-related experimentation (e.g., trachoma eye surgeries in the 1920s), desecration of burial sites, and placement of indigenous children into non-Native custodial care. These and other historically traumatic assaults constitute a "historical trauma response," otherwise known as a "soul wound" (Duran, Duran, Yellow Horse Brave Heart, Yellow Horse-Davis, 1998, p. 341). Historic and current traumatic assaults have enduring consequences—environmentally, socially, culturally, emotionally, biologically, psychologically, and, above all, spiritually, for both indigenous peoples and their perpetrators. The soul wound is the cumulative effect of historical trauma brought on by centuries of colonialism, genocide, and oppression. Psychological ramifications include internalization of the oppressor, unresolved grief and mourning, and suicidality (Yellow Horse Brave Heart, 2000). The succession of traumatic events have left AIAN people plagued with a host of social and health problems, including high rates of poverty, unemployment, substance use, violence, and poor health and mental health indicators.

Many clinically oriented and Western-trained therapists have sought to understand the biological and psychological effects of such traumas among historically oppressed peoples. Diagnostic categories such as post-traumatic stress disorder (PTSD), complicated bereavement, and alcohol and other drug use (AOD) disorders have been postulated to capture the disease and pathology caused by such traumas. Yet, what these diagnostic categories fail to capture is the complete and utter wounding of the spirit that is caused by the trauma. Moreover, the typically proposed treatment for such trauma focuses completely on psychological and behavioral sequelae with little to no attention to the spirit affected by such traumas. As one Yup'ik elder stated, "I have come to the conclusion that the primary cause of alcoholism is not physical but spiritual . . . the cure must also be of the spirit" (Napoleon, 1991, p. 2). Eduardo Duran (2002), a Native psychologist, noted that since the collective colonization of the psyche of the people includes physical, psychological, and spiritual wounding, all three levels—mind, body, and spirit—must be addressed, with the deepest healing work carried out on the spiritual level. This worldview is consistent with many indigenous understandings of historical trauma effects and corresponding healing processes. Any understanding of etiology and change efforts related to historical trauma and corresponding AOD use and family violence among Native peoples has to begin and end with the restoration of spirit.

In this chapter, we present a decolonization practice framework specific to Native families and communities that incorporates the impact of historical trauma as well as the protective functions of family, community, and spirituality. After reviewing the relationships among colonial traumatic stressors, substance use, and family violence, we highlight specific culturally protective factors and conclude with directions for child welfare practice. Our decolonization practice framework is rooted in indigenist thought with a focus on healing rather than treating indigenous families and communities.

The Colonial Context

HISTORICAL TRAUMATIC EVENTS

Kill and scalp all, little and big.

—Colonel John Milton Chivington, before the Sand Creek Massacre

In mid-September 1861, Major Wynkoop escorted about 750 Cheyennes and Arapahos into Camp Weld, near Denver, Colorado (Churchill, 1997). Under Wynkoop's command, the Cheyenne and Arapaho surrendered all of their weapons and were interned under U.S. military supervision along a site known as Sand Creek. In November, Colonel John Milton Chivington and his 900 "Indian fighter" soldiers sought out the Sand Creek settlement to rectify their public embarrassment of not having killed enough Indians during their 100-day tour of duty. At dawn on November 28, Chivington and his men slaughtered the community in a surprise attack, despite the fact that both American and White flags of surrender flew over the sleeping encampment. One lieutenant from the New Mexico Volunteer Cavalry who was a witness to the massacre later testified in congressional hearings on his observations of that day:

> Of from five to six hundred souls [who were killed], the majority of which were women and children . . . I did not see a body of man, woman, or child but was scalped, and in many instances their bodies were mutilated in a most horrible manner—men, women and children's privates cut out, etc. . . . . I heard one man say that he had cut out a woman's private parts and had them for exhibition on a stick . . . I also heard of numerous instances in which men had cut out the private parts of females and stretched them over the saddle bows and wore them over hats while riding in the ranks . . . I heard one man say that he had cut a squaw's heart out, and he had it stuck up on a stick.
>
> —(Churchill, 1997, p. 233)

Such horrific events were commonplace in the latter part of the 19th century. Mutilation of Native bodies, both living and dead, was well documented in such colonialist exploits. For example, Andrew Jackson ordered the mutilation of over 800 Muscogee Indian corpses by slicing their flesh to make bridle reigns, and Tecumseh's skin was flayed to make razor straps (as cited in Smith, 1999; as cited in Wrone & Nelson, 1982; Stannard, 1992.

Genocidal atrocities persist to this day, accompanied by ethnocide (i.e., the systematic attempt to modify or annihilate cultural practices and knowledge; this is a subcategory of genocide). Genocidal events are an integral part of historically traumatic events (HTE). Historically traumatic events consist of communally based incidents that cause catastrophic upheaval or high levels of community distress among and within indigenous communities and/or nations. These events include planned phenomena by government and government-sponsored institutions such as forced relocation, community massacres, forced boarding school attendance, sterilization of Native women, and prohibition of religious activities. HTE also includes strip mining of homelands, radioactive dumping of chemical waste into rivers that sustain communities, flooding of homelands, and the introduction of diseases into indigenous communities by virtue of contact with outsiders. Historically traumatic events can be aimed at communities or families directly, as in the case of boarding schools, or they can be aimed at the environment in which indigenous populations live. Attacks on indigenous communities via the land and environment cuts at the heart of indigenous survival. Land plays a critically sacred role in indigenous life-ways. Not only is it inherently sacred, with particular tribal-specific meaning, it is often directly connected to ritual sacred, sites where ceremonies and obligations are performed. LaDuke (1999) identifies several contempory HTE via land:

> [Native peoples'] lands are subject to some of the most invasive industrial interventions imaginable . . . 317 reservations in the United States are threatened by environmental hazards, ranging from toxic wastes to clearcuts. Reservations have been targeted as sites for 16 proposed nuclear waste dumps . . . seventy-seven sacred sites have been disturbed or desecrated through resource extraction and development activities . . . over the last 45 years, there has been 1,000 atomic explosions on Western Shoshone land in Nevada, making the Western Shoshone the most bombed nation on earth . . . [and, there are] over 1,000 slag piles and tailings from abandoned uranium mines sit on Diné [Navajo] land, leaking radioactivity into the air and water. (p. 3)

CONCEPTUALIZING HISTORICAL TRAUMA

Historical trauma (HT) is the distress and suffering resulting from numerous compounding historically traumatic events experienced by a community over several generations (Yellow Horse Brave Heart, 1999b). The traumas are based on events that are shared by a *collective* and are generally catastrophic in nature. Moreover, the trauma need not be directly experienced for it to have an effect on future generations. Indeed, HT may accumulate over generations as community members retain the trauma of their ancestors while they continue to experience new HTE and other cumulative life stressors.

Historical trauma also results from the inability to complete cultural and spiritual ritual obligations (e.g., potlatch and traditional birthing and funerary rites) as a result of various forms of spiritually based HTE. Native peoples have been subject to systematic government-sponsored Christian proselytization efforts specifically designed to detribalize, deculturate, and assimilate them (Hirschfelder & Molin, 2001). For example, in 1883, the U.S. government established the Court of Indian Offenses on reservations with the explicit directive to abolish indigenous practices and replace them with "civilized" practices under the auspices of Christianity. By 1892, the Court of Indian Offenses decree allowed for strict punishment of AIAN individuals, families, and communities who engaged in indigenous cultural and spiritual practices, including the withholding of food rations from violators' families and imprisonment for up to six months (Hirschfelder & Molin, 2001).

The compounding of spiritual trauma over multiple generations can interact with current traumatic events, thereby triggering or exacerbating preexisting intergenerational historical trauma. For example, victims of massacres and their descendants may have been unable to bury the dead and perform traditional ceremonies to help the dead pass over to the spirit world. As a consequence, these communities may experience profound trauma and guilt over not being able to help their ancestors enter the spirit world, and this trauma may be passed on for successive generations. In some cases, communities may have lost the cultural tools, prayers, and ceremonies that are needed to transition the dead. Consequently, whole communities may feel the guilt and trauma associated with not being able to heal, transition, or protect their ancestors.

Several factors may put AIAN communities at higher risk than non-AIAN communities of having serious reactions to historically traumatic events. First, the extensive nature of interwoven extended-family or clan systems means that traumatic events are likely to affect the entire community (Duran et al., 1998). In addition, the emphasis on ancestor spirits in Native communities means that many Natives experience their ancestors presence in the here and now; consequently, the suffering of ancestors may be experienced in the present. Finally, the sense of time in Native communities may affect the experience of HTE. As Cross (1998) noted, many Native people do not conceptualize events as occurring along a linear timeline. Instead, some events occurring hundreds of years ago may be felt as strongly as events occurring only days before.

According to intergenerational traumatologists, family and community communication is a critical factor in understanding the impact of historically traumatic events on historical trauma (Danieli, 1998). Not surprising, many survivors of HTE tend to avoid talking about traumatic events and their surrounding feelings (Nagata, Trierweiler, & Talbot, 1999). Avoidance of the topic and indirect communication about the trauma are significantly related to poor mental health outcomes such as paranoia, hypochondria, anxiety, and low self-esteem (Lichtman, 1984). However, this is particularly complex for AIAN peoples since indirect communication tends to be culturally valued. In fact, practitioners can inadvertently misdiagnose or pathologize normal cultural practices if they are unaware of these subtle differences in communication patterns. Clinically, it is important that practitioners differentiate between *avoidance* of communication (a trauma reaction) and culturally based indirect communication styles (a culturally appropriate communication style).

HISTORICAL TRAUMA AND CHILD WELFARE POLICY

Child welfare has been a particular target of governmental attempts to destabilize tribal families, and child welfare policies have left a legacy of mistrust regarding any governmental interference in the lives of AIAN peoples. Attempts by Westerners to deculturate Native children began with the arrival of the first European "settlers," who were encouraged to adopt or tutor Native children. Beginning in the early 19th century, the federal government became involved officially in this cultural genocide, providing funds to private programs created to "civilize" young Native people (Cross, Earle, & Simmons, 2000). With the federal government's blessing, numerous private and religious agencies began operating Indian boarding schools with the express purpose of assimilating AIAN children into Western culture. By the turn of the century, thousands of AIAN children were coercively taken and raised in boarding schools. Sadly, many children died in these institutions, and child abuse and neglect were commonplace. Children were often punished by extreme physical means, tortured, or neglected if they spoke their language or engaged in traditional cultural practices. Countless others were sexually abused in the schools. For example, John Boone, a teacher at a Hopi boarding school, is estimated to have sexually abused over 142 Native children, while the principal at that school did not investigate any allegations of the abuse (as cited in Smith, 1999). Moreover, the Bureau of Indian Affairs (BIA), despite knowledge of such abuses in boarding schools, did not issue a policy to strengthen background checks of teachers until 1989 (as cited in Smith, 1999). The abuse suffered in the schools left a harmful legacy of self-doubt regarding parenting skills as well as destruction of culturally specific parenting knowledge (Evans-Campbell, in press). Moreover, as Smith (1999) points out, "through this colonization and abuse of their bodies, Indian people learn to internalize self-hatred. . . The fact that many Native peoples will argue that sexual violence is "traditional" indicates the extent to which our communities have internalized self-hatred" (pp. 40–41).

In the 1930s, the government began to close many boarding schools and promoted alternative ethnocidal governmental policies. Beginning in the 1940s, child welfare agencies actively advocated for the placement of AIAN children into non-AIAN custodial care. Throughout the 1950s and 1960s, Native-White adoptions were widespread, and in 1959, the Child Welfare League of America, in cooperation with the Bureau of Indian Affairs, initiated the Indian Adoption Project, which formalized transracial adoption and ultimately led to the adoption of thousands of Indian children into White, often urban families (Mannes, 1995). By the 1960s and 1970s, the crisis in Indian child welfare had reached epidemic proportions. Federal surveys at the time found that in the five states with the largest Indian populations, between 25% and 35% of all Native children were in out-of-home placement, with most placed in non-Native homes (Byler, 1977; Fischler, 1985). Across the nation, AIAN children were placed in substitute care at a rate between

5 and 25 times higher than non-Native children (U.S. Senate Select Committee on Indian Affairs, 1977). Tribes responded to these alarming conditions by demanding more power over the rights of their own children and began to advocate for federal policy to support their mission. By the late 1970s their efforts resulted in the creation of the Indian Child Welfare Act (ICWA), which was finally passed by Congress in 1978.

The ICWA set forth strict new requirements in child welfare cases involving Indian children and placed authority for Native children within the tribes. Despite the passage of ICWA, the number of AIAN being removed from their homes has continued to rise while the number of children in care for other ethnic groups has decreased (U.S. Department of Health and Human Services [DHHS], 2001). During the mid-1990s, American Indians and Asian Americans were the only two groups in the United States to see a rise in cases documented by child protective services (CPS) of child maltreatment, and the rise for American Indians was 3 times that for Asian Americans (18% compared to 6%; DHHS, 2001). Generations of these traumatic child welfare policies have created a profound and justifiable mistrust of child welfare systems and workers. Every AIAN person has been affected by this historical legacy, and communities continue to grieve the loss of these "stolen" generations. These cumulative multiple losses are contemporary, and their effects can be seen in the levels of violence indigenous communities endure to this day.

CONTEMPORARY VIOLENCE

Today, AIAN peoples are the victims of violent crimes at a rate (124 per 1,000) more than 2.5 times the national average (Greenfeld & Smith, 1999). Women in particular bear the brunt of colonial violence. The rate of violent crime against AIAN women is almost 50% higher than that reported for African American males, and the rate for AIAN males is double that for all males (Greenfeld & Smith, 1999). Moreover, the rate among AIAN women is highest compared to women of any other ethnic or racial group (98 per 1,000; Greenfeld & Smith, 1999). Colonization and subjugation of Native women's bodies has been a historical reality since contact and continues today via other forms of harassment and attack (e.g., "Save a fish; spear a pregnant squaw" was on a sign during White protests of Chippewa spearfishing in the 1980s; Smith 1999). As Smith (1999) points out, "the colonial desire to subjugate Indian women's bodies was quite apparent when, in 1982, Stuart Kasten marketed a new video [game], "Custer's Revenge," in which players get points each time they, in the form of Custer, rape an Indian woman" (p. 37).

Overall, AIAN peoples experience primarily assault-related violence, with 56% experiencing simple assault, 28% aggravated assault, and 6% sexual assault. Perpetration of violence in AIAN communities is at the hands of mostly Whites (60%) and other non-Natives (10% for a total of 70% non-AIAN perpetrators; Greenfeld & Smith, 1999).

MICROAGGRESSIONS AND OTHER FORMS
OF DISCRIMINATION

Microaggressions represent some of the most subtle, insidious, and pervasive forms of colonial discriminatory violence that indigenous peoples endure. Microaggressions include discriminatory acts that are "subtle" (e.g., being rendered invisible); covert (e.g., being followed in a store); and overt (e.g., being spit at or attacked). They also encompass everyday hassles (e.g., being asked permission to touch one's hair) and other forms of anti-indigenous colonial discrimination (witnessing stereotypes such as racist logos, advertisements, and mascots). Other examples include being subjected to "authenticity tests" that question whether a Native person is a "real" Indian, and romanticized stereotypes as demonstrated by comments such as, "My great-grandmother was a Cherokee princess," and "I think I was Indian in a past life." Microaggressions also include "silent" or "spiritual" genocide that involves the appropriation and theft of indigenous ceremonies, sacred objects, and sites. These types of discriminative assaults compound over time and exert a major bio-psycho-social-cultural-spiritual cost to individuals, families, communities, and tribal nations. All forms of epistemic, physical, sexual, and discriminatory (e.g., microaggressions) violence, whether it is subtle, overt, or symbolic, are a fundamental attack on indigenous wellness, stability, and, ultimately, on indigenous sovereignty.

Documentation of the empirical relationship between discrimination and health outcomes on indigenous communities is nearly nonexistent. However, research on non-Natives provides ample evidence that discrimination directly affects health-related outcomes. As Walters, Simoni, and Evans-Campbell (2002) noted in their review of the literature, discrimination has been related to depressive symptoms, global measures of distress, anxiety symptoms, and poor general physical health. Research also shows that everyday discrimination is much more stressful than episodic or time-limited discrimination and, as a result, daily hassles have a greater impact on health outcomes (Williams, Yu, Jackson, & Anderson, 1997). One of the few studies specifically addressing discrimination among AIAN peoples found that perceived discrimination was strongly associated with depressive symptoms and that traditional practices buffered the negative effects of discrimination among AIANs who regularly participated in such practices (Whitbeck, McMorris, Hoyt, Stubben, & LaFromboise, 2002).

The Impact of Colonial Trauma

Although the impact of colonial traumas on wellness cuts across many psycho-bio-spiritual outcomes, for the purposes of this chapter we focus on five main wellness outcomes. Specifically, we discuss historical trauma response, colonial trauma response, PTSD, AOD use, and family violence. In the last half of this section we discuss the relationships among colonial trauma response, AOD use, and family violence, and, ultimately, how these factors relate to family and parenting processes.

Historical Trauma Response

Maria Yellow Horse Brave Heart and her collaborators at the Takini Network developed the Lakota historical trauma response theory (Yellow Horse Brave Heart, 2000). Yellow Horse Brave Heart stated that the indigenous response is similar to the survivor child's complex identified among Jewish Holocaust survivors and their progeny. Yellow Horse Brave Heart contended that the historical trauma response includes obsessive rumination about the deceased; identification with the dead to the point of feeling emotionally dead; transposition or living concurrently in the past and present with a major life focus on ancestor suffering; survivor guilt, including enacting ancestor suffering in one's own life; unresolved mourning; psychic numbing; anger; depression and suicidality; intrusive dreams and thoughts; use of fantasies that project oneself into the past as a form of coping; and cardiovascular problems (Yellow Horse Brave Heart, 1999a, 1999b, 2000). Although there is tremendous heterogeneity in the experience of traumatic events, there are universal symptoms characterizing survivors of historically traumatic events. Such symptoms include depressive and anxiety-related reactions, guilt, unresolved grief and mourning, agitation, insomnia, nightmares, and somatization (Felsen, 1998).

We have elaborated on the work of Yellow Horse Brave Heart and colleagues to identify historical trauma response (HTR) as the bio-psycho-social-cultural-spiritual wounding from historically traumatic events and historical trauma. While historically traumatic events are the cause, and historical trauma is the compounding of multiple historically traumatic events over generations, historical trauma response is the collective wounding response.

INTERGENERATIONAL TRANSMISSION OF HISTORICAL TRAUMA RESPONSE

Although the field of intergenerational traumatology is still emerging, research suggests that a psychological profile of children of Holocaust survivors may capture an intrinsic pattern that does not imply pathological functioning but rather a predisposition or vulnerability to stress. For example, although at baseline there is no clinically significant difference between children of Holocaust survivors and Jewish nonsurvivor controls in terms of PTSD symptoms, when the survivor children are exposed to stressful events, they are significantly more likely than controls to develop PTSD or subthreshold PTSD (Danieli, 1998). Similar multigenerational effects have been documented in other populations after the Japanese-American internment (Nagata, 1991) and the American Indian Holocaust (Robin, Chester, & Goldman, 1996). For AIAN survivor offspring, increased sensitivity or hyperarousal to stressful events, in particular to events that act as reminders of their colonized status, may predispose them to secondary and vicarious traumatization experiences. For example, hearing other Natives discuss their trauma may trigger HTR reactions such as nightmares in the individual who has not had the direct trauma experience. Although there is considerable clinical anecdotal evidence for this stress vulnerability among indigenous populations, future research will need to test this hypothesis.

Colonial Trauma Response

Colonial trauma[1] response (CTR) is a complex set of historical (including HTR) and contemporary trauma responses to collective, individual, and interpersonal colonization-based traumatic events; whereas HTR only focuses on collective traumatic events and responses, colonial trauma response reactions quite often include trauma responses in which the traumatized individual unites with a collective sense of injustice and trauma. For example, a Native woman who is called "squaw" by a stranger might feel rage over her own current experience and see it as another example of the injustices perpetrated on Native women over the centuries. As this example suggests, it is probable that microaggressions trigger a colonial trauma response. Although the traumatic event was targeted at her individually, she may begin to contemplate her ancestors' experiences and connect with collective ancestral pain in a very immediate and visceral way in the here and now. Many of these indigenous trauma responses bear a strong resemblance to PTSD or PTSD-like symptoms. In fact, in addition to HTR and CTR, PTSD symptomatology may be a natural reaction to historical and contemporary colonial traumatic events.

Post-Traumatic Stress Disorder

According to the *Diagnostic Statistical Manual of Mental Disorders* (DSM-IV, 1994), PTSD is diagnosed if the event is a traumatic stressor; if the individual experiences helplessness, terror, or horror; and if significant distress or functional impairment results. Compared to other major psychiatric disorders, PTSD is relatively common, with an overall lifetime prevalence of about 8% in the general population (Kessler, Sonnega, Bromet, Hughes, & Nelson, 1995).

Women are more vulnerable to PTSD than men. Incidence and prevalence rates of PTSD are reported to be twice as high for women and adolescent girls compared to men and adolescent boys (Stein, Walker, & Forde, 2000), with women being more likely to develop a chronic course than men (Norris, Foster, & Weisshaar, 2002). In terms of intergenerational transmission of traumatic stress, research has demonstrated that daughters of Holocaust survivors are more vulnerable to the intergenerational transmission of parental trauma (Felsen, 1998). The mechanisms and pathways for these gender differences remain unclear. One possible explanation involves the type of event. For example, sexual assault has the highest conditional risk for PTSD (Norris et al., 2002), and women tend to be exposed more often to sexual assaults than men. Although untested, research data would suggest that, similar to non-Native women, Native women may also be at higher risk for PTSD and intergenerational transmission of traumatic stress than Native men.

Despite advances in PTSD research, PTSD as a diagnostic category fails to capture the complexity of cumulative trauma experienced day to day as well as trauma that is passed on intergenerationally, both of which are typically found in AIAN communities. The subtleties of the effects of cumulative trauma may simply be undetectable, given how PTSD is currently conceptualized, and, as a result, many studies might yield underestimates of traumatic stress symptoms in AIAN communities. For example, Jones, Daughinais, Sack, and Somervell (1997) found that the majority of Native youth experienced high rates of trauma, yet only 3% met diagnostic criteria for PTSD. Despite such potential underestimates, a recent review of traumatic life events among 477 Native youth revealed high rates of trauma exposure (e.g., car accidents, rape) and PTSD symptomatology (e.g., psychic numbing and avoidance of the event, and automatic hyperarousal; Manson et al., 1996).

Finally, cohabiting partners of individuals with PTSD are also affected by the traumatic stress of their partners via a process known as "secondary victimization" (Figley & Kleber, 1995). Secondary victimization is a process in which the partners or other family members of the traumatized person develop symptoms similar to the traumatized person's symptoms (Byrne & Riggs, 2002). For example, among the wives of Israeli combat veterans, those whose husbands had PTSD symptoms reported higher levels of distress compared to wives of veterans with no PTSD symptomatology (Solomon et al., 1992).

Alcohol and Other Drug Use

Substance use and abuse is another negative health outcome related to colonial trauma among AIAN populations (see Walters et al., 2002, for further discussion on this topic). Although there are high rates of abstention from AOD use among many Native populations (May, 1996), among those who do use, a disturbing picture emerges. Native youths tend to use alcohol earlier, use it more often and in higher quantities, and experience more negative consequences from alcohol compared to non-Native youth (Oetting & Beauvais, 1989). Additionally, Natives are five times more likely to die of alcohol-related causes than non-Natives and have an alcoholism death rate that is seven times the alcoholism death rate of the general population (45.5/100,000; Indian Health Service [IHS], 1999). In terms of illicit drugs, AIAN youth report higher *lifetime* (51% versus 21%–42%), *past year* (30.5% versus 13%–21.6%), and *past month* illicit drug use (18.4% versus 5.5%–9.2%) than other ethnic groups (Substance Abuse and Mental Health Services Administration, 2000). Finally, mortality from drugs among Native populations is 18% higher than for the U.S. population (IHS, 1999).

Co-occurrence of PTSD-AOD Use

Colonial traumas also increase the likelihood of AIAN peoples having co-occurring PTSD and AOD disorders. Traumatic violence exposure places individuals at higher risk for AOD use (Stewart, Ouimette, & Brown, 2002), and, in the case of multiple violent traumas, places individuals at higher risk for dual diagnoses (i.e., PTSD-AOD disorders; Breslau, Davis, Andreski, Federman, & Anthony, 1998). Although women are at greater risk of co-occurrence of PTSD-AOD disorders than men (Stewart et al., 2002), this difference is likely attributable to the type of trauma the individual is exposed to (e.g., chronic childhood abuse) rather than gender per se (Kessler et al., 1995). Study findings also indicate that chronic heavy AOD use may exacerbate existing PTSD arousal symptoms (e.g., startle response; as cited in Stewart et al., 2002).

FAMILY VIOLENCE

Research has also demonstrated that traumatic stress reactions create considerable family stress and leave families prone to violence. For example, veterans with PTSD compared to those without PTSD report greater relationship distress and difficulties with intimacy, greater levels of hostility and less verbal expressiveness, and greater risk for increased aggression toward intimate partners (Byrne & Riggs, 2002). In terms of AIAN families, this "wounding seeking wounding," or lateral oppression, is a dynamic found among populations that have experienced considerable historical trauma and a collective soul wound (Duran, 2002). Lateral oppression is the psychological (and spiritual) internalization of the colonizer or identification with the aggressor, which is then manifested in acting out the colonial process by oppressing others of the same or less powerful status within and between Native institutions, communities, families, and individuals. Duran (2002) stated that manifestation of lateral oppression is found in expressions of learned helplessness (as in the case of not intervening to prevent harm to others or oneself), epistemic violence in tribal or institutional settings where Native leaders or administrators are themselves oppressive "mini-emperors" and abusive to Native staff, and infliction of pain on family members as in the case of intimate partner violence and child maltreatment.

Intimate Partner Violence

The impact of colonial stress on Native families is evident in the relatively high levels of domestic violence. One study exploring domestic violence among a southwestern tribe found much higher rates of intimate partner violence among AIAN women compared to women in the general U.S. population (53% of the AIAN women under age 50 and 28% over age 50 reported being struck at least once by their intimate partner; Robin, Chester, & Rasmussen, 1998). In a community-based sample of urban AIAN women, 40% of respondents reported a history of intimate partner violence (Evans-Campbell, Lindhorst, Huang, & Walters, in press). These rates are significantly higher than the rate of assault by an intimate partner for women of all ethnicities in the United States (22.1%; Tjaden & Thoennes, 2000). Most disturbing, AIAN women experience disproportionately high rates of homicide by their intimate partners (Arbuckle et al., 1996).

Child Maltreatment

Similar to domestic violence, child maltreatment rates reflect familial disruptions in culturally based parenting styles and high rates of colonial distress. Overall, child abuse and neglect rates for AIAN children are significantly higher per 1,000 (21) than for Hispanic (10), White (11), and Asian/Pacific Islander (5) children (Child Welfare League of America, 2004) and vary from tribe to tribe (e.g., 5.7 per 1,000 versus 26 per 1,000; Fischler, 1985; Hauswald, 1987). While Native children make up 1% of all children in the United States, they account for about 1.8% of the substantiated cases of child maltreatment (Child Welfare League of America, 2004). In a review of 2,000 child maltreatment cases involving AIAN children from 17 states, data indicated that 48.9% of the maltreatment reports were based on neglect, 28.1% on sexual abuse, and 20.8% on physical abuse (National Center on Child Abuse and Neglect, 1999). Moreover, Native girls are more likely than Native boys to experience abuse in general (57.1% of victims are female) and sexual abuse more specifically (79.8% of victims are female). Compared to Native boys, Native girls are thus more vulnerable to the pernicious long-term traumatic stress effects from sexual abuse (e.g., PTSD and AOD use) given their higher rates of exposure.

Relationships Among Childhood Violence, PTSD, and Substance Use

In a comprehensive review of studies among non-AIAN populations, Stewart et al. (2002) found consistent evidence of the relationship between the number and severity of childhood trauma exposures and lifetime PTSD. Moreover, studies of both male and female non-AIAN samples suggest a causal connection between childhood trauma exposures and subsequent adulthood drinking problems. In fact, lifetime PTSD is strongly associated with a number of lifetime substance abuse disorders. Indeed, the more severe and chronic the interpersonal trauma, the more likely PTSD-AOD comorbidity will emerge (Stewart et al., 2002). In one study, for example, a history of childhood sexual abuse was related to a doubling of the number of alcohol abuse symptoms experienced in adulthood (Epstein, Saunders, Kilpatrick, & Resnick, 1998).

However, not all individuals exposed to childhood trauma develop subsequent drinking problems. The presence of strong adults in trauma survivors' lives as children has been identified as a key protective factor, buffering the impact of childhood trauma on PTSD and AOD outcomes (Stewart et al., 2002). Thus, this cycle of traumatic abuse exposure, AOD use to cope, and enactment of traumatic abuse in hurting others can be interrupted with strong AIAN parenting figures in the lives of traumatized AIAN children.

COLONIAL TRAUMA RESPONSE AND FAMILY PROCESSES

Indian child welfare scholars point to an erosion of traditional parenting norms and practices as a contributing factor to child maltreatment in AIAN family systems (Horejsi, Craig Heavy Runner, & Pablo, 1992; Mannes, 1995). This breakdown in parenting practices has been attributed to the deprivation of traditional parental role models as a result of high rates of boarding school attendance among AIAN populations (Horejsi et al., 1992). Horejsi et al. suggested that boarding school experiences may not only have interrupted the intergenerational transmission of healthy child rearing practices, they may also have instilled new, negative behaviors in their place. For example, many boarding school students who were beaten and neglected may reenact these practices on their own children. In his study of child maltreatment among the Navajo, Hauswald (1987) found that maltreatment was associated with one or more generations of cultural disruption stemming from dramatic sociocultural changes, including boarding school attendance.

Parenting Roles and Self-Image

The government's continuing practice of removing children from Native communities sends the message that Native families are not appropriate places to raise Native children. The effects of this message can be deleterious for AIAN parents and their offspring, who may internalize it, beginning to doubt themselves, their own culture, and their traditional ways of parenting. Emerging research indicates that parents who attended boarding school feel overwhelmed and inadequate in their parenting roles; are confused about how to raise healthy children (Yellow Horse Brave Heart, 1999b), and are likely to have poor self-images (Metcalf, 1979). Brasfield (2001) has argued for the creation of a diagnostic term to apply to survivors of Indian residential schools in Canada—Residential School Syndrome (RSS). According to Brasfield, RSS survivors not only suffer from PTSD-like symptoms (e.g., intrusive memories, sleep disturbances, flashbacks, anger management issues), they may also often show significant attachment difficulties and may have trouble forming and maintaining relationships with others, including their own children. In his practice, Brasfield found that many parents who attended boarding school had limited parenting skills despite genuine caring for their children.

Parenting Success

The trauma of out-of-home placement has also been shown to have profound effects on parenting success for Native parents. In a small qualitative study of urban Native adults, Spicer (1998) found significant differences in parenting success based on whether mothers had grown up in foster homes, kinship care, or with their birth parents. Tragically, of the seven mothers who had been in foster care, six had lost their own children to foster care. The four mothers raised by kin faired better, with only one having her child permanently removed. Mothers raised by birth parents had the best success; only two had had their children removed, and both had been successful in having them returned.

Parental Attachment

Trauma and abuse may undermine one's ability to attach to others, including one's own children. For example, parents who have experienced childhood trauma or abuse may be unsure about appropriate boundary setting and disciplining. The intense attachments parents have to children may remind Native parents of their own childhood experiences and the lack of nurturing adult caregivers in their lives. Certain parenting behaviors and the intense feelings around them may also provoke anxiety and feelings of shame. For example, some Native practitioners assert that the low rates of breastfeeding[2] in Native communities may stem in large part from attachment issues related to childhood abuse experienced by Native mothers. Today, many Native parents are fighting against this legacy and embracing traditional ways of parenting with success.

Resilience in the Face of Colonial Trauma

Walters et al. (2002) noted that historically, cultural protective mechanisms have been used among Native communities to address various traumas and corresponding symptoms (e.g., the Wiping the Tears ceremony among the Lakota or the Enemy Way ceremony among the Navajo). However, lack of access to these ceremonies because of geography, family dysfunction, poverty, and colonial traumas may decrease the capacity to cope for AIAN communities and individuals. Although a full discussion of this issue is beyond the scope of this chapter we highlight a few key protective factors that are relevant for work with AIAN families (see Walters et al., 2002, for further discussion).

COMMITMENT TO THE COMMUNITY

For Native people, commitment to the community is profound, and this commitment may facilitate healing in several ways. First, Native communities inform personal and familial coping strategies as modes of healing are passed down through the generations. Pathways to healing may be imparted through storytelling, community rituals, and role modeling. Moreover, many Native communities have begun to develop annual community healing rituals and ceremonies. As these ceremonies become part of the fabric of community life, more and more individuals are participating. Second, individuals living in close-knit communities may be more likely to consider how their individual actions—both positive and negative—have an impact on their entire community. By focusing on the communal context, Native people may more readily see how dysfunctional coping strategies such as AOD abuse affect not only their own life but also the lives of all tribal members for generations to come. This communal lens provides a powerful incentive to heal.

IDENTITY ATTITUDES AND ENCULTURATION

For indigenous peoples, a positive identity has long been considered an important factor in Native wellness. In one study, identity attitudes accounted for 10%–21% of the variance in self-esteem, depression, anxiety, and interpersonal sensitivity (Walters & Simoni, 1999). Although researchers have yet to adequately test the stress-buffering role of identity in AOD problems and family violence, the *externalization* of negative colonizing attitudes could be a potential buffer in moderating the effects of colonial trauma on AOD use and family violence. In a similar vein, other researchers have also suggested that enculturation (i.e., immersion into one's culture; Zimmerman, Ramirez, Washienko, Walter, & Dyer, 1996) is a protective factor that can decrease the probability of drinking problems and family violence. Enculturation is associated with retraditionalization in AIAN communities and can be a useful concept in delineating cultural processes that serve as buffers between trauma and health outcomes.

SPIRITUALITY

As Walters et al. (2002) noted, contemporary abstinence and retraditionalization movements are critical mechanisms for individual, communal, and tribal healing. These Nativistic AOD movements emphasize a return to traditional and spiritual practices and sobriety in developing nationalistic pride and survival as a people. All of these movements have at their core revitalization of indigenous traditions accompanied by traditional living. Although there is tremendous ceremonial diversity (including Christian-only, Christian-traditional fusion, and traditional-only practices) among and even within tribes for healing imbalances, reconnecting the "sick" individual with family and community is widely considered integral to healing from historical and colonial traumas. Participation in traditional spiritual practices serves not only to heal mind, body, and soul, but also serves as a critical protective factor in dealing with adversity and other stressors in Native families' lives (see Walters et al., 2002, for a more detailed discussion on the role of spirituality in practice with AIAN populations). Nativistic spiritually based sobriety movements include the Inupiaq Ilitqsat (Eskimo Spirit Movement), the Native American Church (Peyote Way/Road), Gaiwiio (Handsome Lake Movement), the Northwest's Indian Shaker Church movement, and the Red Road sobriety movement.

Decolonizing Practice Competencies

To help Native families in recovery from colonial trauma, we suggest using the decolonizing practice strategies outlined below. These guidelines are not exhaustive and they aim to instigate further exploration in work with families and communities.

1. *Enacting a culturally relevant framework for practice.* All practitioners working with Native families should have training around colonial violence and its impact on family processes and diversity within AIAN communities as well as culturally specific child rearing practices. Research suggests that Native parents have unique cultural beliefs about appropriate child rearing (Evans-Campbell, 2000). In many Native communities, for instance, children are seen as equal beings central to the entire community and are treated accordingly, with direct interventions seen as disrespectful (Green, 1983). Native families are also known for their tendency to share child rearing duties among extended family and community members with the expectation that everyone has a stake in that child's rearing. Accordingly, the importance of including the extended family and community in case plans for First Nations families cannot be overstated.

2. *Learning about precolonial history.* An important element in healing for families who experience HT (Danieli, 1998), this knowledge about colonial history can help AIAN families recognize health in contemporary communities and allow them to connect with precolonial narratives. In exploring cultural narratives and history, practitioners also can assist families in identifying traditional ways of addressing trauma. In addition, working with traditional healers can help reestablish these ancient connections to historic ways of healing.

3. *Dealing with mistrust.* Studies show that AIAN parents have high levels of mistrust around CPS agencies and staff, affecting their ability to work with these agencies and their staff (Horejsi et al., 1992; Evans-Campbell, 2000). Many Native parents hold the belief, for example, that once a child goes into the foster care system, he or she is lost forever. Given the long history of CPS intervention in Native families, such views are not surprising and practitioners should be prepared to encounter them. However, instead of viewing this mistrust as a "hostile" reaction, practitioners should anticipate it, understand it, and even reframe it as a healthy reaction to what in other historical circumstances would have been a real threat.

4. *Documenting historically traumatic events and colonial trauma.* While family members may suffer from historical trauma and colonial trauma responses, they may not be aware of the specific events that contextualize their family functioning. Practitioners can assist families in learning about their histories by completing genograms, cultura-grams, and soul-wounding timelines with families. These charts should document births, deaths, and cultural events as well as specific historically traumatic events and corresponding colonial trauma responses at individual and familial levels. Through these exercises, family patterns of substance use, family violence, and anniversary reactions to historically traumatic events are made explicit and can be clearly linked to traumatic events. The cultural and familial meanings given to historical episodes can also be documented.

5. *Communicating about historical trauma.* Communication around HTE and CTR is an integral piece of healing. Denial and anger may be quite functional and protective responses to trauma, especially while a person is attempting to survive major cata-strophic events such as boarding school or genocide. Yet, the maintenance of such responses will undermine family health and community functioning over time, pro-moting silence over HTEs and constraining critical relationships. Practitioners should assist family members in exploring losses and making links to current family function-ing. Importantly, family members may have quite different beliefs about HTE and their impact. How a family makes meaning out of colonial trauma is critical in heal-ing and identifying familial and tribal resilience. Intergenerational anniversary patterns—conscious and unconscious—are also an important area of exploration. Individuals may become anxious or preoccupied with their mortality, for example, on the anniversary of a community massacre. Unresolved family issues may also mani-fest when a child reaches the same age that a parent or grandparent was at the time of an HTE such as boarding school.

6. *Highlighting resilience.* Practitioners must also help families document their histories of power, resilience, and resistance. Although all indigenous people share a history of CT, they also share tremendous intergenerational resiliencies and strengths.

Recognition of survival and resistance in the face of traumas can inspire and engender a strong sense of pride. Too often, survival strategies are not clearly identified in family stories. Practitioners can illuminate these strategies and identify how they continue to manifest in the family system today, reconnecting people with the power of their ancestors and culture.

7. *Creating new narratives.* In families where violence has prevailed, it is important to identify how and when these behaviors were learned (Duran, 2002). To better explain how one becomes "infected" with lateral oppression, Duran used a vampire metaphor. He pointed out that vampires tend to work at night (i.e., in spiritual darkness), can only be eradicated by spiritual means, and can survive only by infecting others. Once the spiritual injury is introduced to clients via this metaphor, they can begin the deeper search for meaning and healing of the spirit. Duran suggests asking the basic question, "Where did you learn this [hitting, abusing]?" which usually garners the response, "From my parents," and then asking the follow-up question, "Where did they learn this," and so forth. This process will help construct a historical narrative and timeline to identify when the family system "became infected" with the soul wound. Not only will this begin to construct a counternarrative, but it begins to situate the process historically and expulses "the vampire" outside of the person for observation and intervention and ultimately allows for deeper healing. With appropriate supervision and consultation, a parallel narrative can be constructed in which the non-Native practitioner also engages in a serious analysis of his history ("Where did I learn this?"), and in this manner the historical "vessel" of the wounding can also be healed. Ideally, parallel narratives emerge that are liberating to both the client and healer, leading to a collective healing of the soul wound (Duran, 2002).

8. *Supporting community grief ceremonies.* Some communities have lost their cultural tools, prayers, and rituals for addressing trauma or helping the dead pass over to the afterlife. Practitioners can be invaluable as they support community members in mourning these losses, relearning traditions, and creating new ways to heal. In cases where community members are mourning the loss of an important tradition, it is important to remind people that culture is not static but constantly changing. In fact, creating new traditions may be a necessary component of healing. One note of caution—we are not suggesting that practitioners be responsible for imparting cultural or spiritual knowledge or traditions (this would be inappropriate); rather, we are encouraging practitioners to provide emotional support for AIAN families to identify appropriate traditional resources in their respective communities. Opportunities abound in creating collective healing rituals to memorialize traumatic events and to facilitate community healing. Before establishing any community-based intervention, however, it is important to identify the community's level of readiness for the intervention (for an

overview of this model, see Edwards, Jumper-Thurman, Plested, Oetting, & Swanson, 2000).

In summary, decolonizing practice competencies will require stamina, perseverance, creativity, and the ability to incur risk in cocreating new forms of indigenist social work practice. The pursuit of a decolonizing practice is liberating for all involved with rewards for both the practitioner and the AIAN family. In this chapter, we have presented a framework to assist practitioners in assessing and working with Native families. It is our hope that this chapter will provide an empowering context for practice with Native families.

Conclusion

Attempts to destroy the "breath"—the very essence—of Native people have been at the heart of colonial violence. All indigenous nations have a form of Original Instructions given to them by the Creator for living and being in balance with their physical and spiritual worlds. For example, the Yup'ik call their Original Instructions *Yuuyaraq*, "the way of being a human being." These instructions outline the way of living and being in harmony with the spirit world and all beings that inhabit the universe. As indigenous peoples rediscover, uncover, or simply continue to live their Original Instructions, the breath of the people will continue, and healing from historical traumas and the resultant AOD use and family violence will ensue. As social work practitioners committed to the pursuit of social justice, it is our responsibility to support and assist American Indian, Alaska Native, and First Nations communities in catching their breath.

Notes

(The epigraphs to this chapter are drawn from Napolean, 1991.)
1. Colonial trauma encompasses historical and contemporary traumatic events that reflect colonial practices to colonize, subjugate, and perpetrate ethnocide and genocide against contemporary AIAN peoples.
2. It is important to note that some Native communities are affected by radioactive dumping (LaDuke, 1999) making it difficult or impossible for Native mothers to safely breastfeed their infants.

References

Arbuckle, J., Olson, L., Howard, M., Brillman, J., Anctil, C., & Sklar, D. (1996). Safe at home? Domestic violence and other homicides among women in New Mexico. *Annals of Emergency Medicine, 27,* 210–215.

Brasfield, C. (2001). Residential school syndrome. *BC Medical Journal*, *43*(2), 78–81.

Breslau, N., Davis, G., & Andreski, P. (1998). Epidemiological findings on posttraumatic stress disorder and co-morbid disorders in the general population. In B. Bohrenwend (Ed.), *Adversity, stress and psychopathology.* (pp. 319–330). New York: Oxford University Press.

Byler, W. (1977). The destruction of the American Indian family. In W. Byler (Ed.), *The destruction of the American Indian family* (pp. 1–11). New York: Child Welfare League of America.

Byrne, C. A., & Riggs, D. S. (2002). Gender issues in couple and family therapy following traumatic stress. In R. Kimerling, P. Ouimette, & J. Wolfe (Eds.), *Gender and PTSD* (pp. 382–399). New York: Guilford Press.

Child Welfare League of America. (2004). *Children of color in the child welfare system.* National data analysis system. Retrieved July 2005, from http://ndas.cwla.org

Churchill, W. (1997). *A little matter of genocide: Holocaust and denial in the Americas 1492 to the present.* San Francisco: City Light Books.

Cross, T. (1998). Understanding family resilience from a relational world view. In H. McCubbin, E. Thompson, A. Thompson, & J. Fromer (Eds.), *Resiliency in Native American and immigrant families.* Thousand Oaks, CA: Sage.

Cross, T. A., Earle, K. A., & Simmons, D. (2000). Child abuse and neglect in Indian country: Policy issues. *Families in Society: The Journal of Contemporary Human Services*, *81*(1), 49–58.

Danieli, Y. (Ed.). (1998). *International handbook of multigenerational legacies of trauma.* New York: Plenum.

Diagnostic and statistical manual of mental disorders. (1994). Washington, DC: American Psychiatric Association.

Duran, E. (May 2002). *Wounding seeking wounding: The psychology of internalized oppression.* Paper presented at the Healing Our Wounded Spirits Conference, Warm Springs, Oregon, 2002.

Duran, E., Duran, B., Yellow Horse Brave Heart, M., & Yellow Horse-Davis, S. (1998). Healing the American Indian soul wound. In Y. Danieli (Ed.), *International handbook of multigenerational legacies of trauma* (pp. 341–354). New York: Plenum.

Edwards, R. W., Jumper-Thurman, P., Plested, B. A., Oetting, E. R., & Swanson, L. (2000). Community readiness: Research to practice. *Journal of Community Psychology*, *28*(3), 291–307.

Epstein, J. N, Saunders, B. E., Kilpatrick, D. G., & Resnick, H. S. (1998). PTSD as a mediator between childhood rape and alcohol use in adult women. *Child Abuse and Neglect*, *22*(3), 223–234.

Evans-Campbell, T. (2000). *Percpetions of and attitudes towards child neglect among urban American Indian parents in Los Angeles*. Unpublished dissertation, University of California, Los Angeles.

Evans-Campbell, T. (in press). Child welfare practice with urban American Indian families. In T. Wiko (Ed.), *No longer forgotten: Addressing the mental health needs of urban Indians*. New York: American Psychological Association.

Evans-Campbell, T., Lindhorst, T., Huang, B., & Walters, K. (in press). Interpersonal violence in the lives of urban American Indian/Alaska Native women: Implications for health, mental health, and help-seeking. *American Journal of Public Health*.

Felsen, I. (1998). Transgenerational transmission of effects of the Holocaust. In Y. Danieli (Ed.), *International handbook of multigenerational legacies of trauma* (pp. 43–68). New York: Plenum.

Figley, C. R., & Kleber, R. J. (1995). Beyond the victim: Secondary traumatic stress. In R. J. Kleber, C.R. Figley, & B. P. R. Gersons (Eds.), *Beyond trauma: Cultural and social dynamics* (pp. 75–98). New York: Plenum.

Fischler, R. S. (1985). Child abuse and neglect in American Indian communities. *Child Abuse and Neglect, 9*, 95–106.

Green, H. (1983). Risks and attitudes associated with extra-cultural placement of American Indian children: A critical review. *Journal of the American Academy of Child Psychiatry, 22*, 63–67.

Greenfeld, L. A., & Smith, S. K. (1999). *American Indians and crime*. Washington DC: U.S. Department of Justice.

Hauswald, L. (1987). External pressure/internal change: Child neglect on the Navajo reservation. In N. Scheper-Hughes (Ed.), *Child survival: Anthropological perspectives on the treatment and maltreatment of children* (pp. 145–164). Dordrecht, Netherlands: D. Reidel.

Hirschfelder, A., & Molin, P. (2001). *Encyclopedia of Native American religions*. New York: Checkmark Books.

Horejsi, C., Craig Heavy Runner, B., & Pablo, J. (1992). Reactions by Native American parents to child protection agencies: Cultural and community factors. *Child Welfare, 62*(4), 329–342.

Indian Health Service. 1999. *Regional differences in Indian health: 1998–1999*. Rockville, MD: Department of Health and Human Services, Indian Health Service, Office of Planning, Evaluation, and Legislation, Division of Program Statistics.

Jones, M. C., Daughinais, P., Sack, W. H., & Somervell, P. D. (1997). Trauma-related symptomatology among American Indian adolescents. *Journal of Traumatic Stress, 10*(2), 163–173.

Kessler, R., Sonnega, A., Bromet, E., Hughes, M., & Nelson, C. (1995). Posttraumatic stress disorder in the National Comorbidity Survey. *Archives of General Psychiatry, 52*, 1048–1060.

LaDuke, W. (1999). *All our relations: Native struggles for land and life*. Cambridge, MA: South End Press.

Lichtman, H. (1984). Parental communication of Holocaust experiences and personality characteristics among second-generation survivors. *Journal of Clinical Psychology, 40*, 914–924.

Mannes, M. (1995). Factors and events leading to the passage of the Indian Child Welfare Act. *Child Welfare, 74*(1), 264–282.

Manson, S., Beals, J., O'Nell, T., Piasecki, J., Bechtold, J., Keane, E., & Jones, M. (1996). Wounded spirits, ailing hearts: PTSD and related disorders among American Indians. In A. J. Marsella, M. J. Friedman, E. T. Gerrity, & R. M. Scurfield (Eds.), *Ethnocultural aspects of posttraumatic stress disorder: Issues, research, and clinical applications* (pp. 255–283). Washington DC: American Psychological Association.

May P. (1996). Overview of alcohol abuse epidemiology for American Indian populations. In G. D. Sandefur, R. R. Rundfuss, & B. Cohen (Eds.), *Changing numbers, changing needs: American Indian demography and public health* (pp. 235–261). Washington DC: National Academy Press.

Metcalf, A. (1979). Family reunion: Networks and treatment in a Native American community. *Handbook of international sociometry, 32*, 179–189.

Nagata, D. K. (1991). Transgenerational impact of the Japanese-American internment: Clinical issues in working with children of former internees. *Psychotherapy: Theory, Research, Practice, & Training, 28*(1), 121–128.

Nagata, D., Trierweiler, S., & Talbot, R. (1999). Long-term effects of internment during early childhood in third generation Japanese Americans. *American Journal of Orthopsychiatry, 69*(1), 19–29.

Napoleon, H. (1991). *Yuuyaraq: The way of the human being*. Fairbanks: Alaska Native Knowledge Network, University of Alaska Fairbanks.

National Center on Child Abuse and Neglect. (1999). Annual report: *National incidence and prevalence of child abuse and neglect, 1998*. Washington, DC: U.S. Department of Health and Human Services.

Norris, F. H., Foster, J. D., & Weisshaar, D. L. (2002). The epidemiology of sex differences in PTSD across developmental, societal, and research contexts. In R. Kimerling, P. Ouimette, & J. Wolfe (Eds.), *Gender and PTSD* (pp. 3–42). New York: Guilford Press.

Oetting, E. R., & Beauvais, F. (1989). Epidemiology and correlates of alcohol use among Indian adolescents living on reservations. In *Alcohol use among U.S. ethnic minorities* (NIAAA Research Monograph No. 18). Rockville, MD: U.S. Public Health Service.

Robin, R. W., Chester, B., & Goldman, D. (1996). Cumulative trauma and PTSD in American Indian communities. In A. Marsella, M. Friedman, E. Gerrity, & R.

Scurfield (Eds.), *Ethnocultural aspects of posttraumatic stress disorder: Issues, research, and clinical applications* (pp. 239–252). Washington, DC: American Psychological Association.

Robin, R., Chester, B., & Rasmussen, J. (1998). Intimate violence in a southwestern American Indian tribal community. *Cultural Diversity and Mental Health*, *4*(4), 335–344.

Smith, A. (1999). Sexual violence and American Indian genocide. *Journal of Religion and Abuse*, *1*(2), 31–52.

Solomon, Z., Waysman, M., Belkin, R., Levy, G., Mikulincer, M., & Enoch, D. (1992). Marital relations and combat stress reaction: The wives' perspective. *Journal of Marriage and the Family*, *54*(2), 316–326.

Spicer, P. (1998). Drinking, foster care, and the intergenerational continuity of parenting in an urban Indian community. *American Indian Culture and Research Journal*, *22*(4), 335–360.

Stannard, D. (1992). *American holocaust*. Oxford, UK: Oxford University Press.

Stewart, S. H., Ouimette, P., & Brown, P. J. (2002). Gender and the comorbidity of PTSD with substance use disorders. In R. Kimerling, P. Ouimette, & J. Wolfe (Eds.), *Gender and PTSD*. New York: Guilford Press.

Stein, M., Walker, J., & Forde, D. (2000). Gender differences in susceptibility to posttraumatic stress disorder. *Behavior Research and Therapy*, *38*(6), 619–628.

Substance Abuse and Mental Health Services Administration. 2000. *Summary findings from the National Household Survey on Drug Abuse, 1999 and 2000*. Rockville, MD: U.S. Department of Health and Human Services.

Tjaden, P., & Thoennes, N. (2000, November). Full report of the prevalence, incidence, and the consequences of violence against women: Findings from the National Violence Against Women Survey. Washington, DC: U.S. Department of Justice.

U.S. Department of Heath and Human Services,. Administration on Children, Youth and Families. (2001). *Child maltreatment: 1999*. Washington, DC: U.S. Government Printing Office.

U.S. Senate Select Committee on Indian Affairs, 95th Congress. (1977). *Indian Child Welfare Act of 1977: To establish standards for the placement of Indian children in foster or adoptive homes, to prevent the breakup of Indian families, and for other purposes*. Washington, DC: U.S. Government Printing Office.

Walters, K. L., & Simoni, J. M. (1999). Trauma, substance use, and HIV risk among urban American Indian women. *Cultural Diversity and Ethnic Minority Psychology*, *5*(3), 236–248.

Walters, K. L., & Simoni, J. M., & Evans-Campbell, T. (2002). Substance use among American Indians and Alaska Natives: Incorporating culture in an "Indigenist" stress-coping paradigm. *Public Health Reports*, *117*(Suppl. 1), S104–17.

Whitbeck, L. B., McMorris, B. J., Hoyt, D. R., Stubben, J. D., & LaFromboise, T. (2002).

Perceived discrimination, traditional practices, and depressive symptoms among American Indians in the upper Midwest. *Journal of Health and Social Behavior, 43*(4), 400–418.

Williams, D. R., Yu, Y., Jackson, J. S., & Anderson, N. B. (1997). Racial differences in physical and mental health: Socioeconomic status, stress, and discrimination. *Journal of Health Psychology, 2,* 335–351.

Wrone, D., & Nelson, R. (Eds.). (1982). *Who's the savage?* Malabar, FL: Krieger Publishing.

Yellow Horse Brave Heart, M. (1999a). Oyate Ptayela: Rebuilding the Lakota Nation through addressing historical trauma among Lakota parents. *Journal of Human Behavior in the Social Environment, 2*(1/2), 109–126.

Yellow Horse Brave Heart, M. (1999b). Gender differences in the historical trauma response among the Lakota. *Journal of Health and Social Policy, 10*(4), 1–21.

Yellow Horse Brave Heart, M. (2000). Wakiksuyapi: Carrying the historical trauma of the Lakota. *Tulane Studies in Social Welfare, 21–22,* 245–266.

Zimmerman, M., Ramirez, V., Washienko, K., Walter, B., & Dyer, S. (1996). The development of a measure of enculturation for Native American youth. *American Journal of Community Psychology, 24*(2), 295–310.

Part 5

Asians and Pacific Islanders

14

Beginning Dialogue Between Two Research and Practice Fields

MIEKO YOSHIHAMA and JOHN NAKASHIMA

Introduction

Asians and Pacific Islanders (API) is one of the fastest-growing population groups in the United States. Currently, there are about 10.6 million APIs in the United States, which represents 3.7% of the total U.S. population (U.S. Census Bureau, 2001). The API population is expected to reach between 20 million and 40 million by the year 2050 (U.S. Census Bureau, 1999). The API population in the United States is extremely diverse; the U.S. Census Bureau identified 24 Asian and 19 Pacific Islander ethnic groups (U.S. Census Bureau, 2000). Groups differ considerably with respect to socioeconomic status as well as in migratory and historical experiences. Some groups have been in the United States for multiple generations, whereas others are mostly recent immigrants or second generations (Logan, Stowell, & Vesselinov, 2001). Native Hawaiians are an indigenous population colonized by the United States. Different migratory and historical experiences may underlie variations in socioeconomic, educational, and occupational attainment. Some immigrants have come to the United States with transferable professional and technical skills, while others may have been war refugees with limited literacy and employment skills (Center for Substance Abuse Treatment [CSAT], 1999; Kim, McLeod, and Shantzis, 1992).

The great diversity of the API population makes efforts to study and understand the nature of domestic violence and substance abuse in API communities an enormous challenge. Further, sociopolitical and historical factors have contributed to an underrecognition of domestic violence and substance abuse in API American communities—and, subsequently, limited scholarship on these issues. There are few data on API domestic violence and substance abuse, and no studies have focused on the potential relationship between domestic violence and substance abuse in the API communities. This current dearth of scholarship on API domestic violence and substance abuse hinders the development of policy and programs that respond to the needs of API populations. The purpose of this chapter is to present what is presently known about domestic violence and substance abuse in the API communities and identify some key questions and concerns that can be addressed through future scholarship and the development of practice initiatives. First we examine the separate literatures regarding domestic violence and substance abuse in the API communities. Then we discuss how the two phenomena might be interrelated and the subsequent implications for practice and research. Finally, we conclude with some questions to facilitate discussion among researchers and practitioners on domestic violence and substance abuse in the API communities.

Domestic Violence in API Communities

Violence against women by intimate partners (domestic violence) knows no racial, ethnic, or class boundaries (Coomaraswamy, 1996; Heise, Ellsberg, & Gottemoeller, 1999). Domestic violence is not limited to physical violence, but includes sexual violence and a wide range of other acts used to hurt, isolate, intimidate, threaten, and control women. Feminist sociopolitical analysis has uncovered the ways in which patriarchy supports, and is reinforced by, men's use of violence against women in general and domestic violence in particular (e.g., Bograd, 1988; Hanmer & Maynard, 1987; Martin, 1981). In the United States, a grassroots movement against domestic violence, often referred to as the Battered Women's Movement, emerged in the 1970s (Schechter, 1982). This movement has involved a range of consciousness-raising efforts; establishing hotlines, shelters, and safe homes; and advocating for changes in institutional responses to domestic violence.

The proliferation of domestic violence research was parallel to the rise of the women's movement against domestic violence. National and regional studies indicate that 22% to 38% of adult women in the United States experience violence perpetrated by their male intimates during their lifetimes, and approximately 10% of women experience severe violence at the hands of intimate partners (Collins et al., 1999;

Commonwealth Fund, 1993; Schafer, Caetano, & Clark, 1998; Straus & Gelles, 1986; Tjaden & Thoennes, 2000). Because of the underreporting common to survey research and limited attention to nonphysical violence in previous studies, the true extent of domestic violence is probably much higher than these estimates.

One serious limitation of the mainstream scholarship on domestic violence is its "monocultural analysis of domestic violence" (Ho, 1990, p. 131). Most studies have failed to examine the ways in which violence against women interacts with race, ethnicity, and culture, as well as racism and other discriminatory forces in society. Thus, the experience of domestic violence among women of color in the United States, including API women, remains largely unknown. In particular, there are at least three major problems in current mainstream research that have hampered an understanding of the experience of domestic violence among API women: (1) exclusion, (2) aggregation, and (3) lack of socioculturally relevant instruments.

EXCLUSION

APIs are not represented in major studies of domestic violence, such as the National Family Violence Survey of 1975 and 1985 (Straus & Gelles, 1986), the Commonwealth Fund's Survey of Women's Health in 1993 and 1998 (Collins et al., 1999; Plichta, 1996), the National Alcohol and Family Violence Survey (Kantor, Jasinski, & Aldarondo, 1994), and a special domestic violence component of the National Alcohol Survey (Schafer et al., 1998). Reasons for not including API women in studies (or not reporting them as a separate category) vary. Since many studies are conducted in English (sometimes in Spanish as well), many API women who are non-English-speaking or have limited English proficiency are excluded. In addition, APIs are often excluded from analysis because of the small sample size as APIs represent 3%–4% of the general population— unless they are oversampled, they would represent a small proportion of the respondents in most studies.

AGGREGATION

Prevalence studies typically compare the rates of victimization or perpetration of domestic violence among major racial groups in the United States (Collins et al., 1999; Straus, Gelles, & Steinmetz, 1980; Straus & Smith, 1990; Tjaden & Thoennes, 2000). In almost all of these studies, APIs, if not excluded from the analysis, are lumped together with "others." The only exception is the National Violence Against Women Survey (NVAWS; Tjaden & Thoennes, 2000), which includes a large enough number of APIs to permit separate analysis ($n=133$). The NVAWS, funded by the National Institute of Justice and the Centers for Disease Control and Prevention (CDC), is the largest national study specifically examining violence against women, with a national representative sample of 8,000 women (and 8,000 men). The NVAWS found that women of API descent have the lowest reported rate of partner violence (15%) of any major racial or ethnic group: the reported rates were 24.8% for Whites, 29.1% for African American, 37.5% for American Indian/Alaskan Native, and 30.2% for mixed race (Tjaden & Thoennes, 2000). While the NVAWS was laudable for including an API category, it did not go a step further by reporting separately the rates of victimization among the various ethnic groups of API descent in the United States, such as Chinese and South Asian, or variations by immigration status within a single ethnic group. The aggregation of API data regardless of ethnic/cultural groups or generational positions, which is not unique to studies of domestic violence, hampers identifying considerable within-group variations that exist among APIs (Uehara, Tekeuchi, & Smukler, 1994).

While studies that used aggregated racial groups have found higher rates of domestic violence among non-Whites (Straus et al., 1980) and among Mexican Americans (Straus & Smith, 1990) than among Whites, studies that disaggregate subgroups often uncover differences among ethnic subgroups and/or across generational positions within an ethnic group (Jasinski, 1998; Kantor et al., 1994; Sorenson & Telles, 1991). Even within a separate ethnic subgroup, there may be differences in the experience of domestic violence depending on the generational position. For example, in a study of Japanese American women, Yoshihama (2002) found that the perceived effectiveness of coping strategies had opposite effects on women's psychological distress depending on whether they were born in the United States or in Japan. The U.S.-born women were more likely to seek outside help and consider this strategy more effective than were Japan-born women. For Japan-born women, the more effective they considered these "active" strategies, the higher their levels of distress; for the U.S.-born women, the opposite relationship was found. A study of Chinese Americans found a strong association between levels of acculturation and experience of domestic violence (Yick, 2000). These findings underscore the importance of considering within-group differences and warn against aggregation.

LACK OF SOCIOCULTURALLY RELEVANT INSTRUMENTS

Many studies use standardized measures that are developed without regard for sociocultural variations in the manifestations and perceptions of domestic violence across people of different sociocultural backgrounds. While domestic violence itself is not culture specific, there are certain culturally specific ways in which male partners' violence manifests itself. Assaults and murders of brides by their grooms and grooms' families connected to conflicts over dowry in South Asian populations in India and the United States are examples of socioculturally influenced manifestations of domestic violence (Singh & Unnithan, 1999; Stone & James, 1995). A study of women of Japanese descent in Los

Angeles (Yoshihama, 2001) included questions regarding several socioculturally rooted manifestations of domestic violence found in Japan (e.g., the perpetrator throwing liquid, overturning a dining table, or insisting on sexual intercourse in situations where privacy could not be guaranteed). Had these socioculturally rooted items not been included in the investigation, 104 (instead of 109) women would have reported physical violence, and 57 (instead of 63), sexual violence. This means that when socioculturally rooted types of violence were included in the measure, the reported rate of physical violence increased by 4.8% (5/104), and the rate of sexual violence, by 10.5% (6/57). These findings underscore the limitations of mainstream, monocultural instrumentation and its negative impact on correctly assessing the phenomenon of domestic violence in ethnic groups like APIs.

Even in qualitative studies aimed at understanding women's subjective experiences, gender is often given salience, explicitly or implicitly, over race, ethnicity, and cultural background, thereby paying little attention to the sociocultural contexts of women's experiences (e.g., Davis & Srinivasan, 1995; Lempert, 1996). For example, in her study of 32 battered women, 9 of whom were women of color, Lempert (1996) states, "I have *assumed* [italics added] gender salience in the experiences of these women, that is, victimization as female partners transcending issues of race and/or ethnicity, although a larger sample of cross-race comparisons would be needed to test this assumption" (pp. 271–272). This inattention to race, ethnicity, and culture and assumption of salience of gender over them, whether intentional or not, reflect a Euro-centered perspective that permeates research and U.S. society in general.

Magnitude and Dynamics of Domestic Violence in API Communities

The number of empirical studies of domestic violence among API communities in the United States has increased slowly in several areas. Although no national studies have been conducted to date, a few regional studies have examined the prevalence of domestic violence using a random sample of specific ethnic subgroups: Chinese Americans in Los Angeles (Yick, 2000), Japanese Americans in Los Angeles (Yoshihama, 1999), and Korean Americans on the East Coast (Kim & Sung, 2000). Several other studies have used nonprobability samples, such as purposive and convenience samples (Hoagland & Rosen, 1990; Raj & Silverman, 2002; Song-Kim, 1992).

Although methodological variations across these studies make comparing results difficult, findings point to victimization rates among API women that are comparable with or higher than those found in mainstream studies of women in the United States (22%–31%, Collins et al., 1999; Tjaden & Thoennes, 2000). For example, Yoshihama's study found a high prevalence of domestic violence among women of Japanese descent in Los Angeles: 55% of the respondents reported partners' physical and/or sexual violence some time prior to the interview, and 19% reported victimization during the past 12 months (1996, 1999). Similarly high rates of partners' physical and/or sexual violence were found in studies that used nonprobability samples: 60% of Korean women in Chicago (Song-Kim, 1992) and 41% of South Asian women in Greater Boston (Raj & Silverman, 2002). Although these rates are much higher than the 15% obtained in the NVAWS (Tjaden & Thoennes, 2000), the true extent of domestic violence is probably higher than these estimates found in regional studies of API population groups because of underreporting common to survey research.

Attitudinal studies have documented a relatively high degree of tolerance for domestic violence among individuals of API descent in the United States and elsewhere (Family Violence Prevention Fund, 1993; Hanson Frieze & Zubritzky, 1987; Klein, Campbell, Soler, & Ghez, 1997; Yick & Agbayani-Siewert, 1997; Yoshihama, 1993). One study compared the perceptions about partner violence across various racial/ethnic groups and found that APIs in general were less likely to define a husband's shoving or "face smacking" as domestic violence compared to Euro-Americans (Klein, Campbell, Soler, & Ghez, 1997). A self-administered questionnaire study conducted by the Asian Task Force Against Domestic Violence at ethnic fairs in the Boston area found considerable variations across five Asian groups in attitudes toward domestic violence (Yoshioka, 2000). For example, 29% of Korean respondents said a woman being abused should not tell anyone about the abuse, a rate higher than for Cambodian (22%), Chinese (18%), South Asian (5%), and Vietnamese (9%) respondents. In addition, 82% of South Asian respondents indicated that a battered woman should turn to a friend for help, whereas only 44% of Cambodian, 37% of Chinese, 41% of Korean, and 29% of Vietnamese respondents agreed with this statement.

Further, several researchers have investigated the experience of domestic violence through qualitative analysis of women's narratives. Research on sociocultural contexts, in large part, has focused on specific ethnic subgroups, because of the enormous cultural and linguistic diversity among API populations. Studies of Filipinos (Agtuca, 1992; Hoagland & Rosen, 1990), Japanese (Yoshihama, 2000), Koreans (Kim, 1999; Rhee, 1997; Song, 1986; Song-Kim, 1992), South Asians (Abraham, 1999, 2000; Ayyub, 2000; Dasgupta, 2000; Dasgupta & Warrier, 1996; Mehrotra, 1999; Singh & Unnithan, 1999; Stone & James, 1995), Chinese and Southeast Asian (Ho, 1990), and Vietnamese (Bui & Morash, 1999; Segal, 2000; Tran, 1997; Tran & Des Jardins, 2000) have documented the particular experiences of these subgroups in the United States. Some of these studies have reported various examples of socioculturally influenced manifestations of domestic violence: assaults and murder of a bride by a groom and his family connected to conflicts over dowry in South Asian populations (Singh & Unnithan, 1999; Stone & James, 1995); isolation (Abraham, 2000); neglect (Mehrotra, 1999); sexual abuse by flaunting the sexual desirability of other women (Abraham, 1999); and "comparative abuse—when the husband frequently compares his wife to other women and constantly puts her down" (Mehrotra, 1999, p. 630). In many API families, parents-in-law and other extended family members perpetrate violence against their daughters-in-law directly or indirectly (Asian/Pacific Islander Domestic Violence Resource Project, 2001; Dasgupta, 2000; Fernandez, 1997; Mehrotra, 1999; Yoshihama & Yunomae, 2000).

Various sociocultural factors such as cultural values, practices, attitudes toward women, minority status, and institutionalized racism influence the ways in which women experience partners' violence, including the meaning a woman may give to a partner's violence and her patterns of coping and help seeking (e.g., Crenshaw, 1991; Kanuha, 1994; Richie, 1996; West, 1998; Wyatt, 1994). In many API cultures, women's identities are tied to being daughters, wives, and mothers, and young women face tremendous pressure to marry and have children. Ayyub (2000) illustrates the shame that divorce brings not only to the woman but also to her family: "No price the women will pay would be greater than the shame they would bring on the family if they chose to end their marriage" (p. 243). While these factors and values may add to the vulnerability of API women, they also need to be viewed as sources of strength for them to cope with adverse life conditions.

The responses by the perpetrator, family, friends, and their community, as well as the extent to which domestic violence is tolerated, may vary. Furthermore, the availability of personal and social options and resources is not equally distributed among different sociocultural groupings (e.g., Crenshaw, 1991). Thus, individuals' experiences of domestic violence must be understood in their unique sociocultural contexts. Drawing from the emerging literature and practice experience, we discuss sociocultural, sociopolitical, and sociohistorical factors that affect the ways in which API individuals, families, and communities experience and respond to domestic violence.

Transgenerational Influence of the Culture of Origin

Cultural values and norms shared in the country of origin influence how an immigrant woman perceives and responds to a partner's violence behaviorally and cognitively (Bauer, Rodriguez, Quiroga, & Flores-Ortiz, 2000; Jang, Lee, & Morello-Frosch, 1990; Perilla, Bakeman, & Norris, 1994; Torres, 1987). Such influence is often transgenerational. For example, an immigrant woman from a culture that values "endurance" or believes in "fate" may be more likely to view her victimization as a tragedy of life over which she has little control but to endure. In a study of Japanese American women in Los Angeles (Yoshihama, 2000), respondents who do *not* speak Japanese made a specific reference to a term in Japanese, *gaman*, in describing the value of endurance, which is indicative of the centrality of this term in their worldview:

> The Japanese culture teaches you to *gaman*, to tolerate difficulties (age 44, third generation U.S. born).

> The Japanese word *gaman*—bear with it and I did (age 39, third generation U.S. born).

Socialization, especially gender role socialization, in the country of origin may exert a strong influence on how women would respond to partners' violence. In the same study (Yoshihama, 2000), both U.S.-born and Japan-born women described various ways in which power relations between men and women in Japanese culture influenced their response to partners' violence:

> Japanese society is a male-dominated society. It allows men to behave any way they want to. Over the years, I've learned to conform to a cultural expectation that wives ought to defer to their husbands (age 44, Japan born, English translation).

> Being a Japanese woman, I sometimes feel a sense of subservience. I think being Japanese makes me believe that a woman has a certain role in a relationship, and a man a certain role in a relationship. As a result, it causes me to just quietly take the abuse (age 40, third generation U.S. born).

That the pressure to assume a subscribed role of subservience in a relationship operated across generations was particularly noteworthy:

> I think that being Japanese does influence the way I dealt with it even though I'm fourth generation. It still influences me on how women are supposed to act . . . It's important to sacrifice myself and my own happiness . . . Especially, in a relationship with a man, it's your role to give in to him (age 18, fourth generation U.S. born).

> I'm 4th generation, so I'm more American. But I try not to think about myself because he is the man (age 21, fourth generation U.S. born).

For immigrant and refugee API women, legal and institutional responses to domestic violence in their countries of origin also influence significantly the ways in which they respond to domestic violence. For example, a woman from a country in which the legal system represents a social control agent or a corrupt system would be less likely to turn to the legal system in the United States (Bauer et al., 2000). In contrast, a woman from a country where domestic violence is recognized as a social problem or as a crime would be more likely to seek assistance from outside agencies in her new country. In addition, previous experiences with trauma by refugees from war-torn Southeast Asian countries may desensitize some API women to the seriousness of domestic violence they experience. Although the impact of practice and values of the country of origin is strong and long lasting, women (and men) confront those practices and values that they find oppressive and detrimental to their welfare (Yoshihama, 2000).

Institutionalized Racism

Many obstacles confront immigrant women who have experienced a partner's violence. The limited availability and accessibility of culturally and linguistically competent assistance resources hamper help seeking among immigrant API women (Bauer et al., 2000; Ho, 1990; Lai, 1986; U.S. Commission on Civil Rights, 1992). What compounds their difficulties is the racist and discriminatory social structure of U.S. society.

U.S. history is filled with overt discrimination, violence, and injustice toward APIs (e.g., the Chinese Exclusion Act and the internment of Japanese Americans during World War II). Reported hate crimes against APIs are numerous (National Asian Pacific American Legal Consortium, 1998), and probably many more go unreported. Racism and anti-immigrant sentiment and practice (which permeate social, economic, legal, and political institutions in the United States) affect the safety and survival of not only API battered women but also API communities. On a micro, interpersonal level, the experience of racism and discrimination affects the willingness of women to seek assistance from many social and legal institutions, such as the police. Some avoid contact with the police or other agencies because they are afraid of insensitive treatment for themselves or their partners. If the perpetrator is also an immigrant or person of color, an API woman may choose not to call the police because she does not want to subject her partner to discriminatory and often brutal treatment by the criminal legal system. Anti-immigrant and xenophobic attitudes, which were markedly intensified after the terrorist attacks in September 2001, have amplified the already deep-seated fear on the part of immigrant women.

On a community level, the historical and contemporary experiences of overt and covert discrimination and violence toward APIs in the United States as a group lessen the willingness of API community members to address domestic violence. API community leaders and members alike may consider the survival of the community in the face of negative stereotypes and discriminatory treatment the priority over acknowledging and addressing violence against women in the community. For example, a number of Korean community leaders in Los Angeles expressed their strong concern that creating an educational video depicting a Korean American man battering his wife would seriously under-mine their efforts to create a positive image of the Korean American community. In the interest of the collective survival of the community, leaders and members may turn a blind eye to women's suffering. These complex race and gender dynamics in API com-munities in the United States may explain the lack of recognition and communitywide initiatives to address domestic violence.

Additional Institutional Assaults— Anti-immigrant Policy

The political climate and changes in social policy in the past several years add to the assault of immigrant women, many of whom are from Asia or the Pacific Islands. For example, the Personal Responsibility and Work Opportunity Reconciliation Act of 1996 severely reduced benefits to immigrants, which meant that immigrant battered women may not have access to this safety net when they leave their abusive partners, giving many immigrant battered women no choice but to endure an abusive relationship.

The U.S. immigration policy further leaves immigrant women in a vulnerable posi-tion. Under the provisions of the Marriage Fraud Act Amendments of 1986, a foreign spouse of a U.S. citizen is granted a two-year conditional residency status, requiring that the U.S. citizen petition on behalf of his or her foreign spouse in order for the latter to obtain permanent residency. The partner may threaten to divorce or not to petition for her permanent residency. Out of fear of losing legal status, immigrant women may be pressured to remain with their abusive partners. Subsequent laws such as the Immigration Act of 1990, the Violence Against Women's Act [VAWA] (Title IV of the Violent Crime Control and Law Enforcement Act of 1994, P.L. 103-322), and the reau-thorization of VAWA (VAWA, 2000), Victims of Trafficking and Violence Prevention Act, provide some legal recourse for battered immigrant women, such as a waiver for failure to meet the requirements for permanent residency status and the right to self-petition for residency status. However, these legal procedures are complex and require someone with a specialized legal background. In addition, the availability of these legal recourses is not something the average citizen would know, let alone immigrant women with limited English proficiency. Thus, many immigrant, battered women remain unable to access necessary assistance or may not seek outside assistance fearing the loss of their legal status.

Need for API Domestic Violence Programs

The sociocultural, sociopolitical, and sociohistorical factors that affect APIs' experiences with domestic violence call for unique interventions that respect cultural diversity and address their different needs. The "model minority myth" (a stereotype that characterizes all Asians as affluent, well educated, quiet, passive, and nonviolent) promotes the belief that domestic violence does not happen in Asian communities and has hindered service development for Asian battered women (Almeida & Dolan-Delvecchio, 1999; Thomas, 2000). However, across the nation, there are an increasing number of such programs targeted primarily at recent immigrants and refugees of API descent who have limited English proficiency. These programs are mostly in large cities with a high concentration of APIs, such as Los Angeles (e.g., Center for Pacific Asian Family, Inc., and Pacific Asian Women's Center), the San Francisco Bay Area (e.g., Asian Women's Shelter and Narika), New York (e.g., New York Asian Women's Center and Sakhi for South Asian Women), Boston (e.g., Asian Task Force Against Domestic Violence), Chicago (e.g., Apna Ghar), St. Paul (Asian Women United of Minnesota), and Atlanta (Tapistory). In 1998, a national organization, Asian & Pacific Islander Institute on Domestic Violence, was formed, creating a venue for networking and information exchange, collective policy advocacy, and more. Given the rapid and steady population increase, additional programs that are linguistically and/or culturally competent need to be established in other areas with large API populations. Outreach efforts to this population must address cultural barriers to recognition of abuse and help seeking. Needless to say, information regarding the available services must be disseminated in a manner that reaches a target population group—at a minimum, translation into languages spoken in a target community is necessary (Jang et al., 1990). Through public education, community members should be made aware of the multiple ways in which cultural values and behavior norms perpetuate and permit men's violence against women on the one hand, and encourage women to endure in silence on the other.

Substance Abuse in API Communities

As in the field of domestic violence research, there is a lack of needed data and research on API alcohol and other drug (AOD) use. Few, if any, national AOD studies report separate, disaggregated data on APIs. (The National Household Survey on Drug Abuse—one of the standard epidemiological AOD use studies—only started regularly reporting a separate API category in 2000.) A Substance Abuse and Mental Health Services Administration [SAMHSA] summary of 1991–1993 data on substance use among racial and ethnic subgroups did conclude that substance use prevalence, alcohol dependence, and need for substance abuse treatment for APIs are high enough for concern, though not as high as in other ethnic/racial groups in the United States (SAMHSA, 1998).

Factors Associated with Substance Abuse Risk in API Communities

In their perusal of the literature, Kuramoto and Nakashima (2000) identified four factors associated with risk for AOD use among API subgroups: (1) pressure to succeed, (2) immigration and acculturation stressors, (3) discrimination and racism, and (4) shame and denial (CSAT, 1999; Kim et al., 1992; SAMHSA, 1998; Yee, 1999; Zane & Kim, 1994).

1. Pressure to succeed: Educational success is a common value among many API groups. Unfortunately it can also be a source of stress to many API youth. Some API parents may pressure their children to achieve academically and criticize them if they fail to meet expectations (Kim et al., 1992). In response, some youth may see AOD use as a means of coping with their anxiety and anger.

2. Immigration and acculturation stressors: Recently immigrated APIs face many stressors adjusting to life in the United States. Newcomers may struggle with learning a new language, obtaining a job, being poor, and adapting to a new culture while mourning the loss of the life left behind in their original homeland (SAMHSA, 1998). These elements are all potential stimuli to AOD use for adults.

    Immigration and acculturation stressors can damage family cohesion. Immigrant parents working long hours to support their families may not be able to provide needed support and guidance to their children (Kim et al., 1992). Their children, growing up in the U.S. culture of their peers, may not understand or respect the values and authority of the parents (SAMHSA, 1998). API youth may turn to drug use to fit in with their Americanized peers and/or to "rebel" against the parents they do not understand (Yee, 1999).

3. Discrimination and racism: As elaborated upon in this chapter's discussion of the relationship between institutionalized racism and domestic violence, racism has had an impact on APIs from the first wave of immigration to the present day. Hate crimes and other forms of racism are serious stressors that may promote AOD use.

4. Shame and denial: Substance abuse can be a serious source of shame and embar-

rassment to API families and their communities, which may promote denial of the existence of a problem. This denial, in turn, will hinder any attempts to seek help for the problem, thus delaying or stopping efforts for treatment (CSAT, 1999).

API Substance Abuse Services and Promising Practice Models

In spite of the research that suggests that substance abuse rates are significant and that API communities exhibit many high-risk attributes for substance abuse, APIs are still "invisible" when it comes to developing local strategies to address substance abuse problems (CSAT, 1999). API women, who report lower levels of substance use and abuse compared to men, are even less visible: "[if] Asians and Pacific Islanders, as a whole, suffer from a lack of visibility and treatment accessibility, women within these groups are given even less consideration for service" (CSAT, 1999, p. 41). Mainstream drug abuse treatment programs may not have culturally and linguistically sensitive staff and services that can successfully engage API clients.

There are nonprofit agencies that specifically target API populations such as the Asian American Drug Abuse Program in Los Angeles, the Asian Association of Utah in Salt Lake City, and Washington Asian Pacific Islander Families Against Substance Abuse (WAPIFASA) in Seattle. Such programs, unfortunately, are few. It is believed there are about 30 mental health and substance abuse agencies specifically serving APIs in the continental United States.

API agencies and social workers have developed various approaches to address AOD issues in their communities. One example is the family-skills-type substance abuse prevention model (see Kumpfer, 1998). In some programs, this involves working with families that have a parent or a youth with a drug problem. Other programs target families that happen to live in high-risk environments, such as neighborhoods characterized by high unemployment, crime, and drug use. In a family-skills program, focus is placed on families (parents and children), with separate and conjoint activities for children and their parents by trained agency facilitators or counselors. They feature multiweek curricula that emphasize improving the self-esteem and efficacy of both parents and children as well as the parenting skills of the adults to promote higher family functioning and health. In addition to these sessions, extra services such as drug counseling and case management are available. Two examples of API family-skills programs are the Comprehensive Asian Pre-School Services (CAPS), conducted by Asian American Recovery Services in San Francisco, and Coalition for a Drug-Free Hawaii's Strengthening Hawaiian Families (SHF) in Honolulu.

Family-skills-type programs for APIs seem particularly promising for several reasons. First, they focus on the importance of family cohesion, a cultural strength of API families.[1] They also address family stressors (cultural/generational gap) by promoting greater understanding and communication between parents and children. For parents, they potentially mitigate acculturation and immigration stressors by providing concrete information on American norms and values as well as providing a support network among participants. Such programs also emphasize the cultural strengths and rich history of the participant's ethnic group. (Cultural appreciation may help to reduce the sting of perceived discrimination and anti-immigration sentiment in the United States.) Finally, the programs run by API-specific agencies help demystify the nature of AOD prevention and treatment and may promote increased use by the participants and their relatives and friends.

Such local AOD prevention efforts represent concrete, targeted approaches to the specific cultural and geographic needs of the population. Thus, one useful strategy to address substance abuse issues in API communities may be to foster the development of local community-based service organizations that have a deep understanding of the people they serve—and perhaps more important, the trust of their clients. At a micro level, this would involve social workers staffing such agencies and providing direct services. At a mezzo level, social workers may help develop an interagency council to facilitate collaboration of the area's service delivery. At a macro level, social workers can advocate for funding from government agencies to expand existing API community-based organizations' capacities and help establish new agencies. The fact that there are about 30 identified substance abuse and mental health nonprofit agencies specifically targeting the over 10 million APIs in the country indicates there is much real work to be done.

The Relationship Between Domestic Violence and Substance Abuse

Thus far, we have reviewed the separate literatures regarding domestic violence and substance abuse in API communities. Common themes have emerged in both fields, including lack of empirical data regarding prevalence, inattentiveness by mainstream institutions, and the dearth—though not complete absence of—assistance programs addressing domestic violence and substance abuse in the API communities. In searching to explore how these two fields can be integrated, our investigation *has not found a single study that has examined the relationship between domestic violence and substance abuse among any API group*. In the absence of empirical data specific to the API populations in the United States, we examine the available data from the mainstream research and services, which we hope will shed light on future practice and research directions addressing domestic violence and substance abuse in API communities.

Although research on the intersection between domestic violence and substance abuse dates from the 1970s, the scope of research remains limited, and its methodology underdeveloped. In general, available research on the relationship between domestic violence and substance abuse can be separated into four categories: (a) whether substance abuse is associated with perpetration of domestic violence (Barnett & Fagan, 1993; Julian & McKenry, 1993; Van Hasselt, Morrison, & Bellack, 1985), (b) whether substance abuse is associated with being victimized by domestic violence (Gleason, 1993; Kantor & Straus, 1989; McCauley et al., 1995; Miller, Downs, & Gondoli, 1989), (c) whether perpetrators and/or victims were using substances during domestic violence incidents (Kantor & Asdigian, 1997), and (d) whether there is a dose-response type relationship between the level of the substance abuse problem and the severity of domestic violence (Clark & Foy, 2000; Coleman & Straus, 1983). In all lines of research, most studies use a small convenience sample of batterers (or battered women) with one or more comparison groups. Alcohol has been studied more extensively than other drugs, and the interaction of alcohol and drugs has been studied rarely. (Studies by Kantor & Asdigian, 1997; Miller et al., 1990; and Willson et al., 2000, are notable exceptions.) These studies have documented a strong correlation between substance abuse and domestic violence in general, in particular among male perpetrators. Men's substance use is consistently associated with violence toward female partners, whereas women's substance abuse is not always associated with their partners' violence toward them. Kantor and Asdigian assessed substance abuse during episodes of domestic violence against women and found that women were much less likely than men to be intoxicated. Several studies of a community-based random or probability sample have found a more complex relationship between domestic violence and substance abuse, in that the correlation is stronger for certain groups of individuals. For example, Leonard and Blane (1992) used a national random sample of 320 married or cohabiting young men and found that violence toward partners was associated with high scores on the Alcohol Dependence Scale among those with high hostility and low marital satisfaction but not among those with low hostility and low marital satisfaction. Kantor and Straus (1987) found that alcohol consumption was associated with violence toward wives among men with normative approval of violence.

These earlier studies have paid little, if any, attention to the effects of race or ethnicity; only recently have studies begun to pay attention to race, ethnicity, culture, class, or other factors that may affect the link between domestic violence and substance abuse (Caetano, Schafer, Clark, Cunradi, & Raspberry, 2000; Kantor, 1997; Neff, Holaman, & Schluter, 1995). Findings from these studies are mixed at best and illustrate the complexity in the relationship among domestic violence, substance abuse, race/ethnicity, acculturation, and structural factors such as poverty and unemployment. For example, Kantor found that heavy drinking by men was associated with increased rates of domestic violence among Hispanic and Anglo-American couples, whereas there was little or no effect of drinking by African American men on domestic violence, controlling for socioeconomic variables. Similarly, the study by Neff et al. (1995) of a regional probability sample in San Antonio, Texas, found no effect of drinking on rates of domestic violence among African Americans, controlling for financial strains, sex roles, and social desirability. Caetano et al. (2000) focused on Hispanic couples and examined whether acculturation levels affected the relationship between substance abuse and domestic violence. These studies found that domestic violence was associated with increased alcohol consumption only among the high-acculturation group. Findings from the small number of studies reviewed call for an expanded and more systematic investigation of the relationship among domestic violence, substance abuse, race, ethnicity, acculturation, and structural factors across and within diverse population groups.

While variations by race/ethnicity and acculturation remain underexamined, the existing body of literature suggests a general correlation between battering and substance abuse and being battered and substance abuse. Because of the use of a cross-sectional design in most previous studies, whether domestic violence leads to increased substance use or substance use increases the risk of domestic violence remains largely unexamined. However, through using prospective design and/or advanced analytical methods, several past studies began to examine pathways among victimization and substance use (Chilcoat & Breslau, 1998; Kilpatrick, Acierno, Resnick, Saunders, & Best, 1997). Although this type of research did not specifically examine domestic violence, findings indicate that exposure to trauma (e.g., victimization) can lead to post-traumatic stress disorder (PTSD), which in turn can lead to substance abuse (self-medication hypothesis) as opposed to substance abuse leading to increased risk for trauma exposure, leading to PTSD. Taken together, these research findings suggest that (a) under the influence of substances, a person may be more likely to batter his or her partner, and (b) a woman who has experienced domestic violence may resort to substance abuse as a means of coping.

Implications for Social Work Practice

These two hypotheses suggest the need for, and the utility of, addressing the intersection of substance abuse and domestic violence in practice. For example, batterers who come into contact with legal and social service organizations should be screened for substance abuse, and those with substance abuse problems should receive drug and/or alcohol counseling. Residents or outpatients at drug treatment programs should be assessed for a history of perpetration of and/or victimization by partners' violence. Similarly, women seeking assistance from domestic violence programs should be assessed for substance use, and those with such a problem should be provided specific assistance in-house or be referred for specialized substance abuse treatment.

However, like domestic violence and substance abuse research, the fields of domestic violence and drug abuse treatment have remained separate, overall. A study of domestic violence and substance abuse programs in Illinois found that substance abuse programs do not routinely assess clients for domestic violence perpetration or victimization (Bennett & Lawson, 1994). Similarly, domestic violence programs do not always assess clients for substance abuse problems. Not only have domestic violence and substance abuse programs remained separate, they have been at odds with each other at times. Battered women are often denied entry to some shelters if they have substance abuse problems. Considering the high co-occurrence of domestic violence victimization and substance abuse, this practice inevitably leaves many women without much-needed assistance. Regarding API women, the need for culturally or linguistically responsive services adds another layer of difficulty in addressing client need.

Although it may be natural to want to integrate *existing* domestic violence and substance abuse programs, rather than developing a new program, we must first question whether such integration is possible and preferable. What are the advantages and disadvantages of integrating existing domestic violence and substance abuse programs? In what ways, if any, can such integrated programs ensure the safety and empowerment of women and perpetrators' accountability—two pillars of domestic violence programs?

What about the intersection between domestic violence and substance abuse in API communities? API communities are very diverse, significantly and differently affected by sociocultural, sociopolitical, and sociohistorical factors. Prompted by the current dearth of research and programs that specifically address the intersection of domestic violence and substance abuse in API American communities, we pose the following questions, which we hope will stimulate further discussion, research efforts, and practice initiatives and innovations:

1. What is the relationship between domestic violence and substance abuse in the API American communities? Are they comorbid? Does substance abuse by the perpetrator promote battering? Do battered API women use substances as a form of self-medication or coping?
2. Are there variations by ethnicity and/or immigration status in the relationship between domestic violence and substance abuse among API communities? If so, how are such variations associated with sociohistorical factors, such as racism and the anti-immigrant social structure?

3. Do community agencies that serve APIs adequately address domestic violence and substance abuse when both issues are present? If so, in what ways? If not, how can they address these issues effectively?

4. Are family skills substance abuse prevention programs as described in this chapter effective in reducing the risk of violence in the family as well? Are they appropriate in cases where one family member is abusive toward another? Will the safety of an abused woman (or child) be compromised in family-based substance abuse prevention programs that promote family cohesion and shared activities? What alternative models of practice may be possible and promising?

Finally, we conclude by raising another, broader question. Given the diverse cultures and experiences of people of API descent, is "API" a useful category to guide research and practice? What alternative paradigm(s) of research and practice, if any, would be useful?

Note

1. Karen Joe's ethnographic study (1996) has elucidated chaotic family backgrounds in API women who used drugs, pointing to the importance of involving family members. However, a family-centered approach may be contraindicated in certain instances, for example, when abuse is present in the family.

References

Abraham, M. (1999). Sexual abuse in South Asian immigrant marriages. *Violence Against Women, 5,* 591–618.

Abraham, M. (2000). Isolation as a form of marital violence: The South Asian immigrant experience. *Journal of Social Distress and the Homeless, 9,* 221–236.

Agtuca, J. R. (1992). *A community secret: For the Filipina in an abusive relationship.* Seattle, WA: Seal Press.

Almeida, R. V., & Dolan-Delvecchio, K. (1999). Addressing culture in batterers intervention: The Asian Indian community as an illustrative example. *Violence Against Women, 5,* 654–683.

Asian/Pacific Islander Domestic Violence Resource Project. (2001, September). Project AWARE. Washington, DC: Author.

Ayyub, R. (2000). Domestic violence in the South Asian Muslim immigrant population in the United States. *Journal of Social Distress and the Homeless, 9,* 237–248.

Barnett, O. W., & Fagan, R. W. (1993). Alcohol use in male spouse abusers and their female partners. *Journal of Family Violence, 8,* 1–25.

Bauer, H. M., Rodriguez, M. A., Quiroga, S. S., & Flores-Ortiz, Y. G. (2000). Barriers to health care for abused Latina and Asian immigrant women. *Journal of Health Care for the Poor and Underserved, 11*, 33–44.

Bennett, L., & Lawson, M. (1994). Barriers to cooperation between domestic-violence and substance-abuse programs. *Families in Society: The Journal of Contemporary Human Services, 75*, 277–286.

Bograd, M. (1988). An introduction. In K. Yllo & M. Bograd (Eds.), *Feminist perspectives on wife abuse* (pp. 11–27). Newbury Park, CA: Sage.

Bui, H. N., & Morash, M. (1999). Domestic violence in the Vietnamese immigrant community. *Violence Against Women, 5*, 769–795.

Caetano, R., Schafer, J., Clark, C. L., Cunradi, C. B., & Raspberry, K. (2000). Intimate partner violence, acculturation, and alcohol consumption among Hispanic couples in the United States. *Journal of Interpersonal Violence, 15*, 30–45.

Center for Substance Abuse Treatment [CSAT]. (1999). *Cultural issues in substance abuse treatment* (DHHS Publication No. SMA 99-3278). Rockville, MD: Substance Abuse and Mental Health Services Administration, U.S. Department of Health and Human Services, Public Health Service, Substance Abuse and Mental Health Services.

Chilcoat, H. D., & Breslau, N. (1998). Investigations of causal pathways between PTSD and drug use disorders. *Addictive Behaviors, 23*, 827–840.

Clark, A. H., & Foy, D. W. (2000). Trauma exposure and alcohol use in battered women. *Violence Against Women, 6*, 37–48.

Coleman, D. H., & Straus, M. A. (1983). Alcohol abuse and family violence. In E. Gottheil, K. A. Druly, T. E. Skoloda, & H. M. Waxman (Eds.), *Alcohol, drug abuse and aggression* (pp. 104–124). Springfield, IL: Charles C. Thomas.

Collins, K. S., Schoen, C., Joseph, S., Duchon, L., Simantov, E., & Yellowitz, M. (1999). *Health concerns across a woman's life span: The Commonwealth Fund 1998 Survey of Women's Health*. New York: Commonwealth Fund.

Commonwealth Fund. (1993). *The Commonwealth Fund Survey of Women's Health: News release and key tables*. New York: Author.

Coomaraswamy, R. (1996). *Report of the special rapporteur on violence against women, its causes and consequences* (E/CN.4/1996/53). New York: United Nations Commission on Human Rights.

Crenshaw, K. (1991). Mapping the margins: Intersectionality, identity politics, and violence against women of color. *Stanford Law Review, 43*, 1241–1299.

Dasgupta, S. D. (2000). Charting the course: An overview of domestic violence in the South Asian community in the United States. *Journal of Social Distress and the Homeless, 9*, 173–185.

Dasgupta, S. D., & Warrier, S. (1996). In the footsteps of "Arundhati": Asian Indian women's experience of domestic violence in the United States. *Violence Against Women, 2*, 238–259.

Davis, L. V., & Srinivasan, M. (1995). Listening to the voices of battered women: What helps them escape violence. *Affilia, 10*, 49–69.

Family Violence Prevention Fund. (1993). *Men beating women: Ending domestic violence—A qualitative and quantitative study of public attitudes on violence against women.* San Francisco: Author.

Fernandez, M. (1997). Domestic violence by extended family members in India. *Journal of Interpersonal Violence, 12*, 433–455.

Gleason, W. J. (1993). Mental disorders in battered women: An empirical study. *Violence and Victims, 8*, 53–68.

Hanmer, J., & Maynard, M. (1987). Introduction: Violence and gender stratification. In J. Hanmer & M. Maynard (Eds.), *Women, violence, and social control* (pp. 1–12). Atlantic Highlands, NJ: Humanities Press International.

Hanson Frieze, I., & Zubritzky, M. (1987, July). *College students' beliefs about wife battering and marital rape in the United States and Japan.* Paper presented at the Third National Family Violence Research Conference, Durham, New Hampshire.

Heise, L., Ellsberg, M., & Gottemoeller, M. (1999, December). Ending violence against women. *Population Reports, 27*(4), Series L 11.

Ho, C. K. (1990). An analysis of domestic violence in Asian American communities: A multicultural approach to counseling. *Women & Therapy, 9*, 129–150.

Hoagland, C., & Rosen, K. (1990). *Dreams lost, dreams found: Undocumented women in the land of opportunity: A survey research project of Chinese, Filipina, and Latina undocumented women.* San Francisco: Coalition for Immigrant and Refugee Rights and Services, Immigrant Women's Task Force.

Jang, D., Lee, D., & Morello-Frosch, R. (1990). Domestic violence in the immigrant and refugee community: Responding to the needs of immigrant women. *Response to the Victimization of Women and Children, 13*, 2–6.

Jasinski, L. L. (1998). The role of acculturation in wife assault. *Hispanic Journal of Behavioral Sciences, 20*, 175–191.

Joe, K. A. (1996). The lives and times of Asian-Pacific American women drug users: An ethnographic study of their methamphetamine use. *Journal of Drug Issues, 26*, 199–218.

Julian, T. W., & McKenry, P. C. (1993). Mediators of male violence toward female intimates. *Journal of Family Violence, 8*, 39–56.

Kantor, G. K. (1997). Alcohol and spouse abuse ethnic differences. In M. Galanter (Ed.), *Recent developments in alcoholism: Vol. 13. Alcoholism and violence* (pp. 57–79). New York: Plenum Press.

Kantor, G. K., & Asdigian, N. (1997). When women are under the influence: Does drinking or drug use by women provoke beatings by men? In M. Galanter (Ed.), *Recent developments in alcoholism: Vol. 13. Alcoholism and violence* (pp. 315–336). New York: Plenum Press.

Kantor, G. K., Jasinski, J. L., & Aldarondo, E. (1994). Sociocultural status and incidence of marital violence in Hispanic families. *Violence & Victims, 9*, 207–222.

Kantor, G. K., & Straus, M. A. (1987). The drunken bum theory of wife beating. *Social Problems, 34*, 213–230.

Kantor, G. K., & Straus, M. A. (1989). Substance abuse as a precipitant of wife abuse victimizations. *American Journal of Drug Alcohol Abuse, 15*, 173–189.

Kanuha, V. (1994). Women of color in battering relationships. In. L. Cosmas-Diaz, & B. Green (Eds.), *Women of color: Integrating ethnic and gender identities in psychotherapy* (pp. 428–454). New York: Guilford Press.

Kilpatrick, D. G., Acierno, R., Resnick, H. S., Saunders, B. E., & Best, C. L. (1997). A 2-year longitudinal analysis of the relationships between violent assault and substance use in women. *Journal of Consulting and Clinical Psychology, 65*, 834–847.

Kim, J. (1999). Marital conflict and violence in Korean-American families [Electronic version]. *Asian Journal of Women's Studies, 5*(2).

Kim, S., McLeod, J. H., & Shantzis, C. (1992). Cultural competence for evaluators working with Asian-American communities: Some practical considerations. In M. A. Orlandi (Ed.), *Cultural competence for evaluators: A guide for alcohol and other drug abuse prevention practitioners working with ethnic/racial communities* (pp. 203–260). (DHHS Publication No. [ADM] 92-1884). Washington, DC: DHHS.

Kim, J. Y., & Sung, K. (2000). Conjugal violence in Korean American families: A residue of cultural transition. *Journal of Family Violence, 15*, 331–345.

Klein, E., Campbell, J., Soler, E., & Ghez, M. (1997). *Ending domestic violence.* Thousand Oaks, CA: Sage.

Kumpfer, K. L. (1998). Selective prevention interventions: The strengthening families program. In R. S. Ashery, E. B. Robertson, & K. L. Kumpfer (Eds.), *Drug abuse prevention through family interventions* (pp. 160–207). (NIH Publication No. 99-4135.) Rockville, MD: National Institutes of Health.

Kuramoto, F., & Nakashima, J. (2000). Developing an ATOD prevention campaign for Asian and Pacific Islanders: Some considerations. *Journal of Public Health Management Practice, 6*(3), 57–64.

Lai, T. A. (1986). Asian women: Resisting the violence. In M. C. Burns (Ed.), *The speaking profits us: Violence in the lives of women of color* (pp. 8–11). Seattle, WA: Center for the Prevention of Sexual and Domestic Violence.

Lempert, L. B. (1996). Women's strategies for survival: Developing agency in abusive relationships. *Journal of Family Violence, 11*, 269–289.

Leonard, K. E., & Blane, H. T. (1992). Alcohol and marital aggression in a national sample of young men. *Journal of Interpersonal Violence, 7*, 19–30.

Logan, J. R., Stowell, J., & Vesselinov. (2001). From many shores: Asians in Census 2000. Albany, NY: State University of New York, Albany, Lewis Mumford Center for Comparative Urban and Regional Research.

Martin, D. (1981). *Battered wives* (Rev. ed.). San Francisco: Volcano Press.

McCauley, J., Kern, D. E., Kolodner, K., Dill, L., Schroeder, A. F., DeChant, H. K., Ryden, J., Bass, E. B., & Derogatis, L. R. (1995). The "battering syndrome": Prevalence and clinical characteristics of domestic violence in primary care internal medicine practices. *Annals of Internal Medicine, 123*, 737–746.

Mehrotra, M. (1999). The social construction of wife abuse: Experiences of Asian Indian women in the United States. *Violence Against Women, 5*, 619–640.

Miller, B. A., Downs, W. R., & Gondoli, D. M. (1989). Spousal violence among alcoholic women as compared to a random household sample of women. *Journal of Studies on Alcohol, 50*, 533–540.

Miller, B. A., Nochajski, T. H., Leonard, K. E., Blane, H. T., Gondoli, D. M., & Browers, P. M. (1990). Spousal violence and alcohol/drug problems among parolees and their spouses. *Women and Criminal Justice, 1*, 55–72.

National Asian Pacific American Legal Consortium. (1998). *Audit of violence against Asian Pacific Americans* (Fifth annual report). Washington, DC: Author.

Neff, J., Holamon, B., & Schluter, T. (1995). Spousal violence among Anglos, Blacks, and Mexican Americans: The role of demographic variables, psychosocial predictors, and alcohol consumption. *Journal of Family Violence, 10*, 1–21.

Perilla, J. L., Bakeman, R., & Norris, F. H. (1994). Culture and domestic violence: The ecology of abused Latinas. *Violence and Victims, 9*, 325–339.

Plichta, S. (1996). Violence and abuse: Implications for women's health. In M. M. Falik & K. S. Collins (Eds.), *Women's health: The Commonwealth Fund Survey* (pp. 237–270). Baltimore: Johns Hopkins University Press.

Rhee, S. (1997). Domestic violence in the Korean immigrant family. *Journal of Sociology and Social Welfare, 24*, 63–77.

Raj, A., & Silverman, J. (2002). Intimate partner violence amongst South Asian women in greater Boston. *Journal of the American Medical Women's Association, 57*(2), 1–4.

Richie, B. (1996). *Compelled to crime: The gender entrapment of battered black women.* New York: Routledge.

Schafer, J., Caetano, R., & Clark, C. L. (1998). Rates of intimate partner violence in the United States. *American Journal of Public Health, 88*, 1702–1704.

Schechter, S. (1982). *Women and male violence.* Boston: South End Press.

Segal, U. A. (2000). A pilot exploration of family violence among nonclinical Vietnamese. *Journal of Interpersonal Violence, 15*, 523–533.

Singh, R. N., & Unnithan, N. P. (1999). Wife burning: Cultural cues for lethal violence against women among Asian Indians in the United States. *Violence Against Women, 5,* 641–653.

Song, Y. I. (1986). *Battered Korean women in urban America: The relationship of cultural conflict to wife abuse.* Unpublished doctoral dissertation, Ohio State University.

Song-Kim, Y. I. (1992). Battered Korean women in urban United States. In S. M. Furuto, B. Renuka, D. K. Chung, K. Murase, & F. Ross-Sheriff (Eds.), *Social work practice with Asian Americans* (pp. 213–226). Newbury Park, CA: Sage.

Sorenson, S. B., & Telles, C. A. (1991). Self-reports of spousal violence in a Mexican-American and non-Hispanic white population. *Violence and Victims, 6,* 3–15.

Stone, L., & James, C. (1995). Dowry, bride-burning, and female power in India. *Women's Studies International Forum, 18,* 125–134.

Straus, M. A., & Gelles, R. J. (1986). Societal change and change in family violence from 1975 to 1985 as revealed by two national surveys. *Journal of Marriage and the Family, 48,* 465–479.

Straus, M. A., Gelles, R. J., & Steinmetz, S. K. (1980). *Behind closed doors: Violence in the American family.* Garden City, NY: Anchor Press/Doubleday.

Straus, M. A., & Smith, C. (1990). Violence in Hispanic families in the United States: Incidence rates and structural interpretations. In M. A. Straus & R. J. Gelles (Eds.), *Physical violence in American families: Risk factors and adaptations to violence in 8,145 families* (pp. 341–367). New Brunswick, NJ: Transaction.

Substance Abuse and Mental Health Services Administration [SAMHSA]. (1998). *Prevalence of substance use among racial and ethnic subgroups in the United States, 1991–1993* (DHHS Publication No. SMA 98-3202 Analytic series; A-6). Rockville, MD: Substance Abuse and Mental Health Services Administration, U.S. Department of Health and Human Services.

The Immigration Act (P.L. 101-649), November 29, 1990.

The Marriage Fraud Act Amendments (P.L. 99-639). November 10, 1986.

The Personal Responsibility and Work Opportunity Reconciliation Act (P.L. 104-193), August 22, 1996.

The Victims of Trafficking and Violence Prevention Act (P.L. 106-386) (VAWA 2000), October 28, 2000.

The Violence Against Women's Act [VAWA] (Title IV of the Violent Crime Control and Law Enforcement Act of 1994, PL 103-322), September 13, 1994.

Thomas, E. K. (2000). Domestic violence in the African-American and Asian-American communities: A comparative analysis of two racial/ethnic minority cultures and implications for mental health service provision for women of color. *Psychology, 37,* 32–43.

Tjaden, P., & Thoennes, N. (2000). *Extent, nature, and consequences of intimate partner violence: Findings from the National Violence Against Women Survey.* Washington, DC: U.S. Department of Justice, Office of Justice Programs, National Institute of Justice.

Torres, S. (1987). Hispanic-American battered women: Why consider cultural differences? *Response to the Victimization of Women and Children, 10,* 20–21.

Tran, C. G. (1997). *Domestic violence among Vietnamese refugee women: Prevalence, abuse characteristics, psychiatric symptoms, and psychosocial factors.* Unpublished doctoral dissertation, Boston University.

Tran, C. G., & Des Jardins, K. (2000). Domestic violence in Vietnamese refugee and Korean immigrant communities. In J. L. Chin (Ed.), *Relationships among Asian American women* (pp. 71–96). Washington, DC: American Psychological Association.

Uehara, E. S., Tekeuchi, D. T., & Smukler, M. (1994). Effects of combining disparate groups in the analysis of ethnic differences: Variations among Asian American mental health services consumers in level of functioning. *American Journal of Community Psychology, 22,* 83–99.

U.S. Census Bureau. (1999). *Projections of the total resident population by 5-year age groups, race, and Hispanic origin with special age categories.* Washington, DC: U.S. Department of Commerce. Retrieved January 27, 2002, from http://www.census.gov/population/www/projections/natsum-T3.html

U.S. Census Bureau. (2000). *2000 Census of Population and Housing, Summary File 2, Technical documentation.* Washington, DC: U.S. Department of Commerce, Bureau of Census. Retrieved January 27, 2002, from http://www.census.gov/prod/cen2000/doc/sf2.pdf

U.S. Census Bureau. (2001). Census 2000 Summary File 1, Matrices P3, P4, PCT4, PCT5, PCT8, and PCT11. Washington, DC: U.S. Department of Commerce. Retrieved January 27, 2002, from http://factfinder.census.gov/servlet/BasicFactsTable?_lang=en&_vt_name=DEC_2000_SF1_U_QTP3&_geo_id=01000US

U.S. Commission on Civil Rights. (1992). The plight of battered Asian American women. *Civil rights issues facing Asian Americans in the 1990s* (pp. 174–180). Washington, DC: Author.

Van Hasselt, V. B., Morrison, R. L., & Bellack, A. S. (1985). Alcohol use in wife abusers and their spouses. *Addictive Behaviors, 10,* 127–135.

West, C. M. (1998). Lifting the "political gag order": Breaking the silence around partner violence in ethnic minority families. In J. L. E. Jasinski & L. M. E. Williams (Eds.), *Partner violence: A comprehensive review of 20 years of research* (pp. 184–209). Thousand Oaks, CA: Sage.

Willson, P., McFarlane, J., Malecha, A., Watson, K., Lemmey, D., Schultz, P., & Gist, J. F.

N. (2000). Severity of violence against women by intimate partners and associated use of alcohol and/or illicit drugs by the perpetrator. *Journal of Interpersonal Violence*, *15*, 996–1008.

Wyatt, G. E. (1994). Sociocultural and epidemiological issues in the assessment of domestic violence. *Journal of Societal Distress and the Homeless*, *3*, 7–21.

Yee, B. W. K. (1999). Life span development of Asian-Americans and Pacific Islanders. In B. W. K. Yee, N. Mokuau, & S. Kim (Eds.), *Developing cultural competence in Asian-American and Pacific Islander communities: Opportunities in primary health care and substance abuse prevention* (pp. 91–142). Rockville, MD: Substance Abuse and Mental Health Services Administration, U.S. Department of Health and Human Services.

Yick, A. G. (2000). Predictors of physical spousal/intimate violence in Chinese American families. *Journal of Family Violence*, *15*, 249–267.

Yick, A. G., & Agbayani-Siewert, P. (1997). Perceptions of domestic violence in a Chinese American community. *Journal of Interpersonal Violence*, *12*, 832–846.

Yoshihama, M. (1993). *Domestic violence: Experience, knowledge, and attitudes among residents of Tokyo, Japan*. Unpublished manuscript, School of Social Welfare, University of California, Los Angeles.

Yoshihama, M. (1996). *Domestic violence against women of Japanese descent: Understanding the socio-cultural context*. Unpublished doctoral dissertation, University of California, Los Angeles.

Yoshihama, M. (1999). Domestic violence against women of Japanese descent in Los Angeles: Two methods of estimating prevalence. *Violence Against Women*, *5*, 869–897.

Yoshihama, M. (2000). Reinterpreting strength and safety in socio-cultural context: Dynamics of domestic violence and experiences of women of Japanese descent. *Children and Youth Services Review*, *22*, 205–227.

Yoshihama, M. (2001). Immigrants-In-Context Framework: Understanding the interactive influence of socio-cultural contexts. *Evaluation and Program Planning 24*, 307–318.

Yoshihama, M. (2002). Battered women's coping strategies and psychological distress: Differences by immigration status. *American Journal of Community Psychology*, *30*, 429–452.

Yoshihama, M., & Yunomae, T. (2000). *A final report of focus groups research project on domestic violence in Yokohama, Kobe, and Sapporo*. Yokohama and Kanagawa, Japan: Yokohama Women's Association.

Yoshioka, M. (2000, November). *Asian family violence report: A study of the Cambodian, Chinese, Korean, and Vietnamese communities in Massachusetts*. Boston, MA: Asian Task Force Against Domestic Violence.

Zane, N., & Kim, J. H. (1994). Substance abuse and abuse. In N. W. S. Zane, D. T. Takeuchi, & K. N. J. Young (Eds.), *Confronting critical health issues of Asian and Pacific Islander Americans* (pp. 316–343). Thousand Oaks, CA: Sage.

Authors' Note

An earlier version of this paper was presented at the Task Force Meeting, Cultural Competence in Child Welfare Practice: A Collaboration Between Practitioners and Academicians, February 9–10, 2001, University of Texas at Austin. The authors wish to thank Terri Torkko for her editorial assistance.

15

Pacific Islander Americans

Impact of Colonialization and Immigration

**HALAEVALU VAKALAHI, MERIPA GODINET,
and ROWENA FONG**

Introduction

Pacific Islander Americans comprise one of the fastest-growing ethnic communities in the United States today. According to the U.S. 2000 census, Pacific Islanders constitute about 874, 414 (.3 %) of the total U.S. population, a growth of approximately 140% since 1990 (U.S. Census Bureau, 2000). By 2010, the projected population of Asians/Pacific Islanders combined in the United States will be about 16 million (5%); and by 2050, there will be about 38 million (9%) Asians/Pacific Islanders in the United States. While this growth offers tremendous opportunities for progress and contribution to our society, it presents challenges as well. One of the greatest challenges is building a child welfare system that is culturally competent in responding to Pacific Islanders on issues such as substance abuse and family violence (Zane, Takeuchi, & Young, 1994). At the same time, this challenge presents new opportunities to build collaborative partnerships between professionals in the child welfare system and Pacific Islander communities. In a profession that promotes cultural competency, self-determination, and social and economic justice, social workers, with their expertise in prevention and intervention, administration, policy, and research, are needed in the child welfare system to work collaboratively with Pacific Islander communities in advocating for resources to meet the needs of children, their families, and their communities.

The literature on Pacific Islander Americans is sparse, particularly in relation to the involvement with and effects of substance abuse, family violence, and child welfare (Mokuau, 1998; Zane & Sasao, 1992). Because of the lack of information, portrayals of Pacific Islanders can be misleading. Furthermore, the lack of information will continue to hinder the development of culturally sensitive child welfare policies, programs, and research that appropriately and effectively respond to the needs of Pacific Islander Americans regarding substance abuse and family violence. Although limited, the existing literature does indicate that Pacific Islanders are well behind other ethnic minority groups in research, policy, and social work practice concerning substance abuse and family violence. The existing literature also supports the fact that the bio-psycho-social-spiritual well-being of Pacific Islander individuals and groups is often disintegrated as a result of experiences with substance abuse and family violence. Likewise, the general literature is rich in terms of confirming that substance abuse and family violence have stricken all sectors of society, including our most vulnerable populations, children and youth (Kelly, Faust, Runyon, & Kenny, 2002; Morelli, Fong, & Oliveira, 2001; Naar-King, Silvern, Ryan, & Sebring, 2002; Peterman & Dixon, 2001; Yoshihama, 2001).

This chapter discusses what is currently known about substance abuse, family violence, and child welfare among Pacific Islander Americans. The discussion focuses on the sociocultural context, substance abuse, and family violence among Pacific Islanders and relevant action-based research. Key issues are identified as implications for further practice, policy, and research. Information provided in this chapter, although limited, is offered to assist child welfare personnel in designing systems and services that will better meet the needs of Pacific Islander American communities.

Sociocultural Context

For decades, Asians and Pacific Islanders were aggregated in government documents, social services, educational systems, and in other sectors in American society. The political, ideological, and demographical aggregation of these two distinct ethnic/racial groups seems to have had some positive outcomes such as Asians being called model minorities, leading to privileges and greater access to more resources. Unfortunately, the aggregation presented a misleading portrait of Pacific Islanders, thus contributing to the problem of not having their needs met appropriately. For instance, the title of "model minority" given to Asians/Pacific Islanders has actually been in reference to Asians only, whereas Pacific Islanders have often been perceived as lazy, unmotivated, and violent (McDermott, Tseng & Maretzki, 1980). Furthermore, according to the U.S. Census Bureau (2000), Asians/Pacific Islanders are the most highly educated ethnic/racial group with the highest median of household income in the United States. However, Asians/Pacific Islanders have higher rates of poverty for all ages, are underemployed (earning less than Caucasians), and because of larger family size (multiple generations living under one roof), they have less income per household member (Mokuau, 1995; U.S. Census Bureau, 2000). Thus, socioeconomic status is one of the most misunderstood factors for Asians/Pacific Islanders because of its mismatch with high educational achievement (Chow, 2001). Moreover, despite the high educational achievement of the Asians/Pacific Islander group, Pacific Islanders alone generate lower numbers in educational achievement compared to Asians and the larger U.S. population (Mokuau, 1995). For example, Tongans earned the lowest number of high school diplomas, at about 64% compared to Hawaiians, at 80% . Tongans also had the lowest number of bachelor's degree, at 6%, compared to 58% for Asian Indians (U.S. Census Bureau, 2000). Additionally, statistics of the Hawaii school system indicated that Samoan females have the lowest high school completion rate of all ethnic groups in the study. Similarly, the high school completion rate for Samoan males is the second lowest, only surpassed by the rate for Filipino males (Franco, 1991). Nationally Pacific Islander Americans alone are overrepresented in crime, poverty, and health problems (Mokuau, 1998; Zane, Takeuchi, & Young, 1994). Certainly, these aggregate data have hindered the development of culturally competent policy and programs that respond to the needs of Pacific Islanders who live and practice in diverse cultures of origin combined with their American culture.

The U.S. 2000 census was the first time Pacific Islander Americans were recognized on census documents as a separate group. According to the census, Pacific Islanders was the smallest ethnic/racial group in the United States. Because of its size, any misreporting could have a large effect on the Pacific Islander population. Pacific Islanders belong to three major groups, including Polynesians (i.e., Native Hawaiian, Samoan, Tongan, Tahitian, Maori, Fijian, Tokelauan), Micronesians (i.e., Chamorro or Guamanian, Mariana Islander, Saipanese, Palauan, Carolinian, Kosraean, Pohnpeian, Chuukese, Yapese, Marshallese, I-Kiribati), and Melanesians (i.e., Papua New Guinean, Solomon Islander, Ni-Vanuatu). In terms of age, Pacific Islanders are a fairly young population with the largest age group between 25 and 44 years. In terms of gender, Pacific Islanders are about proportional in number for male and female. The largest Pacific Islander group in the United States is Native Hawaiians, followed by Samoans and Chamorros. Three-fourths of the total number of Pacific Islanders in the United States live in the West, mainly Hawaii and California. Other locations with a fair number of Pacific Islanders include the South, Midwest, Northeast, and Puerto Rico (U.S. Census Bureau, 2000).

Issues of Colonization and Immigration

The story of Pacific Islander Americans deals with enormous historical, cultural, political, and socioeconomic diversity that has led to challenges in appropriately meeting the needs of children and families on social issues, including substance abuse and family violence (Zane et al., 1994). The present minority status of Pacific Islanders and the mistrust of foreign systems are linked to historical and cultural experiences of colonization, immigration, oppression, marginalization, and racial discrimination. For example, even today in the 21st century Kanaka Maoli (Native Hawaiians) continue to deal with the destructive effects of colonization, loss of many original cultural values and practices, and the illegal overthrow of their government. Prior to Western influence, the Kanaka Maoli population was about 1 million strong; in the 1870s, the population decreased to about 40,000 because of diseases and other circumstances (Blaisdell & Mokuau, 1991). Today at 140,652 individuals, Kanaka Maoli are overrepresented in prisons and on public assistance (Furuto, San Nicholas, Kim, & Fiaui, 2001; Office of Hawaiian Affairs, 1998; U.S. Census Bureau, 2000). In pre-Western contact time, Kanaka Maoli had the highest literacy rate (Hawaiian language) in the world (Reinecke, 1969), but today, 30% are identified with the highest literacy needs (Omnitrack Research and Marketing Group, 1989). Among other matters, colonizers introduced diseases, guns, alcohol, tobacco, drugs, and corporal punishment to Pacific Island nations, which have led to the disintegration and annihilation of cultures, communities, families, and individuals. Unquestionably, understanding the experience of colonization as a piercing factor in a history and culture is imperative for adequately addressing the needs of Pacific Islander Americans.

In addition, immigration is a major struggle for Pacific Islanders who are either recent immigrants or have lived in the United States for generations or are indigenous populations. Immigration has been a vehicle for at-risk experiences in both their homelands and in the United States. In other words, Pacific Islanders were not only deeply affected by immigrants, but they were also deeply affected as immigrants. For example, early immigrants into Pacific Island nations from Europe brought diseases and foreign practices that destroyed many Native Pacific Islander populations. Likewise, Pacific Islanders who migrate to the United States, depending on their immigration status, experience the consequences of language barriers, poor health, lack of job skills resulting in lower-paying jobs, lack of education, and involvement in criminal activities as a form of survival. Without proper education and training, Pacific Islander Americans are often marginalized and passed up on opportunities. In fact, discrimination by government entities and Caucasian American communities is faced by every new generation of Pacific Islander immigrants (Millett & Orosz, 2001; Yoshihama, 2001). Regarding Samoans, they are overrepresented in prison, juvenile arrests, family violence incidences, family court cases, and public housing. In the state of Hawaii, Samoan high school students have the second-highest rate of suspension of all ethnic groups. Also, the unemployment rate among Samoans is almost as high as 80%. In the workforce, they are underrepresented in professional jobs and in universities (Furuto et al., 2001). With Chamorros, inmigration has contributed to oppression, exploitation, and the disintegration of cultural identity. In Chamorro communities in the United States, there is a clear decline in the cultural practice of reciprocity and sharing of resources, including the sharing of children, or *poksai* (Furuto et al., 2001; Untalan, 1991). Apparently, diversity in historical, migratory, and sociopolitical experiences contributes to differences in socioeconomic status and educational achievements as sources of risk for social problems such as substance abuse and family violence.

Cultural Strengths and Protective Factors

Despite the many challenges faced by Pacific Islander Americans, there are strengths in the values and practices of the culture of origin that may serve as protective factors for social problems. The diversity among Pacific Islanders makes it difficult to identify a set of cultural practices that is adhered to by the entire population. However, common themes emerged from values of all Pacific Islander cultures that emphasize harmony in family relationships, love for children, respect for the elderly, and communal responsibility (Chow, 2001). For instance, in Pacific Islander culture, family is first and the center of all relationships. In the Chamorro family or *y familia*, love and support are not demanded but are simply there. The family is the agent of socialization where individuals learn to trust, respect, and be responsible for each other. Because of such a heavy responsibility, family members do their best to nurture, honor, respect, collaborate with, and sacrifice for the family. Similarly, in the Samoan culture, the unit of organization is the extended family or *aiga* consisting of several nuclear families related by blood, marriage, or adoption and headed by a chief or *matai*. The matai of various *aiga* make up the council or *fono* that governs the family community (Furuto et al., 2001; McDermott et al., 1980). As a result of a sometimes hostile U.S. environment, the extended family and informal networking have become the primary support systems for new Pacific Islander immigrants (Millett & Orosz, 2001). Clearly, interdependency and harmony in relationships in families and communities rather than individual independence is the ultimate achievement in Pacific Islander cultures (Furuto et al., 2001). In addition, Pacific Islander families have great love for children. In fact, Pacific Islanders believe that a house without children is a house without life. Children are embraced, paid attention to, seldom left alone when crying, and raised in the contexts or environments in which the first human bonds are developed into strong ties in adulthood. This love for children is critical in understanding illegitimacy in the Hawaiian culture. To Hawaiians, it doesn't matter that a child was born out of wedlock; that child needs love and care. Thus, the Hanai system is a mechanism for adoption that does not sever ties; instead it extends ties by offering another layer of support. In Samoan culture, children are taught from childhood to respect the elderly, and older siblings are held responsible for their younger siblings. By age three, when children begin involvement in housework, punitive measures are regularly employed. Sometimes child rearing requires direct and overt discipline involving physical punishment and public shaming (McDermott et al., 1980).

Certainly, the range of challenges faced by Pacific Islander Americans in relation to cultural transitions and demographic changes has had an impact on their experiences with substance abuse and family violence and ways of coping and seeking help from professionals in the child welfare system (Furuto et al., 2001). Unfortunately, the system has not recognized and maximized the use of Pacific Islander cultural strengths to meet their needs.

Substance Abuse and Pacific Islanders

Before Western influence, the only addictive substance known to Pacific Islanders was kava, a drink made from a plant traditionally used for medicinal and ceremonial purposes. Today, this tradition is changed; many Pacific Islanders have used Kava in a manner similar to alcohol for purposes of daily relaxation and "talking story." These gatherings have become a daily occurrence for many Pacific Islander Americans, particularly males, and have often led to many social problems, including further substance abuse and family violence. Today, substances such as alcohol, tobacco, marijuana, and other illicit drugs are introduced by Westerners and often readily adopted into Pacific Islander cultures, leading to the disintegration of Pacific Islander families and individual spirituality (Alama & Whitney, 1990; Whitney & Hanipale, 1991). The significance of spirituality in Pacific Islander cultures leads to the perception that substance abuse blocks the path to spirituality (Mokuau, 1995). Although the existing literature is limited, studies have found that serious substance abuse problems exist in Pacific Islander communities that warrant immediate attention (Substance Abuse and Mental Health Services Administration [SAMHSA], 2002). In particular, Pacific Islanders have problems related to alcohol, tobacco, marijuana, and cocaine. For instance, Hawaiians living in Hawaii use alcohol and cigarettes at higher rates than Whites, Filipinos, and Japanese (Substance Abuse and Mental Health Services Administration, 1998). Hawaiians also had the highest percentage of binge and chronic drinking, with Hawaiian juveniles using alcohol at a higher rate. Furthermore, Hawaiians and Samoans are overrepresented in substance-abuse-related crimes (Mokuau, 1995). Hence, despite the declining trend in substance abuse in the nation, caution must be taken in relation to Pacific Islanders, especially given the current statistic that substance abuse is most prevalent in the western part of the United States, where the majority of Pacific Islanders reside (U.S. Department of Health and Human Services [DHHS], 2001).

RISK FACTORS

Evidently, the ethnic/racial minority status of Pacific Islanders amplifies their vulnerability to and the effects of substance abuse (Mokuau, 1995). Risk factors commonly associated with the minority status of Pacific Islanders in relation to substance abuse include low educational achievement, low income, unemployment, criminal activity, and a language barrier (Millett & Orosz, 2001). As the most disadvantaged group in the United States, Pacific Islanders have used and abused substances as a means of coping (DHHS, 2001). Pacific Islander immigrants and refugees with linguistic difficulties are the most at risk for substance abuse because such factors serve as barriers to substance abuse education as well as inhibit the use of available traditional treatment modalities (Mokuau, 1995). Other immigration-based risk factors for substance abuse among Pacific Islanders include family separation during the immigration process, overcrowded housing, poverty, and intergenerational conflicts (National Clearinghouse for Alcohol and Drug Information [NCADI], 2002). The literature confirms the association of these factors with increased substance abuse rates, especially among young immigrant Pacific Islanders (DHHS, 2001; Padilla, Sung, & Nam, 1993).

The intersection of class and race/ethnicity informs substance abuse patterns among Pacific Islanders. According to SAMHSA (1998) Pacific Islander families earning $20,000–$40,000 annually used substances less, whereas families earning less than $20,000 annually used substances at a higher rate. NCADI (2002) contends that major socioeconomic disparities among ethnic/racial groups have contributed to the greater prevalence of substance abuse among Pacific Islanders, especially males. Because males are most likely the breadwinners in Pacific Islander families and communities, there are great implications for increased substance abuse, family violence, and involvement in the child welfare system.

In relation to the child welfare system, Hampton, Senatore, and Gullotta (2000) found that substance abuse is one of the primary family problems that lead to child removal and foster care. Over 70% of child welfare clients are substance abusers. For Pacific Islanders, shame and stigma are core issues for resistance to seeking help from the child welfare system. Also, inattentiveness of the child welfare system and limited culturally competent substance abuse services for Pacific Islander populations have multiplied the problem (DHHS, 2001; NCADI, 2002). Hampton et al. (2000) contend that the substance abuse field and child welfare field must be bridged to collaboratively seek solutions and prevent further suffering of children.

Family Violence and Pacific Islanders

Family violence as an act of misusing power to gain control through fear and intimidation manifests itself in many forms, including child abuse and neglect and domestic violence. In the United States, even though national trends of child abuse and neglect have been declining in the past few years, child abuse and neglect remain the most prevalent forms of violation of children's rights (DHHS, 2001). As such, research, policy, and programs are urgently needed in reducing and preventing child abuse and neglect (Schumacher, Slep, & Heyman, 2001). According to the Administration for Children and Families, in 1999 there were about 2,974,000 referrals for child abuse and neglect; of this number about 1,100 children died (Sedlak & Broadhurst, 1996). According to DHHS (2001), billions of dollars are spent annually in dealing with the emotional, psychological, behavioral, and biological consequences of child abuse and neglect. In regard to domestic violence, according to the National Coalition Against Domestic Violence, a woman is beaten by her intimate partner every 15 seconds. According to the American Medical Association, 50% of all women will experience some type of domestic violence in their lifetime (Peterman & Dixon, 2001). As a public health concern in the United States, treatment for physical injuries from family violence has been estimated to be over $800 million a year. Around the world, these forms of family violence are major social and health problems that have injured the most vulnerable sectors in our society, including children, youth, and other oppressed populations.

In reference to Pacific Islander Americans, there is a dearth of information regarding the issue of family violence, even though the population is at high risk because of historical and cultural experiences (Huisman, 1996; Leake, 2001). In 1999, according to the Administration for Children and Families, Pacific Islanders generated the lowest rate of child maltreatment, at 4%. However, underreporting of family violence, the overrepresentation of children of color in the child welfare population, and the higher incidence of abuse in larger families with lower income must be taken into consideration in reference to Pacific Islanders (Sedlak & Broadhurst, 1996). For Kanaka Maoli, Hammond (1988) and Leake (2001) noted the high rates of child abuse, substance abuse, and school problems. They concluded that cultural loss is the primary contributing factor to such unfavorable outcomes and suggested a return to traditional values and strengthening of cultural identity based on the fact that traditional Kanaka Maoli ways do not promote family violence, substance abuse, and failure in school. Discipline is the duty of the

Ohana, who may punish children for serious misbehavior; however, such harsh punishment is rare, unusual, and done openly (Blaisdell & Mokuau, 1991; Dubanoski, 1981; Pukui, Haertig, Lee, & McDermott, 1979). In Samoan families, physical discipline is used as an external control to assure children's participation in the family system, thus harsh punishment may be common in these families (Mokuau, 1991). The rationale for physical punishment of children as a form of discipline was introduced to Pacific Islanders through Christianity based on the biblical statement, "you spare the rod, you spoil the child" (Mokuau & Tauili'ili-Pemerika 1992).

Furthermore, in relation to domestic violence in Hawaii, where most Pacific Islanders reside, in 1992, of 502 women on the island of Kauai, 14% reported abuse, about 21% of whom were identified as Hawaiian/part Hawaiian. On the island of Maui, about 24% of women who reported abuse were Hawaiian/part Hawaiian. In 1993, in a study of 311 women in Hawaii who were in domestic violence shelters and/or counseling, 19.5% were Hawaiian/part Hawaiian (Hawaii State Commission on the Status of Women, 1993). In 1996, an estimated 20% of all women in Hawaii were victims of domestic violence (Domestic Violence Family Court, 1996). Given these numbers, the actual incidence of domestic violence may be higher as Pacific Islander women are less likely to report abuse because of shame and stigma as well as language and cultural barriers. One of the most significant cultural barriers is the fact that most people in Hawaii are related by blood or through community and spiritual connections (Huisman, 1996; Tjaden & Thoennes, 1998).

RISK FACTORS

Sources of risk for family violence include micro-, mezzo-, and macro-level systems. Research has supported the association among family violence and gender, age, power issues (patriarchy), socioeconomic status, unemployment, relationship instability, and substance abuse (Anderson, 1997; Gelles & Loseke, 1993; Johnson, 1995; Lin, Shah, & Svoboda, 1997; Roizen, 1997). Specifically, child abuse and neglect have been found to be associated with parental behavioral and psychological characteristics such as personality disorder, hostility, aggression, neuroticism, family stress, lack of family support, family history of violence, parental substance abuse, impoverished socioeconomic status, and harmful coping strategy (Black, Heyman, & Slep, 2001; Black, Slep, & Heyman, 2001; Salzinger et al., 2002; Schumacher, Slep, & Heyman, 2001). Furthermore, women who are victims of domestic violence or physical and sexual abuse are most likely to be under the age of 30 or over the age of 50. These women are also more likely to be experiencing poor communication patterns in the family and poor marital adjustment and attachment, have less education, lower income, are unemployed, have a history of child emotional victimization, and live in a disorganized community (Black, Heyman, & Slep,

2001; Schumacher, Feldbau-Kohn, Slep, & Heyman, 2001; Schumacher, Slep, & Heyman, 2001). In relation to Pacific Islander Americans, risk factors for family violence are further complicated by historical and cultural experiences associated with the effects of colonization and immigration that generate systemic barriers. Such systemic barriers may include differential treatment because of language, cultural loss because of the forbidding of traditional practices, lack of education because of financial strains, and lack of cultural competency on the part of the child welfare system. Likewise, the patriarchal system of some Pacific Islander cultures can be a major risk factor for abuse and neglect in that females are considered inferior to males in terms of status, privileges, value, authority, and power (Taylor, Magnussen, & Amundson, 2001).

As stated earlier, the complexity of the intersection of family violence, substance abuse, and child welfare is magnified for Pacific Islander Americans. Family violence and substance abuse are not traditional cultural practices, but are outcomes of assimilation and fusion of Pacific Islander and Western cultures. The introduction of alcohol and drugs by Western cultures has been strongly linked to domestic violence as well as child abuse and neglect and involvement in the child welfare system (McCloskey, Treviso, Scionti, & dal Pozzo, 2002; Peterman & Dixon, 2001).

Action-Based Research: Prevention and Intervention Strategies

CONCEPTUAL FRAMEWORK

Traditional paradigms have proposed a variety of theories to conceptualize prevention and intervention strategies for substance abuse, family violence, and other deviant behaviors for mainstream America (Bandura, 1977; Duvall, 1957; Hawkins, Catalano, & Associates, 1992; Hirschi, 1969; Merton, 1968). Alternative paradigms specifically applicable to prevention and intervention strategies for Pacific Islander Americans are urgently needed. The discussion on conceptual framework offered here does not entirely explain what is required for effective work on substance abuse, family violence, and child welfare among Pacific Islander Americans; however, it does offer some significant suggestions in relation to the concepts of biculturalization, community-based, community-driven, and cultural competency. The multisystemic therapy treatment model is also discussed as a possible option for conceptualizing work with Pacific Islander Americans.

Based on the integration of traditional and alternative paradigms, biculturalization refers to creating bicultural interventions by matching Western interventions with values of ethnic cultures. Biculturalization brings together a mainstream and an indigenous model such as Ho'oponopono and the Ghandi technique (Fong, Boyd, & Browne, 1999).

In creating bicultural interventions for Pacific Islanders, community-based, community-driven, and cultural competency must be present. These concepts emphasize the significance of the environment as a source of influence on Pacific Islander values and behavioral patterns, the importance of relationships in providing resolutions, and the value of focusing on strengths of Pacific Islanders in resolving problems (Mokuau, 1995). As such, community-based refers to establishing the program in the community it serves and hiring staff from the community, whereas community-driven refers to involving people in the community in decision making regarding the structure and content of the program, and cultural competency refers to hiring staff with a deep understanding of the cultural history and characteristics, program content, and policies and procedures (Mokuau, 1995). Furthermore, in Chamorro culture, the concept of *afamaolek* is significant because it calls for developing cooperation and community teamwork as imperative in working with Chamorro communities. Cooperation and collaborative practice require empowerment, recognition of strengths, and instilling in clients and their families a vision of hope to learn and grow (Furuto et al., 2001).

In encompassing the concepts previously discussed, the multisystemic model (MST) has been used in conceptualizing prevention and intervention for social problems, including family violence and substance abuse. The MST model was originally developed in the late 1970s to address gaps in mental health services for juvenile offenders. This model is based on social-ecological perspectives and family systems theories (Bronfenbrenner, 1980). It is an intensive family and community-based practice model for addressing the multiple determinants of antisocial behaviors such as violence and substance abuse, viewing individuals as being nested within a complex network of interconnected systems of family, peer, school, neighborhood, and community. In other words, this model allows an individual to be viewed in context. It promotes behavior change in the natural environment (i.e., home, school, community) using systemic strengths. It is a goal-oriented treatment that considers both risk and protective factors in an individual's social network. In terms of cultural competency, treatment teams commonly reflect the ethnic composition of the population served. Such multicultural teams can provide grounds upon which culturally appropriate practices can be identified, discussed, and, if needed, changed. According to Henggeler, Schoenwald, and Munger (1996), the nine core principles of the MST model are as follows.

1. The purpose of assessment is to understand the fit between the identified problem(s) and the broader systemic context.
2. Therapeutic contacts should emphasize the positive and use systemic strengths as levers for change.
3. Interventions should be designed to promote responsible behavior and decrease irresponsible behavior among family members.

4. Interventions should be present-focused and action-oriented, targeting specific and well-defined problems.
5. Interventions should target sequences of behavior within and between multiple systems that maintain identified problems.
6. Interventions should be developmentally appropriate, meeting developmental needs.
7. Interventions should be designed to require daily or weekly effort by family members.
8. Intervention effectiveness is evaluated continuously from multiple perspectives, with providers assuming responsibility for overcoming barriers to successful outcomes.
9. Interventions should be designed to promote treatment generalization and long-term maintenance of change by empowering families to address their needs across multiple systemic contexts.

In relation to Pacific Islander Americans, the MST model corresponds with cultural themes such as collectivity, empowerment, and community orientation (Mokuau, 1995). However, perhaps the one factor that requires consideration is time, in that it takes a good amount of time to develop trust between Pacific Islander American families and service providers.

POLICY FOUNDATION

Problems of family violence and neglect, substance abuse, and poverty are interrelated and interdependent. For Pacific Islander Americans, approaches to family strengthening and the reduction and prevention of the effects of substance abuse, family violence, and poverty must include the cooperation of families and communities, new training, new systems designs, and capacity-building models that promote family and child welfare goals of safety, protection, and empowerment (Briar-Lawson, 1998; DHHS, 2001).

Prevention and intervention strategies for substance abuse, family violence, and child welfare are founded on policies created to enhance human well-being and eliminate injustices. Title IV-B and Title IV-E of the Social Security Act as amended by the Adoption and Safe Families Act frame most policy decisions on child welfare, substance abuse, and family violence preventions and interventions. Numerous policies serve as a foundation for child welfare services, including the Child Abuse Prevention, Adoption, and Family Services Act of 1988; Child Abuse Prevention Challenge Grants Reauthorization Act of 1989; Drug Free School Amendments of 1989; Victims of Child Abuse Act of 1990; Adoption and Safe Families Act of 1997; Violence Against Women Act (VAWA) of 1994; Family Violence Prevention and Services Act; Individuals with Disabilities Education Act; and many others (DHHS, 2001).

One of the most influential policies affecting child welfare laws is the Child Abuse Prevention and Treatment Act (CAPTA) Amendments of 1996 (CPS Watch, 2002).

From its 1974 version to the 1996 amendment, CAPTA mandates programs and services for child abuse and neglect and contributing factors to abuse and neglect. Child welfare laws as amended by CAPTA require the involvement of law, psychology, social services, medicine, state and local governments, organizations providing services to disabled persons, teachers, parents, self-help organizations, families, and all other systems affecting children and their families. CAPTA established an Office on Child Abuse and Neglect with an advisory board to execute and coordinate the functions and activities of the act. This act provides for assessment, prevention, and intervention; emphasizes help for states and communities in providing child and family protection; and calls for research and evaluation of child and family protection programs. Furthermore, the act creates grants for developing, implementing, and enhancing community-based prevention, family resources, and support programs that assess community resources and needs, community referral services, direct service, parent education, leadership services, and mutual support groups. Explicitly stated in child welfare laws is the provision of grants to provide substance abuse and family violence prevention and intervention services. Also, the Family Violence Prevention and Services Act provides grants for state coalitions dealing with family violence. As a result of these federal policies, each state has child welfare legislation that focus on issues such as family violence and substance abuse prevention and intervention (CPS Watch, 2002).

PREVENTION AND INTERVENTION STRATEGIES

According to Mokuau (1995), providing services to Pacific Islander Americans requires several considerations, including service accessibility, culturally valid content, and culturally valid delivery. For example, in order for services to be accessible, they must be established within the community rather than in areas where driving or plane rides are required. Also, given the high poverty rate among Pacific Islanders, affordability of services is critical. Furthermore, validity in content and delivery requires the incorporation of Pacific Islander cultures (i.e., spirituality, family, cooperation) into the program curriculum and using agencies with high involvement rates of Pacific Islanders to deliver substance abuse and family violence services. Based on these considerations and given the limited literature on Pacific Islander Americans in relation to substance abuse, family violence, and child welfare, a few strategies are highlighted here that encompass key elements relevant to Pacific Islander cultures, in general.

Ho'oponopono

Ho'oponopono is a Hawaiian family-centered, family empowering, problem-solving model (Mokuau, 1990). Ho'oponopono means "to set right." This indigenous model has been used widely in Hawaii in the child welfare system with Native Hawaiians. Many forms of this model are used by other Pacific Islander cultures as well. Stages of Ho'oponopono include the following (Fong et al., 1999):

1. *Pule* (prayer). The process begins by asking God for a blessing in the problem-solving effort. Sincerity and truthfulness are imperative.
2. *Kukulu Kumuhana* (statement of the problem). The *kupuna* (elders) lead the session and reach out to everyone, including any resistant individuals, in order to establish a proper climate for the *hala* (transgression) to be stated. It is critical that the initial transgression is articulated in order to avoid further misunderstandings. The *kupuna* select one issue to focus on throughout the discussion, simultaneously uncovering other concerns and resolving relationship troubles.
3. *Mahiki* (discussion). The *kupuna* lead an in-depth discussion, yet prevent direct confrontations that may generate additional emotional eruption and confusion. Each member is allowed to share his or her *mana'o* (feelings) but with extreme caution in avoiding reproach and recrimination.
4. *Ho'ike i ka hana hewa i hana ia* (confession of wrongdoing). Following the discussion, a sincere confession of wrongdoing and the seeking of forgiveness take place.
5. *Panina* (restitution). When necessary, restitution is discussed and agreed upon.
6. *Mihi* (forgiveness). Mutual forgiveness by both parties occurs.
7. *Kala* (release). A mutual release occurs when there's confession and forgiveness. Both parties are expected to engage in mutual release in order for proper Ho'oponopono to occur.
8. *Pani* (summary). In the final phase, the occasion and the family's strengths are summarized. After the problem is resolved, further discussion about the matter is forbidden. In closure, a closing prayer is offered, and a meal is shared among participants. (p. 98).

Family Decision Making and Family Group Conference

The Family Decision-Making Model originated in New Zealand among the Native Maori people. Many forms of this model are used by other Pacific Islander cultures. This model has a cultural base in that the Maori people developed a culture that included child rearing practices and family decision making, shaped by their relationship to the land. Such a cultural base gives the Maori people the preeminent right to be heard, to participate, and to decide what happens to their own. This model is based on the premise that each family is the "expert" on itself. Each family has the power to make decisions on its own. The family knows itself better than anyone else does, including those in the external environment. The family is the natural and, perhaps, best place to determine needs and resources for addressing areas of family dysfunction. This model proposes that only in the family can the best decisions be made about the family. This model has been successful in helping families resolve social problems, including substance abuse and family violence (Wilcox et al., 1991).

Kamehameha Schools' Safe and Drug-Free Program

The Kamehameha Schools' Safe and Drug-Free Program (SDFP) in the state of Hawaii is dedicated to partnerships with individuals, families, and communities in reducing substance abuse and violence among Native Hawaiians. The high quality of statewide partnerships between SDFP and the communities has contributed to the success of its programs and projects. The SDFP programs and projects are designed according to six research-based prevention and education strategies developed by the Center for Substance Abuse Prevention (CSAP). These strategies include:

1. Information and Dissemination. Culturally appropriate violence and substance abuse prevention materials are developed and disseminated to schools and communities throughout the state.
2. Education. Activities range from implementing curricula, after-school programs, and family-based retreats to providing classroom presentations and workshops.
3. Alternative activities. These include the development of safe and drug-free activities and youth leadership programs.
4. Problem identification. This involves resource and referral services for Native Hawaiian students and families.
5. School/community-based processes and approaches. These include needs assessment and agency collaboration activities in selected communities and schools throughout the state.
6. Environmental. Activities range from providing technical assistance to schools and communities on social impact issues to reviewing policies and legislation as they relate to Native Hawaiians and substance abuse and violence prevention (Kamehameha Schools' Safe and Drug-Free Program, 2002).

The following criteria are used in site selection and developing partnerships:

•Relationship to the mission and goals of the SDFP
•Relationship to the mission and goals of Kamehameha schools
•Number and percentage of Native Hawaiians
•A need for substance abuse/violence prevention services and resources
•Ability and willingness to work with program evaluation requirements (Kamehameha Schools' Safe and Drug-Free Program, 2002)

Discussion

IMPLICATIONS FOR PRACTICE

Any discussion of substance abuse and family violence has implications for the child welfare system and families involved in the system. This is especially true for Pacific Islander Americans, who account for less than 1% of the U.S. population, yet are increasingly engaged in or at risk for abuse of substances and family members. Given the commonality among Pacific Islander cultures, many interventions (e.g., Ho'oponopono, Maori Family Group Conferencing) would be relevant to most or all Pacific Islander cultures. As stated earlier, in order to meet the needs of Pacific Islander Americans, service providers must consider historical and cultural experiences such as colonization, immigration, oppression, and the shame and stigma that occurs on multiple systemic levels during all stages of services (i.e., assessment to treatment). Traditional child welfare modalities have denied adequate service capacities for Pacific Islander Americans, and professionals alone have not been able to meet the needs of Pacific Islander American families.

Despite the many barriers, social workers have long known that indigenous experiences are significant because of their giving and benefiting ethos (Reisman, 1997). Pacific Islander values promote reciprocity, advocacy for the whole, and interdependency. Thus, expansion of professional theories and child welfare practices for Pacific Islander Americans would build family capacity to deal with the effects of substance abuse and family violence. For example, outreach, family conferencing, use of the family hierarchy, and limit setting have been used in dealing with the shame and stigma that comes from seeking professional help for substance abuse and family violence among Pacific Islanders (DHHS, 2001). Both professionals and Pacific Islander communities are sources of expertise for filling gaps in traditional child welfare services, advocacy, and mobilizing Pacific Islander American families and communities. Certainly, in order to make a difference in the lives of Pacific Islander Americans, we must include more people and more skills at more levels (Briar-Lawson, 1998). Furthermore, Dana, Behn, and Gonwa (1992) suggest culturally familiar backgrounds such as Pacific Islander posters, music, and employees in order to reduce the barriers to service use. The bridge between child welfare and Pacific Islander communities must be built at all governmental levels, beginning with the local and state levels. Emphasis should be focused on a holonistic, collaborative, systemic, strengths-based, and multiservice approach reflecting the original cultures of Pacific Islander Americans. Solutions must be focused on all levels, including research, social work practice, policy, organizations, and economic infrastructures (Chow, 2001).

IMPLICATIONS FOR POLICY

In general, the progress of Pacific Islander Americans has been minimal compared to other ethnic minority groups' because the trickle-down effect of existing policies that focus on the progress of ethnic groups has been minimal. In a manner of speaking, the current status of Pacific Islander Americans can be described as being able to "sit anywhere in the bus" with few or no opportunities for progress thereafter. This minimum progress calls for effective policies as interventions for inequality and injustice in the child welfare system and in society as a whole.

In the child welfare system, policies must be culturally relevant with the primary purpose of advancing the interests of vulnerable families and children such as Pacific Islander Americans. As such, child welfare service providers can advocate for funding to create culturally appropriate substance abuse and family violence programs for Pacific Islander families and children. Policies could highlight the need for substance abuse and family violence services for Pacific Islander Americans and provide funding opportunities for integrating original cultural values and practices into program curriculum. Policies could also reflect the need for multisystemic efforts with Pacific Islander Americans, including provisions for higher education, employment training, and mental health services. Likewise, child welfare policy needs to mandate timely decision making in the system. Pacific Islander families and children should receive child welfare services quickly and accurately. In other words, policies could mandate the system to adjust to the needs of Pacific Islander Americans rather than Pacific Islander Americans accommodating the system.

IMPLICATIONS FOR RESEARCH

First, the limited nature of the existing literature on the intersection of substance abuse, family violence, and child welfare for Pacific Islander Americans has major implications for research. Studies are needed to focus on the complexity of social problems intertwined with ethnic cultures and historical experiences. Second, additional research is needed to test specific risk and protective factors for substance abuse and family violence among Pacific Islanders. There is a need to evaluate factors such as satisfaction with relationships with family and friends, higher income, and higher education as a source of protection for substance abuse and family violence among Pacific Islander Americans.

Third, there is a need to evaluate the relevance of conceptual frameworks and their components for Pacific Islanders. For example, in reference to the multisystemic model, evaluation of systems, including all government levels, their influences, and strengths, is crucial. Fourth, there is a need to evaluate existing programs that are

Pacific Islander-focused for effectiveness and as a means to determine allocation of funding. Fifth, there is a need to evaluate the outcomes of the aggregation as well as the separation of Asians and Pacific Islanders (API) in the 2000 census. Perhaps one group of Pacific Islanders that specifically needs attention in relation to the consequences of the 2000 census includes individuals who are mixed race, particularly in Hawaii. Moreover, existing studies rarely include Pacific Islanders, particularly women and children. If they are included, Pacific Islanders are grouped with Asians. Although social problems of Asians and Pacific Islanders overlap, there are also important and distinct differences between the two cultures. As a result of such a grouping, it has been difficult to understand the needs and concerns of Pacific Islanders; therefore, there has been a monocultural approach to meeting their needs. Furthermore, the API group has been found to be the highest-achieving ethnic group in the United States, thus leading to the illusion that API and Caucasian Americans have equal access to opportunities. On the contrary, studies have found that Caucasian Americans have better employment, income, and health. Thus, research is needed to support the elimination of systemic barriers such as institutional racism and promotion of equal access to employment, health care, education, and housing.

References

Alama, K., & Whitney, S. (1990). *Ka Wai Kau Mai O Maleka: Water from America—The intoxication of the Hawaiian people.* Unpublished manuscript.

Anderson, K. L. (1997). Gender, status, and domestic violence: An integration of feminist and family violence approaches. *Journal of Marriage and Family, 59,* 655–669.

Bandura, A. (1977). *Social learning theory.* Englewood Cliffs, NJ: Prentice-Hall.

Black, D. A., Heyman, R. E., & Slep, A. M. S. (2001). Risk factors for male to female partner sexual abuse. *Aggression and Violent Behavior, 6*(2-3), 269–280.

Black, D. A., Slep, A. M. S., & Heyman, R. E. (2001). Risk factors for child physical abuse. *Aggression and Violent Behavior, 6*(2/3), 121–188.

Blaisdell, K., & Mokuau, N. (1991). Kanaka Maoli, indigenous Hawaiians. In N. Mokuau (Ed.), *Handbook of social services for Asians and Pacific Islanders* (pp. 131–154). Westport, CT: Greenwood.

Briar-Lawson, K. (1998). Capacity building for integrated family-centered practice. *Social Work, 43*(6), 539–550.

Bronfenbrenner, U. (1980). Ecology of childhood. *School Psychology Review, 9*(4), 294–297.

Chow, J. C. (2001). Assessment of Asian American/Pacific Islander organizations and communities. In R. Fong & S. B. C. L. Furuto (Eds.), *Culturally competent practice: Skills, interventions, and evaluations* (pp. 211–224). Needham Heights, MA: Allyn & Bacon.

CPS Watch. (2002). *Entire child welfare law as amended by the Adoption & Safe Families Act.* Retrieved May 24, 2002, from www.cpswatch.com/federallaws/iv-b/ 42USC625.htm

Dana, R., Behn, J., & Gonwa, T. (1992). A checklist for the examination of cultural competence in social service agencies. *Research in Social Work Practice, 2,* 220–233.

Domestic Violence Family Court. (1996). *Domestic violence Family Court monitoring project report.* Honolulu: State of Hawaii, Judiciary Court System.

Dubanoski, R. A. (1981). Child maltreatment in European and Hawaiian-Americans. *Child Abuse and Neglect, 5*(4), 457–465.

Duvall, E. (1957). *Family development.* Philadelphia, PA: Lippincott.

Fong, R., Boyd, C., & Browne, C. (1999). The Gandhi Technique: A biculturalization approach for empowering Asian and Pacific Islander families. *Journal of Multicultural Social Work, 7*(1/2), 95–109.

Franco, R. W. (1991). *Samoan perceptions of work: Moving up and around.* New York: AMS Press.

Furuto, S. B. C. L., San Nicolas, R. J., Kim, G. E., & Fiaui, L. M. (2001). Interventions with Kanaka Maoli, Chamorro, and Samoan communities. In R. Fong & S. B. C. L. Furuto (Eds.), *Culturally competent practice: Skills, interventions, and evaluations* (pp. 327–342). Needham Heights, MA: Allyn & Bacon.

Gelles, R. J. & Loseke, D. R. (1993). *Current controversies on family violence.* Newbury Park, CA: Sage.

Hammond, O. W. (1988). Needs assessment and policy development: Native Hawaiians as Native Americans. *American Psychologist, 43*(5), 383–387.

Hampton, R. L., Senatore, V., & Gullotta, T. P. (Eds.) (2000). *Substance abuse, family violence and child welfare: Bridging perspectives.* Thousand Oaks, CA: Sage.

Hawaii State Commission on the Status of Women. (1993). *Domestic violence report.* Honolulu: State of Hawaii.

Hawkins, J. D., Catalano, R. F., & Associates. (1992). *Communities that care: Action for drug abuse prevention.* San Francisco: Jossey-Bass.

Henggeler, S. W., Schoenwald, S. K., & Munger, R. (1996, January/February). Multisystemic therapy proving to be effective treatment model. *Family Matters, 11,* 1–3.

Hirschi, T. (1969). *Causes of delinquency.* Berkeley: University of California Press.

Huisman, K. A. (1996). Wife battering in Asian-American communities. *Violence Against Women, 2,* 260–284.

Johnson, M. P. (1995). Patriarchal terrorism and common couple violence: Two forms of violence against women. *Journal of Marriage and Family, 57,* 283–294.

Kamehameha Schools' Safe and Drug-Free Program—SDFP. (2002). Retrieved May 24, 2002, from http://extension.ksbe.edu/eolapono/programs/index.html

Kelly, D., Faust, J., Runyon, M. K., & Kenny, M. C. (2002). Behavior problems in sexually abused children of depressed versus non-depressed mothers. *Journal of Family Violence, 17*(2), 107–116.

Leake, D. W., Jr. (2001). Cultural models relevant to the problem of anger for youngsters perceived as troubled and troubling in a "tough" community in Hawaii. *Dissertation Abstracts International, 61*(7-A), 2787.

Lin, R. L., Shah, C. P., & Svoboda, T. I. (1997). The impact of unemployment on health: A review of the evidence. *Journal of Public Health Policy, 18*, 275–300.

McCloskey, L. A., Treviso, M., Scionti, T., & dal Pozzo, G. (2002). A comparative study of battered women and their children in Italy and the United States. *Journal of Family Violence, 17*(1), 53–74.

McDermott, J. F., Jr., Tseng, W., & Maretzki, T. W. (1980). *People and cultures of Hawaii: A psychocultural profile.* Honolulu: University Press of Hawaii.

Merton, R. K. (1968). *Social theory and social structure.* New York: Free Press.

Millett, R., & Orosz, J. J. (2001). Understanding giving patterns in communities of color. *Fund Raising Management, 32*(6), 25–27.

Mokuau, N. (1990). A family-centered approach in Native Hawaiian culture. *Families in Society: The Journal of Contemporary Human Services, 71*(10), 607–613.

Mokuau, N. (1991). *Handbook of social services for Asian and Pacific Islanders.* Westport, CT: Greenwood Press.

Mokuau, N. (1995). Pacific Islanders. In *Center for Substance Abuse Prevention, Cultural Competence Series* (special collaborative NASW/CSAP monograph, DHHS Publication No. SMA 95-3075, pp. 159–188). Rockville, MD: Substance Abuse and Mental Health Services Administration.

Mokuau, N. (1998). *Responding to Pacific Islanders: Culturally competent perspectives for substance abuse prevention.* Washington, DC: Substance Abuse and Mental Health Services Administration, Center for Substance Abuse Prevention.

Mokuau, N., & Tauili'ili-Pemerika, P. (1992). Families with Native Hawaiian and Pacific Island roots. In E. W. Lynch & M. J. Hanson (Eds.), *Developing cross-cultural competence: A guide for working with young children and their families* (pp. 301–318). Baltimore, MD: Baltimore Brooks Publication.

Morelli, P. T., Fong, R., & Oliveira, J. (2001). Culturally competent substance abuse treatment for Asian/Pacific Islander women. *Journal of Human Behavior in the Social Environment, 3*(3-4), 263–280.

Naar-King, S., Silvern, L., Ryan, V., and Sebring, D. (2002). Type and severity of abuse as predictors of psychiatric symptoms in adolescence. *Journal of Family Violence, 17*(2), 133–149.

National Clearinghouse for Alcohol and Drug Information [NCADI]. (2002). Asian/Pacific Islander substance abuse: Issues and implications. Retrieved May 1, 2002, from www.health.org/seasonal/asianpi/naomi.htm

Office of Hawaiian Affairs. (1998). *Native Hawaiian data book 1998*. Honolulu: Author.

Omnitrack Research and Marketing Group. (1989). "Hawaii Statewide Literacy Assessment." Presented to Governor's Office of Children and Youth.

Padilla, A. M., Sung, H., & Nam, T. V. (1993). Attitudes toward alcohol and drinking practice in two Vietnamese samples in Santa Clara County. *Horizons of Vietnamese Thought and Experience*, *2*(1), 53–71.

Peterman, L. M., & Dixon, C. G. (2001). Assessment and evaluation of men who batter women. *Journal of Rehabilitation*, *67*(4), 38–42.

Pukui, M. K., Haertig, E. W., Lee, C. A., & McDermott, J. F. (1979). *Nana I Ke Kumu* (Vol. 2). Honolulu: Hui Hanai.

Reinecke, J. (1969). *Language and dialect in Hawaii*. Honolulu: University of Hawaii Press.

Reisman, F. (1997, Spring). Ten self-help principles. *Social Policy*, 6–11.

Roizen, J. (1997). Epidemiological issues in alcohol-related violence. *Recent developments in alcoholism*, *13*, 7–40.

Salzinger, S., Feldman, R. S., Ng-Mak, D. S., Mojica, E., Stockhammer, T., & Rosario, M. (2002). Effects of partner violence and physical child abuse on child behavior: A study of abused and comparison children. *Journal of Family Violence*, *17*(1), 23–52.

Schumacher, J. A., Feldbau-Kohn, S., Slep, A. M. S., & Heyman, R. E. (2001). Risk factors for male to female partner physical abuse. *Aggression and Violent Behavior*, 6(2-3), 281–352.

Schumacher, J. A., Slep, A. M. S., & Heyman, R. E. (2001). Risk factors for child neglect. *Aggression and Violent Behavior*, *6*(2/3), 231–254.

Sedlak, A. J., & Broadhurst, D. D., (1996). Third national incidence study of child abuse and neglect. The National Clearinghouse for Alcohol and Drug Information. Retrieved May 1, 2002, from www.calib.com/nccanch/pubs/statinfo/nis3.cfm

Substance Abuse and Mental Health Services Administration [SAMHSA]. (1998). *Prevalence of substance abuse among racial and ethnic subgroups in the U.S., 1991–1993*. Rockville, MD: U.S. Department of Health and Human Services.

Substance Abuse and Mental Health Services Administration. (2002). Prevalence of substance abuse among racial and ethnic subgroups in the U.S. Retrieved May 1, 2002, from www.samhsa.gov/oas/NHSDA/Ethnic/ethn1007.htm

Taylor, W. K., Magnussen, L., & Amundson, M. J. (2001). The lived experience of battered women. *Violence Against Women*, *7*(5), 563–585.

Tjaden, P., & Thoennes, N. (1998). *Prevalence, incidence, and consequences of violence against women: Findings from the National Violence Against Women Survey*. Washington, DC: National Institute of Justice.

Untalan, F. F. (1991). Chamorros. In N. Mokuau (Ed.), *Handbook of social services for Asian and Pacific Islanders* (pp. 171–182). Westport, CT: Greenwood Press.

U.S. Census Bureau. (2000). Select social characteristics of the population by region and race. Racial Statistics Branch, Population Division. Retrieved May 1, 2002, from www.census.gov.

U.S. Department of Health and Human Services [DHHS]. (2001). *Child maltreatment 1999: Reports from the states to the national child abuse and neglect data system*. Washington, DC: U.S. Government Printing Office.

Whitney, S., & Hanipale, F. (1991). *Feeling strong: Themes in Samoan drinking and recovery*. Unpublished manuscript.

Wilcox, R., Smith, D., Moore, J., Hewitt, A., Allan, G., Walker, H., Ropata, M., Monu, L., & Featherstone, T. (1991). *Family decision making and family group conference*. Lower Hutt, New Zealand: Practitioners' Publishing.

Yoshihama, M. (2001). Immigrants-in-context framework: Understanding the interactive influence of socio-cultural contexts. *Evaluation and Program Planning, 24*(3), 307–318.

Zane, N., & Sasao, T. (1992). Research on drug abuse among Asian Pacific Americans. *Drugs and Society, 6*(3-4), 181–209.

Zane, N. W. S., Takeuchi, D. T., & Young, K. N. J. (1994). *Confronting critical health issues of Asian and Pacific Islander Americans*. Thousand Oaks, CA: Sage.

16

Family Violence, Child Welfare, and Substance Abuse in Southeast Asian Refugee and Immigrant Populations

GWAT-YONG LIE

Introduction

Since 1975, the United States has admitted about 1.25 million refugees from Southeast Asia (U.S. Department of State, 1999). Three distinct waves of migration have been identified, beginning with the first, which took place shortly after the fall of U.S.-supported governments in Vietnam, Laos, and Cambodia. Many of the refugees were people with wealth and power—high-ranking indigenous government officials and other members of the elite (Baker & North, 1984). An estimated 135,000 Vietnamese fled to the United States after the fall of Saigon. In Cambodia, an estimated 34,000 supporters of the old regime made their way to safety in Thailand; subsequently, many resettled in the United States.

In the late 1970s, war, persecution, and poverty in Southeast Asia triggered a second exodus by land and by sea (Ranard & Pfleger, 1993). However, unlike the first group, this wave included large numbers of rural people, many of whom had never attended school or been exposed to modern urban life; "[s]hifting at jet speed from familiar Southeast Asian surroundings to cities and suburbs across the United States, they frequently found themselves in linguistic and cross-cultural confusion" (p. 2). Many Vietnamese, Cambodians, Lao, and Hmong fled by foot or by boat to Thailand and neighboring countries, including the Philippines and Malaysia. After many years in the refugee camps, many were eventually resettled in the United States and France (Southeast Asian Action Resource Center, 2002).

In 1979 through the late 1980s, the composition of Southeast Asian refugees changed again, and two groups of people made up the majority of refugees from Southeast Asia: former political prisoners from Vietnam, and the Hmong, an ethnic minority group from Laos (Ranard & Pfleger, 1993). Most of the Hmong adults had little or no formal education and few vocational skills. According to the Center for Applied Linguistics, most of the Vietnamese were well-educated former military officers and their families (as cited in Ranard & Pfleger, 1993). Kinzie et al. (1990) noted that the educational level of the Cambodians who survived the Pol Pot years of 1975–1979 was low "because of the singling out of leaders, teachers, businessmen, Buddhist monks, and intellectuals for execution" (p. 914). On the other hand, the Laotians had a mix of educational and social backgrounds.

In its annual report to the U.S. Congress in 1999, the Office of Refugee Resettlement (ORR) noted that Southeast Asians were the largest refugee group among recent arrivals. Of the 1,638,000 refugees who arrived in the United States since 1983, about 39% (roughly 637,500) were from the Southeast Asian nations of Vietnam, Cambodia, and Laos (ORR, 2002a). From 1983 through 1999, Vietnamese made up 71% of refugee arrivals, while 18% were from Laos, and 11% from Cambodia.

The term "refugee" is assigned to someone with "a well-founded fear of persecution in their country of origin because of race, religion, nationality, membership in a particular social group or political opinion" (ORR, 2001, p. 1). Because of the life-threatening circumstances surrounding their flight from their home countries, many Southeast Asian refugees continue to reexperience and suffer from their war, escape, concentration camp, and prisoner-of-war experiences. Boehnlein and Kinzie (1996) also noted the extensiveness of the tragedy:

> Vietnamese saw family members killed, possessions confiscated, and villages destroyed. The Laotians, Mien and Hmong had significant irreversible damage done to their social structures and cultures. Cambodians experienced the brutal rule of Pol Pot from 1975 to 1979 when an estimated one million people died from disease, starvation, torture, and execution. No individual or family was spared, directly or indirectly, the trauma of this period. (p. 1)

Besides coping with loss and trauma, Southeast Asian refugees were not only having to adjust to a different physical environment, but also to respond to socioeconomic pressures to secure employment and meet financial obligations. In the process, the integrity of traditional gender roles was subverted. Husbands and fathers, used to being sole breadwinners, were supplanted by wives and daughters who were willing to accept menial and service-sector employment to supplement the family income. Able-bodied adult members of families were having to work more than one job in order to make ends meet. Anecdotal reports of wife abuse, child maltreatment, and substance abuse as coping responses to the stress, strain, and struggle began to surface. Few published studies that document such incidences are available, however.

Given the paucity of published research and findings on the intersection of child welfare, substance abuse, and family violence in Southeast Asian refugee and immigrant families, the purpose of this chapter is to draw on the limited published professional and academic literature to describe the sociocultural context forming the backdrop to the challenges that partner violence, substance abuse, and child welfare present to the Vietnamese, Cambodian, Laotians, and the Hmong; to discuss the social work practice, research, and policy implications that each of these communities faces with respect to those challenges; and to recommend future directions for social work practitioners and scholars.

Sociocultural Context

U.S. Census 2000 (U.S. Census Bureau, 2002) estimates show that among Southeast Asian refugee and immigrant populations, the largest group by national origin was the Vietnamese (1,122,528), followed by Cambodians (171,937), Hmong (169,428), and Laotians (168,707).

In terms of geographic distribution, the Southeast Asian Resource Action Center (2002) reported that the largest number of Vietnamese lived in California, Texas, and Washington, D.C.; Cambodians were concentrated in California, Massachusetts, and Pennsylvania; California, Minnesota, and Wisconsin had the highest Hmong populations; and Laotians were mostly found in California, Wisconsin, and Minnesota. For many, the current state of residence may not be the state to which they first migrated. Employment opportunities, the pull of an established ethnic community, more generous welfare benefits, better training opportunities, reunification with relatives, or a more congenial climate have resulted in secondary migration within the United States.

According to census data, in 1998 1.4 million (13%) Asians and Pacific Islanders, compared to 15.8 million (8%) non-Hispanic Whites, were poor.[1] In 2000, an estimated 25.5% of Vietnamese and 29.5% of "Other Asians"[2] were below the poverty level (Logan, 2001). When looking at employment patterns, ORR computes the employment-to-population ratio (EPR). In October 1999, the EPR for Vietnamese was 74.3%. In other words, 74.3% percent of all Vietnamese in the United States were employed, whereas for "Other Southeast Asians,"[3] it was 38.0% (ORR, 2002b). About equal proportions of Vietnamese males (74.0%) and females (74.7%) were employed. In contrast, more "Other Southeast Asian" males were employed (45.7%) than were females (29.8%) in the group. The labor force participation rate[4] for "Other Southeast Asians" in general was 41.5%; for males, 51.4%; and for females, 31.9%.

Every Vietnamese refugee who wanted to work was gainfully employed (ORR, 2002b). However, for "Other Southeast Asians" the unemployment rate, at 8.3%, was almost three times that for all refugees. The unemployment rate was higher for males (10.8%) than for females (4.5%). Interestingly, the unemployment rate for all refugees was 3.1% in 1999, with a higher unemployment rate for females (3.4%) than for males (2.9%).

Refugees aged 16 years and over were interviewed and asked why they were not looking for employment. Some of the reasons given included attending school (median age of respondents was 18); age (median age of respondents was 70 years); poor health or disability (median age, 57 years); and a combination of limited English and other factors, usually poor health and age (ORR, 2002b).

Upon resettlement in their adopted country, the first and most basic challenge facing refugees is achieving self-sufficiency, especially financial security. Weinstein-Shr and Henkin (1991) noted the plight of Southeast Asian refugee and immigrant families:

> By coming into exile, refugee families lose land, possessions or financial comfort accumulated over generations in their native countries. It is unlikely that skilled professionals will be able to find equivalent jobs in their new settings. Farmers and other unskilled migrants are even less prepared to find and keep work that provides adequate resources for maintaining their families. (p. 355)

Referencing the work of Gozdziak (1988), they further noted that on minimum-wage or low-wage earnings, many gravitated to the inner city, where housing was inexpensive and inadequate and crime rates high. Other factors affecting employment prospects include occupational and educational skills, family size and composition (e.g., number of dependents to support), job opportunities, and resources available in the communities where they reside (ORR, 2002b)

In 1997, 1,327 Southeast Asian families (90% of whom were believed to be Hmong) received cash assistance (Moore & Selkowe, 1999). By December 1998, only 300 Southeast Asian families were receiving public assistance. While these figures document "a drastic drop in the number of Hmong receiving public assistance . . . it is not clear that Hmong heads of household are leaving W-2 [Wisconsin Works, the state's welfare-to-work program] with the experience and skills needed for unsubsidized employment"

(Moore & Selkowe, 1999, p. 3). By comparison, in California 1.9 million people in 1998 received assistance from CalWORKs, about 12% of whom were Asians (Jang & Penserga, 1999). In 1996, the highest number of Asian and Pacific Islander recipients were Southeast Asian: Vietnamese (126,597), Laotian (76,758), and Cambodian (49,091) (Jang & Penserga, 1999).

Because of the horrors encountered and the trauma suffered in their homeland and en route to the United States, refugees also faced the challenge of attaining physical and mental health. Frye (1995, p. 274) noted, "The effects of war on the agricultural and food security systems of Southeast Asia and traumatic injuries resulted in large numbers of malnourished, disabled and physically ill refugees." Kinzie et al. (1990) documented the high rate of post-traumatic stress disorder (PTSD) among Southeast Asian refugees. In 1996, Boehnlein and Kinzie noted that the most common diagnoses since 1978 for the more than 1,000 Southeast Asian refugees over 17 years old were major depression and PTSD.

A third set of challenges that the refugees had to overcome was language and literacy (Weinstein-Shr & Henkin, 1991). Frye (1995) noted that "minimal cultural and language transition" (p. 271) were provided before resettlement. The refugees' lack of English-language skills severely limited employment opportunities and impeded their sociocultural adaptation to life in an urban industrial environment. Nonetheless, Southeast Asian refugees and immigrants "have been enormously resourceful in drawing on family, clan, and community, even when these have had to be reconstructed in the face of death and decimation" to survive in their new surroundings (Weinstein-Shr and Henkin, 1991, p. 358). Mutual assistance among families of similar circumstance and background has resulted in the pooling and sharing of scarce resources such as money and child care.

Further, embedded in Southeast Asian cultures are lifelines for survival. Frye (1995, p. 270) noted that despite their "heterogeneity and culturally differentiated patterns and customs," two dominant cultural themes—kinship solidarity and equilibrium—have been instrumental in assisting Vietnamese, Cambodian, Laotian, and Hmong populations to adjust and adapt to their newfound life situation.

These cultural themes in essence reflect the cultural strengths of Southeast Asian refugee and immigrant populations. They emerged in the course of the comprehensive review that Frye (1995) completed when working on health promotion strategies for Southeast Asian refugee populations. Southeast Asian refugee and immigrant families are family-centered, and filial piety and respect for the elders are assiduously observed. Her work provides a summary of family patterns among the Vietnamese, Cambodian, and Hmong refugee and immigrant communities in the United States.

The concept of "equilibrium" refers to "the search for integrity through balance" (Frye, 1995, p. 270). This search extends to all areas of life, including "balance in emotions, relationships, work and relaxation patterns, food, intake and spiritual life" (p. 270). Frye noted that within the Vietnamese and Cambodian cultures, equilibrium is framed by both Buddhist tenets and belief in the spirit world:

> Buddhism advocates merit-making actions such as feeding the monks or being kind to children and elders as ways to balance the scales for sinful transgressions in this life or past lives. This balance is further promoted through generosity and nonconfrontational behavior in interpersonal relationships. (p. 270)

In the Hmong community, "equilibrium" is framed by "the concept of a world populated with spirits and belief in the need for balance in the natural world" (Frye, 1995, p. 271). Frye further noted that "the individual is believed to possess many souls in constant danger of being separated from the body" (p. 271). Equilibrium is restored by reuniting the soul with the physical body through "balancing behaviors in food intake, activity, and nonconfrontational relations" (p. 271). Thus, from a Southeast Asian perspective, "suffering" represents "an interruption in the idyllic state of equilibrium" and the "lack of equilibrium in one realm of being results in disharmony for the entire being" (p. 271). Within such a worldview then, family violence, child welfare struggles, and substance abuse issues are states of imbalance and, in turn, situations of suffering.

No systematic study of the prevalence or incidence of family violence, child welfare issues, or substance abuse patterns in Southeast Asian refugee and immigrant communities has been done at either the national or local level. Much of the information that is available is based on anecdotal evidence or on the findings of studies that have limited generalizability. The few studies that have been conducted generally focus on one particular group and tend to draw on nonrandomly selected, small samples.

Frye (1995) noted, "domestic violence has not been widely discussed in the literature about the Southeast Asian refugee populations, but there is anecdotal evidence that it is common" (p. 275). Chow, Bester, and Shinn (2001) noted that, "many AsianWORKs participants face multiple family problems [and are involved with], a variety of services, such as mental health, substance abuse, domestic violence counseling, parenting skills training and child care advocacy" (p. 119). Bromley and Olsen (1994), in the course of conducting an evaluation of a project providing early intervention services to Southeast Asian children, likewise noted that "a few of the families experienced such intense family problems (for example, alcoholism, gambling, domestic violence, mental illness and depression) that the family's and staff's energies continued to be absorbed by concrete problem resolution" (p. 254). Segal's (2000a) study, based on a sample of 28 Vietnamese respondents living in the St Louis metropolitan area, reported that "few indicated any use of violence against either children or spouses. Interestingly, some did indicate filial violence, an occurrence that indicates fissures in the traditional hierarchical structure of authority" (p. 531).

Bui and Morash (1999) interviewed a total of 20 Vietnamese women, 10 of whom were known to be in a physically abusive relationship, and an equivalent number from a similar social background but who were not known to be battered. Lie (2000) completed a community needs assessment survey of a Hmong community residing in a mid-size midwestern city. Telephone interviews with 269 Hmong individuals aged 18 years and older were completed; however, not all respondents were willing to answer questions on conflict resolution tactics that they themselves or their spouses used (Straus, 1979, 1990). Because domestic violence is a very sensitive and private/personal issue in the Hmong community, the few reports of its occurrence significantly underrepresent its true incidence and prevalence.

The Conflict Tactics Scale (CTS) (Straus, 1979, 1990) was used to attempt to gauge the extent of the problem in the target sample of Hmong participants. The response rate for this section of the interview ranged from 74.3% (200 respondents) to 85.5% (230 respondents). Lie (2000) found evidence of physical abuse among the few who were willing to admit either to having been the target of such abuse or having themselves perpetrated the abuse in the past year. Responses to the Violence Sub-Scale ranged from refusals to respond to all items (about 25%) and "never" (about two-thirds of participants), to once or more times in the past year (about 10%).

With regard to substance abuse, according to O'Hare and Tran (1998), "preliminary evidence suggests that Southeast Asian immigrants, refugees and their children in the U.S. are at increased risk for abusing alcohol and other drugs" (pp. 69–70) They cite findings from the 1992 National Health Interview Survey (NHIS): 24.4% of Asian American youth (12–21 years of age) consumed alcohol once within the past 30 days, 15% of Asian American youth used marijuana, and 3.7% tried cocaine at least once in their life (National Center for Health Statistics, 1995). They also draw attention to the results of a study by D'Avanzo, Frye, and Froman (1994): almost 7% of the 120 Cambodian women interviewed reported having a family member with a drinking problem, and 17% of the women admitted to abusing prescription drugs. D'Avanzo and Barab (2000) completed a study of 155 Cambodian women residing in France and the United States and found that 23% of the women in the United States (compared to 37% of the women in France) drank alcohol in the first trimester of their pregnancy. During the second and third trimesters, 18% of the U.S. women (compared to 5% of the French sample) continued drinking. Based on a review of several studies between 1987 and 1992, Amodeo, Robb, Peou, and Tran (1997) concluded that alcohol and other drug abuse is "a significant problem among Southeast Asians resettled in the United States" (p. 64).

Aggregated data on Asian and Pacific Islander (API) adolescents reported by the Office of Applied Studies, Substance Abuse and Mental Health Services Administration ([SAMHSA], 2002) showed that

- the number of API adolescent admissions to publicly funded substance abuse treatment facilities increased by 52% between 1994 and 1999;
- about three-quarters of API adolescent admissions were first-treatment episodes; and
- API adolescents were more likely to enter treatment through self-referrals, individual referrals, or school referrals than through the total youth treatment population.

Kuramoto (1997), in his review of the literature, found tobacco and alcohol to be the most prevalent substances used by Chinese populations; other drugs were being used but not at the prevalence rates registered for tobacco and alcohol, which in 1997 were 19.6% (National Center for Chronic Disease Prevention & Health Promotion, 1998). His findings with respect to commonly used substances among specific ethnic groups include:

- Vietnamese: tobacco, marijuana, and cocaine
- Cambodians: alcohol, tobacco, crack cocaine, and methamphetamines
- Laotians: alcohol, tobacco, and marijuana
- Hmong: alcohol, tobacco, and opiates

Participants in the survey by Lie (2000) were responsive to questions about alcohol or tobacco use; very few admitted to the use of illicit substances. Almost 40% imbibed, with beer and wine being the more popular type of alcoholic beverage (versus hard liquor, e.g., whiskey, brandy). About 13.4% used tobacco, four participants reported using pot/marijuana, one participant used opium, and five participants reported using "other substances." The survey did not investigate level, frequency, or consequences of substance use.

Child welfare issues among Southeast Asian refugee and immigrant populations are not well documented. The few publications available tend to focus on the psycho-emotional plight of child abuse, unaccompanied minors, school dropouts, and gangs. Segal (2000b) pointed to factors that placed Southeast Asian refugees and immigrants at risk for spousal and child abuse. She referred to "a constellation of poverty, isolation, issues of acculturation, identity, and poor language proficiency" that exacerbated the stress and distress already being experienced and suggested that it "may have led to violence against spouses and children" (p. 160). In her investigation of child abuse among Vietnamese refugees, she found

About half of the parents indicated that they had used "acceptable" forms of corporal punishment, such as hitting the child on the bottom with a bare hand, but none indicated having engaged in any of the "abusive" forms of violence, such as hitting repeatedly. Nonagressive forms of violence, such as shouting or calling the children names, were admitted (p. 179).

She concluded that "common methods of identifying the occurrence of child abuse may not be valid in its assessment among populations that may fear repercussions of admitting to the use of corporal punishment to discipline their children" (p. 159).

Of the three issues, domestic violence, substance abuse, and child maltreatment, child maltreatment presented as the most agonizing to the sample interviewed by Lie (2000). About 40% of participants had dealt with either law enforcement or child welfare authorities in the preceding year. About a quarter of participants said they knew little to nothing about laws regarding the maltreatment of children. Anguished comments such as, "I don't understand my children any more," "I try hard to be a good parent, but they say I am not," and "My children are too Americanized," point to the fallout from differential acculturation experiences and the increasing estrangement of Hmong children from their parents and elders.

Goldberg (1999) noted that even though it has been more than 24 years since Cambodian refugees fled their homeland and resettled in the United States, the legacy of the war and the passage to their adopted home continues to haunt them and their children. She found published support for the connection between school adjustment problems among Cambodian youth and factors such as lack of parental experience with literacy or education, language learning difficulties, and emotional problems related to family adjustment issues. Her research study at a high school revealed an 11.4% chronic truancy rate for Cambodian students, a rate that is more than five times the rate for the school as a whole. Because chronic truancy usually precedes dropping out of school, Goldberg was motivated to investigate factors associated with truancy and dropouts so that corrective action could be taken.

Knox (1996) contended that refugee parents "often find that they are unable to meet their children's needs within American society" (p. 554). Based on an extensive literature review, she listed factors that have been implicated in refugee parents' alleged compromised ability to care of the children. Examples of contributing factors include lack of employment skills and ability to find stable employment; poor English-language skills and lack of formal education; and the inability to access needed social, educational, and medical resources. She expressed concern about the impact that such critical constraints would have on child development:

> [S]ome children may experience health problems, may be at risk for developmental
> delays, and may be unprepared to enter the school system. These children, as a result of

inadequate attention and supervision, traditional healing practices such as coining and cupping, and physical discipline practices, are also at risk for neglect and abuse, as defined by American standards. (p. 555)

She also directed attention to the magnitude and urgency of the problem, noting that since an estimated 40% to 60% of Southeast Asian refugees in the United States are children under 18 years of age, early intervention to prevent long-term problems was definitely indicated (Knox, 1996).

A growing concern in many Southeast Asian Refugee and immigrant communities is street gangs. A common complaint among Asian youth is the unavailability of parents for support or consultation (Lee, 1996; Long, Ricard, & Ricard, 1997). In many families, parents may not be physically around because of having to work long hours and several jobs in order to make ends meet. Some youth feel that their parents are not psychologically or emotionally accessible, because they are still dealing with the aftermath of the flight from their homelands. Still other youth feel alienated from their parents socially and culturally and find support and solace in the company of other Southeast Asian or neighborhood youth.

Issues and Problems

Is an appreciation of the feminist, social change, and advocacy-based roots of the violence against women movement necessary in order to effectively address the sexism, racism, and classism systems deeply embedded in interventions, policies, research, and culturally competent models of practice? Kanuha (2001) insists that it is; she contends that, otherwise, social workers are at risk of decontextualizing problems, with the end result being neglecting to critically examine the role of structural conditions, such as gender, race, and class and, thus, missing opportunities for structural change. Her concern is that in missing opportunities for advocacy and social change, women and children stand at risk of being revictimized.

Kanuha's concerns are valid and well founded. However, as E. N. Chow (1987) has pointed out, it is important also to understand the social contexts in which the gender consciousness of Asian American women has developed. The following explanation, even though it may no longer hold true for *all* Asian American women, may still be relevant to many, especially recent immigrant and refugee women:

Domination by men is a commonly shared oppression for Asian American women. These women have been socialized to accept their devaluation, restricted roles for women, psychological reinforcement of gender stereotypes, and a subordinate position within Asian American communities as well as in the society at large. (p. 286)

There again, those who have dared to push the envelope paid a price not many are willing to pay:

> Asian American women are criticized for the possible consequences of their protests: weakening of the male ego, dilution of effort and resources in Asian American communities, destruction of working relationships between Asian men and women, setbacks for the Asian American cause, cooptation into the larger society, and eventual loss of ethnic identity for Asian Americans as a whole. In short, affiliation with the feminist movement is perceived as a threat to solidarity within their community. (p. 288)

In radical feminist analysis, the personal is political. Individual women's experiences of injustice and the miseries that women think of as personal problems are actually political issues, "grounded in sexist power imbalances" (Saulnier, 1996, p. 32). Saulnier (1996) explains further that radical feminists posit that separating public from private issues masks the reality of male power and domination. On the other hand, central to the cultural competence framework is the concept of informed choice. Individuals and families make choices based on myriad factors, including values, beliefs, customs. and traditions.

For many the personal and the political may never intersect because past experiences have impressed on them to keep the two separate in order to survive. For many Southeast Asian refugee and immigrant women, their experiences with repressive and brutal government regimes have left an indelible impression: politics is not for the common man or woman. They have learned to shun any action or activity that makes them visible and, thus, vulnerable to becoming targets of political action. On the other hand, they should not be excluded from educational and consciousness-raising opportunities aimed at promoting the welfare and well-being of women and children through social change and community action.

The following case example describes an intervention that met the individual's needs, and at the same time served as instigator for community education and, one hopes, future social and structural change efforts. To the social worker, the intent was to help the woman arrive at a decision that would suit her personal circumstances, honoring her cultural values, beliefs, and practices. At the same time if the opportunity arose, the worker would attempt to encourage her to introduce change in the community at a level and a pace with which she would be comfortable. And if the woman felt otherwise, the worker would respect the decision not to do anything beyond the personal. To the woman involved, her motivation was simple: to stop women from suffering the same fate. It was also important for her that this altruistic act was actualized in ways so that those who needed to hear the message would indeed hear it.

> A Hmong woman presents herself at a primary health care facility with bruises that clearly indicate that she had been traumatized. In response to queries, she hesitantly

admits to having been battered by her spouse. Further questioning reveals that the beatings are a regular occurrence. She cannot remember when they started, but she is certain that it has been going on even before the birth of their oldest child who is now nine years old.

Another thing that she is sure of is that the beatings have resulted in more visible and increasingly severe injuries. She refuses to go to a shelter. She fears that staying away will only fuel her spouse's unfounded suspicions and allegations. Besides, what will her relatives and friends think? Who will take care of her children when they return from school and her husband is away at work? Her neighbor said that she had heard of another person in the neighborhood whose children were taken away by the government when she had left them on their own to go to the corner store.

Her needs are simple: she wants the beatings and verbal abuse to stop. Leaving her spouse is not an option. She would be ostracized not only by her family but by the whole community. She would much rather put up with the beatings than risk losing the support of her family, friends, and the Hmong community. Also, she says, if only the clan leader would talk to her spouse and let him know that the drinking only makes him mean and "bad" to his wife and the children.

She is willing to come in and talk to the social worker at the primary care facility. Her spouse works a second shift, and she can come in as soon as he leaves for the factory. She wants to learn how to make her spouse happy so that he does not beat so frequently and for the most trivial of reasons. She wants to learn how to protect the children so that they do not suffer when he is angry at her.

She is not fluent in English, and she refuses the services of an interpreter. The local Hmong community is small, and she is afraid the interpreter might be someone who knows her and her family, and she is anxious to avoid causing her spouse and their respective families any embarrassment.

The social worker worked on self-protective strategies with her and together they designed a safety plan that included her three children. At the same time, as trust developed, the social worker asked if she knew of other women in the same predicament. She did. While it was uncomfortable for her to talk about herself, she seemed less inhibited in discussing what could be done to help the other women. She wanted to know what non-Hmong women who were beaten did: what did their families do to help them? Why do Americans want wives to leave their husbands when they are beaten? What good can be gained from breaking up the family?

She thought that little could be done to stop beatings by men of her generation and older. However, she had great hopes that much could done with adolescent males and younger male children. If Hmong elders, clan leaders, and mothers could reach these kids and impress on them the importance of dealing with each other and the women and girls in their lives in nonviolent ways, then significant gains would have been made, in her estimation. If the local Hmong association would sponsor youth talk sessions for both boys and girls, these sessions could be geared toward addressing the importance of family and how to treat one another with respect and integrity.

As mentioned previously, no nationally representative studies of domestic violence in the Asian and Pacific Islander or Southeast Asian communities have been conducted. Instead, much of what is known has been informed by case histories, clinical examples, anecdotal reports, and newspaper accounts (West, 1998). The myth that domestic violence does not exist in the Asian community is pervasive (Masaki & Wong, 1997). Ho (1990) noted that while the reported frequency of domestic violence in Asian American communities may be low, it is unclear if these statistics are reflective of an actual lower rate of domestic violence or low use rates of public assistance; inadequate health, behavioral health, and mental health services available to Asian Americans; or other factors. Masaki and Wong (1997) advocate a task-oriented approach: education about domestic violence; the dynamics of relationships; the relationships between physical and emotional health, and options and resources; explaining and teaching the language of feelings; and building a network of supports. As with Ho (1990), Masaki and Wong emphasize the importance of community intervention to make domestic violence unacceptable.

Child welfare and well-being presentations should not be looked upon as symptomatic of poor parenting or *bad* children. Instead, they point to the dynamics of being a recent immigrant/refugee and the difficult process of adjusting to a context of different value and belief systems. The process of adjustment includes intrafamily struggles around whether the family's existing set of sociocultural norms and rules continue to be relevant, and whether new or modified coping mechanisms and survival skills are called for. They also point to the fact that different members of the family, depending on the nature and quality of their contacts with the environment, acculturate at different rates, with children being the most quickly acculturated. Most important, they point to the need for parents and children alike to learn to reach out and talk to each other. While this form of parent-child interaction may not be customary, it may be an option well worth trying, particularly for those who are open and receptive to doing so.

The issue of underuse of health, behavioral health, and/or social services by APIs has been variously documented (e.g., Mokuau & Fong, 1994; Ja & Yuen, 1997; Kitano, 1969; Kitano & Maki, 1996; Min, 1995; Snowden & Cheung, 1990; Sue & McKinney, 1975). The salience of this issue lies in its connection to funding allocations (or their lack) for programs and services. Because funding allocations for programs and services are based on use, and because APIs underuse programs and services in general, the needs of APIs have been consistently underestimated (Min, 1995). Quoting Crystal (1989), Min strives to underscore the importance of distinguishing between need and use:

Underutilization is an important issue for the Asian American community because it is still used by governmental agencies to buttress the belief Asian Americans have low rates of mental disturbance. The criterion of use rather than need determines funding targets and program policy. What must be recognized is the distinction between needs and demand: Low demand as reflected in low utilization should not be misconstrued as an absence of need. (1995, p. 408)

By the same token, it is important not to throw the baby out with the bath water. Within subcommunities where there is an indigenously identified need for programs and services, it becomes important to research and understand the dynamics that have contributed to the phenomenon of why, despite the demonstrated need, use rates are low. Miranda and Kitano (1976) found that the key reasons for the underuse of services include language and cultural barriers (Ja & Yuen, 1997; Min, 1995), specifically, cultural values inhibiting self-referral (Sue & Sue, 1999); financial barriers, principally the lack of health insurance coverage and access (Brown, Ojeda, Wyn, & Levan, 2000); specialization; referrals; location; lack of Asian American professionals at all levels of services; and the discontinuity between clients and the service delivery system (as cited in Kitano & Maki, 1996). With immigrant and refugee subgroups, a reason for not using formal helping resources may simply be attributable to the lack of information on what is available and how to access these resources.

Practice, Research, and Policy Recommendations

Members of Southeast Asian refugee and immigrant communities must be prepared to confront the incidence and prevalence of family violence, child maltreatment, and substance abuse by acknowledging the existence of these issues in their respective communities. With their involvement and input, well-designed, culturally responsive, and well-funded research must become a priority. With well-substantiated information, funding for linguistically accessible and culturally appropriate programs and services must be secured and offered.

A community as large, diverse, and dynamic as the Southeast Asian populations "cannot stay on the edge of obscurity, frustrated by images that have rendered us invisible and voiceless" (Zia, 2000, p. 258). What does it take for Southeast Asians to be at *the* table? It is impossible to discuss the plight and predicaments of Southeast Asians with respect to substance abuse and family violence without also discussing the need for social and political activism. Certainly, more research is definitely indicated, including not only cross-sectional studies but longitudinal projects that examine changes, if any, over time as well.

Southeast Asians should ideally be studied and represented by API scholars and researchers to avoid "the continued marginalization of the 'Other' as object rather than subject" (Takaki, 1994, p. 296). Data collection should be disaggregated so that subgroup-specific information is available. At the same time, it is important to be mindful that

> The very search for the voices of peoples has sometimes reinforced this fragmentation by focusing on specific texts of individuals, which are examined in isolation from larger social and economic contexts. (p. 299)

While "bean-counting" research methods help to substantiate requests for funding and resource allocations, qualitative studies should also be conducted to help understand and appreciate subjective experiences and individual perspectives within the constraints of everyday life and its challenges. In addition, evaluation of culturally competent practice models must be carried out to ascertain if investments of precious resources in treatment/intervention efforts result in improvements in the welfare and well-being of all APIs over the long term and alleviation of pain and suffering in the interim. If not, a mechanism should be in place that provides a comprehensive review with provisions for modifications or discontinuation. At the same time, attention and the necessary resources need to be directed toward prevention initiatives.

Jang and Penserga (1999) summarized the plight of Southeast Asian women and families who were trying to transition from welfare and poverty:

> Much of current welfare policy underestimates the income necessary to truly be self sufficient. Many Asian and Pacific Islander women are concentrated in low-wage service, domestic, manufacturing and clerical work sectors that lack health and other benefits. Finding work means losing health benefits. (p. 6)

The long-term picture is not exactly promising either, because "without job-training programs that incorporate the needs of the limited English speaking populations, many Asian and Pacific Islander women will continue to seek minimum-wage (or less) service industry jobs which lack health benefits" (Jang & Penserga, 1999, p. 7). Unless this gap is addressed, Jang and Penserga issued a warning that is relevant to Southeast Asian welfare-to-work participants all over the United States:

> At a federal minimum-wage of $5.75/hour, women will have little choice but to undertake two or three jobs to stay off welfare. This leaves little time for much else, like learning English, continuing education, or spending time with children. (p. 6)

The connection between poverty and violence was researched by Lyon (1998, p. 1). The outcome of her comprehensive review was documented evidence for high rates of domestic violence among welfare recipients: "[W]ell over half of the women receiving AFDC [Aid to Families with Dependent Children] reported that they had experienced physical abuse" by an intimate male partner at some point in their lives. The proportion of those who had experienced more recent violence from their male partners ranged from 19.5% to 32%. Because "economic independence and employment are central considerations in women's safety options," Lyon (1998, p. 2) joined the call for economic self-sufficiency as an added protective factor from vulnerabilities, such as domestic violence. In addition, she noted:

> States can play a critical role in identifying the prevalence of domestic violence in their caseloads, in tracking and evaluating the granting of waivers or exceptions to TANF [Temporary Assistance to Needy Families] and child support enforcement requirements, and in documenting the success and difficulties of battered women in attaining employment. (p. 6)

Asserting that "racial, sexual, class, age and other differences cannot adequately be conceptualized or practiced through a single framework of cultural competency that emphasizes race and ethnicity as the sole or most important factor in analyzing or addressing social problems," Kanuha (2001) challenged scholars and practitioners to "expand upon the concepts, theoretical frameworks, and operationalizations of 'culturally competent practice'" (p. 13). She suggested the incorporation of Crenshaw's (1994) notion of *intersectionality*—applying multiple lenses of class, gender, sexuality, age, and other salient factors, to understand APIs, and, by implication, Southeast Asian refugee and immigrant families. Her call for multiple-lens analyses or intersectionality is timely and must be heeded. However, a clarification is in order. The cultural competence perspective is *not* dedicated to race and ethnicity as the sole or most important factor. If this is the emphasis that those using the framework have given, the shortcoming is not of the framework, but of the persons applying the framework. For the cultural competence framework to be truly *culturally competent*, the framework cannot adopt a linear approach to the analysis of complex issues.

According to Lum (2000), *culture* "reflects the lifestyle practices of particular groups of people who are influenced by a learned pattern of values, beliefs, and behavioral attitudes" (p. 89). This application of culture allows for the consideration of the plethora of factors, in addition to race and ethnicity, that have an impact on lifestyle practices, including sexuality, age, disabilities, and socioeconomic status. Thus, the challenge is indeed to expand the operationalization of a culturally competent framework to include race, sexual, class, age, and other factors as these intersect with one another and others to more accurately portray the complexities of the human conditions.

At the direct service level, outreach services, including community education initiatives aimed at educating members about laws, penalties, options, and resources available, and how to access services, are critical components in the service delivery continuum. Reframing substance abuse and family violence as a family well-being issue, or more specifically, as a health (versus mental health or behavioral health) issue would, one hopes, remove the stigma associated with both and encourage help seeking and use of social and mental health services. Social workers and other service providers should be challenged to adopt a strengths-based (e.g., Cowger, 1994; De Jong & Miller, 1995; Saleeby, 1995) or an empowerment approach (e.g., Gutierrez & Lewis, 1999) to assessment and intervention, and to see themselves as client advocates. Needless to say, programs and services need to be located in the neighborhood and staffed with, preferably, native-language speakers. If native-language speakers are not available, quick access to professional interpreters must be in place. Models of intervention and prevention should be monitored and evaluated and revised where necessary, so that these models continue to be responsive to the needs of those served.

Beeman, Hagemeister, and Edleson (2001); Edleson (1999); Kantor & Jasinski (1998); and Wolak and Finkelhor (1998) have documented multiple presentations of abuse in violent families: spousal abuse, substance abuse, and child maltreatment. In response, Beeman et al. (2001) offered the following recommendations: "single issue" assessments must be replaced by a comprehensive and holistic assessment of multiple types of family violence by first responders, such as law enforcement and child protection professionals; implement data sharing across systems that work with families experiencing family violence; use the perpetrator's name to record and track cases instead of the custodial parent's, typically the mother; and recommend careful and knowledgeable consideration of risk and protective factors by child protection professionals so that appropriate and effective safety measures can be implemented. Further, the comprehensive assessment must take into account the sociocultural context of family functioning as well as attend to the impact of all the -isms, such as sexism, ageism, and classism. It is also imperative when working with Southeast Asian families to have the professional services of an interpreter and the assurance that all service linkages would be linguistically accessible and culturally appropriate.

Southeast Asian mothers who admit to being abused and to having abused children are afraid to be accused of failure to protect and to face the prospect of having their children taken from their custody. Their lack of knowledge of the workings of the child welfare system and their experience of the system and its staff as being capricious and whimsical have only served to reinforce their silence. For this reason, especially, it is critical that all professionals involved in the child welfare system be educated about the dynamics of abuse, the primal need to self-protect, and the erosion of self-efficacy, and to be willing to serve as advocates for battered women saddled with a failure-to-protect allegation.

Future Directions

Researchers, practitioners, policy makers, and community representatives need opportunities for dialogue, to plan, and to strategize. The need for advocacy and social change efforts at the community and societal levels cannot be emphasized enough. The very institutions and systems that perpetuate oppression and preserve the vulnerabilities of Southeast Asians must be challenged and changed. This can only take place when Southeast Asians are psychologically, emotionally, socially, and economically ready. This makes social, economic, and political investment in and the mentoring of the next generation of Southeast Asians, born and bred in the United States but very distinctly Asian by character and identity, crucial. But they should not stand alone. All Asians must coalesce as a cohesive plurality with a mission. Helen Zia's (2000) optimism is infectious: she believes that the social welfare agenda will be defined by the next generation, which will not be reluctant to immerse itself in unglamourous but compelling causes. This generation will not be seduced by capitalism, nor lured away from the communities that raised them. According to Zia:

> Many will take their energies back into the community. They might be among the young Asian Americans working on environmental justice with Laotian teenage girls in the Asian Pacific Environmental Network who live next door to chemical refineries in Richmond, California; leading street actions against posh boutiques and athletic shoe stores, in conjunction with groups such as Asian Immigrant Women Advocates, to expose designers, manufacturers, and retailers who rely on sweatshop labor; getting trained as organizers by unions or groups like the Center for Third World Organizing; becoming safer-sex educators for HIV/AIDS programs; creating innovative programs for such women's groups as the Asian Women's Shelter in San Francisco to teach survivors of domestic violence; and becoming involved in any number of grass-roots community efforts. (p. 309)

Notes

1. The poverty level in 1999 was $8,501 for a single individual or $17,029 for a family of four (U.S. Census Bureau, 2002). In 1995 dollars, the poverty level was $15,455 per annum for a four-person household (Baugher & Lamison-White, 1996).
2. Excluding Chinese, Filipinos, Japanese, Asian Indians, and Koreans.
3. Including Cambodians, Laotians. and Hmong.
4. Includes individuals looking for work as well as those currently employed.

References

Amodeo, M., Robb, N., Peou, S., & Tran, H. (1997). Alcohol and other drug problems among Southeast Asians: Patterns of use and approaches to assessment and intervention. *Alcoholism Treatment Quarterly*, *15*(3), 63–77.

Baker, R. P., & North, D. S. (1984). *The 1975 refugees: Their first five years in America.* Washington, DC: New Transcentury Foundation.

Baugher, E., & Lamison-White, L. (1996). *Poverty in the United States: 1995.* Washington, DC: U.S. Government Printing Office.

Beeman, S. K., Hagemeister, A. K., & Edleson, J. L. (2001). Case assessment and service receipt in families experiencing both child maltreatment and women battering. *Journal of Interpersonal Violence*, *16*(5), 437–458.

Boehnlein, J. K., & Kinzie, J. D. (1996). Psychiatric treatment of Southeast Asian refugees [Electronic version]. *National Center for PTSD Clinical Quarterly*, *6*(1), 1–6. Retrieved July 24, 2002, from http://www.ncptsd.va.gov/publications/cq/v6/n1/boehnlei.html?printable=yes

Bromley, M. A., & Olsen, L. (1994). Early intervention services for Southeast Asian children. *Social Work in Education*, *16*, 251–256.

Brown, E. R., Ojeda, V. D., Wyn, R., & Levan, R. (2000). *Racial and ethnic disparities in access to health insurance and health care.* Los Angeles: University of California, Los Angeles Center for Health Policy Research and the Kaiser Family Foundation.

Bui, H. N., & Morash, M. (1999). Domestic violence in the Vietnamese immigrant community: An exploratory study. *Violence Against Women*, *5*(7), 769–795.

Chow, E. N. (1987). The development of feminist consciousness among Asian American women. *Gender & Society*, *1*(3), 284–299.

Chow, J., Bester, N., & Shinn, A. (2001). AsianWORKs: A TANF Program for Southeast Asian Americans in Oakland, California. *Journal of Community Practice*, *9*(3), 111–124.

Cowger, C. D. (1994). Assessing client strengths: Clinical assessment for client empowerment. *Social Work*, *39*(3), 262–269.

Crenshaw, K. (1994). Mapping the margins: Intersectionality, identity politics & violence against women of color. In M. A. Fineman & R. Mytiuk (Eds.), *The public nature of private violence: The discovery of domestic abuse* (pp. 93–118). New York: Routledge.

Crystal, D. (1989) Asian Americans and the myth of the model minority. *Social Casework: Journal of Contemporary Social Work*, *70*(7), 405–413.

D'Avanzo, C. E., & Barab, S. A. (2000). Drinking during pregnancy: Practices of Cambodian refuges in France and the United States. *Health Care for Women International*, *21*, 319–334.

D'Avanzo, C. E., Frye, B., & Froman, R. (1994). Culture, stress and substance use in Cambodian refugee women. *Journal of Studies on Alcohol, 55*, 420–426.

De Jong, P., & Miller, S. D. (1995). How to interview for client strengths. *Social Work, 40*(6), 729–736.

Edleson, J. L. (1999). The overlap between child maltreatment and woman abuse. VAWnet Applied Research Forum. Retrieved June 30, 2001, from http://www.vawnet.org/DomesticViolence/ VAWnet/AR_overlap.pdf

Frye, B. A. (1995). Use of cultural themes in promoting health among Southeast Asian refugees. *Health Promotion, 9*(4), 269–280.

Goldberg, M. E. (1999). Truancy and dropout among Cambodian students: Results from a comprehensive high school. *Social Work in Education, 21*(1), 49–63.

Gozdziak, E. (1988). *Older refugees in the United States: From dignity to despair.* Washington, DC: Refugee Policy Group.

Gutierrez, L. M., & Lewis, Z. A. (1999). *Empowering women of color.* New York: Columbia University Press.

Ho, C. K. (1990). An analysis of domestic violence in Asian American communities: A multicultural approach to counseling. *Women and Therapy, 9*(1), 129–150.

Ja, D., & Yuen, F. K. (1997). Substance abuse treatment among Asian Americans. In E. Lee (Ed.), *Working with Asian Americans: A guide for clinicians* (pp. 295–308). New York: Guilford Press.

Jang, D., & Penserga, L. (1999, June). *Beyond the safety net: The effect of welfare reform on self-sufficiency of Asian and Pacific Islander women in California.* A policy brief by the Asian and Pacific Islander American Health Forum. Retrieved July 24, 2002, from http://www.apiahf.org/publications/calworks99.html

Kantor, G. K., & Jasinski, J. L. (1998). Dynamics and risk factors in partner violence. In J. L. Jasinski & L. M. Williams (Eds.), *Partner violence: A comprehensive review of 20 years of research* (pp. 1–43). Thousand Oaks, CA. Sage.

Kanuha, V. K. (2001, February 9–10). Substance abuse, domestic violence, and Asians and Pacific Islanders: Problematizing the intersections of culturally competent social work practice. Paper presented at the meeting on Cultural Competence in Child Welfare Practice: A Collaboration Between Practitioners and Academicians, University of Texas at Austin.

Kinzie, J. D., Boehnlein, J. K., Leung, P. K, Moore, L. J., Riley, C., & Smith, D. (1990). The prevalence of posttraumatic stress disorder and its clinical significance among Southeast Asian refugees. *American Journal of Psychiatry, 147*(7), 913–917.

Kitano, H. H. (1969) Japanese-American mental illness. In S. C. Plog & R. B. Edgerton (Eds.), *Changing perspectives in mental illness* (pp. 256–284). New York: Holt, Rinehart & Winston.

Kitano, H. H. L., & Maki, M. T. (1996). Continuity, change and diversity: Counseling Asian Americans. In P. B. Pedersen, J. G. Draguns, W. J. Lonner, & J. E. Trimble (Eds.), *Counseling across cultures* (pp. 124–145). Thousand Oaks, CA. Sage

Knox, J. (1996). Homebased services for Southeast Asian refugee children: A process and formative evaluation. *Children and Youth Services Review, 18*(6), 553–578.

Kuramoto, F. H. (1997). Asian Americans. In J. Philleo & F. L. Brisbane (Eds.), *Cultural competence in substance abuse prevention* (pp. 98–121). Washington, DC: National Association of Social Workers Press.

Lee, S. (1996). *Unraveling the "model minority" stereotype: Listening to Asian American youth.* New York: Teachers College Press.

Lie, G. Y. (2000, November). *Hmong community needs assessment survey: Report on findings and recommendations for program planning and development.* Unpublished monograph.

Logan, J. R. (2001). *From many shores: Asians in Census 2000.* Report by the Lewis Mumford Center for Comparative Urban and Regional Research, University at Albany. Retrieved July 28, 2002, from http://www.mumford1.dyndns.org/cen2000/AsianPop/AsianReport

Long, D. P., Ricard, P., & Ricard, L. (1997). *The dream shattered: Vietnamese gangs in America.* Boston, MA: Northeastern University Press.

Lum, D. (2000). *Social work practice and people of color: A process-stage approach.* Belmont, CA: Brooks/Cole.

Lyon, E. (1998). Poverty, welfare and battered women: What does the research tell us? *Violence Against Women Online Resources.* Retrieved July 28, 2002, from http://www.vaw.umn.edu/Vawnet/welfare.htm

Masaki, B., & Wong, L. (1997). Domestic violence in the Asian community. In E. Lee (Ed.), *Working with Asian Americans: A guide for clinicians* (pp. 439–451). New York: Guilford Press.

Min, P. G. (Ed.) (1995). *Asian Americans: Contemporary trends and issues.* Thousand Oaks, CA: Sage.

Miranda, M., & Kitano, H. H. L. (1976). Mental health services in third world communities. *International Journal of Mental Health, 2,* 39–49.

Mokuau, N., & Fong, R. (1994). Assessing the responsiveness of health services to ethnic minorities of color. *Social Work in Health Care, 20*(2), 65–72.

Moore, T., & Selkowe, V. (1999). *The impact of welfare reform on Hmong aid recipients.* Milwaukee: Institute for Wisconsin's Future.

National Center for Chronic Disease Prevention and Health Promotion. (1998). *Asian Americans and Pacific Islanders and tobacco.* Retrieved July 24, 2002, from http://www.cac.gov/tobacco/sgr/sgr_1998/sgr-min-fs-asi.htm

National Center for Health Statistics. (1995). *1992 National Health Interview Survey.* Hyattsville, MD: Centers for Disease Control and Prevention.

Office of Applied Studies, Substance Abuse and Mental Health Services Administration [SAMHSA]. (2002). *The DASIS report: Asian and Pacific Islander adolescents in substance abuse treatment: 1999*. Retrieved July 24, 2002, from http://www.samhsa.gov/oas/2k2/AsianTX/AsianTX.cfm

Office of Refugee Resettlement [ORR] (2001). *Fact Sheet*. Administration for Children and Families, U.S. Department of Health and Human Services. Retrieved July 24, 2002, from http://www.acf.hhs.gov/news/facts/orr.htm

Office of Refugee Resettlement. (2002a). II. Refugees in the United States: Population profile. *Annual report to Congress 1999*. Administration for Children and Families, U.S. Department of Health and Human Services. Retrieved July 26, 2002, from http://www.acf.dhhs.gov/programs/orr/policy/99arc8.htm

Office of Refugee Resettlement (2002b). Economic adjustment. *Annual report to Congress 1999*. Administration for Children and Families, U.S. Department of Health and Human Services Retrieved July 28, 2002, from http://www.acf.dhhs.gov/programs/orr/policy/99arc9.htm

O'Hare, T., & Tran, T. V. (1998). Substance abuse among Southeast Asians in the U.S.: Implications for practice and research. *Social Work in Health Care, 26*(3), 69–80.

Ranard, D. A., & Pfleger, M. (1993). Language and literacy education for Southeast Asian refugees.Washington, DC: National Center for ESL Literacy Education (Digest No. EDO LE-93-06). Retrieved July 26, 2002, from http://www.cal.org/ncle/digests/SE_ASIAN.HTML

Saleeby, D. (1995). The strengths perspective in social work practice: Extensions and cautions. *Social Work, 41*(3), 296–305.

Saulnier, C. F. (1996). *Feminist theories and social work: Approaches and applications*. New York: Haworth Press.

Segal, U. A. (2000a). A pilot exploration of family violence among nonclinical Vietnamese. *Journal of Interpersonal Violence, 15*(5), 523–533.

Segal, U. A. (2000b). Exploring child abuse among Vietnamese refugees. In D. de Anda and R. M. Becerra (Eds.), *Violence: Diverse populations and communities* (pp. 159–191). New York: Haworth Press.

Snowden, L. R., & Cheung, F. K. (1990) Use of inpatient mental health services by members of ethnic minority groups. *American Psychologist, 45*, 347–355.

Southeast Asian Resource Action Center. (2002). *Southeast Asian communities*. Retrieved July 26, 2002, from http://www.searac.org/commun.html

Straus, M. A. (1979). Measuring intrafamily conflict and violence: The Conflict Tactics (CT) Scale. *Journal of Marriage and the Family, 41*(1), 75–88.

Straus, M. A. (1990). New scoring methods for violence and new norms for the Conflict Tactic Scales. In M. A. Straus & R. J. Gelles (Eds.), *Physical violence in American families:*

Risk factors and adaptations to violence in 8,145 families (pp. 535–559). New Brunswick, NJ: Transaction.

Sue, D. W., & Sue, D. (1999). *Counseling the culturally different.* New York: Wiley & Sons.

Sue, S., & McKinney, H. (1975). Asian Americans in the community mental healthcare system. *American Journal of Orthopsychiatry, 45,* 111–118.

Takaki, R. (1994). *From different shores: Perspectives on race and ethnicity in America.* New York: Oxford University Press.

U.S. Department of State. (1999). *Summary of refugee admissions for FY 1975–FY 1999.* Retrieved July 26, 2002, from http://www.state.gov/g/prm/rls/fs/2001/5412.htm

U.S. Census Bureau. (2002). *The Asian Population: Census 2000 Brief.* Retrieved July 26, 2002, from http://www.census.gov/population/www/cen2000/briefs.html

Weinstein-Shr, G., & Henkin, N. Z. (1991). Continuity and change: Intergenerational relations in Southeast Asian refugee families. *Marriage and Family Review, 16*(3/4), 351–367.

West, C. M. (1998). Lifting the "political gag order": Breaking the silence around partner violence in ethnic minority families. In J. L. Jasinski & L. M. Williams (Eds.), *Partner violence: A comprehensive review of 20 years of research* (pp. 184–209). Thousand Oaks, CA: Sage.

Wolak, J., & Finkelhor, D. (1998). Children exposed to partner violence. In J. L. Jasinski & L. M. Williams (Eds.), *Partner violence: A comprehensive review of 20 years of research* (pp. 1–43). Thousand Oaks, CA: Sage.

Zia, H. (2000). *Asian American dreams: The emergence of an American people.* New York: Farrar, Straus, & Giroux.

Part 6

Conclusion

17

Cultural Competency and Intersectionality

Bridging Practice and Redirecting Services

CARMEN ORTIZ HENDRICKS and ROWENA FONG

Introduction

Culturally competent practice and research has been moving toward the need to examine domestic and global issues affecting the four ethnic groups of African Americans, Latinos, First Nations Peoples, and Asians and Pacific Islanders (Balgopal, 2000; Dhooper & Moore, 2001; Fong, 2004; Fong & Furuto, 2001; Lum, 1999, 2003) in order to address their diverse but also similar needs and problems. In the arena of child welfare all four ethnic groups have existing and growing problems in substance abuse and domestic violence. Yet, the social work profession has not adequately addressed the intersectionality of these concerns. How do the areas overlap? Why has it been posited that treatment has to be separate rather than integrative, and sequential rather than concurrent? How should interventions differ based upon the cultural variations among and within ethnic groups? Social work practitioners and researchers should be prepared to answer these questions and generate more. The intersection of child welfare, substance abuse, and domestic violence is very important since it is impossible to address one of these problem areas without encountering complications related to the other problem areas. Intersectionality has to be incorporated into social work practice, and cultural competency needs to be reflected in all three problem areas. Each ethnic group will have its unique problems in child welfare, substance abuse, and domestic violence. Cultural values and meanings, indigenous healings, and Western interventions, all need to be considered in the context of how they intersect with the problem areas.

The concept of intersectionality is in a developmental phase. Intersectionality has been associated at the micro and mezzo levels with multiple identities (Fong, 2004; Fong & Wang, 2001; Lum, 2003; Spencer, Lewis, & Gutierrez, 2000) and multiple social group memberships (Spencer et al., 2000). Lum (2003) makes the distinction between internal intersections (such as culture, education, career, family background, sexual orientation, residency, faith and religion, and partnership status) and external intersections (age/life span, ethnicity, language, gender, social class, disability, size, personal appearance). Fong (2003) speaks to the diversification within the Asian and Pacific Islander classifications and advocates that "the single categories need to be broken down into multiple racial combinations and variations within the single ethnic groups. Culturally competent practice also involves the challenge of including the intersection of ethnicity and race with gender, sexual orientation, religion, social class, and physical and mental abilities" (p. 281).

Intersectionality at the macro level is important in the multiple combinations of child welfare, substance abuse, and family violence. The statistics report that 80%–90% of child welfare cases also experience problems in substance abuse and domestic violence, thus mandating that social workers be trained to understand substance abuse and domestic violence issues in order to effectively address child welfare concerns. However, to practice in a culturally competent manner it is necessary to approach the children and families in the child welfare system with knowledge and skills in working with the different ethnic groupings. There certainly will be differences among the four ethnic groups but also within any single entity. The Asian and Pacific Islander groups have much diversity within the different Asian groups alone. This applies to the other three ethnic groups. Discerning differences but recognizing commonalities among the four ethnic groupings is a goal of this final chapter. This chapter summarizes the concerns of the respective ethnic groups (African Americans, First Nations Peoples, Latinos, and Asians and Pacific Islanders) in reference to problems in the areas of child welfare, substance abuse, and family violence. Creating culturally competent services in child welfare is put forth, concluding with redirections in services.

Bridging Practice Among Welfare, Abuse, and Violence

To identify universal concerns in child welfare, substance abuse, and family violence among the African American, Latinos, First Nations Peoples, and Asian and Pacific Islander populations will allow social work practitioners, policy makers, and researchers to have a global picture and reexamine culturally competent practices. In analyzing these chapters in the book, common concerns that were evident across the ethnic groups were child abuse and neglect situations, which emerged in direct response to historical trauma, living in a hostile and unsupportive environment, and dealing with oppression, racism, and economic and social injustice on a daily basis.

Michael Yellow Bird's memories of growing up in his Sahnish/Hidatsa community (chapter 12) powerfully demonstrate the enduring connection between the long-term effects of U.S. colonialism and oppression of First Nations Peoples and modern-day substance abuse and violence among his people. Other authors emphasize the interrelationship of child welfare services with the criminal justice system (McRoy and Vick, chapter 1), substance abuse and treatment programs (Marsiglia, chapter 10), health and welfare services, and the lack of culturally competent and culturally relevant services in all human service arenas. The disproportionate number of families and children of color affected by these systems requires highly skilled and knowledgeable practitioners, supervisors, and administrators who understand and are able to intervene effectively with multiethnic and multiracial individuals and families in crisis. They must also be effective advocates in empowering families, strengthening communities, changing policies, and reforming organizations.

Child welfare specialists need to keep the bigger picture in mind when working with families and their pressing needs. For example, several authors describe the lack of access to and availability of substance abuse treatment programs and domestic violence shelters as significantly affecting increased referrals to child protective services. When parents cannot find help or treatment for their problems or the necessary supports, such as child care, or to take advantage of limited treatment programs, the children are bound to suffer.

McRoy and Vick in the introductory chapter emphasize the correlation between growing numbers of women who are mothers being incarcerated for nonviolent offenses with the escalating need for child welfare services. The consistent message throughout this text is that the underlying causes of substance abuse and family violence are social, economic, and political stress and inequities, and this is why so many children of color are removed from their culturally syntonic homes.

Some authors (Ortega in chapter 8 and Lie in chapter 16) raised concerns about Southeast Asian and Latino immigrant families that arrive in the United States having known nothing but fear, severe economic hardships, and the ravages of war in their countries of origin, experiences that exacerbate the stress and trauma associated with immigration, resettlement, and acculturation.

Child welfare workers need to keep these larger issues in mind when working with families under stress. They must also accept and act on their role as advocate by alerting administrators and policy makers that the children in foster homes and congregate care facilities today will make up the majority of the U.S. workforce by the end of the first quarter of this century (Ozawa, 1997). Everyone needs to protect and strengthen the children of today, even if it is a pragmatic concern for the future of society in general. All of these factors need to be considered when assessing the needs of children and families being served by child welfare agencies.

In reviewing the chapters written by the authors, the following tables represent a summary of the themes found among the four ethnic groups:

TABLE 1

African American Themes in the Intersections Among Child Welfare, Substance Abuse, and Family Violence

POPULATION: AFRICAN AMERICANS

Unlike some stereotypes of this population, African Americans are not monolithic—communities are bicultural and multicultural.

African Americans have a unique history in U.S. African Americans experienced more than three centuries of slavery, a century of legal segregation, 30–40 years of equality by law, differential arrest rates, criminal indictments, incarceration, economic discrimination, negative stereotyping, housing discrimination, police brutality, addictive drug importation, poor education, inadequate health care, inadequate family support.

African American families are disproportionately poor.

Many agencies and programs are not culturally sensitive to the needs of African American families and children.

CHILD WELFARE

African American children are overrepresented in the child welfare system and remain in care longer than White children.

Current social and legal remedies lead to the destruction of families, especially African American families. Most of the families that become involved with child welfare are poor or have limited financial resources and are headed by women. Disproportionately high numbers of these families are African American.

Many African American children in foster care are in care because of substance abuse by a parent. Substance abuse is a barrier to family reunification.

Child welfare workers must be trained in drug abuse screening.

SUBSTANCE ABUSE

African Americans have lower rates of alcohol and illicit drug use than Whites, but more social and health problems related to substance abuse.

Women who abuse alcohol and other drugs are more likely to become victims of domestic violence. They also have less control over their actions and make bad decisions in disciplinary choices and child rearing behaviors.

African American illicit drug use is 50% higher for males than for females.

Workers must explore factors that contribute to substance abuse, such as unemployment, economic deprivation, poverty, racism, discrimination, gender roles, and manhood.

FAMILY VIOLENCE

African American women are more likely to experience the most severe violence compared to other groups. Low income and limited education can increase risk of abuse.

Maladaptive behaviors among some African American men result from violent social learning environments, abusive experiences as children, societal and structural oppression, and violent and high-stress living environments.

African American women are less likely to use domestic violence shelters and other social services than White women. African American men have higher dropout rates in both batterers' treatment and substance abuse treatment than do White males.

African American men must develop skills to negotiate racist and violent oppressive situations and environments in adaptive ways.

TABLE 2

Latino Themes in the Intersections Among Child Welfare, Substance Abuse, and Family Violence

POPULATION: LATINOS

It is the fastest-growing, highly diverse, most youthful population. There are 32.8 million Latinos in the United States, or 12% of the total population. Latinos are three times more likely to live in poverty than non-Hispanic Whites, and the poverty rate is 23%.

Latinos have extensive experiences with historical violence, discrimination, and oppression in both the United States and their countries of origin. Mexicans represent 66% of Latinos; 15% are from Central America and South America; Puerto Ricans account for 6%; and Cubans account for 4% of the Latino population in the United States.

Latinos are a heterogeneous, highly resilient people who have survived centuries of oppression, discrimination, and genocide. Latino culture, language and customs survive to this day.

While considerable empirical evidence exists on risk factors for substance use and family violence, much less is known about protective processes.

TABLE 2 Latinos (continued)

CHILD WELFARE

The presence of Latino children in the child welfare system connotes the fragility of families and how much structural factors such as poverty, stress, substance abuse, psychopathology, trauma, and violence influence child rearing practices.

The main risk factors identified are the lack of family or natural support systems, the child welfare system, polarized gender roles, immigration/migration and internal colonization, socioeconomic status, and acculturation.

Practice and research need to look at cultural values such as the importance of family, respect, dignity, fatalism, and machismo and how these can be protective factors against child maltreatment across the different Latino ethnic groups.

Child welfare practice in Latino communities needs to distinguish among culture and poverty, subgroup differences, acculturation, and language issues.

SUBSTANCE ABUSE

No single cause leads to substance abuse, rather, it takes a series of factors such as lack of educational and employment opportunities, environmental stress, adjustment and resettlement following immigration or migration, and quality of the environment.

Substance abuse is actually lower among Latinos than among their non-Latino counterparts. Latina women account for fewer substance abusers than Latino men do.

Alcohol use is integral to a culture that idealizes family and community, celebration, machismo, hospitality, and generosity.

There is a direct correlation between oppression and the existence of substance abuse within the Latino community.

Substance abuse among Latinos has been attributed to acculturation and subgroup differences. In addition, there are differences in drinking patterns and drug choice among Latinos.

Practitioners need to look at how Latino families are able to survive drug free and the cultural processes that buffer Latinos against drug use.

FAMILY VIOLENCE

There are higher rates of family violence in Latino families than among non-Latino families. The irony is that recent immigrants who are young as well as Latinos who are more acculturated to the United States are the two groups most likely to abuse their spouses.

Family violence and substance abuse have been linked to socioeconomic variables and minority status, and Latinos are overrepresented in both areas. Latino men who cannot provide for their families are most likely to suffer from mental illness, substance abuse, and violence themselves.

Research has documented that drug of choice, prevalence rates, child maltreatment rates, and perception of family violence vary among Latino groups.

How do Latino families survive violence free? What are the cultural processes that buffer Latino families against family violence despite the environmental stress and socioeconomic indicators present?

TABLE 3

First Nations Themes in the Intersections Among Child Welfare, Substance Abuse, and Family Violence

POPULATION: FIRST NATIONS

First Nations populations in the lower 48 United States and Alaska include more than 550 First Nations groups with distinct histories and cultures, or 4.1 million American Indian/Alaska Native peoples.

First Nations Peoples have experienced the effects of historical oppression and historical traumatic events that are passed on from one generation to another.

American colonialism is the key to the intersection among substance abuse, family violence, and child welfare.

The historical traumatic response to cumulative trauma is a "soul wound," a complete and utter wounding of the spirit. Traditional treatments do not work, and the cure must be spiritual, with healing ceremonies that can restore the spirit.

CHILD WELFARE

The need for child welfare services has less to do with child maltreatment than with the excessive rates of death, poverty, depression, unemployment, loss of personal and cultural identity, family and community conflicts, and lack of tribal unity among indigenous peoples.

Historically indigenous children and families have been traumatized by child welfare practices.

Until the passage of the Indian Child Welfare Act of 1978, children were routinely removed from their parents and placed into White homes or Christian boarding schools, where Indian culture was ignored or ridiculed.

Child welfare agencies need to understand indigenous stress-coping models that view cultural factors as a buffer between historical trauma and health and mental health.

Child welfare practices need to incorporate culturally relevant models of practice such as those that

TABLE 3 First Nations (continued)

highlight resiliency and making connections between past and present trauma, reinforce culturally appropriate child rearing practices, support community connections and participation in community grief ceremonies, and examine Native social service programs and their healing methods.

SUBSTANCE ABUSE

The myth of "the drunken Indian" includes many misconceptions and stereotypes. There is no single response by indigenous peoples to alcohol, and the vast majority of indigenous peoples do not drink alcohol or use other substances. One needs to look at age, tribal community, and other factors where alcohol and substance abuse are a severe health hazard.

Research and practice show that there is a positive relationship between the ongoing effects of trauma with substance use, between childhood sexual abuse and adult child maltreatment, and between childhood abuse and adult alcoholism.

Substance abuse programs can use whatever mainstream practice approaches they deem appropriate, but these should be coupled with cultural and spiritual practices consistent with the traditional beliefs and values of indigenous peoples.

Liberation for indigenous peoples from substance abuse, family violence, and child welfare problems requires an aggressive telling of the truth and questioning the role that the colonial structure (the United States of America) has, and continues to have, in the substance abuse and family violence problems among indigenous peoples.

FAMILY VIOLENCE

The stereotype of indigenous peoples being a violent race has been perpetuated by European American society. And while violence does exist among First Nations Peoples, family and intimate violence, overall, is no bigger a problem among these groups than it is in the rest of the population.

The negative effects of historical trauma include high rates of family violence and substance abuse among First Nations Peoples. They do not see the enormous resiliency that keeps families and communities together despite this ongoing trauma.

Research and practice also demonstrate that family and intimate violence experienced by indigenous peoples are more likely to be perpetuated by someone from a different race.

Prevention of family violence programs need to encourage healing by working closely with the victims' families and communities to make family violence publicly known and to encourage the entire community to take responsibility for the violence and come together to create healing and peace among all members.

TABLE 4

Asian and Pacific Islander Themes in the Intersections Among Child Welfare, Substance Abuse, and Family Violence

POPULATION: ASIAN AND PACIFIC ISLANDER AMERICANS

Diversity exists among and within Asian and Pacific Islander populations, distinguishing native-born, immigrant, and refugee status.

Pacific Islanders are an indigenous, colonized population.

Despite high educational achievements among APIs, the "model minority" stereotype tends to mask racism and oppression.

Immigrants and refugees experience problems with acculturation and discriminatory, anti-immigrant laws and policies.

CHILD WELFARE

Asian and Pacific Islander immigrants may lack knowledge and may be unfamiliar with the American child welfare system because they operate under a different context of child rearing practices.

Pacific Islanders tend to be overrepresented in crime, health problems, and poverty. Struggles with overcrowding, unemployment, and lack of formal education exist for Asians, Southeast Asians, and Pacific Islanders.

The Americanization of children and adolescents contributes to child maltreatment attributable to struggles to maintaining traditional values and intergenerational conflict experiences.

SUBSTANCE ABUSE

Substance problems exist, but APIs tend to have an "invisible profile." APIs tend to be excluded from services because of language barriers, small numbers, and the model minority stereotype.

Factors contributing to substance use are acculturation stressors, racism and discrimination, lack of or limited English-speaking skills, PTSD, and trauma.

Family-based treatment centers and spirituality need to be incorporated into prevention and treatment modalities.

FAMILY VIOLENCE

Domestic violence problems of wife beating exist in many API families, but the underuse of social services influenced by shame and stigma avoidance is misconstrued as a lack of need.

TABLE 4 Asian and Pacific Islander (continued)

Domestic violence is not limited to the physical domain but also includes acts of isolation, control, and intimidation. Underemployment and lower-status jobs for men contribute to family stressors.

Insufficient services and resources are attributable to inaccessibility and cultural insensitivities. Community-based programs should include culturally and linguistically appropriate staff.

Common themes among the four ethnic groups are:

• Historical trauma, racism, discrimination
• Disproportionate poverty, unemployment, or underemployment
• Increased risks of abuse because of low income and limited education
• Substance use and domestic violence related to environmental and cultural stressors
• Survival of culture, traditions, and language, despite trauma
• Strong resiliency characteristics
• Within-group differences, bicultural and multicultural communities
• Need for treatment programs using cultural and spiritual practices

In reviewing what is common to all four ethnic groups, culturally competent services and organizations must take into account the need for culturally based treatments, that are sensitive to the historical, social, environmental, and economic stressors affecting these populations.

Creating Culturally Competent Services

Culturally competent child welfare services need to incorporate a multidimensional perspective that recognizes the unique experiences of racially and ethnically diverse children and families in the United States. There is a growing recognition that social agencies, in general, must attend to broader diversity issues. This is attributable in part to the changing composition of the U.S. workforce in which 8 of every 10 new entrants to the workforce can be characterized as women, people of color, immigrants, persons with disabilities, or older workers. "America's workforce therefore will become older, more female, and more ethnically and culturally diverse. Along with the demographic shifts, there are likely to be differences in lifestyles, attitudes, and work ethics, that will affect work and the workplace" (Chernesky, 1997, p. 18). Similarly, child welfare agencies are increasingly composed of workers from different backgrounds, values, and perspectives and face the challenge of managing a diverse workforce while providing culturally competent services to increasingly diverse constituents. "Agencies need to examine their management and program practices at all levels to determine to what extent they are culturally competent and what steps they can take toward becoming more culturally competent" (p. 19). Both child welfare practitioners and child welfare organizations need to change in order to provide effective culturally competent services to diverse client populations and to address the need for better interagency collaborations among the fields of child abuse, substance abuse, and family violence.

Diversity refers to the range of differences and similarities encountered in daily practice, which may include factors associated with culture, gender, race, ethnicity, sexual orientation, social class, religion, age, and abilities. Cultural competency is part of a continuum of social skills and personality development and refers to a set of knowledge and skills that a worker must develop in order to be effective in meeting the needs of a diverse constituency (Lum, 1999). A culturally competent individual possesses a strong personal identity, has knowledge of the beliefs and values of several cultures, displays sensitivity to the affective/emotional components of cultures, communicates clearly in the language of a specific cultural group, performs socially and culturally sanctioned behaviors, maintains active social relations within each cultural group, and negotiates the institutional structures of each culture (LaFromboise, Coleman, & Gerton, 1993). In short, these are many of the skills of a biculturally competent individual.

The development of culturally competent practitioners is dependent on the development of culturally competent organizations or culturally competent systems of care that "acknowledge and incorporate, at all levels, the importance of culture, the assessment of cross-cultural relations, vigilance towards the dynamics that result from cultural differences, the expansion of cultural knowledge, and the adaptation of services to meet culturally-unique needs" (Cross, Barzon, Dennis, & Isaacs, 1989, pp. iv–v). Chernesky (1997) describes the culturally competent agency as one "whose policies, behaviors, and attitudes combine in such a way that the agency and its workers can effectively provide services in multicultural situations" (p. 26). Miley, O'Melia, and DuBois (1998) propose that a culturally competent agency integrates diversity throughout its hiring policies and training programs, program evaluations, and assessment instruments; views culture as a strength and a resource; and strives to develop indigenous helping networks. To have culturally competent agencies dealing with child welfare, substance abuse, and domestic violence issues in Pacific Islander communities, specifically Native Hawaiian ones, the use of *kupunas* or elders is commonly practiced in community-based substance abuse treatment centers (Fong & Morelli, 1998; Morelli, Fong, & Olivera, 2001). Miley et al., (1998) also address the importance of working to develop culturally competent communities that have the potential to celebrate pluralism, diversity, and cross-cultural interactions that promote social justice as opposed to culturally incompetent communities that give voice to discriminatory and segregationist policies and behaviors.

Child welfare organizations have made progress in accepting the premise that recruiting a more diverse workforce, one that resembles the populations served, could increase the delivery of culturally competent services to diverse children and families. However, the powerful benefits of a diverse workforce go beyond increasing access to underrepresented populations in the organization or reaffirming a commitment to affirmative action programs, since diversity and cultural competence are not synonymous. The culturally competent organization taps into the full potential of all its employees. Organizations that value diversity attempt to bring about qualitative changes through increased appreciation of the range of skills and values that dissimilar employees offer and through increased opportunity to include members who are culturally distinct from the dominant group (Loden & Rosener, 1991).

Diversity, by its very nature, pushes an organization to grow and to be creative and flexible in response to the ever-changing cultural backgrounds and identity-group memberships of providers and consumers of their services. For example, the Casey Family Program (2000) has shown its commitment to diversity by writing in Casey's Strategic Plan 2000 a values statement supporting diversity and antiracism. To follow through on this commitment, in October 2000 Casey created an Office of Diversity whose vision is to "facilitate the alignment and integration of diversity and cultural competence throughout the very fabric of the organization" (p. 3). The Office of Diversity has been implementing Undoing Racism workshops for all Casey staff and is manifesting its commitment to culturally competent practice and organizational change.

Child welfare organizations are finding that increasing diversity alone is not enough to promote culturally competent child welfare services. Responding to the complex array of problems that families of color face requires a fundamental change in the attitudes and behaviors that guide training, practice, supervision, and policies in the organization. The entire child welfare system has to broaden its understanding of diversity and cultural competence to appreciate what fundamental changes are demanded of organizations, administrators, and workers. For example, in the First Nations communities, Weaver (2001) speaks of the internalized oppression and the anger that comes with it resulting in internal strife among Native Peoples. But she also advocates that "people do not exist independently of other things" (p. 185). She recommends that organizations working with First Nations Peoples change their methods of assessment to include an ecological and person-in-environment approach to encompass *mitakuye oyasin* (we are all related), which "views all things in creation as related" (p. 185). The need to understand First Nations Peoples and their interrelatedness to the land and creation is important in delivering culturally competent services to them, as Lowery (chapter 3) impresses upon non-Native professionals working with this population.

Child welfare agencies need to continue to actively recruit a diverse workforce, one that includes African Americans, Latinos, First Nations Peoples, and Asians and Pacific Islanders, while simultaneously training all staff to meet the ever-changing needs of diverse children and families. Leung and Cheung (2001) warn that in working with Asian American individuals and families (or most likely any ethnic population), before one evaluates clinical practices, it is necessary that "social workers must evaluate their own cultural values and competencies so that they do not feel overwhelmed by the demand of cultural sensitivity" (p. 430). Leung and Cheung mention five areas of competencies (informational, intellectual, interpersonal, intrapersonal, and intervention) that social workers need to self-assess (pp. 430–433). But requiring self-assessments, increasing demographic representation in the organization, and conducting extensive cultural sensitivity training does not immediately increase effective culturally competent practice. Agencies need to realize that it is how they define diversity and what they do with the experience of being a diverse organization that contributes to their being a culturally competent setting.

Cultural awareness or cultural sensitivity training, although not the only way to address diversity, has been the key component in dealing with diversity in the organization (Motwani, Harper, Subramanian, & Douglas, 1993; Solomon, 1989). It has been popular and widely used to help workers gain an understanding of their own values, personal background, and identities and learn about other cultural traditions, values, and beliefs. There is little empirical evidence that cultural sensitivity training brings about culturally competent services; however, the general assumption is that by learning about another's cultural differences, workers can learn to accept and respect differences between and among people, which will lead them to communicate more effectively and develop strategies for effective intervention (Kavanagh & Kennedy, 1992). In working with Pacific Islander populations, the need to incorporate families in treatment practices using family-centered approaches is mandatory. In chapter 15 Vakalahi, Godinet, and Fong mention the Native Hawaiian family-centered problem-solving approach, called "Ho'oponopono."

To most Western social workers this is a very different treatment approach; to Native Hawaiians it is the most commonly used practice in problem-solving situations. Training in family approaches familiar to the specific ethnic populations should be practiced, not only in cases related to child welfare, substance abuse, and family violence, but also in every problem-related area. While social agencies may argue that they have used this kind of training to help workers examine and overcome their biases; understand the experiences of diverse populations, their attitudes toward their own culture and the majority culture; and to focus on cultural commonality and cultural specificity in working ethnically diverse populations (Stevenson, Cheung, & Leung, 1992), the best kind of training emphasizes that it is not a one-shot deal, but that the goals are to move an agency from a monocultural to a multicultural organization (Solomon, 1989).

Throughout this book, cultural competence has been discussed in terms of specific identity-group membership. The authors provide readers with "insider information" to facilitate effectiveness in delivering child welfare, substance abuse, and family violence services to specific populations. A first step in developing cultural competence is gaining knowledge about a client group's specific cultural background and experiences either from the clients themselves or from workshops or readings. But to stop at this level of conceptualization is too simplistic. Cultural competence is more than how a person looks or where he or she comes from. For example, the assumption that the main virtue Latino or Asian workers have to offer is a knowledge of their own people and culture as well as their bilingual skills is limited and limiting. It is detrimental and exploitative to assign Asian workers only Asian clients or Latino workers only Latino clients. It is a disservice to them and to their clients. Cultural competence should be understood as bringing together the varied perspectives and approaches to the work that diverse members of different identity groups can contribute to the work at hand. Child welfare workers of varying cultural backgrounds bring different, important, and relevant knowledge and perspectives about how to actually do the work, how to problem solve, how to introduce and promote the helping process, how to achieve goals, organize tasks, work on a team, communicate ideas, and supervise and lead others. Culturally diverse workers can challenge basic assumptions about how agencies should function, operate, practice, and proceed in meeting the needs of diverse clients (Thomas & Ely, 1996). If child welfare workers are freed up to bring more of their whole selves to the workplace, and are able to identify more fully with the work they do, then agencies will be more culturally competent and will benefit greatly from fresh and meaningful approaches to the daily work of protecting children and promoting healthy families.

An integrative approach reflecting intersectionality to culturally competent child welfare practice goes beyond earlier efforts to ignore or deny differences in an effort to treat all people equally. This approach does not require workers to abandon their cultural identities and merge with the majority. Instead it requires social workers to be very clear about their cultural identity and competence not just in their own domain of child welfare but also in substance abuse and domestic violence. It may force workers to delve deeper into the knowledge and skills of the ethnic culture because of intersecting variables. In African American cultures Edith Freeman in chapter 6 speaks of a systems approach of both nurturing and task-instrumental environments. She explains that the nurturing environment "serves a cultural resource by helping African Americans to maintain many of the historical cultural traditions. . . . along with support networks such as the black church and community cultural centers." She mentions the need for social workers to simultaneously address the issues of the task environment that "is represented by dominant society, which provides or prevents access to power, basic resources such as food and shelter, employment, education, and often physical survival." Freeman advocates that social workers must simultaneously pay attention to the two systems and not ignore the task environment, which perpetuates oppression.

This constant vigilance to combat oppressive practices is far more than the traditional focus on eliminating prejudice and discrimination against women and certain ethnic group minorities through compliance with federal Equal Employment Opportunity requirements. These equality models expect all workers to assimilate and adapt to the norms and values of the monocultural organization (Cox, 1991) as opposed to the pluralistic organization that "reflects the contributions and interests of diverse cultural and social groups in its mission, operations, and delivery of services. It seeks to eliminate all forms of cultural and social oppression in the organization and its workforce is represented by different cultural and social groups at all levels. Even more significant, diversity in leadership is reflected in the organization's policymaking and governance. Equally important, the pluralistic organization exhibits a sensitivity to issues that affect the larger community and participates in socially responsible activities and programs" (Nixon & Spearmon, 1991, p. 158).

Child welfare organizations have to work toward restructuring the makeup of entire agencies so that they will more closely reflect the pluralistic organization, which in turn reflects the makeup of society and the clientele. They must actively seek to diversify on all levels from management to frontline workers, ensuring that all workers are treated equally and with respect and that some workers are not given unfair advantage over others. Child welfare services also need to engage in mentorship and career development programs specifically for women and people of color while expanding training programs for all workers to learn about and respect cultural differences. There is a need to go beyond affirmative action efforts that are primarily concerned with counting the numbers of underrepresented groups in an organization to determine how well the organization achieves its recruitment and retention goals. In New York City, for example, the Administration for Children's Services (ACS) actively recruited African and South American workers in their countries of origin to work with increasing numbers of African American and Latino children and families in care. In the course of these efforts, ACS discovered wide-ranging cultural differences between Africans and African Americans and among and between Latino groups. As the child welfare workforce becomes more diversified, efforts need to continue to change entrenched cultures within bureaucratic, hierarchical agencies, and to make child welfare practice more culturally relevant and effective.

Organizations can no longer avoid issues of diversity, rather, they are encouraged to address diversity in all its forms (Goldstein & Leopold, 1990). Administrators and staff need to view cross-cultural conflicts or tensions as opportunities for increased dialogue about differences. Creating a fair and respectful agency environment does not always mean it is safe for staff to be themselves, nor does it automatically eliminate sexist, racist, ethnocentric, or homophobic behaviors. Newly diversified workforces are changing the agencies in which they work, and in some instances pulling the organization away from its original culture and mission (Thomas & Ely, 1996). It may take the form of workers advocating for different training programs or denying the relevance of certain training programs to the realities of their practice. In a child welfare agency, it may take the form of supervisory or peer-to-peer conflicts. Agencies need to undergo a cultural shift that leads to understanding what to do with their newly diversified workforces.

Cultural Competence Standards and Self-Assessment

In order to assist professionals in agencies, the National Association of Social Workers established the *NASW Standards for Cultural Competence in Social Work Practice* (2001) for "the advancement of practice models that have the relevance for the range of needs and services represented by the diverse client populations" (p. 7). The implementation of these standards has begun with extensive national and local training efforts to help social workers integrate the 10 standards, which include the social workers' ethical responsibility for providing culturally competent services. The Child Welfare League's Cultural Competence Self-Assessment Instrument (CWLA, 1993) provides a useful format for agencies to use to determine whether their policies, practices, and programs are culturally competent. It is designed to assist agencies in identifying strengths and weaknesses in their response to culturally diverse staff and client populations and in developing action steps for specific changes to become more culturally competent. The following self-assessment questions (CWLA, 1993) illustrate the kinds of issues that agencies are asked to examine in regard to delivering culturally competent services.

1. Do the agency's mission statement and goals include reference to cultural diversity and competence?
2. Do the policy statements and the work of the agency board of directors incorporate the agency's mission statement and goals, including reference to cultural diversity?
3. Does the agency's board of directors consult organizations that represent culturally diverse groups as part of the board recruitment process?
4. Do agency executives report regularly to the board of directors on progress made in the area of cultural competence and on the impact of cultural issues on the agency?
5. Does the agency collaborate with culturally diverse organizations on special projects of benefit to the agency's clientele?
6. Does the agency have a clear process for evaluating the short-term and long-term impact of its programs and policies on culturally diverse families and communities?

7. Does the agency provide opportunities for advancement for staff members who demonstrate, among other skills, cultural competency?
8. Does the agency use when appropriate the expertise of community leaders, natural healers, elders, and other cultural resources in planning and delivering services?
9. Do staff members regularly examine their own cultural beliefs and attitudes to better understand the dynamics of cultural difference and interaction?
10. Do staff members work with families in settings that are comfortable and familiar to them, i.e., home, neighborhood, reservation, community facility?
11. Do agency interventions make use of culturally diverse natural helping networks in the process of delivering service?
12. Is the agency involved in efforts to advocate for programs, policies, and services that directly or indirectly affect the cultural groups it serves?

Intersectionality and Collaboration Across Agency Cultures

Cultural competence is most often analyzed and studied from the perspective of the worker's interactions with diverse clients, and it is given less attention from the point of view of the organizational context. Adding to this complex and misunderstood dynamic in practice, cultural competence is rarely examined as a factor in facilitating interagency cultures. "The culture of an organization is reflected in the pattern of beliefs, values, and expectations shared by organization members that establish norms and rules governing acceptable and unacceptable employee behaviors" (Chernesky, 1997, p. 24). When examining the intersection of child welfare practice with substance abuse and family violence services, each service delivery system has its own unique way of approaching clients, defining problems, and intervening and providing services. In essence each system has its own organizational culture and history that guide how workers are trained and supervised and how services are administered. Each system has a particular view of human behavior, theories that inform that view, and a historical mission and culture. In order to achieve integrated child welfare services, there needs to be an exchange of knowledge that leads to child welfare, substance abuse, and domestic violence practitioners understanding each other's culture and effectively working together to benefit diverse children and families.

Local, statewide, and federal child welfare programs, alcohol and substance abuse treatment services, domestic violence initiatives, and criminal justice systems need to establish partnerships in order to better serve shared, mutual constituents. This involves discussions about how to more effectively coordinate service plans for families with child abuse and neglect, substance abuse, and family violence problems. Community-based organizations also have to commit to partnerships that integrate service delivery to families and children in their communities. The creation of the Adoption and Safe Families Act (ASFA) has placed renewed importance on a child's need for permanency and recognizes that substance abuse has become endemic to the child welfare system. Statistics point to the increasing incidence of family violence and the growing number of women prisoners, many of whom have children. All of these factors point to the critical need for human service systems to examine their effectiveness in providing parents and their children fair opportunities to live in safe, stable, and nurturing environments. The intended outcome of any collaborative effort is to create system integration and improve provider relationships in order to offer families and youth opportunities to move into recovery and family reunification.

This collaborative process between major service delivery systems and community-based organizations is highly complex and time consuming. It requires the establishment of a protocol that identifies the values and shared principles inherent in creating and improving partnerships as well as how to share information, make referrals, and ensure continuity of care between providers. Building common ground and clarifying expectations are also essential to the partnership. If the collaboration is to succeed, there is a need for (1) best practice pilot projects to evaluate how to interface practice with organizational structures, including guidelines on how to communicate and coordinate service delivery; (2) joint training programs that foster and support collaboration and define certain terms and acronyms used by each member of the partnership; and (3) ongoing feedback from agencies and workers on how the referral process is working, including how each member screens and intervenes with clients. Basically the protocol establishes who does what and when, and how responsibilities are distributed between and among provider systems. Because many people are involved in the decision-making process of a case, it is crucial that one person within an agency be identified as the key contact person responsible for a case. This person, whether the alcoholism counselor or child welfare worker, is responsible for coordinating services with other provider agencies and seeing that the protocol is followed. This process seeks to ensure accountability, continuity of care, and minimize duplication of services. There will be a need for continued work on refining each provider's role and incorporating practical suggestions for enhanced integrated services.

An example of an effort to intersect child welfare and substance abuse is the collaboration involving an integrated service delivery system being attempted between the New York City Administration for Children's Services and the New York State Office of Alcoholism and Substance Abuse Services (OASAS). In a May 2001 memorandum describing the operational protocol for client referral and communication between the two agencies, the following guiding principles for the collaboration were issued:

1. All children deserve safe, nurturing and permanent families who can provide an unconditional lasting commitment to them.
2. All parents affected by substance abuse deserve a fair and timely opportunity to receive needed services that will assist them in providing themselves and their children with safe, nurturing and permanent homes.
3. We believe a safe and supportive living environment for the parent affected by substance abuse and for his/her family is essential to the recovery process.
4. All children and families deserve to receive services in a timely and coordinated fashion that meet their specific needs and respect their strengths.
5. Every person and service provider involved with a family's care must work as partners to ensure positive outcomes for children and families.
6. In order to protect children, the needs of their parents affected by substance abuse and their families must also be met.
7. We understand that relapse may occur and may even be part of the process and progress of moving into recovery.
8. We believe that keeping parents and children affected by substance abuse closely connected (when appropriate) is important to enhancing and preserving their relationships, aiding their move into recovery, and assuring children's healthy development.
9. We believe that substance abuse must be addressed in the context of other issues which may be impacting the parent affected by substance abuse and their family including parenting, domestic violence, health, mental health, criminal justice involvement, nutrition, housing, family services, budgeting and employment readiness training.
10. We are concerned about and committed to the parent affected by substance abuse and their family and will promote an integrated treatment plan of sufficient length and quality whose goal is to eliminate substance abuse as an obstacle to parenting.
11. We acknowledge the strong connection between substance abuse and women abuse/domestic violence, specifically the large percentage of substance abusing women who are both battered and addicted. In recognizing this phenomenon, we will work together to ensure both safety and stability for this parent and her child.
12. We will communicate and share information about the parent affected by substance abuse and his/her child(ren) in a respectful and purposeful manner and in compliance with the client's right to confidentiality. (New York City Administration for Children's Services and New York State Office of Alcoholism and Substance Abuse Services Collection, 2001, p. 1–9).

In addition, this collaborative process requires efforts at values clarification and discussions of how a worker's values manifest themselves in the work he or she does. Just as culturally competent workers need to look at barriers to working effectively with clients, major human service systems need to examine some of the barriers to working effectively across systems on behalf of mutual consumers or shared clients. For example, ask a worker from each system to identify three child-welfare-related issues, three substance abuse treatment issues and three domestic-violence-related issues that they would address in their work with a particular individual or family. They will quickly prioritize the issues, and their unique approach to working with clients will be readily evident. Then ask them, if they shared a mutual client with these problems, how would they collaborate effectively as well as support their mutual client. Their responses may well be slower and less coherent. They have not been trained to work collaboratively as a team or to overcome and resolve barriers to collaborative practice. Each worker will view the client from a particular lens, whether it is child protection, sobriety or detoxification, or partner safety, and each will have difficulty seeing the whole picture.

Redirecting Services

Intersystemic partnerships need to begin with where the workers are, helping them see that families with substance abuse problems are often jointly served by child welfare and domestic violence systems, and that their role is to provide better integration and coordination of services in order to significantly expedite appropriate treatment and permanency goals for families. A sound and comprehensive assessment is the most important first step in developing an effective intervention strategy and plan of action. A lifetime of trauma is often a common thread in clients' lives regardless of where they enter the human service arena. This theme has been echoing throughout the chapters of this book, and child welfare workers need to seriously consider and inquire into experiences with trauma that affect their clients' daily lives. Sometimes the trauma is perpetrated by the very human service systems established to help children and families. Prolonged and variable foster care treatment, unfair policies and practices that prevent family reunification, inaccessible drug treatment programs, or unavailable safe homes can be as traumatic as maltreatment or violence. Workers concerned with children at risk of addictive and violent behaviors may do well to appreciate the underlying trauma that may be shared by their client. While success is not guaranteed, and there may be problems in the implementation of this collaboration, this is an example of a child welfare agency's attempt to intersect with another organization dealing with substance abuse. More of these collaborative intersection efforts are needed in the social service delivery systems of child welfare, substance abuse, and family violence. It is hoped that this book will guide future services in these three areas and others to further culturally competent approaches in working with African Americans, Latinos, First Nations Peoples, and Asians and Pacific Islanders.

References

Balgopal, P. (Ed.). (2000). *Social work practice with immigrants and refugees*. New York: Columbia University Press.

Casey Family Program. (2000). Casey's strategic plan 2000. Seattle, WA: Author.

Chernesky, R. H. (1997). Managing agencies for multicultural services. In E. Congress (Ed.), *Multicultural perspectives in working with families* (17–33). New York: Springer.

Child Welfare League of America [CWLA]. (1993). *Cultural competence self-assessment instrument*. Washington, DC: Author.

Cox, T. (1991). The multicultural organization. *Academy of Management Executive, 5*(2), 34–47.

Cross, T., Barzon, B., Dennis, K., & Isaacs, M. (1989*). Towards a culturally competent system of care*. Washington, DC: Georgetown University Child Development Center.

Dhooper, S., & Moore, S. (2001). *Social work practice with culturally diverse people*. Thousand Oaks, CA: Sage.

Fong, R. (2003). Cultural competence with Asian Americans. In D. Lum (Ed.), *Culturally competent practice: A framework for understanding diverse groups and justice issues* (pp. 261–281). Pacific Grove, CA: Brooks/Cole.

Fong, R. (Ed.). (2004). *Culturally competent practice with immigrant and refugee children and families*. New York: Guilford Press.

Fong, R., & Furuto, S. (2001). *Culturally competent practice: Skills, interventions, and evaluations*. Boston, MA: Allyn & Bacon.

Fong, R., & Morelli, P. (1998). *Fifth year evaluation of the NaWahine Makalapua: Pregnant and postpartum women and their infants in Hawai'i*. Demonstration grant. Honolulu, HI: Department of Health, State of Hawaii, Alcohol and Drug Abuse Division.

Fong, R., & Wang, A. (2001). Adoptive parents and identity development for children. In N. K. Choi (Ed.), *Psychosocial aspects of the Asian American Experience* (pp. 19–34). New York: Haworth Press.

Goldstein, J., & Leopold, M. (1990, November). Corporate culture vs. ethnic culture. *Personnel Journal*, 83–92.

Kavanagh, K., & Kennedy, P. (1992). *Promoting cultural diversity*. Newbury Park, CA: Sage.

LaFromboise, T., Coleman, H., & Gerton, J. (1993). Psychological impact of biculturalism: Evidence and theory. *Psychological Bulletin, 114*, 395–412.

Leung, P. & Cheung, M. (2001). Competencies in practice evaluations with Asian American individuals and families. In. R. Fong & S. Fumto (Eds.), *Culturally competent practice: Skills, interventions and evaluations*, (pp. 426–437). Boston, MA: Allyn & Bacon.

Loden, M., & Rosener, J. B. (1991). *Workforce America! Managing employee diversity as a vital resource*. Homewood, IL: Irwin.

Lum, D. (1999). *Culturally competent practice: A framework for growth and action.* Pacific Grove, CA: Brooks/Cole.

Lum, D. (Ed.). (2003). *Culturally competent practice: A framework for understanding diverse groups and justice issues.* Pacific Grove, CA: Brooks/Cole.

Miley, K., O'Melia, M., & DuBois, B. (1998). *Generalist social work practice: An empowering approach.* Boston, MA: Allyn & Bacon.

Morelli, P., Fong, R., & Olivera, J. (2001). Culturally competent substance abuse treatment for Asian and Pacific Islander women. In N. Choi (Ed.), *Psychological aspects of the Asian-American experience* (pp. 19–34). New York: The Haworth Press.

Motwani, J., Harper, E., Subramanian, R., & Douglas, C. (1993). Managing the diversified workforce: Current efforts and future directions. *SAM Advanced Management Journal, 58*(3), 16–21.

National Association of Social Workers. (2001). *NASW Standards for Cultural Competence in Social Work Practice.* Washington, DC: Author. National Committee on Racial and Ethnic Diversity.

New York City Administration for Children's Services and New York State Office of Alcoholism and Substance Abuse Services Collaboration. (2001, May). Training memorandum, 1–9.

Nixon, R., & Spearmon, M. (1991). Building a pluralistic workplace. In R. L. Edwards & J. A. Yankey (Eds.), *Skills for effective human services management* (pp. 155–170). Washington, DC: National Association of Social Workers.

Ozawa, M. (1997). Demographic changes and their implications. In M. Reisch & E. Gambrill (Eds.), *Social work in the 21st century.* New York: Pine Forge Press.

Solomon, C. M. (1989, August). The corporate response to workforce diversity. *Personnel Journal, 68,* 43–53.

Spencer, M., Lewis, E., & Gutierrez, L. (2000). Multicultural perspectives on direct practice in social work. In P. Allen-Meares & C. Garvin (Eds.), *The handbook of social work direct practice* (pp. 131–149). Thousand Oaks, CA: Sage.

Stevenson, K., Cheung, K. M., & Leung, P. (1992). A new approach to training child protective services workers for ethnically sensitive practice. *Child Welfare, 70*(4), 291–305.

Thomas, D. A., & Ely, R. J. (1996, September–October). Making differences matter: A new paradigm for managing diversity. *Harvard Business Review, 74,* 79–90.

Weaver, H. (2001). Organization and community assessment with First Nations People. In R. Fong and S. Furuto (Eds.), *Culturally competent practice: Skills, interventions, and evaluations.* (pp. 178–195). Boston, MA: Allyn & Bacon.

Index